CATHERINE DE' MEDICI

. . . . .

CATHERINE DE' MEDICI

R. J. Knecht

Longman

An imprint of **Pearson Education**

Harlow, England · London · New York · Reading, Massachusetts · San Francisco
Toronto · Don Mills, Ontario · Sydney · Tokyo · Singapore · Hong Kong · Seoul
Taipei · Cape Town · Madrid · Mexico City · Amsterdam · Munich · Paris · Milan

Pearson Education Limited
Edinburgh Gate,
Harlow, Essex CM20 2JE
England
and Associated Companies throughout the world

Visit us on the World Wide Web at:
http://www.pearsoneduc.com

© Addison Wesley Longman Limited 1998

First published 1998

ISBN 0-582-082412 PPR
ISBN 0-582-082420 CSD

British Library Cataloguing-in-Publication Data

A catalogue record for this book is available from the British Library

Library of Congress Cataloging-in-Publication Data

Knecht, R.J. (Robert Jean)
Catherine De' Medici / R.J. Knecht.
p. cm. – (Profiles in power)
Includes bibliographical references and index.
ISBN 0-582-08241-2. – ISBN 0-582-08242-0
1. Catherine de Médicis, Queen, consort of Henry II, King of France,
1519-1589. 2. Queens–France–Biography. 3. France–Kings and
rulers–Mothers–Biography. 4. France–Church history–16th century.
5. France–Civilzation–1328–1600. I. Title.
II. Series: Profiles in power (London, England)
DC119.8.K64 1997
944'.028'092—dc21
[B]   97-37451
                                                        CIP

10   9   8   7   6   5   4   3
0+ 03 02 01 00

Set by 7 in 11/12 New Baskerville
Printed in Malaysia (PP)

CONTENTS

CONTENTS

CONTENTS

LIST OF MAPS AND GENEALOGICAL TABLES

MAPS

GENEALOGICAL TABLES

To J.A.S.G.
in gratitude

LIST OF ABBREVIATIONS

AGS   Archivo General de Simancas, Spain

BN   Bibliothèque Nationale, Paris

BSHPF   *Bulletin de la Société de l'histoire du protestantisme français*

CSPF   *Calendar of State Papers, Foreign*

FH   *French History*

GBA   *Gazette des Beaux-Arts*

HJ   *Historial Journal*

Note: The names of French kings are given in French before their accession and in English thereafter: e.g. Henri duc d'Anjou becomes Henry III and Henri de Navarre becomes Henry IV.

PREFACE

Catherine de' Medici is only the third woman to figure in the series of 'Profiles in Power', the others being Elizabeth I of England and Catherine the Great of Russia, yet the power she wielded was quite different from theirs. Whereas they ruled as queens in their own right (even allowing for the fact that Catherine the Great usurped her husband's throne), Catherine was debarred from the French throne by the Salic law which restricted the royal succession to the male line of descent. Yet for forty years she helped to shape France's destiny either as queen consort or as regent or as queen-mother. Following the accidental death of her husband, Henry II, in 1559, she had to protect the inheritance of her four sons, aged fifteen, nine, eight and four respectively. Three of them became kings of France within Catherine's lifetime and her main contribution may have been to ensure dynastic continuity at a time of unprecedented political turmoil in France.

Few historical reputations have fluctuated as wildly as that of Catherine de' Medici. No historian would question the importance of her role in the Wars of Religion, which tore France apart in the second half of the sixteenth century. Opinion, however, is sharply divided regarding her policies. Very different answers have been given to two questions: did she consistently strive to bring peace to the kingdom by healing its religious divisions or did she inflame an already perilous situation by playing one side against the other and using violent means to get rid of her political opponents? Traditionally, historians have been critical of Catherine, arguing that after she had failed to

xi

secure a religious settlement at the Colloquy of Poissy in 1561 and to impose a measure of religious toleration in a series of royal edicts, she sided with the Catholic extremists in 1572 and instigated the Massacre of St. Bartholomew in which thousands of Protestants or Huguenots were butchered in Paris and elsewhere, including their leader, Admiral Coligny. The great nineteenth-century historian Jules Michelet, who has had such a lasting influence on popular perception of the past in France, felt nothing but contempt for Catherine, describing her as that 'maggot which came out of Italy's tomb'. In his view the massacre was an elaborate plot by 'the very secret Italian council of the queen-mother' to use the Guises to wipe out the Châtillons, and then the Châtillons to wipe out the Guises. Tradition is echoed in the more recent work of Janine Garrisson, the historian of sixteenth-century French Protestantism, who thinks it 'more or less certain that the decision to assassinate [the Huguenot leaders] was taken by Catherine de' Medici with the backing of her younger son, the duc d'Anjou'.

Recently, there has been an attempt – initiated by Nicola Sutherland and continued by Jean-Louis Bourgeon – to rehabilitate Catherine. They see her as the victim of a 'Black Legend'. An even more passionate defender was the late Dame Frances Yates, who maintained that Catherine was always an Erasmian and a 'politique', who sought harmony between Catholics and Protestants by involving them in extravagant festivals. Catherine was undoubtedly victimized by propagandists in the late sixteenth century. Propaganda is seldom more effective than when it blames a single individual for all the ills of this world. In sixteenth-century France, Catherine offered the perfect target to a hate campaign fuelled by xenophobia, social snobbery and misogyny. As a Florentine, she was seen as deceitful by nature and a skilled poisoner; as the scion of a family deemed to be upstart (the Medici had risen socially through trade and banking), she was regarded as jealous of France's ancient nobility; and, as a woman, she exemplified the 'monstrous regiment' denounced by John Knox and other male preachers and political theorists as unfit to rule.

Catherine's unpopularity developed late. In the early stages of the Wars of Religion, she was praised by the poet Ronsard for her peace-making efforts. The turning-point came with the Massacre of St. Bartholomew in 1572, a crime so heinous that it released a flood of pamphlets, mostly by Huguenots, condemning the perpetrators. Many believed that Catherine had planned the slaughter as far back as 1565, when she had met the duke of Alba, the chief minister of Philip II of Spain, who was soon to make his mark on history as the butcher of the Netherlands. No contemporary document has yet come to light proving that a plot had been hatched by Catherine and Alba, but its absence cannot clear Catherine from some responsibility at least for the massacre. Her reputation inevitably hinges around this event. If she was guilty to any extent, how can this departure from her earlier efforts to heal the religious divisions be explained? Was her policy less consistent than her defenders have claimed?

I have approached Catherine with an open mind. As I have followed each twist and turn in her long and eventful life, I have come to suspect her motives but also to admire her superhuman efforts on behalf of her children. Even towards the end of her life, as her health began to break down, she continued to travel far and wide across the kingdom in pursuit of some diplomatic objective or other. Her enormous correspondence, often displaying a lively sense of humour even in adversity, bears witness to her physical stamina which contrasted so sharply with the sickliness of her male offspring. Whatever we may think of Catherine herself, there is no denying that her children were all dreadful. Even her favourite son, Henry III, showed signs of mental derangement, for all his intellectual gifts. Catherine's fate also elicits sympathy. Having been plucked from her native land for an arranged political marriage with a man she had never met, she had to tolerate his gross infidelity. Then, suddenly, he was killed, leaving her with six young children (the seventh had just become queen of Spain) and virtually no experience of government in an environment poisoned by aristocratic faction and growing religious antagonisms. As Nicola Sutherland has demonstrated, Catherine had to grapple with a multiplicity of problems – some rooted in the past, others springing from the Reformation – which even a mature king would have found daunting. In Sutherland's phrase, Henry II's death 'revealed with tragic force the total dependence on the king of the society and state of France, so that the loss of his person not only presented grave new problems, but also revealed hitherto controllable tensions, permitting the stream of public life to surge towards a reach of chaos'. As a woman, unable ever to command more authority than that of regent, Catherine may have done her best, but was that good enough in the circumstances? This brief study will seek to answer this question.

Among friends who have assisted my efforts to probe the chaos, Joseph Bergin and Mark Greengrass have been especially kind and helpful. I have also profited from conversations with Denis Crouzet, whose knowledge of the period is unrivalled, and Penny Roberts, whose research is now reaching out from Troyes to the rest of provincial France. I am once again grateful to Professor Keith Robbins for inviting me to contribute to his series and also to Andrew MacLennan for his unfailing good humour and encouragement. My greatest debt, as always, is to my wife, Maureen, without whose generous support no scholarship would be possible.

Birmingham 1997

Chapter 1

DAUGHTER OF FLORENCE
(1519–33)

Catherine de' Medici owed her life and marriage to King Francis I of France. From the start of his reign in 1515, he planned to conquer the duchy of Milan, to which he had inherited a claim from his great-grandmother, Valentina Visconti. Within a few months he assembled an army, crossed the Alps and inflicted a crushing defeat at Marignano on the Swiss, who had been defending Milan. The duchy was conquered and its ruler, Lodovico Sforza, packed off to France. Having taken Milan, Francis set his sights on the kingdom of Naples. He hoped to replace its ruler, King Ferdinand of Aragon, who died in January 1516, by invoking an old Angevin claim. In order to reach Naples, however, Francis needed to gain the support of Pope Leo X, who was not only head of the church but also ruler of the Papal States, a band of territory stretching diagonally across central Italy. Leo belonged to the Florentine family of Medici and maintained a close interest in its fortunes.

. . .

FLORENCE AND THE MEDICI

Italy in the early sixteenth century was not yet a unified nation. Politically it was divided into many independent states of which the republic of Florence was among the most important. Others were the duchy of Milan, the republic of Venice, the Papal States and the kingdom of Naples. By modern standards Florence was not a large city. Its population was about 65,000; one could walk across it in twenty minutes. The most important organ of government was the

Signoria, which comprised eight priors and a chairman, called the gonfalonier of justice. It met daily, usually with two other bodies – the twelve 'goodmen' and the sixteen 'standard-bearers', whose assent to any proposed legislation was mandatory. These three bodies were collectively called the *tre maggiori*. *Ad hoc* bodies of citizens were summoned from time to time to advise the Signoria on matters of great moment. Specific aspects of the administration, such as war or law and order, were supervised by various committees. Legislative powers were vested in the Council of the People and the Council of the Commune.

All officers of state in Florence (except for the Chancery staff) served for only a few months at a time. Most were chosen by lot, their names being drawn from a bag. To qualify for election to the three leading offices, a man had to be solvent, to have paid his taxes, to be over thirty and a member of one of seven major guilds or fourteen minor guilds. Although the Florentine constitution promoted political awareness among a large proportion of the population, it was not democratic. Only 5,000 or 6,000 people qualified for office.[1]

The Medici were one of many prominent Florentine families which rose through commerce. In the early fourteenth century, some of its members served on the chief council, but they were not yet important enough to advise the government in times of crisis. Other families, notably the Strozzi, were far wealthier. After 1343 some Medici held leading offices of state, but quarrels and litigation among the family's nine branches may have damaged their political standing. By 1400 only two were allowed to hold public office. Eventually, the family of Averardo de' Medici emerged as leader of the Medici clan. It was his son, Giovanni di Bicci, who founded the Medici fortune by his banking activities. He also built up a political party whose core was formed by the various branches of the family, and broadened by careful marriages with more prestigious families. The methods adopted by the party to advance its power were unspectacular yet effective.

---

1   J.R. Hale, *Florence and the Medici: The Pattern of Control* (London, 1977), pp. 15–20.

Giovanni's son, Cosimo, combined a devotion to learning with an active and conscientious concern for public affairs. He encouraged humanists, collected many books and founded the Laurentian library. Among the visual arts he was especially fond of sculpture, Donatello being his favourite artist; but it was architecture which really fired his enthusiasm. He chose Michelozzo to design the Medici palace in the Via Larga. Narrower than it is today, it served as both fortress and strongbox at a time when street-fighting was still rife in Florence. The palace's austere style powerfully influenced other domestic buildings in the city, notably the Pitti and Strozzi palaces.

After 1429 the Medici bank expanded steadily. In addition to the head office in Florence, it threw out branches in Rome, Geneva (transferred to Lyon in 1464), Bruges, Ancona, Pisa, London, Avignon and Milan. Much initiative was left to the firm's branches, which provided Cosimo with an unrivalled information service and contacts with influential men throughout western Europe. He was on terms of intimacy with popes and princes, and it was largely under his influence that Florence was chosen in 1439 as the venue for the general council of the church which proclaimed the short-lived reunion of the Roman and Byzantine churches. Not surprisingly, Cosimo came to be regarded as the republic's effective ruler. When he died in August 1464 he was given the title of *Pater patriae* by public decree.[2]

Cosimo's son, Piero, seemed destined to inherit his influence as well as his fortune. He was allowed by Louis XI of France to add the fleur-de-lis to one of the Medici's *palle* (the coat of arms of the Medici, consisting of six balls on a gold field). His rule, though brief (he died in December 1464), left its mark on Florence's heritage. Piero commissioned Gozzoli to decorate the chapel of the Medici palace and was an early patron of Andrea della Robbia and Verrocchio.[3]

The 'golden age' of Medicean Florence is associated with the rule of Piero's son Lorenzo 'the Magnificent'. Highly

2 Ibid., pp. 20–42.
3 Ibid., pp. 43–8.

educated, the friend of humanists and a poet in his own right, he staged elaborate festivals and tournaments drawing on the skills of famous artists. He was drawn to a princely life-style, and his wife, Clarissa, who gave him eight children, belonged to the aristocratic Roman family of Orsini. Lorenzo, however, was not an enthusiastic builder. The villa at Poggio a Caiano is the only surviving building of note for which he was responsible. A keen huntsman, he often visited the Medici villas in Tuscany. At the time of his death he owned many paintings by famous Italian and Flemish artists, but he seldom ordered any for himself; preferring to collect ancient gems, cameos and *objets d'art.*

Lorenzo's relations with other Italian powers depended on the Signoria, a situation which they did not always appreciate. His position was further hampered by a sharp decline in the fortunes of the Medici bank. He alienated Pope Sixtus IV by refusing him a loan, thereby pre-cipitating the Pazzi conspiracy. This was a plot by a Florentine faction to assassinate Lorenzo and his brother. The latter was killed, but Lorenzo escaped. The plotters were rounded up and executed, and the Florentine constitution was made even less democratic: a Council of Seventy, whose members were carefully picked and not subject to rotation, was made responsible for electing the Signoria. Lorenzo was passionately devoted to his family. One of his earliest ambitions was to have one of his sons made a cardinal. In 1489 Innocent VIII agreed to give a red hat to Lorenzo's second son, Giovanni, although he was only thirteen.[4]

After Lorenzo's death, on 8 April 1492, his son Piero was admitted to the Council of Seventy. Although well educated, he lacked his father's political judgment. In 1494 Charles VIII of France invaded Italy with the aim of conquering the kingdom of Naples. He had no designs on Florence as such but wanted to secure his communications. He requested some fortresses in Tuscany as well as the ports of Pisa and Leghorn. Acting on impulse, Piero agreed to his demands without first consulting the Signoria. When summoned by this body to explain his action, he came with an armed

---

4   Ibid., pp. 49–75.

escort. The doors of the palace were barred against him and its bell called the people to the piazza. As a mob sacked the Medici palace, Piero and his brothers, Giovanni and Giuliano, fled.

Piero's exile was followed in Florence by a new republican government headed by Piero Soderini, which lasted till 1512. He resisted pressure from Pope Julius II to join a league which had been formed to drive the French out of Italy. The French alliance was useful to Florentine trade, but it isolated her diplomatically. After the French had been driven out of Italy in 1513, the victorious pope decided to punish Florence. The League's army invaded Tuscany, provoking an uprising in the city. As Soderini fled, the Medici – Giuliano and Cardinal Giovanni – returned to Florence in triumph. They were welcomed back with verses linking them to the days of Cosimo, Piero the Elder and Lorenzo the Magnificent, especially the latter, and his symbol, the laurel. The feast of SS. Cosmas and Damian, patron saints of the Medici, once more became a public festival.

.   .   .

POPE LEO X (1513–21)

On 11 March 1513 cardinal Giovanni de' Medici, the son of Lorenzo the Magnificent, became Pope Leo X. This obliged him to find a suitable kinsman to represent him in Florence. While the pope's brothers-in-law, Jacopo Salviati and Piero Ridolfi, acted as caretakers in the city, Leo discussed its future with relatives and ardent Mediceans who had come to Rome to congratulate him on his election. By August they had decided on a new regime. While Giuliano, Leo's brother, became archbishop of Florence and a cardinal, the pope's nephew, Lorenzo, was put in charge of state affairs. In May 1515 the Council of Seventy sanctioned his appointment as captain-general of the armed forces of Florence.[5]

This, roughly, was the situation in Florence when Francis I invaded Italy in 1515. Charles VIII's invasion in 1494 had led to the overthrow of Piero de' Medici, as we have seen. Leo was keen to avoid a repetition of that event. In fact, he

---

5   Ibid., p. 99.

had nothing to fear, for Francis had his own reasons for wanting his friendship. Recent history had shown that no French ruler could hope to establish his authority permanently in Italy without papal co-operation. Even after Marignano, the king's position in the peninsula was precarious: the Emperor Maximilian and King Henry VIII of England seemed willing to join the Swiss cantons in a new offensive against France. The threat of such a coalition made it imperative for Francis to gain Leo's friendship. What is more, the pope, as the suzerain of Naples, had its investiture in his gift. Thus a treaty was easily arranged: in exchange for Parma and Piacenza, Francis gave the duchy of Nemours and a large pension to Leo's brother, Giuliano, and another pension to his nephew, Lorenzo. This, however, was only the first step towards closer union. In December 1515 the king and the pope met in Bologna. Their most important decision was to sign a concordat whereby the papacy recovered its authority over the French church, which had been curtailed in 1438, while the king was authorized to appoint to the chief benefices in his kingdom. More to the point, Leo promised to support Francis's Neapolitan ambitions.[6]

When Giuliano de' Medici died in 1516, Leo X secured Lorenzo's recognition as head of the Florentine republic. He also appointed him captain-general of the church and gave him the duchy of Urbino. On 26 September 1517 Francis congratulated Lorenzo on his success, which, he hoped, would soon be followed by others. 'For my part', he said, 'this is what I fervently desire and I intend to help you with all my power. I also wish to marry you off to some beautiful and good lady of noble birth and of my kin, so that the love which I bear you may grow and be strengthened.'[7] As fairly recent parvenus, the Medici were bound to feel awed by the prospect of becoming associated with the royal house of France. Lorenzo, after all, was nothing more than a privileged citizen among Florentines. His predecessors had

6   R.J. Knecht, *Renaissance Warrior and Patron: The reign of Francis I* (Cambridge, 1994), pp. 62–8, 79–83.
7   A. de Reumont and A. Baschet, *La jeunesse de Catherine de Médicis* (Paris, 1866), p. 251.

been content to marry into important Florentine or Roman families, such as the Orsini, Cibo, Salviati, Ridolfi and Strozzi.

Another result of the Franco-papal meeting in Bologna was the marriage of Lorenzo de' Medici and Madeleine de La Tour d'Auvergne, comtesse de Boulogne. She was the daughter of Jean III de La Tour and of Jeanne de Bourbon-Vendôme, a princess of royal blood, whose first husband had been Jean II, duc de Bourbon. Jean III de La Tour, who died in 1501, owned, in central France, the counties of Clermont and Auvergne and the baronies of La Tour and La Chaise, and, in the Midi, the counties of Louraguais and Castres. He also had some seigneuries in Limousin and Berry. He and his wife shared an annual revenue from their domain estimated at around 120,000 *livres*. Madeleine's elder sister, Anne, married the Scotsman, John Stuart, duke of Albany.[8]

Francis gave Madeleine a wedding at Amboise as magnificent as if she had been his own daughter. It was preceded on 25 April 1518 by the Dauphin's baptism. Lorenzo, acting as the pope's proxy, held the infant over the font. The nuptial celebrations, which began three days later, lasted ten days. Francis gave the bridegroom a company of men-at-arms and the collar of the Ordre de Saint-Michel, and the bride a pension of 10,000 *écus*. In return, Lorenzo distributed gifts from the pope valued at 300,000 ducats, including two paintings by Raphael – the *Holy Family* and *St. Michael slaying the dragon*.[9] For the wedding, the courtyard of the château of Amboise had been transformed into a banqueting hall; it was covered by a huge awning adorned with garlands of box and its walls were hung with tapestries. After the Dauphin's baptism, it served as the setting for a ballet performed by seventy-two ladies. The wedding was also followed by dancing and a banquet which lasted till 2 a.m. The celebrations comprised a week of jousting in which

---

8   J.-H. Mariéjol, *Catherine de Médicis* (Paris, 1920), p. 3.
9   Both paintings are now in the Louvre. See C. Scalliérez, *François Ier et ses artistes* (Paris, 1992), pp. 106–9. The paintings were actually given to Francis at Nantes by the papal legate, Cardinal Bibbiena. *The Holy Family* was a gift to Queen Claude.

Lorenzo distinguished himself despite a head wound which he had recently sustained besieging Urbino. The climax of this entertainment was a mock battle so realistic that several participants were killed.[10]

In May Lorenzo accompanied Francis on a progress through Brittany. He and his wife then toured her estates in Auvergne before travelling to Italy. They reached Florence on 7 September. According to Florange, the contemporary French memoirist, Lorenzo was riddled with syphilis at the time of his marriage and passed it on to his wife. Be that as it may, he fell seriously ill in November and was sent by his doctors to the Villa Sassetti, where the air was supposedly better than in Florence. On 13 April 1519 Madeleine gave birth to a daughter, who was baptized a few days later at San Lorenzo. She was christened Caterina Maria Romula (after Romulus, the legendary founder of Fiesole, the cradle of Florence). Unfortunately, on 28 April, Madeleine died, and, on 4 May, she was followed to the grave by her husband.

Lorenzo's death destroyed Leo X's hopes of establishing a Medici dynasty in Florence with French support. He did not immediately break his friendship with Francis, but began drawing closer to Charles, King of Spain, soon to become Holy Roman Emperor. Meanwhile, the infant Caterina (we shall now call her Catherine) was taken to Rome by her grandmother, Alfonsina Orsini, and her cousin, cardinal Giulio de' Medici, whom Leo had appointed to administer Florence after Lorenzo's death. Francis I claimed Catherine's tutelage, but the pope refused to hand her over, allegedly because he planned to marry her off to Ippolito, bastard son of Giuliano, duc de Nemours.[11] Actually, Leo was playing for time. Feeling that he had gained nothing from his alliance with France, he looked for a pretext to break it.

On 8 June 1519 Charles of Habsburg was elected Emperor, but he needed to receive Charlemagne's crown from the pope. Francis tried to divert his attention from Italy by stirring up trouble for him elsewhere. Reacting with vigour,

---

10 *Mémoires du maréchal de Florange*, ed. R. Goubaux and P.-A. Lemoisne (Paris, 1913), i. 222–6; *Journal de Jean Barrillon, secrétaire du chancelier Duprat, 1515–21*, ed. P. de Vaissière (Paris, 1897–99), ii. 85.

11 Mariéjol, p. 7.

8

Charles unleashed a war which lasted intermittently until the peace of Cateau-Cambrésis in 1559. On 29 May 1521 Leo signed a treaty with him, promising to crown him Emperor and signifying his willingness to invest him with Naples. Denouncing Leo's ingratitude, Francis banned the dispatch of church revenues to Rome and imposed a heavy fine on Florentine bankers in France. On 19 November the French were driven out of Milan. On 1 December Leo died and Francis awaited the result of the next conclave with bated breath: he threatened to sever his allegiance to Rome if Giulio de' Medici were elected. Instead the cardinals chose the Emperor's old tutor, Adrian of Utrecht, who took the name of Hadrian VI.[12]

. . .

CLEMENT VII (1523–34)

Hadrian's pontificate was short-lived: he died on 14 September 1523 and was succeeded on 19 November by Giulio de' Medici, who became Pope Clement VII. He had been governing Florence since Lorenzo's death, and his election created a vacuum at the heart of the Medicean regime in Florence. The family was now represented by Giuliano's bastard son, Ippolito, aged thirteen, Lorenzo's four-year-old daughter, Catherine, and Alessandro, also about thirteen, given out by Giulio as Lorenzo's bastard but widely rumoured to be his own. Though hardly impressive, this cast list was accepted by the Florentines, who saw economic and political advantages to be gained from the links with a Medici pope. Ippolito was installed at the Medici palace as the family's leading representative, while Alessandro and Catherine moved to Poggio a Caiano. Though age restrictions had been lifted to allow Ippolito to hold public office, he was little more than a puppet, being virtually under the tutelage of Clement VII's personal representative in the city, Cardinal Passerini. The new regime, however, soon became unpopular. Passerini could not conceal the fact that he was under direct orders from Rome. Clement

---

12 Knecht, *Renaissance Warrior*, pp. 175–7, 182.

used his cultural patronage to stress the continuity between the new regime and that of the fifteenth-century Medici. He invited Michelangelo to press ahead with the building of a new sacristy at San Lorenzo which would house monuments to Lorenzo and Giuliano de' Medici and to their illustrious forebear, Lorenzo the Magnificent. Michelangelo began work on the statue of the younger Lorenzo in 1525, but the political situation obliged him to stop for a time.[13]

Clement VII was quite devout and fond of scholarship and the arts; but at a time when Italy was being turned into a battlefield by the rivalry of France and the Empire, he needed to be also a statesman. He proved instead to be timid and shifty. His position became especially difficult when Francis I was defeated and taken prisoner at Pavia in February 1525 and Charles V became all-powerful in Italy. In 1526 Francis was released after promising, in the treaty of Madrid, to give up Burgundy to the Emperor. He was allowed to return to France but obliged to hand over two of his sons as hostages. Having regained his freedom, Francis refused to cede Burgundy; at the same time he tried to put pressure on Charles to release his sons in return for a cash ransom by allying with Henry VIII and Clement VII. A league of Italian states was formed aimed at expelling the imperialists from Italy, but Francis failed to back his Italian allies. Clement consequently found himself at the mercy of Charles V, whose army sacked Rome in May 1527. As the pope was imprisoned in Castel Sant'Angelo. an anti-Medicean faction seized power in Florence.[14]

In August 1527 a French army under marshal Lautrec crossed the Alps and, after overrunning Lombardy, marched on Naples. Clement VII, meanwhile, regained his freedom with Charles V's connivance. In April 1528 Lautrec laid siege to Naples but his army was soon decimated by plague or cholera. Lautrec himself died on 17 August, and his successor sounded the retreat. Other disasters then befell France in north Italy, culminating in the defeat of her army at Landriano in June 1529. The French collapse convinced the pope that he had nothing to gain from being neutral: only

---

13 H. Hibbard, *Michelangelo* (Harmondsworth, 1978), pp. 177–96.
14 Hale, *Florence and the Medici*, pp. 113–16.

the Emperor could provide him with the military support needed to restore the Medici to power in Florence. 'I have quite made up my mind', said Clement, 'to become an Imperialist, and to live and die as such.' On 29 June 1529 he signed the treaty of Barcelona with Charles V, which provided for the restoration of Medici rule in Florence. Clement, for his part, promised to crown Charles Emperor. A marriage was arranged between his nephew, Alessandro de' Medici, and Charles V's illegitimate daughter, Margaret of Austria. By December 1528 Francis I was keen to come to terms with the Emperor. Talks, held at Cambrai, resulted in the so-called Peace of the Ladies (3 August 1529). Charles released Francis's sons in return for a huge ransom, and Francis gave up all his claims to Italy. Early in November Charles and Clement met in Bologna. Charles was crowned Emperor on 24 February and a league of Italian states was formed, only Florence being omitted because of its refusal to restore the Medici. Charles placed an army at the pope's disposal, which soon afterwards laid siege to the city.[15]

While Florence was under siege, Catherine de' Medici was brought back from Poggio a Caiano and placed in a convent of Benedictine nuns, called le Murate, which provided the daughters of the rich Florentine families with a sound education. A diary kept by one of the nuns, Giustina Niccolini, tells us that little Catherine endeared herself to the nuns, who sent gifts of food to her imprisoned kinsmen. As conditions in the city deteriorated during the siege, the Medici pope and his relatives became extremely unpopular. Some political hotheads allegedly wanted Catherine killed or exposed on the town walls as a target for enemy gunfire; others suggested that she should be sent to a brothel. The Florentine government decided instead to transfer her to the greater security of the convent of Santa Lucia, where she remained until the siege was over. Meanwhile, the city's rulers made a clean break with the Medici regime by introducing puritanical legislation recalling the austere days of Savonarola: many material remains of the Medici past were also vandalized.[16]

---

15 Knecht, *Renaissance Warrior*, pp. 253–60, 272–4, 278–85.
16 Mariéjol, pp. 11–14.

While Florence withstood the enemy bombardment, it was forced to surrender on 12 August 1530 by hunger and plague. It was agreed that a new government would be set up by the Emperor within four months. On 27 April 1532 a reform commission wrote the Medici into the Florentine constitution as its hereditary rulers. The Signoria was abolished and Alessandro de' Medici was given the title of duke. His mother was a Roman servant girl, but the identity of his father is uncertain. He may have been Lorenzo, Catherine's father, or, more probably, Pope Clement VII before he became cardinal and pope.[17]

In October 1530 Clement VII arranged for his niece, Catherine, whom he had not seen for five years, to be brought to Rome. He welcomed her with open arms and tears in his eyes. As the pope's niece, the little girl may have been able to explore freely the Vatican library, the Sistine chapel and the gardens, where recently discovered Roman sculptures, such as the *Laocoön*, were on display. This, however, is pure conjecture.

Early in 1531 the rumour circulated that Cardinal Ippolito de' Medici, Catherine's uncle, wanted to marry her. Being slightly older than Alessandro, he viewed himself as the rightful ruler of Florence, a claim which he would have strengthened by marrying his young niece, who was Lorenzo's legitimate heiress. But he could not do so as long as he remained a churchman. He was willing enough to be unfrocked, but Clement had other ideas. He gave him rich benefices and got him out of the way by sending him to Hungary as legate. A famous portrait by Titian shows Ippolito wearing an elegant Hungarian riding outfit with a diamond spray in his cap; he holds a baton in one hand and a sword in the other.[18]

The pope regarded his niece, Catherine, as a useful pawn in the game of international diplomacy. Before the siege of Florence, a number of possible suitors for her hand had been considered by the pope: Ercole d'Este, son of the duke of Ferrara; James V of Scotland; Henry, earl of Richmond,

---

17 Hale, *Florence and the Medici*, pp. 118–24.
18 Mariéjol, pp. 15–16; I. Cloulas, *Catherine de Médicis* (Paris, 1979), pp. 44–5. Titian's portrait of Ippolito is now in the Pitti museum, Florence.

Henry VIII's bastard. During the siege, Clement thought of rewarding Philibert de Chalon, prince of Orange, who led the assault on the city, by marrying him to his niece; but the prince was killed before this plan could be given effect. After the siege, other names were suggested as possible husbands for Catherine, including Federico Gonzaga, duke of Mantua, and Guidobaldo delle Rovere, prince of Urbino. The most serious contender was Francesco Sforza, duke of Milan, who had the Emperor's backing, but the pope did not relish an arrangement which would increase his dependence on Charles V.[19]

It was at this juncture that Francis I put forward the candidature of his own younger son, Henri, duc d'Orléans. Gabriel de Gramont, bishop of Tarbes, was sent to Rome in 1531, with instructions to broach the matter. A draft contract, drawn up on 24 April, laid down that Catherine would live at the French court until she was old enough to consummate the marriage. The pope was to give her a dowry that included Pisa, Leghorn, Reggio and Modena, along with Parma and Piacenza. He was to help Henri reconquer Milan and Genoa, and assist in the reconquest of Urbino. In June 1531 it was reported from Rome that Clement had accepted the contract, but would not send Catherine to France ahead of her marriage. On returning to Paris in July, Gramont urged Francis to send a high-powered embassy to Rome without delay. The king chose for this mission cardinal François de Tournon, an experienced diplomat and a distant cousin of Catherine. He left the French court on 6 August, hoping to reach Rome by mid-September, but fell ill on the way and decided to remain in France for the winter.[20] In the meantime, Henry VIII and Francis met at Boulogne and formed an alliance. Though ostensibly directed against the Turks, it was really aimed at putting pressure on the pope to concede Henry VIII's divorce from Catherine of Aragon. The two monarchs agreed to make a joint approach to Clement. Tournon accordingly resumed his mission to Italy, this time in the company of Gramont, now also a cardinal; they were instructed to

---

19 Cloulas, *Catherine*, p. 46.
20 M. François, *Le cardinal François de Tournon* (Paris, 1951), pp. 94–7.

propose a meeting between the pope and the kings of England and France.

Clement VII spent the winter at Bologna, negotiating with the Emperor. Though anxious not to offend him, he nevertheless hoped that the presence of the French cardinals would serve to stiffen his resistance to Charles's demands. They reached Bologna on 3 January 1533 and were soon able to report progress to Francis I. On 10 January they wrote that Clement had agreed to meet him provided this was kept secret from the Emperor; on 21 January they announced that the pope had agreed to the marriage between Catherine and the duc d'Orléans.[21]

During 1532 Catherine returned to the Medici palace in Florence, which was being looked after by an aged kinsman, Ottaviano de' Medici. Her governess was Maria Salviati, the widow of Giovanni delle Bande Nere. As the duke's sister, Catherine attended many public ceremonies and festivals. In the spring of 1533 she was among the young ladies who welcomed Margaret of Austria, the future duchess. Her visit was celebrated with fireworks, bullfights and a magnificent banquet. Unfortunately, almost nothing is known about Catherine's education. She began to learn French about 1531 and may have been able to speak and write it by the time she left Florence two years later. She also knew some Greek and Latin and continued to study these languages in France.[22]

It was about this time that Catherine's portrait was painted by Sebastiano del Piombo, Giorgio Vasari and possibly Bronzino. A Venetian ambassador described her as small and thin, without fine features, and with bulging eyes shared by other members of her family. She seems, however, to have been quite mischievous. One day, as Vasari was painting her portrait for the king of France, he went out for lunch, leaving the canvas unattended. Catherine and some friends sneaked into the room and, seizing the artist's brushes, began to add bright colours to his work. He seems not to have been upset. 'I am so devoted to her . . . ', he wrote to a friend, 'on account of her special qualities and of the

---

21 Ibid., pp. 98–105.
22 K. Gebhardt, 'Catherine de Médicis (1519–1589) et la langue française' in *Henri III et son temps*, ed. R. Sauzet (Paris, 1992), p. 23.

affection she bears not only me but my whole nation, that I adore her, if I may say so, as one adores the saints in Heaven.'[23]

Preparations for Catherine's marriage ran into snags. On 23 July it was reported in Rome that the king of France had fallen gravely ill as he was travelling to Provence. This was followed by another report to the effect that the duke of Savoy, acting under pressure from Charles V, had refused to allow Nice to be used as the venue for the meeting between the king and the pope. However, these were only hiccups. On 28 August Catherine received a gift of beautiful jewels from Francis I. Her dowry had been carefully prepared by the French and papal negotiators. Clement gave her 100,000 gold *écus* plus another 30,000 *écus* in exchange for her rights to the Medici patrimony. This money was to be paid in three equal instalments. From Francis, Catherine received an annuity of 10,000 *livres* and the château of Gien. A clause in the contract listed the items in her trousseau, such as fine lace, precious cloths, bed-hangings of cloth of gold and much jewellery. A forced loan of 35,000 *écus* which Duke Alessandro had levied on Florence for the refurbishment of its fortifications helped to pay for the trousseau. Caterina Cibo, Catherine's great-aunt, came from Rome to help prepare it. She wrote to Isabella d'Este, asking for bodices and skirts, and also purchased sheets of black silk. From the pope, Catherine received jewels of an estimated value of 27,900 gold *écus*, including a gold belt studded with rubies and diamonds and some of the largest pearls ever seen.[24]

Catherine left Florence on 1 September after giving a farewell banquet to the city's leading ladies. Accompanied by Maria Salviati, Caterina Cibo, Paola Rucellai and Filippo Strozzi, she arrived on 6 September at La Spezia. From here, her cousin, the duke of Albany, transported her on his galleys to Villefranche where she waited for the pope to arrive. Clement left Rome on 9 September with thirteen cardinals, including Ippolito de' Medici, whose pages were dressed like Turks armed with bows and scimitars. Albany again provided the transport to Villefranche, where Clement arrived on 9 October. Two days later, his fleet with

---

23 Mariéjol, pp. 19–20; Cloulas, *Catherine*, p. 49.
24 Cloulas, *Catherine*, pp. 50–1.

Catherine on board arrived off Marseille, where it was greeted by a flotilla of small boats carrying French noblemen and musicians. As the papal fleet entered the harbour, gun batteries fired a welcoming salvo. Marshal Montmorency led Clement to 'the king's garden', next to the abbey of Saint-Victor, where four French cardinals and many other clerics welcomed him. On 12 October he entered Marseille on his *sedia gestatoria* behind a white horse carrying the Blessed Sacrament. The pope was followed by cardinals, riding mules, and by Catherine, escorted by lords and ladies. A temporary palace had been prepared for the pope next to the old palace of the counts of Provence, where Francis was due to stay; the two buildings being linked by a wooden bridge. The road beneath was sealed off to form a large audience chamber and reception hall. The apartments in both palaces had been adorned with tapestries and furniture borrowed for the occasion from the Louvre and other royal palaces.

On 13 October Francis I arrived and prostrated himself at the feet of the Holy Father. The two men immediately got down to business, but the only clue we have as to the nature of their talks is a draft agreement in Francis's hand anticipating an offensive alliance. Other topics certainly discussed were the spread of heresy in France, the calling of a General Council of the church, and Henry VIII's divorce. In the meantime, the nuptial festivities began. On 27 October the contract for Catherine's marriage was signed; next day she and Henri were married amidst great pomp. That night the newly-weds, both aged fourteen, were led by Queen Eleanor and her ladies to a sumptuous nuptial chamber, where they allegedly consummated their union in the presence of Francis, who declared that 'each had shown valour in the joust'. Next morning Clement found them still in bed and noted their satisfied expressions.[25]

---

25 Catherine's marriage is commemorated in one of a cycle of paintings by Giorgio Vasari in the *Sala di Clemente VII* in the Palazzo Vecchio, Florence. Besides the bride and groom, this shows Pope Clement and Francis I, Maria Salviati, Cardinal Ippolito de' Medici and the king's dwarf, Gradasso. See Janet Cox-Rearick, *The Collection of Francis I: Royal Treasures* (New York, 1995), p. 78.

An exchange of gifts rounded off the celebrations. Clement gave Francis a beautiful casket with panels of crystal engraved by Valerio Belli depicting scenes from the Life of Christ; also a unicorn's horn (actually a narwhal's tusk). Traditionally, the unicorn was thought to expel poisonous creatures from fountains and to purify their waters by dipping in its horn. A seventeenth-century commentary explains: 'Pope Clement VII made him [Francis] a gift of a unicorn's horn, which expels poisons, to make him understand that he should keep his kingdom safe from heresy.'[26] Francis gave the pope a Flemish tapestry depicting the Last Supper. He also distributed pensions to the cardinals in the papal entourage. Ippolito de' Medici was given a tame lion which the Barbary corsair, Barbarossa, had recently presented to the king. On 7 November Clement created four French cardinals. The meeting ended on 12 November, when Francis and his court left for Avignon. The pope's departure was delayed until 20 November. Travelling by sea, he was back in Rome by 11 December.[27]

---

26 BN, ms. fr. 10422, f. 22, cited by Cox-Rearick, *Collection of Francis I*, p. 81.
27 Cloulas, *Catherine*, pp. 53–8; Knecht, *Renaissance Warrior*, pp. 299–302; Reumont and Baschet, *La jeunesse*, pp. 325ff; Le P. Hamy, *Entrevue de François Ier avec Clément VII à Marseille, 1533* (Paris, 1900); L. von Pastor, *The History of the Popes*, trans. F. Antrobus and R. Kerr (London, 1891–1933), x. 229–37.

Chapter 2

DAUPHINE (1533–47)

Catherine de' Medici was to spend fourteen years at the court of her father-in-law, Francis I. In 1533 he was thirty-nine years old and had been on the throne eighteen years. His greatest triumph, the battle of Marignano, his worst defeat, the battle of Pavia, and his humiliating imprisonment in Spain lay behind him. In 1529 he had signed the peace of Cambrai with his great enemy, the Emperor Charles V. As a result, he had recovered his two sons, François and Henri, who had taken his place as hostages in Spain. He had also taken Charles's sister, Eleanor of Portugal, as his second wife (the first, Claude de France, had died in 1524). Yet the international situation was far from settled: Francis continued to hanker after the duchy of Milan, and, despite the peace treaty, he seized every opportunity of embarrassing the Emperor. He was given a chance to meddle in the affairs of Germany by the Lutheran Reformation, which posed a serious challenge to the Emperor's authority. While drawing closer to Pope Clement VII, Francis sought the friendship of the German Protestant princes and towns. He also intrigued with the Ottoman Sultan, Suleiman 'the Magnificent'. Meanwhile, within France, problems of a different kind occupied the king's attention. Above all, he needed money to pay for his army and diplomacy. As the yield from taxation was insufficient to serve his needs, he was obliged to resort to various fiscal expedients: he created and sold offices, alienated crown lands, raised loans and imposed forced levies on towns and on the church. Another matter of growing concern to the king was the growth of Protestantism in France. Religious

18

uniformity was deemed essential to political unity; any religious dissent smacked of disobedience, even treason. As 'the Most Christian King', Francis was bound to eradicate heresy, but in its initial stages at least it was not easily defined. The king was torn between his sympathy for the New Learning, as exemplified by the writings of Erasmus of Rotterdam and Jacques Lefèvre d'Etaples, and his duty of defending orthodoxy.[1]

Such, in a nutshell, was the political and religious background against which Catherine de' Medici spent her first years at the French court. As a young girl, she was probably more interested in her immediate environment and in the people with whom she was in daily contact. Her father-in-law, Francis I, was a tall, well-built man, who could be charming and eloquent, but at the same time strongly authoritarian. He was above all a man of action, keen on fighting and hunting; but he also liked art, literature and music, and was one of the outstanding patrons of the Renaissance north of the Alps. The beautiful châteaux which he built in the valley of the Loire and around Paris bear witness to his passionate interest in architecture. In the popular imagination, however, Francis is primarily remembered as a great lover. His taste for erotic art seems to have accurately reflected his private life. His second marriage, like so many royal marriages of the time, was determined by political considerations: Eleanor never won a place in his affections. She was eclipsed from the start by his official mistress, Anne de Pisseleu, duchesse d'Etampes, but Francis also had a 'fair band' of ladies, who accompanied him on hunts. Outstanding among other ladies of the court was the king's sister, Marguerite, author of the *Heptaméron*, a collection of stories modelled on those of Boccaccio's *Decameron*, and of various religious poems. She had a strongly evangelical faith, although she never broke officially with the Catholic church.[2]

Catherine's own generation was represented at the French court by the king's three sons, François, Henri and Charles,

---

1 R.J. Knecht, *Renaissance Warrior and Patron: The reign of Francis I* (Cambridge, 1994), *passim*.
2 Ibid., pp. 105–17, 161, 286–90.

and two daughters, Madeleine and Marguerite. The Dauphin François, aged fifteen, and Henri (Catherine's husband) had only recently returned from Spain, where they had been held as hostages for nearly four years. They had been harshly treated, and Henri, for one, seems never to have forgiven Charles V. Francis I had high hopes regarding his eldest son, who was already being compared to Louis XII, 'father of the people'. One of the reasons for the extensive royal progress in 1532 was to introduce the Dauphin to his future domain and subjects. At Rennes, the young man performed his ducal duties impeccably, winning all hearts. His brother, Henri, was more involved in foreign affairs: being only second in line to the throne, he offered fewer risks as a diplomatic counter. Following his marriage, he became a key figure in talks over the future of Milan. Although both princes were still only adolescents, each already had a small group of clients. The third son, Charles, duc d'Angoulême, was only eleven in 1533. He had not shared his brothers' Spanish imprisonment and, perhaps for this reason, was less subject to melancholia; he seems to have been far more extrovert.[3]

Catherine seems to have adapted well to her new environment. She admired her father-in-law, and much later, when she herself had to govern France, she cited his court and government as examples for her children to follow. Francis, for his part, seems to have liked Catherine. She shared his taste for the great outdoors and was apparently an outstanding rider. She is even credited with the introduction into France of the side-saddle. Previously, the women had used a saddle, called a *sambue,* which was a kind of armchair in which they sat sideways with their feet resting on a board. This meant that they could only amble along. Women were now able to ride as fast as men.[4] At Catherine's own request, she accompanied Francis everywhere along with the rest of his 'fair band'. In March 1537 she was one of the princesses who wrote to the king after he had captured Hesdin. Their letter, which was probably written by Marguerite de Navarre, is an eloquent testimony of their

---

3   Ibid., pp., 304, 331, 338, 349–50.
4   J.-H. Mariéjol, *Catherine de Médicis* (Paris, 1920), p. 34.

20

love for the king. It tells of their fear at the thought of what might happen to him and of their intense joy on learning of his victory. They beg to be allowed to see him wherever he may choose.[5]

Catherine was capable of sharing the literary life of Francis's court. She had good command of French, although she spelt it phonetically and never lost her Italian accent. Although she never used Latin in her correspondence, this does not mean that she did not know the language. She certainly had some Greek. In 1544 the Florentine envoy, Bernardino de' Medici, wrote that her knowledge of that language was astonishing (*che fa stupire ogni uomo*)[6]. Catherine may have been taught by the great French Hellenist, Pierre Danès. However, it was her scientific knowledge which aroused the admiration of Ronsard, who praised her expertise in geography, physics and astronomy in a poem.[7] In this respect Catherine would have been unusual among the ladies of the French court, whose scholarly interests tended to be literary.

The king's sister, Marguerite de Navarre, states in the Prologue of the *Heptaméron* that Catherine and her close friend, Francis I's daughter, Marguerite, had thought of writing some stories modelled on those of Boccaccio, but they wanted them to be 'true stories' unlike his. They planned to bring together ten good raconteurs, but the Dauphin advised them against including any 'men of letters', who might sacrifice truth to effect.[8] The project, however, was abandoned as more important business intervened. In sixteenth-century Italy all kinds of poems were sung by four, five, six or eight voices with an instrumental accompaniment. The vogue soon spread to France. Composers, like Janequin, set to music Clément Marot's verse translations of the first thirty Psalms of David. Such songs became popular at court and the Dauphin was especially

---

5 *Lettres de Catherine de Médicis,* ed. H. de La Ferrière and G. Baguenault de Puchesse (Paris, 1880–1909), x. 1–2.
6 *Négotiations diplomatiques de la France avec la Toscane,* ed. A. Desjardins (Paris, 1859–86), iii. 140.
7 *Oeuvres de Ronsard,* ed. Blanchemain, ii. 182.
8 Marguerite de Navarre, *L'Héptaméron,* ed M. François (Paris, 1960), p. 9.

enthusiastic. He had them sung or sang them himself to the accompaniment of lutes, viols, spinets and flutes. He and each member of his circle chose a personal Psalm. Catherine's was 'Vers l'Eternel des oppressez le Père/ Je m'en irai ... '. Soon, however, singing Psalms became so popular among the early Protestants that the practice became suspect. The court abandoned them in favour of erotic poems by Horace.[9]

Catherine had experienced court life in Rome and Florence. She had spent some time with her papal uncles, Leo X and Clement VII. Although their court was staffed mainly by clergy and its ceremonies were mainly religious, it was far from austere. Leo loved music and hunting; he also enjoyed vulgar horseplay by jesters and scabrous plays. Clement had more dignity, while sharing the tastes of many a Renaissance prince. The Florentine court of Alessandro de' Medici was more modest than the papal court: it lacked traditions or etiquette and was contained within the Palazzo Medici in the Via Larga; the duke simply had more followers than other Florentine nobles and also his own bodyguard.[10] The court of France was different again in both scale and magnificence: a large number of princes, officers of state, prelates, lords and councillors revolved around the monarch and followed him on progresses across the kingdom. France had in effect two capitals: all important decisions were taken by the king and his council and it was to the court, wherever it might be, that foreign ambassadors brought their credentials, and that petitioners came, seeking a pension, a benefice or an office.

. . .

THE COURT OF FRANCIS I

It is impossible to say how large the court of France was at any given moment, for its population fluctuated: it was generally larger in peacetime than in war, when the king and his chief nobles would depart, leaving behind a rump of women, elderly men and clerics. Even in peacetime, its

---

9 Mariéjol, pp. 36–7.
10 Ibid., pp. 30–1.

population was variable. As it moved about the kingdom, nobles from one region would tag on for a few days or weeks, then depart, to be replaced by others from another region. Only the greatest nobles could afford to remain at court for long, as living there was not cheap. Furthermore, many liked to go home to their own estates. Even so, the court was on average as large as a small town of, say, ten thousand people. As Francis became a key figure south of the Alps, Italians flocked to his court looking for his protection or assistance. At the same time many Frenchmen went to Italy as soldiers, administrators or diplomats. They noted that women were regarded as an essential adornment of court society and that close attention was also paid to literature and the arts. In the light of their experience, the court of France acquired refinement and elegance. Francis wanted its ladies to be as beautiful and as fashionable as their Italian sisters. He asked Isabella d'Este to send him dolls dressed in the latest Mantuan fashions, which might be copied and worn by his own ladies. He also asked her for some of her famous soaps and other cosmetics. Francis, who was himself half-Italian, and spoke the language fluently, had many Italians on his household staff, including musicians and stable grooms. Many fine Italian horses were to be found in his stables, some being gifts from the duke of Mantua. Thus Catherine would have found much that was familiar at the French court. As the king's daughter-in-law, she was given her own household and her own team of female companions and servants.

One aspect of Francis's court, however, may have surprised Catherine. Unlike the Italian courts, it remained peripatetic, as it had been throughout the Middle Ages.[11] There were several reasons for this. France being a huge kingdom, it was easier for the court to find its food where it was produced than to have it brought from afar. The king also needed to show himself to his subjects and display his authority. Each year he tried to visit a new set of provinces: whenever he visited a major town for the first time, he was given a solemn entry (*entrée joyeuse*). The leading citizens

---

11 *Relations des ambassadeurs vénitiens sur les affaires de France*, ed. N. Tommaseo (Paris, 1838), i. 107–11.

would meet him outside the walls and offer him some gift in return for confirmation of their privileges. The king would then ride into the town under a canopy through streets that had been cleaned and decorated for the occasion. Tapestries would cover the façades of the houses and tableaux-vivants would be staged at different points along the route. There might also be temporary monuments, such as triumphal arches, bearing mottoes and symbols flattering the royal guest. Another reason for the court's wanderlust was the king's love of hunting. A single forest did not satisfy him: he wanted to encompass as many species of animals as possible.

The court was like an army on the move. It comprised a huge number of people and horses. In his *Autobiography*, Benvenuto Cellini tells us that the court sometimes had 18,000 horses and another contemporary witness speaks of stabling being provided for 24,000 horses and mules. Yet only the more important courtiers travelled on horseback; some of the ladies travelled in waggons and many servants had to walk. Waggons carried the court's plate, furniture and tapestries, for only palaces regularly visited by the court were permanently furnished: the rest were left empty and only furnished for the duration of its stay. Where roads were poor, Francis and his entourage would use rivers. His barge on the Seine was equipped with a kitchen. Finding accommodation was not easy. The king might stay in one of his own châteaux or be the guest of a nobleman or prelate or again he might stay at an abbey or an inn. Only privileged courtiers could share his roof; the rest had to look for other lodgings over a wide area or would sleep under canvas.[12] We can safely assume that Catherine, as a royal princess, was spared such hardships.

The court's movements following Catherine's marriage are precisely known. From Marseille, it travelled to Lyon. After spending Christmas at Pagny, the home of Admiral Chabot, it moved early in 1534 to Dijon, Joinville and Troyes. It then returned to Paris. Later that year the court stayed at Fontainebleau, Saint-Germain-en-Laye and Amboise.[13] Francis

---

12 *The Life of Benvenuto Cellini Written by Himself*, trans. J.A. Symonds, ed. J. Pope-Hennessy (London, 1949), p. 264.
13 *Catalogue des actes de François Ier*, vol. viii (Paris, 1905), pp. 484–5.

was at the château of Amboise on 18 October 1534, when some radical Protestants put up in various public places in Paris and elsewhere printed broadsheets (*placards*) attacking the Catholic Mass; one was allegedly displayed on the door of his bedchamber. The Affair of the Placards, as this event has been called, provoked a savage campaign of persecution in France. In January 1535, following its return to the capital, the court took part in a huge religious procession in which a large number of precious relics were displayed. Catherine was probably among the noble ladies who watched the event, and attended Mass at Notre-Dame and also the banquet held in the bishop's palace. Francis made a speech in which he called on everyone to fight the heretics. Thus, even as a young girl, Catherine would have been made aware of the mounting religious crisis in France.[14]

In the course of Francis I's progresses, Catherine would have seen some of the châteaux which he had commissioned and which were still being built. One of the newest was situated in the Bois de Boulogne, outside the walls of Paris. Although officially called the château of Boulogne, it became popularly known as the château of Madrid. It was a relatively small building, intended as a hunting-lodge. Unusually, it had neither courtyard nor moat. The elevation comprised Italianate and French features. The high pitched roofs and the spiral staircases were traditionally French, but the horizontal tiers of open loggias running round the entire building on two floors were distinctly Italian, as was the decoration of brightly coloured glazed terracotta. One of the artists responsible was Girolamo della Robbia, a member of the famous Florentine family of ceramists.[15] He was the youngest

---

14 G. Berthoud, *Antoine Marcourt* (Geneva, 1973), pp. 174–6; R. Hari, 'Les placards de 1534' in *Aspects de la propagande religieuse*, ed. G. Berthoud *et al.* (Geneva, 1957), pp. 114, 119–20; Knecht, *Renaissance Warrior*, pp. 313–21.

15 M. Chatenet, *Le château de Madrid au Bois de Boulogne* (Paris, 1987); F. Marias, 'De Madrid à Paris: François Ier et la Casa de Campo', *Revue de l'art*, vol. 91 (1991), pp. 26–35. Various explanations of the name have been given. It seems now that the building's unusual design was inspired by the Casa de Campo, a villa near Madrid, which Francis I may have seen during his captivity. See Knecht, *Renaissance Warrior*, pp. 404–5.

son of Andrea della Robbia and the grand-nephew of Luca, who had carved the *Singing Gallery* for Florence cathedral in 1431 as well as numerous reliefs of the Virgin and Child adorning other Florentine buildings.

At Fontainebleau, by far the most important château built by Francis after 1528, Catherine would have found other reminders of her native land. Here, the interior decoration was carried out from 1531 onwards by two Italian artists, Giovanni-Battista Rosso and Francesco Primaticcio. Between them they invented a style consisting of a skilful combination of painting and stucco. Rosso was another Florentine, who had come under the influence of Michelangelo and Raphael. His art is best seen today in the *Galerie François Ier* at Fontainebleau, a long gallery decorated on both sides by large mural paintings, depicting often obscure mythological subjects, framed by work in stucco, including nudes, putti, garlands of fruit and strap-work. The gallery's iconography is clearly intended to glorify the reigning monarch. Primaticcio's art is less well represented at Fontainebleau, much of it having been destroyed in the eighteenth century. In Catherine's day, however, it was very much in evidence, notably in the ballroom and the *Galerie d'Ulysse*. In 1540 the artist was sent to Rome on an art-collecting spree for the king, which brought him into contact with ancient sculpture and the art of Parmigianino. On returning to Fontaine-bleau, he developed a style of figure drawing exemplified by the elongated female nudes of the *Chambre de la duchesse d'Etampes*.[16]

In addition to being a great builder, Francis I was also an outstanding collector of works of art.[17] Among his artistic agents were two Italians: Battista della Palla and Pietro Aretino. Della Palla's activities were closely related to Florentine politics. He had lived in France as a political exile

---

16 Knecht, *Renaissance Warrior*, pp. 407–18; *La Galerie d'Ulysse à Fontainbleau*, ed. S. Béguin, J. Guillaume and A. Roy (Paris, 1985), pp. 9–42. The best account of the *Galerie François Ier* is in the *Revue de l'art*, special no. 16–17 (1972). See also E.A. Carroll, *Rosso Fiorentino: Drawings, prints and decorative arts* (Washington, DC, 1987).

17 Knecht, *Renaissance Warrior*, pp. 425–61; C. Scailliérez, *François Ier et ses artistes* (Paris, 1992).

between 1522 and 1527 and had given Marguerite d'Angoulême a portrait of Savonarola along with the friar's complete writings. In 1528 he returned to France as an envoy of the Florentine republic, and was asked by Francis to buy antiquities and works of art. Among statues sent by Della Palla to the king were Tribolo's statue of *Nature* (now at Fontainebleau), Bandinelli's *Mercury holding a Flute* and Michelangelo's *Hercules,* an early work by the artist, which had been in the Palazzo Strozzi and was now set up as part of a fountain at Fontainebleau. Another work obtained by Della Palla for Francis was Rosso's *Moses and the Daughters of Jethro,* now in the Uffizi gallery. Della Palla was imprisoned by the Medici in 1529, and died in the following year.[18] Yet even without his help Francis continued to add Florentine works to his collection, including Michelangelo's painting of *Leda and the Swan* (now lost) and possibly Bronzino's *Venus and Cupid* (now in the National Gallery, London).

Sculpture entered the royal collection later than painting. In 1541 Primaticcio returned from Rome with a number of plaster casts of ancient statues, mostly from the papal collection at the Belvedere. Almost certainly, Catherine would have seen the originals at the Vatican during her childhood. They included the *Ariadne,* the *Laocoön,* the *Apollo Belvedere,* the *Cnidian Venus,* the *Hercules Commodus* and the *Tiber.* They were turned into bronzes by Vignola, who set up a foundry at Fontainebleau in 1541. The statues, displayed initially in the *Galerie François Ier,* were much admired by the king and his entourage.

Some of the most valuable objects in Francis I's collection were made by Benvenuto Cellini, the Florentine goldsmith and sculptor. He has achieved immortal fame not only on account of his artistic creations, but also for his *Autobiography,* which offers a unique picture of Francis I's artistic patronage. Cellini visited France twice, in 1537 and 1540. The first visit proved a disappointment, although he gained

---

18 Caroline Elam, 'Art and Diplomacy in Renaissance Florence', in *Royal Society of Arts Journal,* vol. 136 (1988), 'Art in the service of liberty: Battista della Palla, art agent for Francis I', in *I Tatti Studies – Essays in the Renaissance,* v (1993) pp. 33–109.

the patronage of Cardinal Ippolito d'Este, the future Cardinal of Ferrara, another Italian prominent at the French court. Cellini's second visit lasted five years. He was given a workshop in the *Petit Nesle*, a medieval building in Paris on the left bank of the Seine, and one of his first works for the king was a statue of Jupiter in silver, one of twelve life-size statues of gods and goddesses which Francis intended for use as candelabra. Cellini was working on his statue one day, when he was visited by the king and members of the court, including Catherine. Among other works made by the artist for Francis was the famous salt-cellar now in Vienna.[19]

. . .

DIFFICULT YEARS

Catherine's marriage was fraught from the start. It had come about for political reasons. By forming an alliance with Pope Clement VII, Francis evidently hoped to consolidate and enhance his prospects in Italy; but Clement fell ill soon after returning to Rome from Marseille and died on 25 September 1533. In the ensuing conclave, the pro-French faction, led by Jean de Lorraine, made known its opposition to any candidate favourable to the Emperor, but it was ready to accept a neutral one. Clement had repeatedly designated Alessandro Farnese, Dean of the Sacred College, as his most suitable successor. The fact that Farnese was sixty-seven years old and in poor health commended him to the younger cardinals. On 12 October he was elected and took the name of Paul III. The election of a Farnese pope, however well disposed towards France, destroyed the *raison d'être* of Catherine's marriage. Her status was immediately reduced to that of a foreigner of relatively modest origins. Francis I allegedly remarked: 'The girl has been given to me stark naked.'[20] According to a Venetian report of 1535, all of France disapproved of her marriage, and Catherine's position was soon made even more difficult by a tragedy

---

19 J. Pope-Hennessy, *Cellini* (London, 1985), pp. 104–15, 133–46, 269, 280–1.
20 I. Cloulas, *Catherine de Médicis* (Paris, 1979), p. 57.

which befell the French royal family. On 10 August 1536, the Dauphin François died suddenly at Tournon after drinking a glass of ice-cold water. He had just finished playing a vigorous game of tennis with his secretary, Sebastiano de Montecuculli, and was seriously over-heated. A post-mortem concluded that he had died from natural causes; but contemporaries suspected foul play and Montecuculli was accused of poisoning the Dauphin. Some people believed that the crime had been instigated by the Emperor Charles V, while the imperialists looked for culprits nearer home. They pointed to Henri, the Dauphin's younger brother, and his wife, Catherine, who stood to gain most from his death. No substantive evidence has ever been produced to justify either charge. Montecuculli was nevertheless put on trial, made to confess his guilt under torture and publicly executed in Lyon.[21]

Stunned by the Dauphin's death, Francis had to face the prospect of being succeeded on the throne by Henri, whose wife had lost all her political significance. Only by producing a son, who would perpetuate the Valois line, could she hope to regain some prestige, but the first ten years of her marriage failed to produce offspring. Catherine's predicament became even worse, when her husband's virility was confirmed. In 1537, during a military campaign in Piedmont, he had an affair with Philippa Duc, the daughter of one of his grooms. She gave birth to a daughter, whom Henri legitimized under the name of Diane de France. He eventually married her off to Ercole Farnese, duke of Castro.[22]

Critics of Catherine's marriage tried to exploit the situation. According to Brantôme, 'many people advised the king and the Dauphin to repudiate her, since it was necessary to continue the line of France'.[23] Brantôme was relying on hearsay (he was not yet born in 1538), yet his

---

21 Knecht, *Renaissance Warrior*, pp. 337–8; M. François, *Le cardinal François de Tournon* (Paris, 1951), p. 132; V.-L. Bourrilly, *Guillaume du Bellay, seigneur de Langey (1491–1543)* (Paris, 1905), pp. 229, 233.
22 Mariéjol, p. 37.
23 Brantôme, *Oeuvres*, ed. L. Lalanne (Paris, 1864–82), vii. 341.

story seems to have substance. The Venetian ambassador, Lorenzo Contarini, writing thirteen years after the crisis, reported that Francis and Henri had both decided on a divorce. Catherine allegedly told the king that she owed him so much that she would not stand in his way: she was ready to enter a nunnery or to become the companion of the lady who would be fortunate enough to wed her husband. Francis was apparently so moved by Catherine's gesture that he promised never to banish her.[24] Even so, she could not be certain that reason of state would not oblige Francis or his son to set her aside. Her best safeguard was to become pregnant. She took medicines prescribed by her doctors and listened to her lady-in-waiting, Catherine de Gondi, who had produced a large brood. Happily for Catherine, on 20 January 1544 she at last produced a son. The event was greeted with tears of joy by Francis I and loudly acclaimed by court poets.[25]

Catherine's relations with her husband were, of course, bedevilled by his love for Diane de Poitiers, the widow of Louis de Brézé, *grand sénéchal* of Normandy, who became Henri's mistress about 1538, when she was thirty-eight and he only nineteen. It has been suggested that Henri's love for Diane was platonic. She has been compared to the *parfaite amie* of contemporary romances, the inspirer of noble thoughts and deeds. This view was advanced by the Venetian ambassador, Marino Cavalli, in 1546. In his opinion, Henri was not interested in the opposite sex and was content with his wife.[26] But there is evidence that Henry's love for Diane was far from platonic; nor was he indifferent to women: he had several love affairs in the course of his life and fathered at least two bastard sons.[27] It seems that Cavalli was taken in by Diane's propaganda. Under Francis I, her morals were frequently impugned by friends of the duchesse d'Etampes. In 1551 Lorenzo Contarini reported popular gossip to the

24 E. Albèri, *Relazioni degli ambasciatori veneti al Senato* (Florence, 1839–63), Series la, vol. iv, p. 73.
25 Mariéjol, p. 38.
26 Albèri, *Relazioni*, Series la, vol. i, p. 243; *Relations des ambassadeurs vénitiens*, ed. Tommaseo, i. 287.
27 *Lettres inédites de Dianne de Poytiers*, ed. G. Guiffrey (Paris, 1866), pp. 220, 223, 226, 228.

effect that Diane had been the mistress of Francis I and of many courtiers before becoming Henri's.[28] Diane's real personality is not easily disentangled from the myth which she helped to promote. By encouraging her identification with Diana, the chaste goddess of hunting, she effectively raised herself above the level of an ordinary royal mistress and disguised the true nature of her relations with Henri.

. . .

THE END OF AN ERA

In January 1543 William Paget, the English ambassador to France, explained to Henry VIII the difficulty of knowing Francis I's designs in Scotland. 'This king', he wrote, 'never sojourns two nights in one place, disposing himself as the report of great harts is made to him, and continually removing at an hour's warning so that no man can tell where to find the Court'.[29] Similar complaints can be found in other diplomatic dispatches of the time. The old king was continually dashing about the countryside, usually in the company of his 'fair band'. Yet he was a desperately sick man, plagued by abscesses which caused him much suffering. Although Francis maintained his grip on power, every courtier knew that his days were numbered and prepared for the inevitable palace revolution that would follow his passing. In August 1546 Nicholas Wotton wrote: 'the Court everywhere is the Court, that is to say, a place where is used good shouldering and lifting at each other'.[30] A major cause of strife was the bitter rivalry between the king's two surviving sons, Henri and Charles. The rift between them widened after Montmorency's fall in 1541. Henri remained the Constable's friend, while Charles became the darling of the Constable's inveterate foe, Madame d'Etampes. Each prince became the focus of a court faction. While Montmorency's friends rallied round Henri, his enemies gathered around Charles. In addition to

---

28 Albèri, *Relazioni*, Series la, vol. iv, pp. 77–8.
29 *Letters and Papers . . . of the reign of Henry VIII*, ed J.S. Brewer, J. Gairdner and R.H. Brodie (London, 1862–1910), vol. xviii (pt. 1), 29.
30 *State Papers of Henry VIII* (London, 1830–52), xi. 277.

Madame d'Etampes, these included Admiral Chabot and the king's sister, Marguerite. After the outbreak of war in 1542, the rivalry between the brothers was exacerbated by their military performance: whereas Charles conquered Luxemburg, Henri failed to capture Perpignan. The latter's hopes of redeeming his reputation were dashed by the peace of Crépy, which laid down that Charles would marry the emperor's daughter and become duke of Milan. He was also promised four French duchies as apanages. Had the peace been implemented, Henri's inheritance would have been seriously curtailed. He would have lost his rights in Italy and possibly much of his kingdom as well. Fortunately for him, the threat was removed when Charles died in September 1545. Thereafter, Francis drew closer to Henri, admitting him to his council and giving him more administrative responsibilities. The old wounds, however, were not easily healed, and Henri preferred to remain in the wings until the stage could be truly his.[31]

In February 1547 Francis fell gravely ill at Rambouillet, as he was travelling to Paris, and prepared for death. According to the imperial ambassador, Saint-Mauris, the king confessed to his son, Henri, that he had injured his subjects by going to war on trifling pretexts and asked him to repair the injustice done to Carlo III of Savoy. Francis also warned him not to be ruled by others as he himself had been ruled by Madame d'Etampes.[32] In another dispatch, Saint-Mauris says that Francis urged his son to take care of his sister, Marguerite, and to find her a worthy husband. He instructed him to defend the faith, to abstain from taxing his subjects too heavily and to take care of Queen Eleanor, whom he had treated badly. On 31 March the king breathed his last. Next day, Henri (whom we shall now call Henry II) ordered his funeral, which lasted several weeks.[33] While the king's heart and entrails were removed and buried in the

---

31 Knecht, *Renaissance Warrior*, pp. 453–86, 493–4.
32 C. Paillard, 'La mort de François Ier et les premiers temps du règne de Henri II d'après les dépêches de Jean de Saint-Mauris (avril–juin 1547)', in *Revue historique*, vol. v (1877), pp. 84–120.
33 R.E. Giesey, *The Royal Funeral Ceremony in Renaissance France* (Geneva, 1960), pp. 1–17. 193–5.

priory of Haute-Bruyère, his body was taken in procession to Paris for a solemn requiem mass at Notre-Dame and lastly to the abbey of Saint-Denis, traditional resting-place of French monarchs and their wives. During much of this ceremonial Henry remained out of sight. His self-effacement was essential to the ritual which involved honouring a life-like effigy of the late king. This was fed and wined for eleven days as if Francis were still alive. Eventually his coffin was lowered into a vault and his stewards cast their wands of office into it. '*Le Roy est mort! Vive le Roy!*' cried a herald.

Chapter 3

QUEEN OF FRANCE
(1547–59)

Catherine de' Medici became queen of France at the age of twenty-eight, yet her political influence was minimal during the lifetime of her husband, King Henry II. He looked to others for political advice, notably his mistress, Diane de Poitiers, and his chief minister, Anne de Montmorency. Catherine's role was essentially to perpetuate the dynasty. Having already produced two children – François and Elisabeth – during Francis I's reign, she produced eight more during the twelve years of Henry's reign: Claude, born at Fontainebleau on 12 November 1547; Louis, duc d'Orléans, on 3 February 1549 (he died on 24 October 1550); Charles-Maximilien – the future Charles IX – on 27 June 1550; Edouard-Alexandre – the future Henry III – at Fontainebleau on 20 September 1551; Marguerite – the future 'Reine Margot' – at Saint-Germain-en-Laye on 14 May 1553; Hercule – the future François, duc d'Anjou – at Fontainebleau on 18 March 1555; and lastly twin daughters, Jeanne and Victoire, on 24 June 1556. According to the Spanish ambassador, Simon Renard, this birth nearly killed Catherine. Victoire lay dead in her womb for six hours and her leg had to be broken to save her mother's life. Jeanne died seven weeks later.[1] Catherine was a very devoted mother, as is revealed by her correspondence: a high proportion of her earliest letters are addressed to Jean d'Humières, the governor of the royal children.[2] Yet, even if she was

---

1   J. Héritier, *Catherine de Médicis* (Paris, 1940), pp. 83–4.
2   *Lettres*, i. 17–18, 20–2, 26, 28, 31–2.

excluded from any significant role in state affairs, her future was largely determined by the events of Henry II's reign. Without entering into all the details of his policies at home and abroad, we must examine certain happenings which shaped Catherine's destiny.

. . .

THE PALACE REVOLUTION OF 1547

The death of Francis I was followed by a palace revolution. The forces of faction which had been building up in the last years of the reign were now released. Henry II had not forgiven the duchesse d'Etampes and Francis's ministers for the peace of Crépy. As the close friend of Anne de Montmorency, he would not allow any of the Constable's enemies to remain at court. He also cashiered Francis's 'fair band', some of whom took refuge in the household of the long-suffering Queen Eleanor. Madame d'Etampes, who had retired to Limours shortly before Francis's death, was refused accommodation at court. She retired to one of her châteaux and devoted herself to pious works. Eleanor returned to Spain, where she died in 1558.

The person who benefited most from Madame d'Etampes' overthrow was Diane de Poitiers. She was soon receiving gifts and distributing favours as unscrupulously as her predecessor had done. In addition to jewels and lands confiscated from Madame d'Etampes, Diane received from Henry the accession gift, which may have amounted to 100,000 *écus*. Other royal gifts included several lordships and property confiscated by the crown. In June 1547 she received the château of Chenonceaux, which Francis I had acquired in 1535. On 8 October 1548 Henry created her duchesse de Valentinois, the highest dignity any lady could receive who was not a princess.[3] It was in this capacity that Diane walked among the princesses of the blood at Catherine's coronation, on 10 June 1549, at the abbey of Saint-Denis.[4] Henry was also generous to his wife. He confirmed the right given to

3   *Actes de Henri II*, vol. 1, nos. 52, 518, 592, 767, 1089; vol. 2, nos. 3755, 3774; vol. 3, nos. 4925, 5896; vol. 4, no. 6465.
4   For a detailed account of Catherine's coronation see I. Cloulas, *Henri II* (Paris, 1985), pp. 228–31.

her by Francis I to appoint a master in every guild throughout France and renewed it when her second daughter was born. She was also allowed to dispose freely of the lands she had inherited from the house of Auvergne. In addition Catherine received an allowance of 200,000 *livres*. Important royal favours were also distributed among her relatives and friends.[5]

The palace revolution did not only affect the distaff side of the court. Anne de Montmorency, who had lived in retirement since 1541, now returned. On 12 April he took the oath of Constable and was confirmed as Grand Master and as captain of several fortresses. His arrears of pay, amounting to 100,000 *écus*, were settled. He also recovered the governorship of Languedoc, while his brother, La Rochepot, was reappointed governor of Paris and the Ile-de-France. In July 1551 Montmorency was created duke and peer, placing him on a par with the highest in the land. His nephews, too, benefited from his rehabilitation: the eldest, Odet de Châtillon, who was already cardinal-archbishop of Toulouse, acquired more benefices, including the see of Beauvais; his brother, Gaspard, became colonel-general of the infantry.[6] Montmorency's return to power automatically caused the fall of Admiral Claude d'Annebault and Cardinal de Tournon, who had run the government in Francis I's last years. Annebault remained Admiral but lost his salary and had to give up his marshalship to Jacques d'Albon de Saint-André. Tournon was replaced as Chancellor of the Ordre de Saint-Michel by Charles de Lorraine. After spending some time in his diocese of Auch, he went to Rome, where he championed French interests. His reward came in 1551, when he became archbishop of Lyon. Two years later, he and Montmorency were reconciled.[7]

Politically, the most sinister aspect of the palace revolution of 1547 was the emergence of the house of Guise as a serious rival to the houses of Bourbon and Montmorency. Within a few months, Charles de Lorraine became a cardinal, and his brother, François duc d'Aumale. They were the sons of Claude, first duc de Guise, and the nephews

5   Ibid., p. 144.
6   F. Decrue, *Anne, duc de Montmorency* (Paris, 1889), pp. 5–7.
7   M. François, *Le cardinal François de Tournon* (Paris, 1951), pp. 228–35, 254, 301.

of another royal councillor, Jean, Cardinal of Lorraine. Their eldest sister, Mary, had married James V of Scotland in 1538, by whom she had a daughter, also called Mary, the future Queen of Scots. François was a soldier, nicknamed 'scarface' (*le balafré*) after he had been seriously wounded at the siege of Boulogne in 1545. He was not only a brilliant tactician – but also a clever politician. His younger brother, Charles, was highly intelligent and a fine orator. His appointment as archbishop of Reims in 1538 had given him the highest position in the Gallican church and one of the richest. Both brothers had the backing of Diane de Poitiers, who needed to balance the Constable's influence. She gave them property, including Meudon, which had belonged to Madame d'Etampes' uncle, Cardinal Sanguin. Her daughter, Louise de Brézé, married Claude, marquis de Mayenne, the youngest son of Claude, first duc de Guise.[8]

The house of Bourbon fared less well in Henry II's distribution of honours. It comprised Antoine, duc de Vendôme and his three brothers: Jean, comte d'Enghien, Charles, the future Cardinal de Bourbon, and Louis, prince de Condé. The Albrets too were left in the cold. Henry, king of Navarre, hardly set foot in the new court, nor did his wife, Marguerite. As a close friend of Madame d'Etampes, she was unwelcome, and spent her last years mainly in Navarre. She died at a château near Tarbes in December 1549.

. . .

HENRY II AND DIANE DE POITIERS

Henry II has not, in general, been given a good press by historians. Michelet described him as a gloomy monarch, yet a Venetian ambassador described him as 'joyful, rubicund and with an excellent colour'. He was tall and muscular, and loved sport, particularly tennis, riding and jousting. Less intelligent than his father, he was less keen on the arts, yet musical.[9] His private life was a shade more respectable than Francis

---

8   J.-M. Constant, *Les Guise* (Paris, 1984), pp. 20–3; H. Forneron, *Les ducs de Guise* (Paris, 1893), i. 80–112.
9   L. Romier, *Les origines politiques des guerres de religion* (Paris, 1913), i. 20–9; Cloulas, *Henri II*, p. 338; F.C. Baumgartner, *Henry II* (Durham, NC, 1988), pp. 23–5, 39–40, 64–5, 103.

I's. He shared it with his wife, Catherine, and his mistress, Diane, but he also had a number of love affairs.[10] The most notorious was with Jane Stuart, Lady Fleming, a beautiful Scottish widow, who accompanied Mary Stuart to France (see below, p. 41) It took place at Saint-Germain-en-Laye when Diane was at Anet recovering from an injury. When she was told about it (allegedly by the Guises), she summoned Henry to Anet and insisted on Lady Fleming's banishment. Early in 1551 Lady Fleming gave birth to a boy, whom the king acknowledged as his own, giving him the name of Henri d'Angoulême, but the lady was packed off to Scotland.[11] In 1558 another of the king's bastards was born, this time to Nicole de Savigny. The boy was christened Henri, but not legitimized, perhaps because his mother was married and the king's paternity might have been challenged. The title of Saint-Rémy was conferred on the child, and much later he was given 30,000 *écus* by Henry III and allowed to incorporate three gold fleurs-de-lis into his coat of arms.[12]

A kind father and a loyal friend, Henry could also be vindictive and pig-headed. In exercising his kingly duties, he was conscientious and hard-working, but relied heavily on advisers. He allegedly trembled like a child whenever Montmorency appeared, yet at council meetings he listened carefully, spoke clearly and sensibly, and, once he had come to a decision, stuck to it.

Henry allowed Diane de Poitiers to exercise a considerable political influence. In 1547 an agent of the duke of Ferrara said that Henry II spent a third of each day in her company.[13] According to Saint-Mauris, he gave her an account of all the important state business he had transacted that day. Then, sitting on her lap, he would play the cittern, fondle her breasts and invite Montmorency or the duc d'Aumale to admire her charms.[14] Diane's influence was

---

10 *Lettres inédites de Dianne de Poytiers*, ed. G. Guiffrey (Paris, 1866), pp. 220, 223, 226, 228.
11 Antonia Fraser, *Mary Queen of Scots* (London, 1969), pp. 53–4.
12 J.H. Mariéjol, *Catherine de Médicis* (Paris, 1920), p. 40.
13 Romier, *Les origines politiques*, I. 26 n. 1.
14 C. Paillard, 'La mort de François Ier et les premiers temps du règne de Henri II d'après les dépêches de Jean de Saint-Mauris', *Revue historique*, vol. 5 (1877) p. 112.

most tellingly manifested in her château of Anet, which contemporaries described as a new Olympus. It was praised as
an enchanted palace by du Bellay, Ronsard and other poets.
Begun under Francis I, it was transformed by the architect
Philibert de l'Orme after Henry II's accession. Surrounded
by a forest, the château served as a magnificent hunting
lodge and as the venue for elaborate court festivals. The
gardens, filled with exotic plants, and the cryptoporticus (a
vaulted gallery with openings on one side) were much
admired by visitors. Yet it was the architecture itself, particularly the entrance portico, crowned by a bronze stag, and
the frontispiece of the main *corps de logis* which gave Anet its
unique character.[15] The design of the building and its
decoration paid homage to the owner, expressing the divine
self-image which she wished to propagate.

Catherine adored Henry and lived in fear of losing him.
Whenever he set off on a military campaign, she went into
mourning and insisted on her ladies doing likewise. She
begged Montmorency to send frequent news of the king's
health. Though deeply saddened by her husband's love for
Diane, Catherine concealed her feelings during his lifetime.
In 1584 she told Bellièvre: 'If I was polite to Madame de
Valentinois, it was for the king's sake, yet I always told him
that it was against my will, for no wife who loves her husband
has ever loved his whore; such a woman deserves no other
name, though it is an ugly word for us to use.'[16] Diane, for
her part, was too intelligent not to realize her proper place
at court. She nursed Catherine when she fell ill or was in
labour, sang her praises to the king, and even encouraged
him to sleep with his wife.[17]

Henry II was extremely interested in projecting his image.
He appointed a 'general engraver of coins' to design medals
and coins, bearing appropriate inscriptions and symbols.
The crescent moon, which was his personal device, implied
the fullness of an achievement yet to come. Henry was power-

---

15   A. Blunt, *Philibert de l'Orme* (London, 1958), pp. 28–55.
16   *Lettres*, viii. 181.
17   Catherine fell seriously ill at Joinville of puerperal fever
     in March 1552 and, according to her doctor, Guillaume
     Chrestien, owned her life to Diane's nursing and prayers. See
     Mariéjol, p. 43.

fully influenced by the cult of Antiquity which swept through the arts and literature in sixteenth-century France. His entry into Lyon in September 1548 resembled a Roman triumph: as he entered the city, he was met by some 160 soldiers wearing Roman uniform.[18] Diane's importance was openly acknowledged on this occasion. All the coats of arms and hangings adorning the route were embroidered with the letters 'H' and 'D' interlaced. An allegorical tableau showed Diana, goddess of hunting, holding a mechanical lion captive with a rope of black and white silk, the personal colours of the king's mistress. On the following day an identical pageant was performed for Catherine's entry, but the participants wore green instead of black and white. The mechanical lion was again produced.[19] This time it was presented to the queen by Diana and its breast opened to reveal a heart bearing Catherine's coat of arms. Among Henry II's other entries, that into Paris on 16 June 1549 made the greatest artistic impact. The programme, devised by the humanist Jean Martin, was carried out by a team of distinguished artists, including the sculptor, Jean Goujon, and the painter, Jean Cousin. Philibert de l'Orme, the superintendent of buildings, also took part. A beautiful monument handed down to us by that entry is the *Fontaine des innocents*, still to be seen in Paris, albeit in a new position and much altered.[20]

Although Henry II may not have been passionately interested in the arts, he nevertheless undertook a fair amount of building. He continued the reconstruction of the Louvre, erected the Château-Neuf at Saint-Germain-en-Laye, added a ballroom to Fontainebleau, and made improvements

---

18 Margaret McGowan, *Ideal Forms in the Age of Ronsard* (Berkeley, Calif., 1985), pp. 23–6, 143–4.
19 Was this the same lion as was produced for Francis I's entry into Lyon in 1515? See my *Renaissance Warrior and Patron: The reign of Francis I* (Cambridge, 1994), p. 131.
20 *The Entry of Henri II into Paris 16 June 1549*, with an introduction and notes by I.D. McFarlane (Binghamton, NY, 1982), *passim;* L.M. Bryant, *The King and the City in the Parisian Royal Entry Ceremony: Politics, ritual and art in the Renaissance* (Geneva, 1986), pp. 172–3; J. Chartrou, *Les entrées solennelles et triomphales à la renaissance, 1484–1551* (Paris, 1928), pp. 80-100.

at other royal palaces, including Chambord. He also took a close interest in Diane's château of Anet.[21] Catherine too indulged in building. Needing a château of her own where she might entertain her husband and the court outside Diane's orbit, she persuaded Henry to acquire the château of Montceaux-en-Brie, not far from Meaux, in 1555. He gave it to Catherine in August 1556 (see below pp. 228–9).

.　.　.

INTERNATIONAL AFFAIRS

Henry II could not forget the humiliation inflicted on French arms by Henry VIII's seizure of Boulogne in 1544. However, it was in Scotland, not in the Boulonnais, that he made his first significant move against England. In December 1542 Scotland had been plunged into a royal minority by the death of James V. He was succeded by his infant daughter, Mary, who soon became a pawn in the international marriage market. Henry VIII wanted to marry her off to his son, Edward, but the Scots preferred to link their fortunes to France. They reached an agreement with Henry II providing for the marriage of Mary with the Dauphin François. Soon afterwards, Henry II sent an army to Scotland which captured St. Andrews. In August, a French fleet picked up Mary at Dumbarton and carried her off to the French court.[22]

Once the English threat to Scotland had passed, Henry was able to attend to Boulogne. He declared war on 8 August 1549 and blockaded Boulogne. In October, however, Somerset was replaced as head of Edward VI's government by the earl of Warwick, who decided to end the war. A peace treaty was signed in March 1550 in which England handed

---

21　A. Blunt, *Art and Architecture in France, 1500–1700* (Harmondsworth, 1957), pp. 44–8; D. Thomson, *Renaissance Paris. Architecture and growth, 1475–1600* (London, 1984), pp. 84, 88, 90, 93, 96; J.-P. Babelon, *Châteaux en France au siècle de la Renaissance* (Paris, 1989), pp. 403–6.

22　Jenny Wormald, *Mary Queen of Scots: A study in failure* (London, 1988), pp. 61–3; Fraser, *Mary Queen of Scots*, pp. 27–35; Cloulas, *Henri II*, pp. 185–8.

back Boulogne in return for an indemnity of 400,000 crowns. In July 1551 an alliance provided for the marriage of Henry's daughter, Elisabeth, to the English king. He agreed to be godfather to Henry's son, Edouard-Alexandre, the future Henry III. These good relations lasted until Edward VI's premature death in July 1553.[23]

Like his father, Henry II wanted to rule northern Italy. At his accession, the French controlled much of Piedmont, but Milan was in the hands of the Emperor Charles V. As always, French fortunes in the peninsula depended to a large extent on the Holy See. Fortunately for Henry, Pope Paul III, having recently fallen out with the Emperor, was keen to draw closer to France. A link between them already existed in the person of the pope's grandson, Orazio Farnese, who had been brought up at the court of Francis I. The pope also strengthened French representation in the Sacred College. At his suggestion, seven French cardinals, led by Jean du Bellay, took up residence in Rome, and new ones were created. Charles de Lorraine became a cardinal in July 1547, and Charles de Bourbon in January 1548. The Franco-papal alliance was sealed on 30 June 1547 by a marriage between Orazio Farnese and Henry II's natural daughter, Diane de France.

In August 1545 Paul III had given to his son, Pier Luigi Farnese, the duchies of Parma and Piacenza, which the Emperor regarded as part of his duchy of Milan. Two years later, on 10 September, Pier Luigi was assassinated in Piacenza by imperial agents and the city handed over to Ferrante Gonzaga, the imperial governor of Milan. Henry II promptly assured the pope of his support, and Charles de Lorraine was asked to persuade the pope to sign a defensive alliance with France. The refusal of Venice to join it deterred Henry from going to war, but he decided to show himself in Italy. He left Fontainebleau in April 1548 with a large escort, leaving Catherine as regent. Among the Italian princes who came to salute him in Turin was Ercole d'Este duke of Ferrara, who used the occasion to arrange a marriage between his daughter, Anna, and François de Guise. This

---

23 Cloulas, *Henri II*, pp. 263–4, 270–1, 302–3.

brought the Guise family into closer union with the French royal family, as Anna was King Louis XII's granddaughter.[24]

Henry's interest in Italy was not restricted to the north: he was also concerned with the situation in Tuscany. Among the many Italian political exiles (*fuorusciti*) at his court, Florentines were prominent. They were led by the four sons of Filippo Strozzi, who had rebelled against Cosimo de' Medici. His rebellion had been crushed and he had died in prison. The eldest son, Piero, who was related to Catherine by marriage, was appointed captain-general of his Italian infantry. The second son, Leone, was a knight of Malta and captain-general of the French galley fleet in the Mediterranean. His brother, Roberto, was head of the Strozzi bank, which had advanced a major part of Catherine's dowry and assisted the French crown with loans. The fourth son, Lorenzo, was abbot of Saint-Victor in Marseille and bishop of Béziers; he became a cardinal in 1557.[25]

Henry's interest in Italy, however, was merely a facet of the protracted power struggle between the houses of Valois and Habsburg which had dominated international politics since 1521. Henry remained implacably hostile towards the Emperor, whom he had never forgiven for the hardships he had suffered as a hostage in Spain between 1526 and 1529. In October 1551 Henry signed the treaty of Chambord with the German princes who were opposing Charles V within the Empire.[26] In return for subsidies, they allowed him to administer the towns of Cambrai, Metz, Toul and Verdun as imperial vicar. In February 1552 he announced that he would lead his army to avenge the injuries inflicted by Charles and to restore German liberties.

For the second time Catherine was appointed regent in her husband's absence. She was dismayed to find, however, that she was expected to share the presidency of the council with Jean Bertrand, Keeper of the Seals, and that all decisions were to be taken by a majority of councillors. The

---

24 Ibid. pp. 174–9, 181–5.
25 Mariéjol, pp. 48–9.
26 G. Zeller, *La réunion de Metz à la France (1552–1648)* (Paris, 1926), i. 162–9; Cloulas, *Henri II*, pp. 308–10, 317–25.

responsibility for raising troops in an emergency was divided between herself and Admiral Annebault. Catherine refused to allow her commission to be published by the Parlement, believing that such a step would diminish her authority. She pointed out that Louise of Savoy had not been so restricted when Francis I had made her regent.[27] With his usual bluntness Montmorency warned her not to overstep her authority: 'You should not incur any expense or order any additional disbursement of money without telling him [Henry] first and knowing his pleasure.'[28] Catherine retorted that even if she had been given full powers, she would have acted only in accordance with the king's wishes.

Catherine took her duties as regent seriously. She supervised supplies for the army and proudly informed her husband that she had become a fully-fledged *munitionnaire*.[29] On 21 April she complained to Cardinal de Bourbon of some Parisian preachers who were preaching sedition in Paris. A Cordelier at Notre-Dame was criticizing the king's alliance with the German princes and the aid he was sending them. He also denounced an inventory of church treasures which had been ordered by the crown. At the church of Saint-Paul, a Jacobin preached on the text *principes sacerdotum concilium fecerunt adversus Jesum*. It was not God's will, he said, that the king should tax churches. This was not the way to perpetuate his title of 'Most Christian King'; benefactors would be deterred from making gifts to the church, and people would say that the king was so poor that he had to rifle the pockets of beggars. Catherine asked the cardinal to silence the preachers 'without noise or public scandal' and to appoint others to explain why the king needed to tax churches.[30]

On 5 April 1552 the van of the French army under Montmorency occupied Toul. Next to fall was the imperial city of Metz. The king, meanwhile, visited Nancy, capital of

---

27 Ribier, *Lettres et mémoires d'Estat des roys, princes, ambassadeurs et autres ministres sous les règnes de François premier, Henry II et Françoys II* (Paris, 1666), ii. 389; Mariéjol, p. 46; I. Cloulas, *Catherine de Médicis* (Paris, 1979), pp. 110–11.

28 Decrue, *Anne, duc de Montmorency*, p. 115.

29 *Lettres*, i. 56.

30 *Lettres*, i. 50–1.

Lorraine. The young duke Charles was sent to be educated at the French court, while his mother, the duchess Christina, was replaced as regent by the comte de Vaudémont. Having in effect taken possession of Lorraine, Henry pushed towards the Rhine but was warned by the German princes not to go further. He accordingly withdrew, having 'watered his horses in the Rhine', as he had pledged to do. He entered Verdun on 12 June and later that month returned to France. His 'German Voyage' has been described as 'one of the most successful military excursions in French history'.[31] At little cost in lives or money, he had gained three strategic bases on France's north-east border and secured a permanent foothold in Lorraine. In November, however, Charles V mounted a counter-offensive. He laid siege to Metz with a huge army, and bombarded the city for forty-five days. It was defended by François de Guise, who had only 6,000 men and a few guns. On 2 January Charles was forced to withdraw under the combined effects of cold, hunger and penury. Guise became a national hero, his victory being compared to David's over Goliath.[32]

Meanwhile, important developments were taking place in Italy. On 26 July 1552 the Sienese rebelled, expelling the Spanish garrison which had occupied their city for twelve years. It was well placed to serve as base for an attack on Florence. Taking Siena under his protection, Henry II appointed Cardinal Ippolito d'Este to represent him in the city. Then, on 29 October 1553, Piero Strozzi was appointed in place of the cardinal. All the *fuorusciti* were invited to join him and the Florentine bankers opened their purse-strings. Well provided with troops and money, Piero travelled to Rome, where he conferred with the pope. On 2 January 1554 he entered Siena. Frenchmen in Rome boasted that the king would soon be master of Tuscany, but on 8 May a Hispano-Florentine army prepared to besiege Siena. Florentine exiles everywhere stepped up their war preparations. In July the French court learnt that Piero Strozzi had invaded Florentine territory. However, on 2 August, he was

---

31 Baumgartner, *Henry II*, p. 153.
32 Cloulas, *Henri II*, pp. 326–9.

crushed at Marciano. Siena surrendered on 17 April 1555, much to Henry II's disgust.[33]

Although Catherine had left Italy for good in 1533, she retained territorial rights in the peninsula and continued to take an interest in its affairs. She was kept informed of Florentine events by correspondents in the duchy and by Italian political exiles at the French court. Her secretaries, almoners, domestic servants, messengers and astrologers were all Florentines. The poet Luigi Alamanni was her steward, and his wife, Maddalena, became Catherine's lady-in-waiting in 1552. Such people were happy to serve her, while other Italian exiles awaited the chance to return to their homeland and looked to the French king to make this possible. Catherine took a close interest in her husband's activities in Italy. Although she wrote politely to Cosimo de' Medici, she sided with the Strozzi. She was particularly fond of Piero. When Leone Strozzi suddenly decamped to Malta on the eve of Henry's German voyage, he not only angered the king but nearly dragged his entire family into disgrace. Catherine promptly reassured Montmorency about Piero's loyalty.[34] Her intercession seems to have been successful. In October 1553, as we have seen, Piero was appointed as Henry's representative in Siena. As for Leone, he was eventually pardoned and given command of the king's galleys in Italian waters. When he was killed, Henry promoted Piero to the rank of marshal of France 'to augment his renown and to console him for his brother's death'.[35] When Piero was defeated and wounded at Marciano, the news had to be withheld from Catherine for a few days because she was pregnant. On being told, she wept profusely but soon regained her composure. She sent a servant to commiserate with Piero and wrote letters of encouragement to the Florentine exiles in Lyon and Rome. She told them that Henry had decided to send more assistance to Tuscany than ever before.[36] Catherine some-times tried to influence her husband's policy. Thus in 1553 she imagined that he no longer cared about Florence, and

---

33 Romier, *Les origines politiques*, i. 322–450.
34 *Lettres*, i. 43–4.
35 Romier, *Les origines politiques*, i. 422.
36 *Lettres*, x. 13.

complained that she had not been consulted, but he showed that her suspicions were unfounded. When Piero Strozzi was appointed to defend Siena, Catherine raised money to help pay for his expedition by mortgaging some of her lands in Auvergne.[37]

Opinion at the French court was sharply divided on the question of French intervention in Italy. The Guises were strongly in favour, as their ancestors had once ruled Naples and Sicily and they longed to reassert themselves there. Montmorency, on the other hand, regarded Italian adventurism as a costly distraction. The fall of Siena enabled him to seek a general peace. Talks between Henry II and the Emperor opened at Marcq, near Calais, in May, but both sides proved uncompromising. By now the Emperor's health was failing, and his son Philip seemed ready to take over the burdens of government. Charles accordingly decided to abdicate. Having given up his titles, he retired to Spain in September 1556. One of Philip II's first moves was to sign a five-year truce with France at Vaucelles (5 February 1556). A breathing space suited Henry II, who was in a serious financial predicament.[38]

Charles V's abdication coincided with big changes in Rome: on 23 May Giampiero Carafa became Pope Paul IV. Although reputed to be a reforming churchman, he used his new-found authority to advance his nephews, particularly Carlo Carafa, whom he appointed as a cardinal and secretary of state. Paul demanded the see of Naples for him. When Philip II refused, the pope excommunicated him. In August 1555, following the breakdown of the talks at Marcq, Henry II decided 'to force the Emperor and his allies to shift the main burden of the war to Italy in order to relieve our territories and subjects on this side [of the Alps].'[39] A Franco-papal alliance was signed on 15 December. In exchange for French assistance, Paul IV agreed to bestow Naples on one of Henry's two sons and Milan on the other.

---

37 Romier, *Les origines politiques*, i. 418. She allegedly raised 100,000 *écus*.

38 M.J. Rodriguez-Salgado, *The Changing Face of Empire: Charles V, Philip II and Habsburg authority, 1551–1559* (Cambridge, 1988), pp. 126–32, 149–51.

39 Romier, *Les origines politiques*, ii. 22.

The pope was promised Siena in return. In May Cardinal Carafa travelled to France ostensibly to complete 'the holy task of peace', but in reality to urge Henry II to fight in Italy. Paul IV then threw down the gauntlet by excommunicating the Colonna, who supported Spain, and seizing their property.

On 1 September the duke of Alba, Philip II's viceroy in Naples, invaded the Campagna and, pushing northwards, threatened the Holy City. Responding to an urgent call for help from Carafa, Henry II decided to intervene. On 14 November he appointed François de Guise as his lieutenant-general in the peninsula. Although ostensibly a move to rescue the pope, Guise's expedition was ultimately aimed at the conquest of Naples. Ever since 1555 the Cardinal of Lorraine had been secretly working towards that end. Guise left Turin on 9 January 1557 with a small army, dependent on Italian allies for supplies and subsidies. In mid-February he met his father-in-law, the duke of Ferrara, and Cardinal Carafa, but they could not agree on his next move. Ercole wanted him to attack the duke of Parma, but Carafa opposed this move. Guise thought of invading the duchy of Florence, but was skilfully deflected by Cosimo de' Medici. So his only remaining course was to march on Naples. He hoped to be assisted by the French and Turkish navies, but was refused money by his Italian allies.[40]

In the summer of 1557 following the collapse of the truce of Vaucelles, Philip II attacked northern France. His army was commanded by Emmanuel-Philibert, duke of Savoy. His way south was barred at Saint-Quentin by the Constable Montmorency. On 10 August, battle was joined and the outcome was a shattering defeat for France, Montmorency being taken prisoner.[41] Guise was recalled from Italy and given wide powers as lieutenant-general throughout France. His brother, the Cardinal of Lorraine, replaced Montmorency as the minister principally concerned with domestic and foreign affairs. The Guises thus gained a firm grip on government.

After Saint-Quentin, Henry II urgently needed cash to rebuild his forces. From Compiègne, he wrote to Catherine,

---

40 Ibid. ii. 108–87.
41 Decrue, *Anne, duc de Montmorency*, pp. 203–5.

asking her to seek help from the Parisians. Surrounded by many lords and ladies, she went to the *Bureau de la Ville* and asked for enough money to pay for 10,000 troops. She explained that, the peasants being too poor, the king had to rely on help from the 'good towns', among which Paris was pre-eminent. After her speech, the queen was asked to withdraw, while the Parisian notables considered her request. They soon agreed to raise 300,000 *livres*. She thanked them with tears in her eyes and promised to recommend their privileges to the king.[42]

The battle of Saint-Quentin galvanized Henry II into making an exceptional effort. In January 1558 he explained at a meeting of the Estates-General that money was urgently needed to secure a good and lasting peace. Meanwhile, on 31 December, Guise pulled off a spectacular military coup by capturing the English enclave of Calais.[43] The estates were so excited by the news that they voted a large subsidy, which enabled the duke to press on with his campaign. He soon captured Thionville. An even greater triumph for his family was the marriage of Mary Stuart to Henry II's eldest son, the Dauphin François. They were betrothed on 19 June and the wedding was celebrated at Notre-Dame on 24 April 1558. The ceremony was followed, as usual, by lavish festivities, in which Guise acted as Grand Master instead of Montmorency. The prestige of the Guises was further enhanced by the marriage of Henry II's daughter, Claude, to Charles III, duke of Lorraine on 20 January 1559. Both marriages served to bring the Guises into closer union with the French royal house.

By the autumn of 1558 the belligerents badly wanted peace. Henry was anxious to free Montmorency and bring him back to court in order to check the fast-growing power of the Guises. He was also too poor to continue the war and needed time to deal with the growing menace of heresy within his kingdom. Philip II, too, was impecunious and keen to end the fighting, particularly as he disposed of a

---

42 *Registres de délibérations du Bureau de la Ville de Paris*, ed. Bonnardot, iv. 496–7.

43 D.L. Potter, 'The duc de Guise and the fall of Calais, 1557–58', *English Historical Review*, 118 (1983), 481–512.

marvellous bargaining counter in the person of the Constable. In December 1558 Montmorency was released after paying the first instalment of his huge ransom to the duke of Savoy. He was warmly welcomed at court by Henry and Diane, and recovered his old authority. While providing for the defence of the kingdom, he continued to work for peace.[44]

. . .

THE GROWTH OF PROTESTANTISM

Henry II carried repressive religious legislation further than his father had done. On 8 October 1547 he set up a special tribunal in the Parlement of Paris to deal with heresy cases. It became known as the *Chambre ardente* (Burning chamber) on account of the severity of its sentences.[45] The new tribunal was opposed by the church courts, which re- sented the loss of their traditional jurisdiction. On 19 November 1549 a new edict attempted to satisfy them, but conflicts over jurisdiction continued, causing Henry to issue the Edict of Châteaubriant (27 June 1551), which repre- sented a draconian tightening up of the heresy laws. In the light of reports that the judiciary was itself being infiltrated by the new religious ideas, the parlements were required to investigate their own personnel every three months, in a session called a *mercuriale*.[46]

One effect of the persecution was to swell the number of French people who fled to Geneva, where Calvin was seeking to create a city 'governed by God'. The flood became significant in the late 1540s. In 1549 the Genevan city council opened a register of people who applied for the status of *habitant*. This listed 5,000 names by the time the register was closed in January 1560, but the real number may have been around twice as many. Although Geneva's

---

44 Decrue, *Anne, duc de Montmorency*, ii. p. 221.
45 N. Weiss, *La Chambre ardente* (Paris, 1889, repr. Geneva, 1970), *passim*. See also Baumgartner, *Henry II*, pp. 264–6; J.H.M. Salmon, *Society in Crisis: France in the sixteenth century* (London, 1975), pp. 87–9.
46 N.M. Sutherland, *The Huguenot Struggle for Recognition* (New Haven, 1980), pp. 45–7, 342–3.

economy was not markedly affected by the immigrants, they did boost its printing industry. This employed many French exiles, including the lawyer-turned-printer Jean Crespin, author of the *Livre des martyrs* (1554), who, along with other Protestant martyrologists, promoted the idea that persecution conferred special blessings on a religious élite.[47]

Despite mounting persecution, heresy – now more clearly in the form of Calvinism – spread to many parts of France. In February 1557 Henry II was sufficiently alarmed to ask the pope to set up the Inquisition in France. Paul IV responded by appointing three French cardinals to serve as inquisitors–general for all the kingdom, but opposition from the Parlement frustrated this move.[48] He was especially disturbed by the changing social complexion of Protestantism; whereas he had always regarded it as a proletarian faith, nobles were now being drawn to it in increasing numbers. Nor were the exiles content to practise their faith abroad: they wanted to convert their countrymen. In 1555 Calvinist missionaries, trained in Geneva, began to slip back into France. They came in response to Calvinist churches looking for instruction and leadership. The distribution of the missions shows that the movement was mainly centred in towns, like Poitiers, Orléans or Rouen. Paris was the first city to have a properly constituted Calvinist church with its own pastor. Among the provinces, Calvinism was strongest in Guyenne, Gascony, Normandy, Dauphiné and Languedoc; it made little or no headway in the north and north-east where powerful Catholic families, like the Guises, were dominant.[49]

On 24 July 1557 Henry II issued the Edict of Compiègne, which has been called 'a declaration of war' on the heretics.[50] However, fierce opposition from the Parlement and the defeat at Saint-Quentin prevented it from being implemented. The Genevan missionaries were thus able to

---

47 R.M. Kingdon, *Geneva and the Coming of the Wars of Religion in France, 1555–1563* (Geneva, 1956), pp. 60, 93–105; M. Greengrass, *The French Reformation* (Oxford, 1987), pp. 31–2.

48 Romier, *Les origines politiques*, ii. 244; N.M. Sutherland, *Princes, Politics and Religion, 1547–89* (London, 1984), pp. 27–9.

49 Kingdon, *Geneva*, pp. 5–12, 31–40.

50 Sutherland, *Huguenot Struggle*, pp. 55–6, 344–5.

continue their activities. They tried at first to be as discreet as possible, holding services in heavily curtained rooms or in forest clearings. Sooner or later, however, they were bound to attract notice. This happened in Paris on 4 September 1557, when an angry mob broke up a Calvinist meeting in a house in the rue Saint-Jacques. The police intervened and some 132 people were arrested, including some noble-women. They were sent for trial and three were executed.[51] The affair gave the Calvinists, or Huguenots, unwelcome publicity. They also wondered how they should react to persecution by the crown. Were they to abide by St. Paul's injunction: 'The powers that be are ordained of God'? If so, resistance could be seen as sinful. They looked to Calvin for guidance. While pitying their plight, he told them that prayer was their only recourse. He warned that it would be preferable for them all to die than that the Gospel should be accused of fomenting sedition.[52]

In May, the Huguenots, taking advantage of an apparent softening of the king's attitude, staged a mass demonstration in a meadow, called the Pré-aux-clercs, on the left bank of the Seine, opposite the Louvre. It lasted several days and was attended by Antoine de Bourbon, king of Navarre, whom the Calvinists wanted to win over. The Cardinal of Lorraine secured a royal prohibition on access to the meadow. Numerous arrests were made, but, as the king did not want to stir up trouble at home just as he was about to go to war, most of the victims were released. Yet the rally convinced

---

51 Cloulas, *Henri II*, pp. 556–9; B. Diefendorf, *Beneath the Cross: Catholics and Huguenots in sixteenth-century Paris* (Oxford, 1991), pp. 50–1; N. Weiss, 'L'assemblée de la rue Saint-Jacques, 4–5 septembre 1557' *BSHPF* 65 (1916), 195–235.

52 *Corpus Reformatorum (Opera Calvini)*, ed G. Baum, E. Cunitz and E. Reuss (Brunswick, 1863–80), Vol. XLIV, cols. 629–30. A translation is given in G.R. Potter and M. Greengrass, *John Calvin* (London, 1983), pp. 154–5. On the Protestant doctrine of non-resistance, see Q. Skinner, *The Foundations of Modern Political Thought* (Cambridge, 1978), ii 219–21. The French Reformers began to be called 'Huguenots' around 1557. The word seems to come from the Swiss *eidgenossen*. See e.g. Léonard, *Histoire Générale du Protestantisme* (Paris, 1961), vol I, pp. 97–8.

him that his authority was under threat. He resolved that once peace was made he would cause blood to flow and heads to roll.[53]

Without wishing to interfere with the Parlement's judicial procedure, Henry expected the court to purge itself of heretics. On 10 June 1559 he turned up unexpectedly at a *mercuriale* and was shocked by the views of some young councillors. Anne du Bourg suggested that all heresy trials should cease pending a General Council; he also denounced as evil the burning of people who had merely invoked the name of Christ, while adulterers, blasphemers and murderers went unpunished. Taking the charge of adultery personally, Henry flew into a rage and ordered the arrest of du Bourg and five other councillors.[54] They were sent to the Bastille and commissioners were appointed to try them.

The Huguenots, meanwhile, were becoming more united. In May 1559 they held their first National Synod in Paris. It drew up a Confession of Faith and Ecclesiastical Discipline. The former was closely modelled on a confession which Calvin had drafted in 1557; the Ecclesiastical Discipline resembled the Genevan Ordinances which he had helped to draft. The main result of the Synod was to tighten up the organization of the French Reformed church. The authority of the National Synod was supplemented by provincial synods, regional colloquies and local consistories in descending order of geographical importance. Local churches could appeal from one body to the next or by-pass them all by appealing directly to the Geneva Company of Pastors, whose authority was accordingly enhanced.[55]

Where did Catherine stand in respect of religion in general and of heresy in particular? The evidence is scanty. She seems not to have shared her husband's orthodox militancy. As a young newcomer to the court of France she had joined the circle of Francis I's sister, Marguerite de Navarre, who had strongly evangelical leanings and who, in later years, offered protection to religious dissidents at her court

53 Cloulas, *Henri II*, pp. 561–2.
54 Ibid., pp. 585–8.
55 Kingdon, *Geneva*, pp. 46–7; Salmon, *Society in Crisis*, pp. 118–19.

at Nérac. Catherine apparently owned a French bible – either the translation by Lefevre d'Étaples (1523) or that of Olivétan (1535), which she read and allowed her servants to read. Her closest companion was Marguerite de France, the future duchess of Savoy, whose Catholicism was so tepid that Calvin later sought to convert her. Other friends included Madeleine de Mailly, comtesse de Roye, Jacqueline de Longwy, duchesse de Montpensier and Madame de Crussol, duchesse d'Uzès, who all became Protestants. On 27 September 1557 three pastors wrote to the council of Berne urging it to intercede on behalf of the Cantons in favour of the victims of the rue Saint-Jacques. Several members of the French court, they said, sympathized with their cause, but were timid; they begged the council to write at once to Catherine, to Marguerite de France, to the king of Navarre and to the duc de Nevers so that they might speak to the king. This suggests at least that Catherine was not regarded as hostile to the reformers. Evidence also exists that she was upset by the cruel punishments suffered by them at the end of Henry II's reign. Françoise de La Bretonnière, one of the ladies arrested in the rue Saint-Jacques, may have been released from prison as a result of Catherine's intercession.

. . .

THE PEACE OF CATEAU-CAMBRÉSIS (3–4 APRIL 1559)

Peace talks betweeen France, England, Spain and Savoy, begun at Cercamp on the Flemish border in October 1558, were concluded at Cateau-Cambrésis in April 1559. France was represented by Montmorency, the Cardinal of Lorraine and marshal Saint-André. Two issues were particularly contentious: Piedmont and Calais. Philip I wanted Piedmont to remove a possible springboard for further French aggression in Italy and to reward the duke of Savoy, who had commanded his army so brilliantly. While Henry was determined to keep Calais, Philip, as the husband of Mary Tudor, owed its recovery to his English subjects. But the problem was eased on 17 November 1558, when Mary Tudor died, releasing Philip from his obligation. The differences between the commissioners seemed irreconcilable at first; but Henry suddenly announced that he had decided to make peace, even at the cost of ceding

Luxemburg, Italy and Corsica. His announcement profoundly shocked the Guises and Catherine, who had so far kept her views to herself, implored Henry not to give up the French positions in Italy. She blamed Montmorency, saying that he had been wrong in the past about everything, but Henry disagreed: the Constable, he said, had always given him sound advice; the real wrongdoers were those who had broken the truce (i.e. the Guises).[56]

The peace of Cateau-Cambrésis (3–4 April 1559) consisted of two treaties: one between France and England; the other between France, Spain and Savoy. Calais was left in French hands for eight years after which France would return it to England or pay an indemnity of 500,000 *écus*. In Italy, France returned Bresse, Savoy and Piedmont to the duke of Savoy, retaining only the marquisate of Saluzzo and, for a time, five fortified towns in Piedmont, including Turin. Spain's rights to Milan and Naples were recognized. In Tuscany, all French positions were ceded to the duke of Mantua or to the duke of Florence. Genoa regained Corsica.[57] The treaty was sealed by two marriages: that of Henry II's daughter, Elisabeth, aged thirteen, to Philip II of Spain, and that of Henry's sister, Marguerite, aged thirty-six, to Emmanuel-Philibert, duke of Savoy. Marguerite, who was four years younger than Catherine, had always been one of her closest companions at the French court.

The peace treaty brought to an end the long sequence of Italian wars which Charles VIII had launched in 1494. It marked a turning-point in the fortunes of France and was

---

56 Romier, *Les origines politiques*, ii. 314 n. 1. The source is a dispatch by the Ferrarese envoy, J. Alvarotti, dated 18 Nov 1558. He also tells the story that Diane de Poitiers, who wanted peace, asked Catherine one day what she was reading. She replied: 'the histories of this kingdom in which she found that always from time to time the policies of kings have been decided by whores (*donne putane)*'. Mariéjol (p. 56) rejects this story as implausible: 'Ces bravades', he writes, 'ne sont pas de sa façon' (Such blustering was not her style).

57 For an excellent account of the treaty and of the negotiations leading up to it, see Rodriguez-Salgado, *Changing Face of Empire*, pp. 305–25.

extremely unpopular among the French captains. They deplored the loss of places in Italy which had been conquered at the cost of much blood and from which new campaigns might be launched. The duc de Guise was particularly upset and reproached the king with brutal frankness. Marshal de Brissac showed reluctance in handing over Piedmont, which he had defended so well. His most invidious task was to disband 12,000 veterans. Many captains had come to regard Italy as a second homeland. They poured obscene abuse on Henry's sister, Marguerite, alleging that Piedmont was, in effect, her marriage dowry. By July Piedmont had ceased to be French, and Brissac, refusing to be governor of merely five towns, stood down in favour of the seigneur de Bourdillon.[58]

Although news of the peace caused public jubilation in Paris, few French contemporaries had a good word for it. For Monluc it was 'a great misfortune' for the king and the nation and the origin of the civil wars. Agrippa d'Aubigné viewed it as 'glorious for the Spaniards, damaging to France and dreadful for the Protestants'. Pasquier deplored the fact that France had given up thirty years of conquests with a mere stroke of the pen. Outside France, the peace was received with dismay. French ambassadors attending the Diet of Augsburg were so embarrassed that they asked to be recalled. In Italy, France's allies – the duke of Ferrara and the Venetian republic – felt abandoned. In Rome, the peace was taken to mark the end of France's greatness as an international power. The pope merely said that he hoped it would enable Henry to give more time to religion. The opinion of modern historians has been, on the whole, kinder to the peace. 'In spite of its appearance,' writes Cloulas, 'the treaty of Cateau-Cambrésis did not mark a diminution of France, but a strategic retrenchment which made her less vulnerable.'[59]

On 15 June the duke of Alba, the prince of Orange and the count of Egmont, Philip II's proxies for his marriage with Elisabeth de Valois, arrived in Paris. Emmanuel-Philibert came a few days later. The wedding took place at Notre-

---

58 Decrue, *Anne, duc de Montmorency*, pp. 228–32; Cloulas, *Henri II*, p. 574.
59 Cloulas, *Henry II*, p. 582.

Dame on 22 June in the presence of all the court. It was followed by festivities, balls and masques at the Palais, the Tournelles and the Louvre. On 28 June the betrothal of Emmanuel-Philibert and Marguerite was celebrated and the marriage contract signed. The wedding itself was to be preceded by magnificent jousts lasting five days (28 June– 2 July). The preparations were closely supervised by Henry II. The lists, triumphal arches and galleries for spectators were set up in the rue Saint-Antoine outside the Tournelles. Rich hangings draped over the timbers bore the arms of France, Spain and Savoy; and statues symbolized war and the blessings of peace.

The first two days of jousting passed off well. Catherine and Diane watched from a gallery surrounded by their ladies. One night, however, the queen dreamt that her husband lay injured, his face covered with blood. Next day, she begged him not to enter the lists, but he would not listen. On a warm afternoon, he and three other combatants entered the lists. Henry wore Diane's colours of black and white, and rode a horse, called *Malheureux* (Unfortunate), a gift of the duke of Savoy. At first, the jousters did marvels. Though tired, Henry insisted on fighting off a challenge by the dukes of Nemours and Guise. He got the better of them, but then had to face another challenger in the person of the comte de Montgomery. He nearly unhorsed the king, whereupon Henry insisted on having his own back. Catherine again tried to restrain him but to no avail. Without even waiting for the traditional trumpet signal, Henry hurled himself on his opponent. Their lances broke as they collided violently. The horses reared. Montgomery regained his balance, but Henry fell heavily against the list. Montmorency and Tavannes, who acted as judges, rushed to his assistance. They found him unconscious with a long splinter of wood jutting from his helmet. Removing it carefully, they saw that Henry's face was covered in blood flowing from wounds caused by more splinters. The longest had struck his forehead above the right eyebrow and pierced the left eye. At the sight of the king's injuries, the Dauphin and the queens fainted, and a loud cry of anguish rose from among the ladies. A disorderly crowd invaded the lists. Montgomery threw himself at the king's feet in a frenzy of guilt: he asked the king, who had regained consciousness, to cut off his hand or behead him, but Henry said he had no cause to seek a pardon; he had only obeyed his king, like a good knight. Henry was then carried to the Tournelles. He tried to walk up the main staircase but had to be supported. His physician wiped blood from his face and applied soothing lotions to his wounds, pending the arrival of more eminent doctors. Vesalius, Philip II's own physician, hastened from Brussels at the request of the duke of Savoy; the famous surgeon Ambroise Paré also hurried to the king's bedside. Five large splinters of wood were removed from his head without anaesthetic, yet he cried out only once. Catherine remained at his bedside with Emmanuel-Philibert and the Cardinal of Lorraine. The duc de Guise, Alfonso d'Este, the Constable Montmorency all took turns at the vigil, but not Diane de Poitiers who was afraid of being driven away by the queen. She was never to see her lover again.

On 1 July the king rallied: he was able to sleep, eat and drink a little. Next day, he spoke a few words and again exonerated Montgomery. On 3 and 4 July he listened to some music, ordered Marguerite's wedding to take place and dictated a letter to his ambassador in Rome informing him of the arrest of Anne du Bourg and other 'Lutherans' in the Parlement. Later that day, however, the king's fever returned. He dictated another letter, but soon lost both sight and speech. On 9 July after receiving Extreme Unction, Henry clasped the Dauphin's hand. That night the wedding of the duke of Savoy and Marguerite was celebrated in another room of the palace. On 10 July Henry died. He was forty years old and had reigned for just over twelve years.[60] French queens traditionally wore white on being widowed, but Catherine was in black as she took leave of her husband's corpse. She remained in mourning for the rest of her life, a broken lance becoming her emblem.

---

60 Ibid., pp. 588–94; Romier, *Les origines politiques*, ii. 378–90.

Chapter 4

QUEEN-MOTHER
(1559–62)

The untimely death of Henry II revealed the weakness of an essentially personal monarchy. Whereas he and his father had been strong men who could lead their armies in battle and command the loyalty of the nobility, Francis II was a mere boy of fifteen and a sickly one at that. Under an ordinance of King Charles V, he was old enough to rule, but lacked experience and judgment. Yet, because of his age, Catherine could not be regent. It is wrong, therefore, to assume, as historians, have often done, that she was responsible for the change of regime after Henry II's death. This is not to be compared with the palace revolution of 1547. True, Diane de Poitiers was banished from the court just as the duchesse d'Etampes had been; but this had been Henry II's decision. What happened in 1559 was a *coup d'état* by the Guises. They quite simply seized power while Catherine was grieving the loss of her husband and Montmorency was occupied standing guard over his body.[1]

The essential feature of the *coup d'état* was Montmorency's exclusion from the central government. This would have pleased Catherine, who allegedly hated him. According to the Venetian ambassador, Giovanni Michieli, he had offended her by his accord with Diane and also by describing Catherine as 'a merchant's daughter'.[2] Montmorency re-

---

1 E. Pasquier, *Lettres historiques pour les années 1556–1594*, ed. D. Thickett (Geneva, 1966), p. 35.
2 E. Albèri, *Relazioni degli ambasciatori veneti al Senato* (Florence, 1839–63), series la, vol. iii, p. 438.

mained Constable, but was made to surrender the Grand Mastership to the duc de Guise. This gave the duke and his brother, the Cardinal of Lorraine, control of the court. They moved the king to the Louvre, where they themselves resided, and Catherine, not to be marginalized, followed him there, breaking the tradition whereby the widow of a French king was expected to remain at the site of his death for forty days afterwards.

Even if the Constable ceased to exercise political influence at the centre of government, he remained a power in the land. He was the richest nobleman in France, owning, it was said, more than 600 fiefs, and was related to some of the most prestigious families in the land. As governor of Languedoc, he continued to hold sway over the Midi. His eldest son, François, was governor of Paris and the Ile-de-France, and two of his nephews held important offices: Gaspard de Coligny was Admiral of France and François d'Andelot was colonel-general of the infantry. Catherine would have been unwise to alienate the old Constable. She preferred to undermine his authority by subtle means: she persuaded him to give up the Grand Mastership in exchange for the promotion of his son François as marshal of France.[3]

As for Diane de Poitiers, she suffered the inevitable fate of a royal mistress: having left the court before the death of Henry II, she never returned. Her daughter, the duchesse de Bouillon, was also banished, but not her other daughter, the duchesse d'Aumale, presumably because she was the duc de Guise's sister-in-law. Diane was also obliged to hand over the crown jewels and to sell Chenonceaux to Catherine in exchange for Chaumont. Her fall from grace also entailed the dismissal of her creature, Jean Bertrand, as Keeper of the Seals, and the return of François Olivier as chancellor.[4]

The *coup d'état* mounted by the Guises was swift. Within a few days the English ambassador reported: 'the house of Guise ruleth and doth all about the French king'. In less than two months the cardinal was described by the Floren-

---

3   J.-H. Mariéjol, *Catherine de Médicis* (Paris, 1920), pp. 59–60.
4   Ibid., p. 61; Y. Cloulas, *Catherine de Médicis* (Paris, 1979), pp. 125–6.

tine envoy as both pope and king in France. An examination of the registers of the royal secretariat for April and June 1560 shows the domination of the Guises. The *Épargne*'s accounts are filled with gifts of money, payments of arrears and reimbursements of loans to their relatives, clients and servants.[5] For many noblemen the obvious response to this situation was to become Guise clients themselves, but this option was not open to all. Protestant nobles, in particular, could not expect fair treatment from men who had championed their persecution under the late king.

The Guises were related to the royal family in several ways. Their grandmother was Antoinette de Bourbon, sister of the king of Navarre, and the duc de Guise was married to Anne d'Este, granddaughter of King Louis XII. They were also, as we have seen, the uncles of Mary Stuart, Francis II's queen. Yet they were not deeply rooted in the old French nobility: their origins lay in the duchy of Lorraine, which still formed part of the Holy Roman Empire.[6] For this reason many Frenchmen regarded them as aliens and usurpers; they failed to see by what right they assumed control of the kingdom instead of Antoine de Bourbon, king of Navarre and first prince of the blood. But he was in Guyenne when Henry II died and took a long time reaching the court. As he travelled slowly to Paris, he was urged by his brother, Louis, prince de Condé, and by friends to assert his rights, but Antoine was indolent: he wriggled and hedged so that by the time he arrived at court the Guises were firmly in control. They found a pretext for denying him accommodation, and, although allowed to sit in the king's council, he was excluded from the inner circle of ministers who decided policy. He feebly accepted this snub and even agreed to accompany Elisabeth de Valois to Spain following her marriage to King Philip II. By so doing he hoped to ingratiate himself with her husband as a first step towards recovering Spanish Navarre, which Ferdinand of Aragon had seized from his ancestor, Jean d'Albret, in 1513.[7] Even

5 R.R. Harding, *Anatomy of a Power Elite* (New Haven, 1978), pp. 34–5.
6 J.-M. Constant, *Les Guise* (Paris, 1984), pp. 20–2.
7 N.M. Sutherland, *Princes, Politics and Religion, 1547–1589* (London, 1984), pp. 55–64; L. Romier, *La Conjuration d'Amboise* (Paris, 1923), pp. 17–27.

Condé, who was far more dynamic, allowed himself to be sidelined by accepting a diplomatic mission to the Netherlands. So the Guises were left to govern France as they wished.

Henry II had been obliged to sign the peace of Cateau-Cambrésis for two main reasons: his serious financial predicament and the growing threat of heresy. Both problems were now taken in hand by the Guises. They estimated the public debt to be 40 million *livres*, half of which was due for immediate repayment. Royal revenue from taxation was estimated at 12 million *livres* and this was probably an over-estimate. Faced with the choice of increasing taxes or curbing expenditure, they chose the latter. Various highly unpopular measures were taken: royal troops were disbanded, the payment of their wages was deferred, pensions were suppressed, free alienations of royal lands revoked, and the interest on royal debts arbitrarily curtailed. Many nobles suspected that these measures were being taken, not in the interest of the kingdom, but of the Guises themselves and their clients. They wondered if they reflected the wishes of the boy-king or whether he was being manipulated by his ministers. Lower down the social scale, the high-handed way in which the Guises treated those who protested at their policy caused deep offence. When disbanded soldiers petitioned the Cardinal of Lorraine for their wages, they were sent packing under threat of the noose. Discontent was particularly rife among the turbulent nobles of south-west France.[8]

The Guises also tightened up the heresy laws. As Protestants continued to meet in secret, wild rumours circulated regarding the nature of their activities. Public concern was reflected in increasingly draconian legislation. On 4 September 1559 an edict ordered houses used by them for illegal meetings to be razed to the ground. Two months later, the death penalty was prescribed for anyone holding or attending illicit meetings. The authorities claimed that the meetings were being used to stir up sedition. Also in November, the denunciation of such meetings was made

---

8   Harding, *Anatomy*, pp. 47–9; Romier, *La Conjuration d'Amboise*, pp. 6–9.

obligatory on pain of death. Informers were to be protected and rewarded.[9] An early victim of the repression was Anne du Bourg, the *parlementaire* who had been arrested under Henry II.[10] The pastor François Morel appealed on his behalf to Catherine, who was believed to have some sympathy for the reformed faith. She promised to work for an improvement in the lot of Protestants 'provided that they did not hold assemblies and that each lived secretly and without scandal'. The persecution, however, continued, whereupon Morel wrote again to the queen. 'She could be assured', he said, 'that God would not allow such an injustice to go unpunished, seeing that He knew his [du Bourg's] innocence; and that just as God had begun by punishing the late king, so she should realize that His arm was still raised to complete His revenge by striking her and her children.' Such impertinence was counter-productive. Catherine said that the goodwill she had shown to the reformers had stemmed only from pity and compassion, not from any desire on her part 'to be otherwise instructed or informed as to the truth or falsehood of their doctrine'.[11] Du Bourg was burnt on 23 December. Yet the queen-mother did not sever relations with the Huguenots. She knew that Navarre was being urged by his friends to demand his rightful place in the government, and wished to know how much Huguenot support he could expect. Through the good offices of Eléonore de Roye, Condé's mother-in-law, a secret meeting was arranged between Catherine and the Parisian pastor, Antoine de la Roche-Chandieu. She was supposed to meet him on her way to Reims for her son's

9 Isambert, *Recueil des anciennes lois françaises*, xiv, pp. 9, 11; N.M. Sutherland, *The Huguenot Struggle for Recognition* (New Haven, 1980), pp. 346–7.

10 Pasquier, *Lettres*, pp. 39, 43; P. Champion, *Paris au temps des Guerres de Religion* (Paris, 1938), pp. 57–80; R.M. Kingdon, *Geneva and the Coming of the Wars of Religion in France, 1555–1563* (Geneva, 1956), p. 64.

11 *Calvini opera*, xvii, cols, 590–1, 597; Régnier de La Planche, *L'Histoire de l'Estat de France tant de la République que de la Religion sous le règne de François II*, ed. Buchon (1836), pp. 211, 219–20; Mariéjol, pp. 67–8.

coronation (18 September), but failed to do so for some unknown reason.[12]

. . .

THE TUMULT OF AMBOISE (MARCH 1560)

On 15 August Morel wrote to Calvin, complaining of Navarre's lethargy. He asked if other means existed of liberating the Reformed church from its current sufferings. The law laid down that if the king died, leaving only minors, the estates should be called to appoint administrators of the realm until they came of age. If Navarre failed to call the estates, could someone else do so? And if legal means failed, could force be used to win back what the tyrants had seized? Calvin's reply was uncompromising: only the first prince of the blood was authorized by law to act.[13] But enemies of the Guises soon despaired of Navarre, who seemed more interested in the recovery of his southern kingdom. They consequently decided to overthrow the Guises by force. Who instigated their conspiracy is not clear. It may have been Condé, but this has been disputed.[14] Historians have traditionally focused on the political aims of the conspirators, but their primary objective may have been to present their Confession of Faith to the king.[15]

Whatever Condé's role in the plot may have been, its preparation, involving the recruitment of troops, was entrusted to the seigneur de La Renaudie, a petty nobleman from Périgord, who had become a Protestant in the course of an adventurous career. He did not impress Calvin on a visit to Geneva, but received encouragement from his right-hand man, Théodore de Bèze. On 1 February 1560 the plotters held a meeting at Nantes in which their loyalty to the king was emphasized alongside their resolve to bring the

---

12 Mariéjol, pp. 69–70.
13 *Calvini opera*, xviii, cols 425–6; on Calvin and non-resistance see Q. Skinner, *The Foundations of Modern Political Thought* (Cambridge, 1978), ii. 191–4.
14 Romier, *La Conjuration d'Amboise*, pp. 10–16, 30–36; Sutherland, *Huguenot Struggle*, pp. 84–6.
15 J. Poujol, 'De la confession de foi de 1559 à la Conjuration d'Amboise, BSHPF 109 (1973), 158–77.

Guises to justice. La Renaudie was confirmed as commander of the coup, scheduled to take place on 10 March. This date, however, had to be postponed for six days.[16]

Secrecy was seldom achieved in sixteenth-century France, and rumours of an impending coup soon reached the ears of the court.[17] It decided to move to the château of Amboise, which was deemed strong enough to withstand a siege. Meanwhile, on 2 March, the king issued the Edict of Amboise, which offered an amnesty to all peaceful reformers.[18] A few days later he ordered the release of all religious prisoners and allowed religious dissenters to petition him. Historians are divided over the authorship of this surprisingly generous move. Sutherland believes that 'it was the work of Catherine de' Medici and the chancellor l'Hospital – possibly also of Coligny', but L'Hôpital did not become chancellor till June. Cloulas ascribes the edict to the queen-mother. It was she, he points out, who sent Jacques de Moroges to the Parlement with a demand that the edict should be registered forthwith. Evennett believes that the Cardinal of Lorraine had some responsibility for it. He confessed as much to the pope, and two years later the bishop of Valence declared that the Guises had first come to recognize the failure of persecution as a means of dealing with heresy early in 1560.[19]

The Edict of Amboise implied no weakening by the government in the face of the Protestant challenge. As groups of conspirators gathered in woods surrounding the château of Amboise, they were set upon by royal troops. Some, like La Renaudie, were killed on the spot; others were rounded up, put through summary trials and executed. Many were drowned in the Loire; others were hanged from

---

16 Kingdon, *Geneva*, pp. 68–72.
17 Pasquier, *Lettres*, pp. 40–1. The plot was betrayed to the Cardinal of Lorraine by a lawyer, called Pierre des Avenelles, who had housed La Renaudie in Paris.
18 Sutherland, *Huguenot Struggle*, pp. 104–5, 347–48; J. Shimizu, *Conflict of Loyalties: Politics and religion in the career of Gaspard de Coligny, Admiral of France, 1519–1572* (Geneva, 1970), p. 38.
19 Sutherland, *Huguenot Struggle*, p. 348; Cloulas, *Catherine*, p. 145; H.O. Evennett, *The Cardinal of Lorraine and the Council of Trent* (Cambridge, 1930), p. 99.

the château's balconies and battlements. The king and the ladies of the court watched the grisly spectacle. Catherine's reaction to the slaughter can only be glimpsed in the records. She allegedly tried to save the life of a captain Castelnau by humbling herself before the Guises, but found them implacable.[20]

The immediate aftermath of the conspiracy is surprising. A savage onslaught on the Huguenots might have been expected. Instead, the policy of moderation initiated by the Edict of Amboise was maintained. At the same time the government looked for ways of restoring religious unity. It began to toy with the idea of calling a national council to reform the church. Writing to the pope on 21 March, Lorraine argued that the recent crisis had shown that heretics were a grave threat to Catholicism in France. He felt that a General Council of the church would take too long to assemble and asked the pope to send Cardinal Tournon to France as legate with powers to reform the French church and, if necessary, to convene a national council. The prospect horrified Pius IV, who viewed a national council as the first step towards a national church. While agreeing to send Tournon as legate, he harshly criticized the religious policy of the French government; the king, he said, had no right to pardon convicted heretics.[21]

Catherine wanted to know what lay behind the current crisis. She accordingly ordered Admiral Coligny to look into the religious situation in Normandy, where he had been sent to prepare a military expedition to Scotland. As yet, he had not declared his allegiance to the Reformed church, but he evidently sympathized with it. He allegedly wrote to Catherine advising her to take charge of the government and to stop the religious persecution.[22] She also tried to arrange a meeting with Chandieu, the Huguenot pastor, but her agents were informed that he was no longer in France. When they asked for a substitute, the Huguenots of Tours refused. They offered to send their views in writing instead. On 24 May a certain Le Camus handed Catherine a remonstrance under

---

20 Romier, *La Conjuration d'Amboise*, pp. 117–19; Mariéjol, p. 75.
21 Evennett, *Cardinal of Lorraine*, p. 100.
22 Shimizu, *Coligny*, pp. 38–9.

the pseudonym of Théophile. This explained that the Amboise plotters had intended no action against the king or his family: they had been driven to use force by the Guises, who had blocked their path to the king and had usurped the place rightfully belonging to the princes of the blood. They advocated two solutions to the current crisis: a council to solve the religious problem and a meeting of the Estates-General to topple the Guises in favour of the princes. The Guises were told of the remonstrance (allegedly by Mary Stuart) and Le Camus was thrown into prison.[23] Yet Catherine pursued her enquiries. She questioned Régnier de La Planche, a councillor of Marshal Montmorency, in the hope of finding out where the Constable and his supporters stood in respect of the princes of the blood. He boldly declared that the Guises should not ride in harness (*tirer au collier*) with the Bourbon princes, but should allow them to lead. He distinguished between two sorts of Huguenots: 'religious' ones, who were only interested in their own salvation, and 'political' ones, who wanted to get rid of the Guises. The former, he believed, could be appeased by means of a council; the latter would not rest until the Guises had been replaced at the head of the government by the princes of the blood.[24]

Catherine was, it seems, mainly responsible for the Edict of Romorantin (May 1560), which tried to turn the judicial clock back. No royal court, not even the Parlement, was to judge heresy cases; these were now left to the ecclesiastical courts. As the church did not impose the death penalty, this was a simple way of unwinding the savage persecution unleashed under Henry II. Bishops were ordered to reside in their dioceses and to attend to the problem of heresy. The edict also effectively nullified the inquisitorial clauses of the Edict of Châteaubriant (1551). In short, Protestants were implicitly tolerated as long as they behaved discreetly. At the

---

23 La Planche, *L'Histoire*, pp. 299–302, 304; Sutherland, *Huguenot Struggle*, pp. 112–13 (where the petition is wrongly dated August 1562); Mariéjol, pp. 76–7.
24 La Planche, *L'Histoire*, pp. 316–18. On his reliability see Mariéjol, p. 77 n. 4. Sutherland writes: 'La Planche is known to have been anti-Guise, but there is no evidence that he was unreliable' (*Huguenot Struggle*, p. 74 n. 26).

same time, the edict banned 'illicit assemblies'. Presumably these were assemblies under arms. Participants in such assemblies were to be prosecuted as rebels before the presidial courts. Informers on such meetings were to receive a reward of 500 *livres*. The edict, however, was fiercely resisted by the Parlement. During a month of debates, all the old arguments over the Concordat of 1516 resurfaced. The *parlementaires* objected to church courts being given so much authority at the expense of the royal ones, particularly as their judges had proved so inefficient. Although the edict was eventually registered, it only produced jurisdictional confusion and was consequently a dead letter.[25]

Meanwhile, discontent mounted in the kingdom at large. The Guises were targeted by popular demonstrations. Lorraine was hanged in effigy in Paris and his château of Meudon was attacked by arsonists. Fearing assassination, he surrounded himself with arquebusiers. A flood of abusive pamphlets poured forth from clandestine presses. Catherine herself was denounced as a whore who had brought a leper into the world. Such propaganda, however, could not destroy the government. Far more sinister was the build-up of a Huguenot military organization. Legislation against heresy, however harsh, was largely ineffective, because the officials responsible for its enforcement were themselves Protestants or Protestant sympathizers. Here and there, more especially in the south, Huguenots demonstrated their faith more provocatively than ever.

· · ·

THE FONTAINEBLEAU ASSEMBLY (AUGUST 1560)

In June 1560 Michel de L'Hôpital, a distinguished lawyer who had studied in Italy and acquired an interest in humanism, was appointed Chancellor of France, the highest public office under the king. He is remembered mainly for his moderation in the midst of bitter religious divisions, but he did not advocate religious toleration. In his judgment, two faiths could not coexist in France without seriously damaging

---

25 E. Maugis, *Histoire du Parlement de Paris* (Paris, 1914), ii. 25–6; Sutherland *Huguenot Struggle*, pp. 113–14, 349–51.

the kingdom's unity; but he knew that Protestantism was too deeply rooted to be violently eradicated. This was not an option he would even contemplate. 'Force and violence', he said, 'pertain to beasts not to man. Justice derives from reason, that most divine part of our being.' In ordering his priorities, L'Hôpital put state before church; political unity before religious conformity. He believed that the best solution to France's domestic problems lay in a reform of the judicial system and of the church. However, before reform could take place, order needed to be restored by giving the Bourbons and other great nobles a stake in government and by convincing the people that genuine reform was on the way.[26] It was with a view to achieving these ends that an Assembly of Notables, including royal councillors, princes of the blood, great officers of state and knights of the Ordre de Saint-Michel, met at Fontainebleau on 20 August.[27] Montmorency turned up with an escort of 800 horsemen, but the king of Navarre and his brother chose to stay in Béarn, thereby implicitly negating their assertion that they were being excluded from a share in the government.[28] Early in August Navarre held a meeting of his council at Nérac, which was attended by François Hotman, the eminent jurist from Strassburg, and Théodore de Bèze. A remonstrance was drawn up in which historical arguments were marshalled in support of the princes' claims while the Guise tyranny stood condemned.[29]

Catherine opened the Assembly of Fontainebleau on 21 August by calling on its members to act in such a way that the king would keep his sceptre, his subjects would be relieved of their sufferings and the malcontents, if possible, would be satisfied. The chancellor followed with a speech in

---

26 R. Descimon (ed.) *L'Hospital: Discours pour la majorité de Charles IX* (Paris, 1993), pp. 7–36; J.H.M. Salmon, *Society in Crisis* (London, 1975), pp. 151–62; Seong-Hak-Kim, 'The Chancellor's Crusade: Michel de L'Hôpital and the Parlement of Paris', *FH* 7 (1993), 1–29.

27 Pasquier, *Lettres*, pp.45–7; Shimizu, *Coligny*, pp. 39–42.

28 See Catherine's letter earnestly entreating him to attend: *Lettres*, i. 146–7.

29 La Planche, *L'Histoire*, pp. 318–38; Mariéjol, p. 83; D.R. Kelley, *François Hotman* (Princeton, 1973), pp. 120–1.

69

which he compared the state to a sick man whose cure depended on finding the cause of his illness. Guise and Lorraine then reported on their respective government responsibilities: the army and finance. On 23 August Coligny submitted two petitions – one to the king, the other to his mother – from the Protestants of Normandy on behalf of all their French co-religionists. The one asked for a suspension of the persecution and for the right to assemble for worship and to build churches (or *temples*) pending a General Council. The petition to Catherine called on her to follow the example of Esther by freeing God's elect from the perils they faced and by banishing the errors and abuses which prevented God from being properly served and honoured. According to Pasquier, who mentions only the first petition, Guise complained that it was unsigned. When Coligny offered to obtain ten thousand signatures, the duke retorted that he could get 100,000 people to sign a counter-petition in their own blood and that he would be their captain.[30]

Jean de Monluc, bishop of Valence, then praised Catherine for her part in frustrating the recent plot and also using gentleness rather than force. He endorsed the punishment of rebels who used religion as a cover for their activities, but argued against the persecution of dissenters loyal to the crown. He pressed for more toleration and advocated a national council to reform the church. Another speaker was Charles de Marillac, archbishop of Vienne, who pointed to the damage being done to France's relations with her Protestant neighbours by the persecution of Huguenots. The state's security, he explained, rested on two pillars: the integrity of religion and popular goodwill. The one required a church council, the other, a meeting of the Estates-General.[31] On 24 August Coligny spoke of the need for church reform, but above all of political action. He backed

---

30 Shimizu, *Coligny*, p. 40; Mariéjol, p. 80; Sutherland, *Huguenot Struggle*, p. 116; *Mémoires de Condé*, ii. 647–8.
31 Pierre de La Place, *Commentaires de l'estat de la Religion et Republique sous les Rois Henry et François second et Charles neuviesme, 1556–1561* (Paris, 1565), pp. 55–8; La Planche, *L'Histoire*, pp. 352–60; P. de Vaissière, *Charles de Marillac* (Paris, 1896), pp. 383–4.

the call for the Estates-General and allegedly angered Guise by complaining of the heavy guard which had been thrown about the king. He concluded that Protestants should be allowed to worship publicly in certain places pending a national council.[32] As for Lorraine, he backed the demand for the Estates-General and promised to pave the way for a church council by setting up an enquiry into church corruption.[33] This received the assembly's assent and Francis II ordered the Estates-General to meet on 10 December. An assembly of the clergy was called for 20 January 1561.

The Fontainebleau assembly revealed Catherine's statesmanship. While the Guises had emerged unscathed, the opposition had been given hope of redress. Distrust, however, remained among the Huguenots, who continued to affirm the pre-eminence of the princes of the blood over all other councillors. In several pamphlets, they argued that foreigners were debarred from the government by the Salic law and by custom. Yet Catherine had no wish to get rid of the Guises. While fearing their extensive clientage and military potential, she knew that, if they were unseated, she would become dependent on the Constable, whom she disliked, or on the princes of the blood, whom she distrusted. In either case, the Estates-General might give the king a new council over which she would no longer preside.

Meanwhile, in various parts of France the Huguenots took to arms. Condé called on the Constable and François de Vendôme, vidame de Chartres, to assist him. Montmorency refused, but the vidame agreed to help the prince against everyone save the king and his family. His letter was intercepted and he was sent to the Bastille.[34] As the prospect of civil war loomed larger each day, Catherine appealed for assistance to Philip II of Spain, and to the duke of Savoy. At the same time, Francis II ordered Navarre to bring Condé to court. He was reported to be raising troops, and the king wanted to know why.[35] Faced with the choice of rebellion or submission, Navarre decided to bring his brother to court.

---

32 Shimizu, *Coligny*, pp. 41–2; Sutherland, *Huguenot Struggle*, p. 118.
33 Evennett, *Cardinal of Lorraine*, pp. 144–9.
34 Pasquier, *Lettres*, p. 45; La Planche, *L'Histoire*, pp. 345–46; Mariéjol, p. 84.

Condé was arrested at Orléans, and on 13 November his trial began. He was entitled to be tried by his fellow peers in the Parlement, but the Guises set up a special tribunal. Catherine was afraid that a guilty verdict followed by the death sentence would destroy any chance of pacifying the Huguenots. On 26 November Condé was found guilty of *lèse-majesté*, but two of his judges – L'Hôpital and du Mortier (both significantly devoted to Catherine) – failed to sign the death sentence.[36] This gained precious time, just as the king fell seriously ill. On 17 November he passed out during Vespers. A fistula was found inside his left ear for which the physicians could offer no cure. Meanwhile, the deputies to the Estates-General began to arrive in Orléans.[37] Fearing that, in the event of the king's death, they might vote Navarre into power, Catherine acted swiftly. On 2 December she summoned him to her presence, and accused him, in front of the Guises, of plotting against the crown. Rebutting the charge, he offered to give up his claim to be regent as proof of his loyalty. Catherine promptly accepted the offer, and secured its confirmation in writing. In return, she promised to appoint Navarre as lieutenant-general of the kingdom. She also bought off the Guises by exculpating them for Condé's imprisonment. It had been ordered only by the king, she explained; whereupon Navarre made peace with the Guises, sealing it with a kiss. On 5 December the king died and Condé's life was accordingly spared.[38]

. . .

THE MINORITY OF CHARLES IX

Francis II's death obliged the Guises to give up the reins of government, for his brother, Charles IX, being only ten years old, was too young to rule. He had to be given a regent.

---

36 Pasquier, *Lettres*, pp. 49–50; La Planche, *L'Histoire*, p. 401; Mariéjol, pp. 85–6.

37 The venue had been changed to Orléans, whose merchants had apparently helped to fund the Conspiracy of Amboise. The king took punitive action as soon as he arrived in the city. Pasquier, *Lettres*, pp. 49–50.

38 La Planche, *L'Histoire*, pp. 415–17; Mariéjol, pp. 86–7; Pasquier, *Lettres*, pp. 53–6.

Custom prescribed that this should be the first prince of the blood, but Navarre had surrendered his right. Many people looked to the Estates-General, who had been gathering at Orléans, to appoint a regent, but the deputies were not sure that their powers allowed them to do so. Catherine did not want a new round of elections, which might return supporters of Navarre; so the deputies were told that their powers remained valid. In any case, they were not invited to choose a regent. On 21 December the *conseil privé* ruled on the matter without consulting them. Catherine was appointed 'governor of the kingdom' with sweeping powers. She was forty-one years old and without commitment to either of the two great rival houses of Guise and Bourbon.[39]

Catherine in her new role was no figurehead. She took charge of the government as effectively as if she had been king. 'My principal aim', she wrote to her daughter, 'is to have the honour of God before my eyes in all things and to preserve my authority, not for myself, but for the conservation of this kingdom and for the good of all your brothers.'[40] She presided over the king's council, initiated and controlled state business, directed domestic and foreign policy, and appointed to offices and benefices. She was the first to receive and open dispatches, and had letters patent read out to her before they were signed by the king. Each of his replies was accompanied by a letter from his mother. She also gave herself a great seal in keeping with her new status.[41]

Catherine's principal concern was to restore peace to the kingdom. As she explained to her envoy in Spain, religious persecution over two or three decades had merely served to fuel religious division. She was being advised to try to win back those who had erred by 'honest remonstrances, exhortations and preaching', while punishing severely those who were guilty of 'scandals and seditions'.[42] On 28 January 1561 Catherine issued *lettres de cachet*, confirming, but also modifying the Edict of Romorantin. She ordered the release

---

39 Mariéjol, p.88; Cloulas, *Catherine*, pp. 154–5.
40 *Lettres*, i. 158.
41 Cloulas, *Catherine*, p. 155.
42 *Lettres*, i. 577–8.

of all religious prisoners and suspended all cases of heresy, even those involving people who had taken up arms or contributed funds to the recent commotion. In other words, she pardoned those who had taken part in the Tumult of Amboise, except the leaders. Significantly, pastors were not excluded from the amnesty as they had been from the Edict of Romorantin.[43]

The regent's conciliatory stance was misconstrued by the Huguenots, who imagined that she was coming over to their side. On 10 March, at their second national synod, held in Poitiers, they called for the establishment of a king's council capable of enforcing royal edicts; they also decided to app-oint representatives at court, who might serve as a pressure group. Meanwhile, in the kingdom at large, Huguenots held large public meetings. Sympathizers, who had hesitated before joining them, now did so with confidence. At the same time, they hurled abuse at their religious opponents, damaged images of saints, made fun of the Host, and refused to adorn their houses for processions on the feast of Corpus Christi.[44] The 'Huguenot Lent' predictably provoked a Catholic backlash spearheaded by the parlements. They dragged their feet about registering recent edicts of toleration and tampered with the wording to diminish or nullify their effectiveness. The Parlement of Paris ordered the destruction of houses used by Huguenots for their assemblies. Catholic preachers denounced their nocturnal conventicles as sexual orgies.[45]

Early in 1561 Navarre tried to get the duc de Guise expelled from court. He threatened to go himself along with Montmorency and the Châtillons, but his bluff was called after the young king had persuaded Montmorency not to desert him. Rather than go off on his own, Navarre re-mained at court. Condé was soon acquitted on all charges and, following his release from prison on 8 March, was

---

43 Sutherland, *Huguenot Struggle*, pp. 121, 351–2.
44 Kingdon, *Geneva*, pp. 85–6; P. Benedict, *Rouen during the Wars of Religion* (Cambridge, 1981), pp. 60–62; L. Romier, *Catholiques et Huguenots à la cour de Charles IX* (Paris, 1924), pp. 71–87.
45 Benedict, *Rouen*, pp. 62–8.

admitted to the king's council. On 25 March Navarre was confirmed as lieutenant-general of the kingdom and again renounced his claim to be regent. His role in the government was quite subordinate: he had to deal with dispatches from provincial governors and captains of fortresses referred to him by Catherine.[46]

Angered by these developments, the Guises returned to their estates pending the king's coronation, but Montmorency, whose Catholicism remained unshaken, disliked the regent's conciliatory policy. On 7 April he, the duc de Guise and Marshal Saint-André formed an alliance, known as the Triumvirate, to defend the Catholic faith. Their immediate aim was to detach Navarre from the Huguenots and win his support; their long-term objective was the destruction of Protestantism throughout Europe with the assistance of the papacy, Spain, Savoy and the Empire. Far from being intimidated, Catherine tried to win over Navarre herself. A prolonged struggle for his allegiance ensued.[47]

On 19 April a new edict banned the use of the words 'huguenot' and 'papist', thereby echoing sentiments which L'Hôpital had voiced in his opening address to the Estates-General. The right to enter houses in search of assemblies was restricted to magistrates, and the edict of 28 February was confirmed. This measure, however, far from pouring oil on troubled waters, caused more trouble, for it was sent to the local authorities without first being submitted to the parlements for registration.[48] Catholics feared that Catherine was becoming a Protestant. Philip II warned her not to allow the 'new ideas' which had arisen in France to make further progress, while his ambassador, Chantonnay, watched her every move like a hawk, bombarding her with reproaches. She justified her policy of 'clemency for past deeds' by pointing to the need to bring peace to the kingdom and to assure it of a better future. She blamed the Guises for spreading lies about her in Spain and condemned their

---

46 Cloulas, *Catherine*, p. 159; Mariéjol, pp. 93–4.
47 Romier, *Catholiques et Huguenots*, pp. 99–109; M. François, *Le Cardinal François de Tournon* (Paris, 1951), p. 407; Sutherland, *Huguenot Struggle*, pp. 122–4.
48 Sutherland, *Huguenot Struggle*, pp. 124–5, 351; *Mémoires de Condé*, ii. 334–5.

effort to marry their widowed niece, Mary Stuart, to Philip II's son, Don Carlos. Such an alliance would threaten all that she was trying to achieve. She suggested her own daughter, Marguerite, as a possible bride for Carlos. Catherine also proposed a way of detaching Navarre from the Huguenot cause: let Philip give him back Spanish Navarre or some other territory in Italy, perhaps Siena or Sardinia. She offered to meet Philip soon after Charles IX's coronation, believing that such a meeting would serve to clear up misunderstandings, but he declined.[49]

On 15 May Charles IX was crowned at Reims. Meanwhile, as the situation in the kingdom remained chaotic, L'Hôpital called a meeting of legal and theological experts to look into ways of solving the crisis. On 18 June he frankly admitted that the king's council was uncertain as to the best course to follow. It needed to know if the edicts regarding Protestant assemblies should be softened, stiffened or replaced altogether. The Edict of Romorantin had achieved nothing. The chancellor urged everyone to speak his mind freely. The immediate upshot was a plenary session of the *Cour des Pairs,* comprising all the chambers of the Parlement, the princes and the king's council. It had twenty-two sessions in Paris between 23 June and 11 July. At the end, the views were carefully noted down, majority decisions reached, and the findings taken to the king.[50] By a majority of only three votes, a ban was imposed on all conventicles and assemblies. But, instead of giving effect to this decision, L'Hôpital produced an edict on 30 July which tried to steer a middle course between severity and leniency. While banning all Protestant worship, it abolished the death sentence for religious offences. The church courts were allowed to judge cases of heresy, but not to search houses on any pretext. Nor could preachers stir up the people. The edict also offered an amnesty and a pardon for all offences, religious or seditious, committed since the death of Henry II as long as the people concerned undertook to lead peaceful and catholic lives in future.[51]

---

49 *Lettres,* i. 189, 576, 581, 587, 597; Mariéjol, pp. 96–8.
50 Maugis, *Histoire,* ii. 28–9.
51 Sutherland, *Huguenot Struggle,* pp. 127–8; Pasquier, *Lettres,* pp. 65–6.

The new edict marked a notable advance on the earlier situation since it carried the approval of Catholics who had taken part in the Paris discussions; but the Huguenots were not satisfied. They wanted permission to expound and defend their Confession of Faith and to recall some of their exiles under safe-conduct. They also asked for an end to persecution, protection from violent outrages, the release of religious prisoners, permission to hold public services and the right to build churches of their own. As evidence of their loyalty to the crown, they offered to admit royal representatives to their services.[52] The edict of 30 July answered only some of these demands. But if the Huguenots remained frustrated, they were encouraged by reports reaching them from the court. Pastors were preaching freely there, and the queen's son, Henri (the future Henry III), was in the habit of snatching prayer-books from the hands of his sister Marguerite and teasing her by singing psalms.[53] Navarre and Coligny were so hopeful that the 'new religion' would soon be recognized that they advised their deputies to the Estates-General no longer to press for a change of regency.[54]

. . .

THE COLLOQUY OF POISSY (SEPTEMBER 1561)

On 27 August 1561 the Estates-General met at Saint-Germain-en-Laye, and after the opening session the deputies split up: the nobility and third estate reassembled at Pontoise and the clergy at Poissy. The lay estates launched a vigorous attack on the clergy's wealth. Only by confiscating church revenues, they believed, would the public debt be cleared. They consequently proposed a general sale of church temporalities which would yield 120 million *livres*. The clergy's representatives at Poissy, understandably alarmed by this proposal, countered it by entering into an agreement with the crown, called the Contract of Poissy (21 September 1561). They undertook to pay 1,600,000 *livres* over six years

---

52 Sutherland, *Huguenot Struggle*, pp. 125–6; *Mémoires de Condé*, ii. 370–2.

53 *Mémoires de Marguerite de Valois*, ed. Y. Cazaux (Paris, 1971), p. 38.

54 Cloulas, *Catherine*, pp. 162–3.

for the redemption of royal domain and of indirect taxes which had been alienated. Thereafter, they would clear the king's debt in respect of the *Rentes sur l'Hôtel de Ville de Paris* to the tune of 7,650,000 *livres*. Never before had the Gallican church agreed to giving the crown an annual subsidy.[55] Catherine could feel satisfied, but she still had to settle the religious divisions which were tearing her son's kingdom apart. Persecution had been tried and had failed. Siding with the Protestants would only provoke the Catholics to fight. The only possible solution was compromise.

In November 1560 Pope Pius IV recalled the Council of Trent, but Catherine was afraid that this would come too late to solve the situation in France. It also seemed likely to confirm Catholic dogma and result in a hardening of religious divisions. While signifying her acceptance of the papal summons, she pressed on with her own plans for a national council. This was anathema to Pius IV, who instructed his nuncio, Viterbo, to secure its postponement by every possible means or at least to restrict its agenda to secondary matters. He also dispatched to France Ippolito d'Este, Cardinal of Ferrara, as legate *a latere*, and Diego Lainez, general of the Jesuits, a fervent opponent of theological compromise. Catherine, meanwhile, argued that a national council was nothing more than a preparation for the general one at Trent. She assured the Emperor that she would never agree to a change of religion in France. On the other hand, she believed that a national council, by reforming the church, would bring back the sheep that had strayed from the fold.[56] On 25 July she announced that 'all subjects' who wished to present their views would be welcome.

The clergy assembled at Poissy agreed to a proposal, originally mooted by Jean de Monluc, of inviting Geneva to send representatives. The invitation was well received and de Bèze was chosen to go to France. As a skilled diplomat, a

---

55 Ibid., pp. 163–4.
56 *Lettres,* i. 209; D. Nugent, *Ecumenism in the Age of the Reformation: The Colloquy of Poissy* (Cambridge, Mass., 1974), pp. 42–3, 51–3, 58, 60–2, 64–7. The charge of Machiavellism which he levels at Catherine rests on a misreading of her letter to the bishop of Rennes.

polished orator and a nobleman, he was thought preferable to Calvin, who was known for his tetchy manner and uncompromising attitude.[57] De Bèze was cordially received by Catherine following his arrival at Saint-Germain-en-Laye on 23 August.[58] She expressed the hope that his coming would bring peace to the kingdom. Lorraine then asked him to clarify certain statements which had been imputed to him. Had he written that 'Christ is no more in the Eucharist than in mud'? The pastor denied the existence of such a statement in his writings. Lorraine then asked him to explain the words: 'This is my body'. De Bèze replied that he held for a real but sacramental presence. Lorraine said that he believed in transubstantiation, but did not think the term was indispensable. He obliquely mentioned the Lutheran interpretation, whereupon de Bèze stressed that Calvinists and Lutherans were at one in condemning transubstantiation. However, he acknowledged a true reception in the sacrament. 'Do you confess then', asked Lorraine, 'that we communicate truly and substantially the body and blood of Jesus Christ?' De Bèze replied affirmatively, though with the qualification 'spiritually and by faith'. 'This also do I believe', said the Cardinal, and, turning to Catherine, he expressed his satisfaction with the meeting. De Bèze then spoke to her directly. Referring to his co-religionists, he said: 'Behold, Madam, these, then, are the Sacramentarians that you have so long vexed and oppressed with all kinds of calumnies.' She turned to Lorraine and said: 'Do you hear Lord Cardinal? He says that the Sacramentarians have no other opinion than this with which you agree.' As he took his leave, Lorraine embraced de Bèze, saying: 'I am very happy to have seen and heard you, and I adjure you in the name of God to confer with me, in order that I might understand your reasons and you mine', adding, 'and you will find that I am not as black as they make me out to be'. Expressing his own gratitude, de Bèze thought the forthcoming colloquy

---

57 Ibid., pp. 67–70; P.F. Geisendorf, *Théodore de Bèze* (Geneva, 1949), pp. 128–9.
58 Nugent, *Ecumenism*, pp. 70–3; *Mémoires de Claude Haton*, ed. F. Bourquelot (Paris, 1857), i. 155–6; *Mémoires de Condé*, ii. 17.

might bear fruit if Lorraine continued in the same spirit.[59] In the days that followed, Catherine was very friendly towards de Bèze. She asked about Calvin's health, and about her compatriot, Peter Vermigli, alias Peter Martyr, one of the most learned Calvinist pastors, who was soon to attend the colloquy. The queen also allowed de Bèze to preach in the apartments of Condé and Coligny, and assured the Calvinist ministers that the bishops at the forthcoming colloquy would not sit in judgment on them, as they feared.[60]

Catherine, it seems, could not understand religious fanaticism. Having been born and brought up as a Catholic, she practised her faith out of habit and also because the liturgy was to her taste. But religion did not enter her soul. Neither gratitude nor love seems to have prompted her prayers but rather a desire to secure God's goodwill or to placate His wrath. When she tried to justify her actions or, later in life, advised her daughter Marguerite on her conduct, she drew her precepts from human wisdom, never from Christian dogma. Although she must often have heard talk of heresy since she had come to France, she never tried to find out about the errors imputed to the victims of persecution. The Reformation only began to interest her once it had become politicized, and even then its doctrine passed her by. She was not hostile to Protestant thought, merely indifferent, which explains why she underestimated the strength of religious conviction, imagining that all would be well if she could only get the party leaders to agree. Guise and Condé were reconciled on 24 August as a result of her mediation, but their accord did not begin to reach the heart of the religious problem.[61]

On 9 September the colloquy opened in the refectory of the Dominican convent at Poissy. It was attended by the royal family, princes of the blood, the king's council, six cardinals, over forty archbishops and bishops, twelve theologians and many canon lawyers. Although most of the prelates were staunchly orthodox, all but five accepted the

---

59 Nugent, *Ecumenism*, pp. 85–9; La Place, *Commentaires*, pp. 155–7; *Histoire ecclésiastique*, i. 492–7: Geisendorf, *Théodore de Bèze*, pp. 136–40; Evennett, *Cardinal of Lorraine*, pp. 295–9.
60 Mariéjol, p. 103.
61 Ibid., pp. 101–2; *Calvini opera*, xviii, col. 631.

government's proposal that the Calvinists should be allowed a hearing. In addition to their party at court, the Protestants were represented by twelve pastors assisted by twelve laymen. They were escorted into the hall by archers and made to stand behind a barrier dividing them from the prelates sitting on either side. The first full-length oration of the colloquy was elegantly delivered by de Bèze. Having outlined the beliefs shared by both sides, he focused on the differences, notably concerning the Eucharist. 'We say', he declared, 'that His body is as far removed from the bread and the wine as heaven is from the earth.' This caused a commotion among the prelates. Standing up with tears in his eyes, Tournon asked the regent how she could suffer such blasphemy to be spoken in her son's presence. The spell which de Bèze's eloquence had cast upon his audience was broken. He hastily concluded his address and Tournon asked that it should be printed so that the bishops might prepare a reply within eight days.[62]

Next morning, the prelates discussed their next move. The obvious person to reply to de Bèze was Tournon, who was dean of the Sacred College as well as legate *a latere*, but Lorraine persuaded the prelates to choose him instead. On 16 September he proclaimed the infallibility of the Catholic church and the Real Presence of Christ in the Eucharist.[63] De Bèze was not impressed 'Never have I heard such impudence, such ineptitude . . . ' he said; 'the old arguments a thousand times refuted . . . nauseated me.' He also poured scorn on efforts sponsored by Navarre to bring Lutherans into the debate. About the same time the Cardinal of Ferrara, and Diego Lainez, general of the Jesuits arrived from Rome. The cardinal, who was related to the Guises by marriage, could look back on a long association with France. He came 'to cast his line into troubled waters which Catherine de Médicis had reserved for herself . . . not only to ruin her tackle and to rob her of her prize, but also to serve her with a notice of trespass' (Evennett). His main purpose was to entice Catherine towards the Council of

---

62 Nugent, *Ecumenism,* pp. 94–102; M. François *Le Cardinal François de Tournon* (Paris, 1951), pp. 411–12.
63 François, *Le Cardinal François de Tournon,* pp. 412–13.

Trent, and Navarre towards Catholicism. Lainez arrived soon after the assembly at Poissy had legalized the Society of Jesus in France.[64]

The legate's arrival obliged the government to change the form of the colloquy. On 22 September it was reduced to a tête-à-tête between twelve Calvinists and an equal number of Catholics. The king was absent as were most of the prelates. Catherine, however, continued to be a spectator. This time de Bèze avoided talking of the Eucharist, focusing instead on the church, the ministry, authority and tradition. Claude d'Espence (a moderate Catholic theologian), who had come well prepared for a campaign against the Calvinist doctrine of the Eucharist, replied. He was followed by the bishop of Evreux, Claude de Sainctes, who was far less polite. This prompted de Bèze to appeal to the queen. It was a sheer waste of time, he said, to continue the debate without a fixed order and at the mercy of insults from any speaker who liked to rise, with neither books of reference nor secretaries to record the proceedings. The discussion, however, became even more acrimonious. An attempt by Lorraine to persuade the pastors to subscribe to the Confession of Augsburg was interpreted by them as a ploy to divide the Protestants. They were also offended when Lainez attacked the legality of the national council. He drew tears from Catherine as he warned her that the Calvinists would destroy the kingdom unless she expelled them.[65] Late in September, she made a last attempt to save the colloquy. Five theologians from either side were appointed to discuss the Eucharist, but they still could not agree. On 13 October the colloquy dissolved itself.

. . .

THE EDICT OF JANUARY (17 JANUARY 1562)

Protestantism seemed to be making headway everywhere in France; yet in spite of dire warnings from Philip II, Catherine did nothing to halt the process. She seemed even to

---

64 Nugent, *Ecumenism*, pp. 108–16, 118–20; Evennett, *Cardinal of Lorraine*, p. 337.
65 Ibid., pp. 123–60; Evennett, *Cardinal of Lorraine*, pp. 337–93.

encourage it. De Bèze was allowed to preach at the French court, while other pastors were active elsewhere.[66] Among great lords and ladies who were converted were Renée, dowager-duchess of Ferrara, the comtesse de Roye and her daughter, the princesse de Condé and Jeanne d'Albret, queen of Navarre. Catherine's children were reported to be saying their prayers in French. Charles IX had mocked the clergy in a masque and had confided to Jeanne d'Albret that he only went to mass to please his mother. D'Andelot was invited to join his brother, Coligny, in the *conseil privé*. On 30 October de Bèze wrote to Calvin: 'Thanks to God I have won permission for our brethren to meet in complete safety, but the permission is only tacit until a solemn edict gives us better and more secure terms.' He was afraid, however, that the impatience of some Huguenots would demolish in a day more than he had built in a month.[67] Violence was erupting in many parts of France. In the south-west, priests were hunted down and killed by Huguenot mobs; saints' images were destroyed, and noblemen who tried to keep the peace, themselves came under attack. In December there was a bloody riot in Paris involving Protestants, who had gathered for worship in a house near the church of Saint-Médard.[68]

Catholics were understandably outraged. At the end of October the Guises showed their disgust by quitting the court. They may even have planned to kidnap the king's young brother, Edouard-Alexandre (the future Henry III) as a hostage to be used in the event of Catherine becoming a Protestant. The boy was her favourite, and she wrote to Philip II expressing her dismay. When she demanded an explanation from Guise, he coldly disclaimed any knowledge of the plot. In Spain, too, the progress of Protestantism in France caused alarm. Elisabeth de Valois presented her mother with a grim choice: either ally with Philip against the Huguenots or he would ally with the French Catholics against her. The same message was conveyed to Charles IX by Chantonnay.[69]

---

66 Pasquier, *Lettres*, pp. 74–5.
67 *Calvini opera*, xix, col. 88.
68 B. Diefendorf, *Beneath the Cross: Catholics and Huguenots in sixteenth-century Paris* (Oxford, 1991), pp. 61–2.
69 *Lettres*, i. 245–6, 250, 601 n.; Mariéjol, p. 108.

Catholics were not the only victims of violence in France. In several regions Protestants came under attack from Catholic mobs. It became urgent for the government to separate the rival groups within urban areas. The king's council accordingly decided to allow Protestant worship only outside the walls of towns and not on Catholic feast-days.[70] Even at this stage, however, Catherine continued to hope for a religious compromise. She announced that twenty-six bishops had been chosen to go to Trent as representatives of the Gallican church. Six would leave before 11 November; the rest would be at Trent by 3 March. But Catherine was not in earnest. While keeping Rome in play, she embarked on a series of efforts to change the Council's character and to organize opinion in favour of a new and less committed assembly. She worked for a provisional toleration of Huguenot worship and the ultimate reunion of Catholic and Calvinist by means of wide concessions in ceremonial and discipline and the mutual acceptance of doctrinal formulae. In the words of Evennett, 'She did not ask herself whether she might not be pursuing a mirage. Her policy, she believed, was the only possible one for her under the circumstances, and she saw its pragmatic value without stopping to question its first principles.'[71] Having come to realize that she would never get what she wanted from the French bishops, she now swung round towards Rome in a desperate, last-minute attempt to secure the pope's help before the Council should open at Trent and spoil everything. She asked him on 24 October to allow the laity to take communion in both kinds. Other concessions to the Huguenots were suggested by Jean de Monluc, Jean de Saint-Gelais and Cardinal de Châtillon, but they were not well received in Italy, where the Council of Trent reopened on 18 January 1562 without a single French prelate being present.[72]

Meanwhile, Catherine called a meeting of senior members of the sovereign courts to Saint-Germain. They had been carefully picked for their moderate views. The chancellor explained that their role was not to choose between the rival faiths but to find the best way of restoring

---

70 Cloulas, *Catherine*, p. 167.
71 Evennett, *Cardinal of Lorraine*, pp. 396–7.
72 Ibid., pp. 402–3.

order to the kingdom. A good citizen, he said, did not need to be a Christian; he could even be an excommunicate. At the end of the conference, which lasted from 7 until 15 January, a vote was taken: 22 members were in favour of allowing the reformers to have temples; 27 against, although they were prepared to allow Protestant worship. Catherine rounded off the proceedings by making a speech which the papal nuncio, Prospero di Santa Croce, hailed as the most eloquent he had ever heard. She declared that she, her children and all members of the king's council wished to live in the Catholic faith and in obedience to Rome.[73]

The result of the discussions at Saint-Germain was the famous Edict of January, which allowed Huguenots to gather for worship in the countryside but not inside walled towns or at night pending a decision by the General Council.[74] This did not please Catholics. The Parlement refused at first to register the edict. The Spanish ambassador complained that religion was being left to the chancellor's discretion and urged the queen to expel Protestant preachers with Spanish help. She replied that she did not want to bring foreigners into the kingdom or to provoke a war. When the envoy complained that religion was being freely discussed in front of her sons, she angrily retorted that this was her business and that she would punish those who spread such slanders.[75] On 5 March, as unrest grew in Paris, the Parlement decided to give way to royal pressure; it registered the edict the next day.

If many Catholics were upset by the new edict, they were consoled by the news that Navarre, after much vacillation, had decided to join them, thereby depriving the Huguenots of their main claimant to the regency. De Bèze vented his fury in a letter to Calvin. 'This wretch', he said,' is completely lost and is determined that all should be lost with him. He is driving away his wife and hardly dares to look at the Admiral to whom he owes everything.' He did not blame Catherine – our 'autocrat' as he calls her. She was at first much upset by the news and blamed Montmorency so harshly that he left

---

73 Mariéjol, p. 112.
74 Sutherland, *Huguenot Struggle*, pp. 133–5, 354–6; Pasquier, *Lettres*, pp. 81–3.
75 *Mémoires de Condé*, ii. 601, 603.

the court.[76] Even at this late stage, she hoped for conciliation. She held another colloquy at Saint-Germain which brought together prelates and a few theologians holding moderate views. De Bèze was there as well. The discussion focused on religious images, but tradition prevailed.[77] Catherine now confounded Huguenot expectations by asserting her orthodoxy. Her ladies were ordered to lead Catholic lives under threat of expulsion from court, while she herself went to communion and took part along with the rest of the court in religious processions. Her children were made to attend church services.[78] And at long last Catherine ordered French bishops to attend the Council of Trent.

The Cardinal of Lorraine, who led the French delegation at Trent, had been instructed by Catherine to seek an understanding with the Germans, to propose the reform of the church in its head and its members, and to demand as a first step communion in both kinds, prayers in the vernacular and clerical marriage. 'Articles of reformation', submitted to the Council by the French representatives, repeated some of these demands. They asked for communion in both kinds, improved religious instruction, prayers and hymns in French, an end to superstitions associated with the cult of saints, pilgrimages and indulgences. The French also called for an end to papal marriage dispensations in return for money, and reservations of ecclesiastical benefices. In return, the king of France was ready to abandon certain practices, which enabled laymen to acquire benefices.

These proposals were strongly opposed by the Italians and Spaniards at Trent. The papal legates put forward a counter-proposal for the 'reform of princes' which would ensure the superiority of the spiritual over the temporal, notably in the financial and judicial spheres. Princes would not be allowed to levy taxes, tolls or even subsidies except in the event of a war against the Infidel or in times of grave

---

76 *Calvini opera*, xix, col. 275.
77 *Histoire ecclésiastique*, i. 692; *Calvini opera*, xix, cols. 273–5; Mariéjol, p. 114.
78 Mariéjol, p. 115.

necessity. These proposals were made just as Catherine decreed the confiscation of the temporalities of the Gallican church. When the French government heard of the papal proposals, it ordered its representatives to leave the council. Eventually, ignoring the French proposals, the Council of Trent confirmed the principal tenets of the Catholic faith, notably the Real Presence in the Eucharist, salvation by good works, the intercession of saints, the value of indulgences, and Purgatory. In other words, the schism of Christendom was now completed. The council's disciplinary decrees restored to the church many powers of jurisdiction which in France had long ago been taken over by the crown.[79]

French participation in the Council of Trent was not enough to satisfy the Triumvirs. They wanted the Edict of January to be rescinded, and agreed to meet in Paris in order to put pressure on the queen-mother.

. . .

THE MASSACRE OF VASSY (1 MARCH 1562)

François, duc de Guise was travelling to Paris from Joinville on 1 March 1562, when he stopped at Vassy, a small walled town which formed part of Mary Stuart's dowry. Although forbidden to do so by the recent edict, Huguenots were worshipping in a barn close to the church. A skirmish developed between the duke's men and the congregation, which ended in bloodshed. According to one account, seventy-four of its members were killed and 104 injured. The duke himself and about a dozen of his men were slightly wounded.[80] News of the massacre travelled ahead of Guise, forcing him to take evasive action as armed Huguenots tried to intercept him. Catholics, meanwhile, celebrated the massacre as a great victory. The *prévôt des marchands* offered to supply the duke with an army of 20,000 men and a subsidy of 2 million gold *écus* so that he might pacify the kingdom; but he politely declined, saying that he was content to obey the queen and Navarre as lieutenant-general of the kingdom.

---

79 Cloulas, *Catherine*, pp. 186–7.
80 Pasquier, *Lettres*, pp. 97–104; *Histoire ecclésiastique*, i. 805–11; Romier, *Catholiques et Huguenots*, pp. 320–1.

Also in Paris was Condé, who had become the leader of the Huguenot movement following his brother's defection. De Bèze hurried to Saint-Germain to demand justice against the perpetrators of the Vassy massacre. Catherine tried to defuse the situation, which had become explosive. She appointed Cardinal de Bourbon as governor of Paris in the hope that he might prove acceptable to both sides. He ordered Guise and Condé to leave the capital, but Guise stayed put, knowing that he had the support of Montmorency and of most Parisians. Condé, on the other hand, fearing an attack by the mob, left on 23 March.

Between 16 and 24 March Catherine wrote four times to Condé from Fontainebleau. 'I see so much that upsets me', she said, 'that if it were not for the trust which I place in God and in the assurance of your help to keep this kingdom and to serve the king my son, I would feel even worse; but I hope that we shall be able to find a remedy for everything with your good advice and help.'[81] However, instead of going to Fontainebleau to protect the queen, Condé left the way clear for his enemies to go there. Guise, Navarre and a thousand horse descended on Fontainebleau and asked Catherine to return to Paris with her son. She pleaded with them to stay put, but their will prevailed in the end. On 27 March, Catherine and the king were back in the capital. Meanwhile, Condé, who had raised an army of 1,800 men, was joined at Meaux by Coligny. The Huguenots were now determined to obtain by force what they had failed to secure by negotiations. On 2 April Condé captured Orléans. The Wars of Religion had begun.[82]

---

81 Catherine's letters to Condé were later published in the Empire in support of a claim that the Protestants had taken up arms on her orders, but the letters, being only copies, may not be complete or accurate. See Sutherland, *Princes, Politics and Religion*, p. 144.
82 Mariéjol, pp. 118–19; *Lettres*, i. 281–4; Cloulas, *Catherine*, p. 171.

Chapter 5

WAR AND PEACE
(1562–66)

Having seized Orléans, Condé published a manifesto (8 April) claiming that he, not the Guises, was on the right side of the law. He and the other Huguenot nobles, who signed the declaration, set themselves the aim of freeing the king, his brothers and the queen-mother; they also wanted to safeguard the freedom of conscience which recent edicts had granted them. While the manifesto was sent to foreign governments in advance of a demand for their armed support, Condé sent agents to various parts of France to raise an army.[1]

Catherine found herself willy-nilly on the side of the Triumvirs. She could not allow the Huguenots to mount a rebellion, and took active steps to increase the size of the king's army, yet was reluctant to fight without making a final attempt at negotiation. She urged Condé and Coligny to come to court. On 9 June Catherine met Condé at Toury and, later that month, she saw the Huguenot leaders at Talcy; but they refused to give up the free exercise of their faith. Despairing of a peaceful outcome, Catherine said: 'Since you rely on your forces, we will show you ours.' Meanwhile, the Huguenots seized several strategic towns, including Rouen and Lyon.[2]

---

1 Q. Skinner, *The Foundations of Modern Political Thought* (Cambridge, 1978), ii. 302.
2 M.P. Holt, *The French Wars of Religion* (Cambridge, 1995), p. 53; P. Benedict, *Rouen during the Wars of Religion* (Cambridge, 1981), pp. 96–7.

As violence spread, Catherine appealed to the pope, Philip II and the duke of Savoy for help. The Huguenots, for their part, looked to Elizabeth I of England, who saw an opportunity of regaining Calais, which had been ceded to France for eight years under the peace of Cateau-Cambrésis.[3] On 20 September Condé's envoys signed a treaty at Hampton Court: Elizabeth promised them money and troops in exchange for the port of Le Havre. This was to be exchanged for Calais before the eight years were up. Meanwhile the king's army began to recover lost ground, capturing Poitiers and Bourges, then moving into Normandy and laying siege to Rouen. Catherine came to Fort Sainte-Catherine, which overlooked the city, to confer with her captains and watch the city's bombardment. Guise and Montmorency warned her of the risks involved, but she merely laughed. 'My courage', she said, 'is as great as yours.' An important victim of the siege was Antoine de Bourbon, king of Navarre, who was fatally wounded by an arquebus shot. He died on 17 November after Rouen's capitulation. Guise planned to follow up this success by advancing against the English, who now occupied Le Havre, but he had to change his plan when Condé suddenly left Orléans and marched on Paris. The race to the capital was won by Guise so that Condé had to change his own plan of campaign: he now advanced on Normandy, hoping to link up with the English, but found his way barred by Montmorency at Dreux. A battle ensued during which marshal Saint-André was killed, and the two rival commanders, Condé and Montmorency, were captured. Guise, who remained as the only effective Triumvir, assumed command of the king's army.

Catherine now sought a negotiated peace, but Catholic opinion was not disposed to accept a tolerant one. On 5 February the municipality of Paris urged the queen to teach the Huguenots that there could be only one religion in the kingdom. Parisian obstinacy was seen by the English ambassador as a serious obstacle to peace. While the municipality took steps to prevent Huguenots entering the

---

3   N.M. Sutherland, *Princes, Politics and Religion, 1547–1589* (London, 1984), pp. 73–96.

capital, the populace seized any pretext to molest Huguenot suspects. Catherine deplored this state of affairs, and, on 8 February, she advised marshal Montmorency to station more troops in the capital.[4]

Guise, meanwhile, laid siege to Orléans, but, as he was returning from a camp inspection on 18 February, he was fatally shot by Poltrot de Méré, a Huguenot nobleman. The duke's assassination has been fairly described as a 'seminal event', for he had become a national hero following his capture of Metz (1552), his conquest of Calais and his victory at Dreux. His death, moreover, effectively decapitated the house of Guise, for his son, Henri, prince de Joinville, was only thirteen years old, and his brother, the Cardinal of Lorraine, was attending the Council of Trent. The duke's other brothers were relatively insignificant politically. His assassination also added a new dimension to the civil unrest in France by creating an aristocratic vendetta as savage as it was protracted. His widow, Anne d'Este, and her family set themselves up as avenging angels. Rightly or wrongly, they believed that Admiral Coligny had instigated the duke's murder. Poltrot implicated him in his first confession, but subsequently contradicted himself.[5] While denying his complicity in the crime, Coligny freely admitted to Catherine (12 March 1563) that he viewed Guise's death as the greatest good that could have befallen the kingdom, the Reformed church and, in particular, his own family.[6]

The Admiral's responsibility for Guise's assassination has been hotly debated. The evidence is inconclusive and need not concern us here. However, we should note that Catherine too was blamed. Some strangely incriminating statements are imputed to her. She allegedly said to marshal Tavannes: 'the Guises wished to make themselves kings, but I stopped them outside Orléans'. To the Venetian ambassador, she said:

---

4   *Lettres*, i. 498–99.
5   J. Shimizu, *Conflict of Loyalties: Politics and religion in the career of Gaspard de Coligny, Admiral of France, 1519–1572* (Geneva, 1970), p. 105.
6   The best account of the duke's assassination and its implications is Sutherland, *Princes, Politics and Religion*, pp. 139–55.

'If Monsieur de Guise had perished sooner, peace would have been achieved more quickly.' In March 1563 she told Condé that 'Guise's death had released her from prison as she herself had freed the prince; just as he had been the duke's prisoner, so she had been his captive given the forces with which Guise had surrounded her and the king.'[7] Such remarks, however, even if true, do not prove Catherine's complicity in Guise's murder.

News of the duke's assassination caused dismay and anger in Paris. Catherine urged the municipal authorities to prevent rioting by keeping a firm hand on the situation.[8] The popular fury was directed not only at the Huguenots but at the crown, for it was rumoured that Catherine was negotiating a peace harmful to the Catholic church. Sir Thomas Smith reported that Parisians 'now say themselves that they are utterly undone; and as their great champion is overthrown, the Huguenots will have all'.[9] Poltrot de Méré was executed before an enormous crowd on the Place de Grève in Paris on 18 March. Next day, the city staged an elaborate funeral procession for the duc de Guise. It was led by twenty-two town criers ringing bells and included many bourgeois and merchants carrying flaming torches. In addition to sizeable groups of clerics and nobles, rank after rank of bourgeois militiamen armed with arquebuses or pikes and wearing chain-mail escorted the duke's coffin.[10]

Catherine, however, did not allow Catholic opposition to prevent the pacification which she so earnestly desired. The fact that she was now rid of the principal party leaders, except for Coligny, offered her the opportunity of reaching a settlement. Montmorency and Condé were temporarily released from captivity in order to negotiate it. The outcome

---

7   F.-W. Ebeling, *Archivalische Beiträge zur Geschichte Frankreichs unter Carl IX* (Leipzig, 1872); E. Marcks, 'Catherine de Médicis et l'assassinat du duc François de Guise', *BSHF*, Vol. XL (1891), pp. 153–64; P. de Vaissière, *De quelques assassins* (2nd edn. Paris, 1912), pp. 84–92; Shimizu, *Coligny*, p. 108 n. 24; G. de Saulx-Tavannes, *Mémoires*, ii. 394.
8   *Lettres*, i. 517–18.
9   *CSPF.* 1563, Vol. 6, pp. 164.
10 B.B. Diefendorf, *Beneath the Cross: Catholics and Huguenots in sixteenth-century Paris* (Oxford, 1991), pp. 71–2.

was the Edict of Amboise (19 March 1563), which conceded freedom of conscience to the Huguenots throughout the kingdom, but regulated their right of worship according to social status. Noblemen with rights of high justice were allowed to worship freely on their estates while those with inferior rights could worship in their homes. Protestant worship was allowed in all towns held by the Huguenots before 7 March and in one town per *bailliage*. They were forbidden to hold services anywhere in Paris or the surrounding *vicomté* and *prévôté*, although residents were allowed to return home. Property taken from the Catholic church was to be returned.

Once peace had been officially restored, Catherine set about undoing the damage done to France's interests by the treaty of Hampton Court. She wanted to keep Calais, yet at the same time recover Le Havre, which the English now occupied. Elizabeth, however, flatly refused to recall her troops. She allegedly said that she had taken Le Havre, not for religious reasons, but to avenge the injuries which she had received from France and to indemnify her for the loss of Calais, which was rightfully hers.[11] Catherine, who at first kept a low profile, had to come out into the open. She rallied Huguenot and Catholic troops against the English, and Montmorency, aided by Condé, besieged Le Havre, which surrendered on 28 July 1563. Feeling betrayed by the Huguenots, Elizabeth never trusted them again. Neither she nor Catherine wanted war, but Elizabeth, out of spite, dragged out the peace talks for as long as possible. Eventually, under the peace of Troyes, France retained Calais in return for an indemnity of 120,000 crowns, a far smaller sum than had been envisaged at Cateau-Cambrésis.

· · ·

ENFORCING THE PEACE

The peace was highly unpopular among Catholics everywhere. The Parlement agreed to register the Edict of Amboise on 27 March, but hesitated about publishing it. The town criers who announced it were pelted with mud. The Easter season, always a time of heightened religious

---

11 Aumale, *Histoire des princes de Condé,* i. 497.

tension, was marked by violence. At the same time, the Bureau de la Ville refused to allow Huguenots to return to their homes and work. Instructions given to the gaoler of the Conciergerie on 7 April indicate the Parlement's reluctance to implement liberty of conscience. Hostility to the pacification, however, was not confined to the Catholics. Huguenots viewed it as a 'sell-out' by Condé. Coligny accused him of destroying more churches 'by a stroke of the pen than all the enemy forces would have succeeded in destroying in ten years'.[12] Calvin accused the prince of betraying God 'out of vanity'.[13] By allowing social criteria to determine the legality and distribution of Protestant worship, he had taken care of the interests of the upper nobility at the expense of Huguenots lower down the social scale. The Protestant faith had been made to look exclusively aristocratic.

The tense, even violent, situation which prevailed in Paris in the wake of the edict was reflected elsewhere. In Rouen resistance was fierce. The parlement only registered the edict after a stinging rebuke from the central government. When a petition from the town council to the queen-mother had been turned down, a law was passed barring all Huguenots who had helped to seize the city from returning, and disarming those who were allowed back. Even after the edict had been registered, relations between the two faiths remained tense. Huguenots complained that their efforts to recover their property and to resume work were being hampered by the civic authorities.[14] In Troyes, the local council countered the edict by conducting a door-to-door survey of religious opinion. Huguenots either absented themselves or gave ambiguous replies; while many Catholics declared that they would rather die than allow Protestant services in or near their city. Several argued that the co-existence of two religions would divide it as well as the realm. By contrast, a similar survey in the Protestant stronghold of Millau, in the Midi, was unanimous in opposing the restoration of the Mass.[15]

---

12 *Histoire ecclésiastique*, ii. 335.
13 *Calvini opera*, xix, col. 686.
14 Benedict, *Rouen*, pp. 114–15.
15 Penny Roberts, *A City in Conflict: Troyes during the French wars of religion* (Manchester, 1996), pp. 123–5.

Although neither side was satisfied by the Edict of Amboise, Catherine pressed for its acceptance. In June 1563 she set an example of conciliation: on the eve of the feast of Corpus Christi, she and the king stayed with Condé. As they travelled with him across the capital, the people seemed docile enough. Catherine concluded that the prince was no longer an object of suspicion and enmity. Next day, however, his wife was stopped by a gang of armed Parisians on her way to Vincennes. A scuffle ensued and one of her attendants was killed. The princess herself escaped unharmed, but Condé was furious: suspecting an ambush by the Guises, he threatened to leave the court and was dissuaded only with difficulty by Catherine. A few days later, she informed the duchesse de Guise that she had reconciled Condé with the duc de Nemours and the Cardinal de Guise. It was her hope that the kingdom at large would follow their example.

Within her limited capacity, Catherine tried to promote a more peaceful climate at court. She persuaded high-ranking nobles to give up their Protestant services (*prêches*), but the task of persuading Huguenots in general to observe the peace was less simple. Goodwill alone could not eradicate the legacy of hatred left by the civil war. Huguenot nobles who had taken advantage of the conflict to plunder churches and seize church goods were not inclined to surrender their gains. Catholics, for their part, attacked reformers as they returned to their homes. In various provinces gangs of hired killers operated with impunity, while magistrates turned a blind eye to their activities if they did not actually instigate them.

By April 1563 it was clear that people would not lay down their arms voluntarily. Charles IX accordingly sent out the marshals of France, with instructions to find out how the edict was being applied, to receive complaints about infringements of its terms and to sort out problems. Twenty-eight commissioners were appointed to assist them. Their task did not prove easy. Marshal de Vieilleville, who was sent to Lyon, Dauphiné, Languedoc and Provence, spent a whole year bringing Lyon into conformity with government policy.[16]

---

16 *Lettres*, ii. 33; J. Boutier, A. Dewerpe and D. Nordman, *Un Tour de France royal. Le voyage de Charles IX (1564–1566)* (Paris, 1984), pp. 185–9.

Catherine ordered Montmorency-Damville, governor of Languedoc, on 8 January 1564 to ensure that the edict was 'inviolably observed'. He was to do so without partisanship to any person or faith and to punish disobedience in an exemplary manner.[17]

The composition of the king's council was also made to reflect more accurately the different interest groups. Membership lists for the years 1563 to 1567 yield the names of sixteen Catholic zealots (the Cardinals of Lorraine and Guise; the dukes of Montpensier and Nevers; Gaspard de Saulx-Tavannes, René de Birague); six Protestants (Condé, the three Châtillon brothers, d'Estrées, La Rochefoucauld) and about twenty moderates (e.g. Michel de L'Hôpital, Artus de Cossé, bishop Morvillier of Orléans and Jean de Monluc). These so-called 'politiques', to whom we can add the Constable and Cardinal de Bourbon, shared Catherine's hatred of violence and her desire to see the edict applied. Their number, which balanced that of the other councillors, reflected the government's aim of ensuring that the crown was an impartial defender of public order.[18]

. . .

CHARLES IX'S MAJORITY DECLARED

The age of majority for a French king had been fixed at fourteen by an ordinance of King Charles V. Although Charles IX was only thirteen years old, Catherine was anxious to have him proclaimed of age, as a king commanded more authority than a regent. The council decided that Charles, being in his fourteenth year, was old enough to rule, and his majority was proclaimed on 17 August 1563, not in the Parlement of Paris, as might have been expected, but in that of Rouen. What is more, the declaration was tied to a formal confirmation of the Edict of Amboise. By linking the two laws and submitting them to the Parlement of Rouen for registration, L'Hôpital evidently hoped to secure speedy registration of the edict without having to face more tiresome remonstrances from the Parlement of Paris. As the

---

17 *Lettres*, ii. 129–30.
18 J.-H. Mariéjol, *Catherine de Médicis* (Paris, 1920), pp. 134–5.

96

Spanish envoy, Chantonnay, pointed out, the move was intended to detract from the authority of the Parlement of Paris, which the queen-mother and her chancellor disliked on account of its opposition to their policies.

Charles went to the Parlement of Rouen on 17 August accompanied by his mother, the princes of the blood, the Constable and marshals of France and a throng of nobles and royal councillors. Once the doors of the chamber had been shut, the young king declared that now that he was of age he would tolerate no disobedience among his subjects. He ordered them to observe the recent pacification and forbade them to have any dealings with foreign powers without his permission or to raise taxes except by his command. L'Hôpital then announced the incorporation of Calais into the royal domain and praised the wisdom of Charles V's law whereby regencies, which had always proved troublesome, could be terminated without anticipating the natural course of maturation. He explained that Charles IX wished to be regarded as major in all things everywhere and in respect of everyone save his mother, to whom he reserved the power to command. L'Hôpital concluded his address by repri- manding the magistrates for putting themselves above the law. He urged them to apply the king's ordinances without partisanship, injustice or cupidity.

The ceremony of homage followed. Catherine announced that she was handing over the government to her son. As she took a few steps towards him, he left his throne and came forward cap in hand. He declared that she would govern and command as much or more than she had done in the past. The duc d'Orléans, the prince of Navarre, Condé and other princes of the blood, cardinals, great officers of state and noblemen then walked up to the king, who had returned to his throne; each in turn making a deep bow and kissing his hand. The doors of the chamber were then thrown open and a proclamation read out aloud, confirming the peace and ordering all the king's subjects to give up their arms. Only nobles were allowed to keep them in their homes, and only royal troops were authorized to carry firearms.

The Parlement of Paris, much offended by these proceedings, refused to endorse the king's majority or to confirm the Edict of Amboise. It complained that their

97

linkage conferred permanency on the edict and implied the recognition of two religions within the state. The Parlement also asked that Parisians be allowed to keep their arms. Charles IX received these remonstrances politely, but chose to ignore them. When the Parlement raised more objections, he reprimanded its representatives: their job, he said, was to administer justice fairly and expeditiously, not to act as his mentors, as protectors of the kingdom or as custodians of Paris.

The Parlement's mood reflected that of the Parisians. On 1 January 1564 Captain Charry, a Catholic member of the king's guard, was murdered by Huguenots as he was crossing the Pont Saint-Michel. Catherine mourned the loss of a devoted servant, but thought it advisable not to hunt for the murderers. Meanwhile, the Guises continued to blame Coligny for the second duke's assassination. As they pressed for justice, the king evoked the case to his council. On 5 January 1564 he suspended the lawsuit for three years, hoping that tempers would cool. Catherine was delighted. 'The king my son', she wrote, 'of his own volition without anyone's prompting has issued a decree that is so beneficial that all the council said that God had spoken through his mouth.'[19] She acclaimed him as a new Solomon. But the Admiral continued to fear for his life. In October 1563 he reported that Aumale had sent two men to kill him. In the following month, the Guises tried to prevent him from going to court near Fontainebleau. He went to the Louvre, where he narrowly missed being assassinated.

On 29 January the Cardinal of Lorraine returned from Trent determined to regain control of the king's council.[20] He asked it to endorse the Tridentine decrees, but was vehemently opposed by L'Hôpital.[21] Catherine shared her chancellor's hostility to papal pretensions. On 18 October she wrote to her envoy in Spain complaining that some Tridentine decrees contradicted the prerogatives of the French monarchy, including one that deprived princes who

---

19 *Lettres*, ii. 128.
20 Sutherland, *The Huguenot Struggle for Recognition* (New Haven, 1980), pp. 146–7.
21 *Calvini opera*, xx, cols. 262–3.

tolerated heretics. Catherine was furious when the pope summoned seven French prelates to Rome to answer a heresy charge.[22] She was equally indignant when Pius IV condemned Jeanne d'Albret for heresy, summoning her to appear before the Inquisition in Rome under threat of severe penalties. Catherine complained that the pope's action was 'against the ancient rights and privileges of the Gallican church'.[23] The sieur d'Orsel was instructed to tell Pius that he had no authority or jurisdiction over kings or queens and no right to give away their states to the first comer, especially the queen of Navarre, who held the larger part of her goods of the king of France. The pope decided to drop the matter. Jeanne was duly grateful for Catherine's protection: 'I put myself wholly under the wing of your powerful protection', she wrote. 'I will go to find you wherever you may be and shall kiss your feet more willingly than the pope's.'[24]

Catherine was anxious that her religious policy should not be misconstrued. The Huguenot leaders seemed to think that once peace had been restored, she would revert to the toleration which she had practised at Saint-Germain. Condé was holding *prêches* at court and the duchess of Ferrara had turned her houses in Paris and Fontainebleau into places of Protestant worship (*lieux de culte*).[25] Chantonnay complained that courtiers were being allowed a freedom that was denied even to nobles with rights of high justice. Catherine waited patiently for Condé voluntarily to stop holding Protestant services in royal residences; but ordered the duchess of Ferrara not to do so while the king was in residence at Fontainebleau.[26] De Bèze was aware of a change in her attitude. Following his return to Geneva in May 1563, he praised the tolerance of Charles IX and his brothers, but was silent about their mother. On 2 July Calvin wrote about her 'flightiness' and 'cunning'. Two weeks later, he accused her of stirring up Catholic fanatics in Paris. Her

---

22 *Lettres,* ii. 119.
23 *Lettres,* ii. 153–4; x. 128–9.
24 N.L. Roelker, *Queen of Navarre: Jeanne d'Albret, 1528–1572* (Cambridge, Mass., 1968), pp. 221–3.
25 *Calvini opera,* xx, col. 6; *Mémoires de Condé,* ii. 160.
26 *Calvini opera,* xx, col. 267.

perfidiousness, he wrote, was allowing them to disregard the king's edicts. 'In drawing them up', he said, 'the Chancellor treats us very liberally, for at the bottom of his heart he favours us. But because of the queen's hidden tricks all the good decisions taken by the council are avoided.' De Bèze echoed these sentiments. 'The greatest misfortune that can befall a people', he wrote on 20 July, 'is to be ruled by a woman, especially one of that kind.'[27]

A royal decree of 13 January 1564, allowing heads of households in Paris to retain their arms, was seen as a threat by the Huguenots. Catherine tried to reassure them. In a letter to Coligny (17 April), she denied that the government was planning to attack his co-religionists. She pointed to the orders which she and her son were sending out each day to magistrates, while admitting that they were not always being obeyed. She urged the Admiral to assure the Huguenots that the edict of pacification would be 'inviolably observed', promising to use every means (*le vert et le secq*) against any source of trouble regardless of religion, person or anything else.[28]

L'Hôpital is often given credit for the crown's policy of moderation, but Catherine's role should not be underestimated. As her correspondence demonstrates, she paid close attention to administrative details as well as important issues of public concern. Her letters, even those written by secretaries, contain marginal notes in her hand; many are entire autographs. L'Hôpital has left many fine speeches calling for concord, gentleness and charity, but his papers contain none of the orders to great officers of state, provincial governors, parlements, *baillis* and *sénéchaux*, or treasurers which are to be found among Catherine's papers. Though L'Hôpital was an able minister, he stood almost alone, being regarded as a crypto-Huguenot by Catholics and distrusted by the Protestants as a former client of the Guises. He depended entirely on Catherine's support. Furthermore, signally lacking Catherine's diplomatic skills, he could be tactless. The government's policy of religious moderation was almost certainly hers rather than his.[29]

---

27 Ibid., xx, cols. 21, 54, 64, 67, 133.
28 *Lettres,* ii. 177.
29 Mariéjol, pp. 140–2.

. . .

THE GRAND TOUR OF THE KINGDOM
(MARCH 1564–MAY 1566)

In an effort to impose Charles IX's authority, Catherine took him on an extended progress through France.[30] She hoped that the sight of the young king would revive loyalty to the crown after the damage it had sustained in the civil war. The progress may be seen as rounding off the campaign to impose the edict of 1563. As Catherine wrote to Coligny from Troyes on 17 April 1564: 'One of the main reasons for which the king, my lord and son, has undertaken his travels is to show his intention regarding that matter so clearly wherever he passes that no one will have any pretext or occasion to contravene it.'[31] The progress also had a diplomatic purpose. Catherine hoped to meet her son-in-law, Philip II, and to clear up differences which had arisen between them. At the same time she hoped to arrange marriages for two of her children and looked forward to seeing again her daughter, Elisabeth, now Philip's queen.

The progress started from Paris on 24 January 1564 and lasted until 1 May 1566. It was chronicled by a certain Abel Jouan, a member of the royal kitchen staff whose *Recueil et discours du voyage du roy Charles IX* was published soon afterwards. This records the various places visited by the court, the dates of arrival and departure, the distances covered, and meal stops on the way. Using this evidence as well as the correspondence of the various participants, three historians have examined the progress from every angle. Only a few statistics need be cited here. The progress lasted 829 days. The court moved on 201 days and stayed put on 628. In other words, it travelled on average one day in every four. Twenty-one stops lasted one week or more, accounting for a

---

30 The best accounts of this tour are P. Champion, *Catherine de Médicis présente à Charles IX son royaume (1564–1566)* (Paris, 1937); Boutier, Dewerpe and Nordman, *Un Tour;* and V.E. Graham and W. McAllister Johnson, *The Royal Tour of France by Charles IX and Catherine de' Medici. Festivals and entries, 1564–6* (Toronto, 1979).

31 Boutier, Dewerpe and Nordman, *Un Tour,* p. 177.

total of 486 days; 57 lasted between one and six days; 118 lasted less than one day (these were mostly overnight stops). The court covered 907 leagues (a league = three English miles or 4.83 kilometres). The average distance between stops was 4 leagues, the minimum being one and the maximum 12. The pace of travel increased on the return leg, as the court drew nearer to Paris. The progress fell neatly into two sections: before and after Bayonne.[32]

On 24 January 1564 the court, consisting of several thousand people, accompanied by a multitude of horses and other beasts of burden and a veritable army, set off from Paris. Although its itinerary had probably been mapped out in advance, some stops were apparently chosen at the last moment. The means of transport was determined mainly by social status. The king and his mother travelled either by coach or litter, or they rode horses as did most of the nobles. Where rivers were navigable, boats were used, but the rank and file travelled on foot. The speed of travel was leisurely by modern standards: the van often reached the next stop before the rearguard had left the last. Nor did the court travel as one body: its members would part company, take short cuts, travel across fields and meet up on the way. Halts varied in duration from one night only to one week or more. The court, for example, spent 90 days at Moulins, 46 at Toulouse, 39 at Bayonne-Saint-Jean-de-Luz, 31 at Bordeaux and 29 at Lyon.[33] Among reasons for the variations were the king's health (he fell ill twice), bad weather, the state of the roads and feast-days. In overall charge of the progress was the Constable Montmorency, who maintained discipline, issued instructions to town governors and rode ahead of the main company to ensure that all was in order for the king's reception.

After stopping at Sens, the scene of a recent massacre of Huguenots, the royal caravan moved to Troyes, where the peace treaty with Elizabeth I was signed. The progress enabled Charles IX to inspect his local officials: they were required to account for their activities and to receive his instructions. The success of the pacification depended on their willingness to enforce it. At Troyes, the local judges

---

32 Ibid., pp. 13–23.
33 Ibid., pp. 19–21.

were accused of not pulling their weight and warned that the king would replace them unless they mended their ways.[34] From here, the court moved to Bar-le-Duc, where Catherine attended the baptism of her first grandchild, the son of the duke and duchess of Lorraine. He was christened Henri.[35] The king and queen-mother acted as godparents for four other infants of noble birth during the progress. All the girls were christened Charlotte-Catherine, one being Monluc's daughter.[36] From Bar-le-Duc, the court moved south. On 22 March Charles IX made his entry into Dijon, whose governor, Gaspard de Saulx-Tavannes, staged a military pageant of quite alarming verisimilitude.[37] There were over one hundred formal entries into towns during the progress. Often they took the form of a traditional welcome at the town gates, the presentation of keys to the town, a speech and a procession in which the king would ride under a canopy carried by civic dignitaries. Some entries were far more lavish, involving a programme of triumphal arches, inscriptions and other features. Descriptions were published in commemorative albums while others are recorded in civic annals and memoirs of various kinds. Well-known poets and artists were often called upon to assist with the programmes and decorations. The entry programmes drew themes from classical mythology, the Bible or French history. Because of Charles IX's dependence on his mother's counsel, he was often compared to Saint Louis, who was guided in his early years by his wise and prudent mother. From classical mythology the same idea was evoked by comparisons with Ariadne, who helped Theseus to find his way through the labyrinth. Alternatively, Catherine might be compared to Pallas, who helped support the pillars of Hercules, or Juno, who suckled the young Hercules.[38]

An aim of the progress was to curb the independence so often shown by the parlements and municipal authorities. On 23 May at Dijon, the duc d'Orléans, acting in the king's

---

34 Roberts, *City in Conflict*, p. 130.
35 Champion, *Catherine de Médicis*, pp. 83–9.
36 B. de Monluc, *Commentaires*, i. 17–18.
37 Ibid., p. 92.
38 Graham and Johnson, *Royal Tour*, pp. 8–9, 11–13.

name, sent for the Parlement's registers. Next day L'Hôpital checked that the Edict of Amboise had been duly published and examined recent trials to ensure that the Parlement had acted fairly. The activities of the municipal authority were also scrutinized. The king intervened in the affairs of almost every town visited on his progress and tried as far as possible to strike a fair balance between the religious parties.[39] From Chalon-sur-Saône, the royal family sailed down the Saône to Mâcon, where they met Jeanne d'Albret, queen of Navarre. A proud and dignified woman, she was accompanied by eight Calvinist ministers and a military escort, necessitated, so she claimed, by Monluc's lawless activities in Guyenne.[40] Jeanne was greeted outside Mâcon by some 1,200 Huguenots. Her servants disgraced themselves by hurling insults at the Corpus Christi procession.

In the course of the progress foreign dignitaries attached themselves to the court, but only two – the papal nuncio and the Spanish ambassador – stayed the whole of its duration. Nobles tagged on or dropped off as they pleased. Political or religious affiliations determined their movements. Thus, as long as the court was in Lorraine or in territories dominated by the Guise family, Huguenots made themselves scarce. The council consequently fell under the influence of Catholics, the party of moderation being represented only by the Constable and the Chancellor. This may explain why some anti-Protestant measures were taken during the progress, though they may have been intended simply to maintain order.[41]

The next major stopping place was Lyon, a city with a large Protestant population. Montmorency, riding ahead of the royal party, took charge of its fortifications, artillery and keys before introducing a royal garrison. As a further safeguard, Protestant services were forbidden for the duration of the royal visit. This ban was soon extended to other towns soon to be visited by the court. Its stay in Lyon was accompanied by pageants and celebrations in which mem-

---

39 Boutier, Dewerpe and Nordman, *Un Tour*, pp. 241–6, 248–53.
40 Roelker, *Queen of Navarre*, pp. 229–30; J.-P. Babelon, *Henri IV* (Paris, 1982), p. 127.
41 Boutier, Dewerpe and Nordman, *Un Tour*, pp. 254–60.

bers of Lyon's colonies of Italian and German merchants figured prominently. Here too the court was joined by Emmanuel-Philibert, duke of Savoy, and his wife, Marguerite. Pleased as Catherine was to see her sister-in-law again, she refused to hand over Pinerolo and Savigliano to her husband.[42]

A plague epidemic forced the court to leave Lyon on 8 July. It moved on to Crémieu, where an important edict regarding French towns was issued on 14 July. L'Hôpital felt sure that municipal independence had been getting out of hand. Under the new edict, the choice of municipal magistrates in the chief towns was left to the king. Electors were required to submit two lists of candidates, leaving him to make the final choice. This was a major step in the subordination of towns to royal control.[43] It was during the court's stay at Crémieu that Jeanne d'Albret asked Catherine for permission to return to Béarn with her son. Her request was categorically refused. Instead, she was given 150,000 *livres* and asked to retire, not to Béarn, but to Vendôme. Her son, Henri, had to remain at court.[44]

The next port of call was Roussillon, where on 4 August Charles IX ruled on the application of the Edict of Amboise. Protestant worship in defiance of the restrictions laid down in the edict was made punishable by heavy fines and property confiscations. Married priests were ordered to leave their wives on pain of banishment. Royal officials, however, were instructed to see that Protestant worship, where permitted, was taking place.[45] On 15 August the court resumed its progress: travelling down the valley of the Rhône, it reached Romans. On 5 September the king's council examined a complaint from the Huguenots of Bordeaux about breaches of the peace. After a short break to allow Charles IX to recover from a chill, the court travelled to Montélimar (14 September), Orange (22 September) and Avignon, where it was hosted by the papal vice-legate. On 16 August the king and his mother called on

---

42 Ibid., pp. 88–9; Champion, *Catherine de Médicis*, pp. 99–111.
43 Boutier, Dewerpe and Nordman, *Un Tour,* p. 249.
44 Roelker, *Queen of Navarre*, p. 231.
45 A. Fontanon, *Les édits et ordonnances des rois de France,* 4 vols. (Paris, 1611), iv. 280–1.

Nostradamus at Salon de Crau. The old man was given 200 *écus* and appointed a royal councillor and king's physician. He prophesied that the king would live as long as the Constable.[46] In fact, Charles was to outlive him by seven years.

On 23 October the royal caravan arrived at Aix-en-Provence, whose parlement had refused to register the Edict of Amboise. Charles IX suspended the court, replacing it by a commission of Parisian *parlementaires*.[47] The next stage of the progress was less contentious. At Brignoles, the king was greeted by young girls who danced the *volta* and *martingale*. In Provence, he was able to admire the local flora, including orange and palm trees as well as pepper and cotton plants. The local Roman remains taught him a practical lesson in ancient history. On 3 November, at Toulon, he took a trip out to sea on a galley. At Marseille, he and his companions took part, disguised as Turks, in a mock naval battle. Crossing the Camargue, the royal party saw flamingoes. At Arles, where it was delayed for three weeks by floods, the king visited Les Alycamps – the famous avenue of Roman sarcophagi – and watched bullfights in the arena. Catherine, meanwhile, tried to persuade the provincial estates to accept the edict of pacification. After crossing the Rhône at Tarascon, the court visited the Pont du Gard. At Nîmes, a staunchly Protestant town, Charles was given an entry notable for its ingenious mechanical devices. He celebrated Christmas at Montpellier, set off on 1 January for Toulouse, but was held up at Carcassonne for ten days by a heavy fall of snow.[48] In Guyenne, Henri de Navarre rode ahead of the main party in order to welcome the king in each town in his capacity as provincial governor.

Throughout the progress Catherine kept in close touch with Paris. No less than 110 letters of the 413 which she wrote at this time were addressed to Parisians. They included 74 to Marshal Montmorency, governor of Paris and Ile-de-France, 22 to the *prévôt des marchands* and *échevins*,

---

46 Champion, *Catherine de Médicis*, pp. 159–60; I. Cloulas, *Catherine de Médicis* (Paris, 1979), p. 201.
47 Boutier, Dewerpe and Nordman, *Un Tour*, p. 242.
48 Mariéjol, pp. 146–7; Champion, *Catherine de Médicis*, pp. 161–206.

and 14 to the Parlement. Her principal concern was law and order, but she was also interested in her building programme, especially the Tuileries.[49] During her stay in Toulouse, some bad news arrived from the capital. Marshal Montmorency had refused to allow the Cardinal of Lorraine to enter the capital with an armed escort. The cardinal had defied the ban, whereupon his escort had been forcefully dispersed by the governor. Lorraine had found shelter in a merchant's house. While the Guises gathered their forces, Coligny brought 500 horse into Paris to assist Montmorency. To avert another civil war, Catherine ordered the Guises and the Admiral to leave the capital forthwith, but only Coligny obeyed.[50]

On 11 March, after forty-six days in Toulouse, the royal caravan resumed its travels. Passing through Montauban and Agen, it reached Bordeaux, where, on 12 April, Charles IX held another *lit de justice*. The Chancellor reprimanded the local *parlementaires*. 'All this disorder', he said, 'stems from the contempt in which you hold the king and his ordin-ances, which you neither fear nor obey except at your own pleasure.' L'Hôpital reaffirmed Charles IX's resolve to impose the edict of pacification. The same treatment was meted out to all the parlements, except those of Grenoble and Rennes. An epidemic of plague kept the king away from the former, and he was prevented from going to Rennes by revolts in towns along the Loire valley.[51]

On 3 May the court left Bordeaux for Bayonne, where Catherine planned to meet her daughter, the queen of Spain. She went there in disguise on 31 May to supervise preparations for Elisabeth's reception. Charles IX followed on 3 June and six days later his brother, Henri, set off to meet his sister in Spain and escort her back to France. The Franco-Spanish meeting in Bayonne was the diplomatic climax of the progress.[52] Catherine hoped to forge closer

49 Boutier, Dewerpe and Nordman, *Un Tour*, pp. 217, 223–4, 261–4.
50 Ibid., p. 262; *Lettres*, ii. 253–5; Mariéjol, p. 149.
51 Boutier, Dewerpe and Nordman, *Un Tour*, pp. 245–6; Champion, *Catherine de Médicis*, pp. 248–52.
52 Boutier, Dewerpe and Nordman, pp. 87–104; Champion, *Catherine de Médicis*, pp. 262–93; Mariéjol, pp. 149–54; Graham and Johnson, *Royal Tour*, pp. 29–57.

CATHERINE DE' MEDICI

links with Spain. She had long wanted to meet her son-in-law, Philip II, believing that a tête-à-tête would clear up difficulties which had arisen between France and Spain, but Philip had evaded her entreaties. In his place he sent the duke of Alba, whose hawkishness was soon to be demonstrated in the Netherlands. He was instructed to persuade Catherine to accept the Tridentine decrees and to scrap the Edict of Amboise in favour of a policy of religious persecution. She came to Bayonne hoping to arrange marriages for some of her children. She wanted Marguerite to marry Philip's son, Don Carlos, and Henri d'Orléans to marry Juana, Philip's sister, but Alba refused to discuss these proposed marriages. In another respect too the Bayonne interview was unhelpful. Although nothing was done against the Huguenots, their exclusion from the talks bred suspicion in their minds. Later on, after the Massacre of St. Bartholomew, many convinced themselves that it had been planned by Catherine and Alba at Bayonne. Some members of the French court undoubtedly expressed hawkish sentiments in private conversations with Alba, but Catherine seems not to have compromised her existing policy in any way.

After the Bayonne meeting, Catherine allowed Jeanne d'Albret to return to Nérac, capital of the duchy of Albret. Here the two ladies met again, and during four days Catherine tried in vain to persuade Jeanne to tolerate Catholicism in Béarn. As the court resumed its journey northward, Jeanne managed to keep her son for a short time. She introduced him to such Huguenot militants as his uncle, Condé. After visiting their domains of La Flêche and Vendômois, Jeanne and her son rejoined the court at Blois.[53]

The court, meanwhile, travelled through Angoumois and Saintonge to Nantes. Then, after stopping at Châteaubriant, it reached Angers and sailed up the Loire to Blois. It then crossed Berry to Moulins, the former capital of the dukes of Bourbon, where it stayed for three months (December 1565 –March 1566). The government had planned to cap its programme of administrative and judicial reform by promulgating a major ordinance. To this end, an Assembly

53 Babelon, *Henri IV*, pp. 131–2.

108

of Notables was called, consisting of princes of the blood, king's councillors, great officers of state and the First Presidents of six parlements. For the first time since 1564, the Guises and the Châtillons met face to face, and Catherine worked hard to heal their enmity. On 29 January Charles IX formally acquitted Coligny of any part in the assassination of the duc de Guise, and Catherine persuaded the Cardinal of Lorraine and the Admiral to kiss each other.

Opening the assembly, L'Hôpital pointed to judicial corruption as the underlying cause of France's troubles. Private greed and ambition, he said, had taken hold of the judiciary. He complained of too many laws, overlapping jurisdictions, and venal offices. He wanted fewer appeals and evocations, and thought courts should be ambulatory rather than stationary. He also believed that municipal authorities were misusing their powers and that these should be handed over to royal officials. Most of the points made by L'Hôpital found their way into the famous Ordinance of Moulins (February 1566), whose 86 clauses covered most aspects of government. Its overriding aim was to strengthen and extend the king's authority, and, although it was never applied, it did serve as a launching pad for future attempts to reform the government of France.[54]

At the end of the winter, the court left Moulins for the Auvergne. It stopped on 31 March at the Mont-Dore, then returned north by way of Clermont, La Charité, Auxerre and Sens. On 1 May it was back in Paris. Peace seemed to have returned to the kingdom. Letters written by Catherine during the progress expressed her optimism. In March 1565 she wrote: 'all things are as peaceful here as we may hope: the further we go, the more is obedience established, and the damage caused by disorder and confusion to the minds of the people is purged and cleansed, so I hope that with God's help all things will revert to their original state'.[55] Writing from Cognac in August 1565, she rejoiced over the fact that she had seen Huguenots and Catholics dancing together at a ball. That autumn she wrote: 'How much I

---

54 J.H.M. Salmon, *Society in Crisis: France in the sixteenth century* (London, 1975), pp. 155–6.
55 *Lettres*, iii. 59.

would like to see this kingdom revert to the state it was in when the mere sight of a white wand was enough for the whole kingdom to obey the king [. . .] The king, *Monsieur* my son, has the will to restore it to that state and I hope, if God allows him to live, that he will succeed.'

Following the court's return to Paris, Jeanne d'Albret spent eight months there attending to a great deal of business, including a lawsuit with Cardinal de Bourbon. She also did her utmost to prevent the handsome duc de Nemours from marrying Anne d'Este, the widow of François de Guise. He had promised to marry Jeanne's cousin, Françoise de Rohan, who was pregnant by him. It was at this time that the queen of Navarre revealed to the full her litigious nature. Aubigné described her as having the sex of a woman and the soul of a man. As the daughter of Marguerite de Navarre, she was highly literate and wrote a text-book for her children, which was printed by Robert II Estienne. Eventually, Jeanne was allowed by the king to take her son to parts of his patrimony which he had not yet seen. After a first trip to Picardy, they went to Maine, Vendôme, Beaumont-sur-Sarthe, Sainte-Suzanne and La Flêche. Jeanne and her son then travelled in haste to Poitou and Gascony. The Spanish ambassador warned Catherine that she had been deceived: the queen of Navarre and her son would not be returning to court for a long time. By taking the first prince of the blood to Béarn without the king's leave, Jeanne d'Albret crossed the Rubicon. She was telling the world that he was a Protestant Albret, not a Catholic Bourbon. Her action was in effect a rebellion. The links which Catherine had tried so assiduously to forge between Henri and her own sons were suddenly broken. Henceforth he assumed the role, under his mother's powerful influence, of a semi-foreign ruler. Soon he was also to become leader of the Huguenot party. The omens for peace were not good.[56]

56 Babelon, *Henri IV*, pp. 132–7.

Chapter 6

THE END OF COMPROMISE (1567–70)

In 1566 a serious revolt broke out in the Netherlands. As yet, it was not an exclusively religious movement. It began as opposition by the local nobility against the government of Margaret of Parma, Philip II's sister and regent in the Netherlands. But Calvinists figured prominently among the rebels, for some of the new laws introduced by the government were aimed at the eradication of heresy. The leaders of the opposition demanded their repeal and the government referred the matter to Philip II. Meanwhile, the protest spread to the lower orders of society, who were being hard pressed economically. Calvinist pastors whipped up popular feelings at huge public gatherings. In August 1566 a mob smashed religious images in Ghent, and the violence soon spread to other Flemish cities. The 'iconoclastic fury', as this outbreak was christened, was, in fact, quite discip- lined, yet it posed a serious challenge to the authorities. As the situation in the Netherlands seemed to get out of control, Philip II decided to send an army under the duke of Alba to restore order. The duke joined his army in north Italy and began to march north in June 1567. His route ran through Philip's dominions of Lombardy and Franche-Comté and those of his allies, the dukes of Savoy and Lorraine.[1]

---

1   G. Parker, *The Dutch Revolt* (London, 1977), pp. 68–103.

. . .

THE *SURPRISE DE MEAUX* (27 SEPTEMBER 1567)

Alba's expedition posed a threat to France's security, which the French government took seriously. Catherine ordered the garrisons in Champagne to be strengthened, and Charles IX raised a force of 6,000 Swiss mercenaries. He and his mother also spent part of the summer of 1567 inspecting urban defences in Picardy. Catherine complained that Philip II had kept her in the dark about his intentions.[2] He, for his part, took offence at the defensive measures being taken in France. Frances de Alava, the Spanish resident in France, expressed surprise at French suspicions of the forces his master was sending to impose obedience on his own subjects. He could not see why Charles IX needed to hire 6,000 Swiss troops.[3] Yet Catherine, being anxious to remain on good terms with Philip, sent six thousand bales of grain to Alba's army as he marched north. She also avoided sending the Huguenot leader, the prince de Condé, to Picardy in case his presence so close to the Flemish border might seem provocative.[4]

Suspicion of Spain was not confined to the French government. The Huguenots shared the fears of their co-religionists in Flanders and wondered if Alba's expedition heralded a crusade against Protestantism generally. They had not forgotten Catherine's meeting with the duke at Bayonne in 1565 and still suspected them of having planned some anti-Protestant coup. They were especially alarmed by the arrival in France of the Swiss troops.[5] Alba, in the event, did not attack France. He reached the Netherlands on 3 August, entering Brussels on 22 August. There he unleashed a savage campaign of repression which culminated in the arrest on 9 September of two leading noblemen, Counts Egmont and Hornes (Coligny's cousin), and their public execution in Brussels on 5 June 1568. Thousands of people were condemned by the Council of Troubles set up by Alba.

---

2   *Lettres*, iii. 41–2.
3   *Lettres*, iii. 42–3.
4   *Lettres*, iii. 7–8, 24.
5   J.-H. Mariéjol, *Catherine de Médicis* (Paris, 1920), pp. 160–1.

About a thousand were put to death; many more were imprisoned; others escaped to France.[6] The border between the Netherlands and France became a highly sensitive area, which Catherine watched closely. She undoubtedly felt relief when Alba reached the Netherlands, thereby lifting the threat of a Spanish invasion of France. But the Huguenots were not reassured, for the 6,000 Swiss troops were not sent home once the emergency had passed. They were brought into the heart of the kingdom so that Charles IX might see for himself how his money had been spent. The Huguenots wondered why they were being retained.[7] Denying that her son was planning to suppress religious liberty, Catherine solemnly assured Condé that as long as the king listened to her advice, the edict of pacification would be strictly observed.[8]

In August 1567 Catherine's main concern was the health of her daughter Elisabeth, the queen of Spain, who was several months pregnant. But other worries soon impinged. On 4 September she was told that 1,200 to 1,500 Huguenot horsemen had assembled near Montargis and Châtillon. She asked marshal Cossé to investigate and report to her in secret at Montceaux.[9] On 16 September news reached her of the arrest in the Netherlands of Counts Egmont and Hornes, but she seems not to have realized the impact this would have on the Huguenots. On the 18th she informed Fourquevaux, the French resident in Spain, of a report that the Huguenots were rearming, but brushed it aside. 'It was just a small scare', she explained, 'which has now blown over.' Next day she told M. de Gordes, the lieutenant in Dauphiné, that she was planning to spend some time in Montceaux. All the council was there, she added, ready to act in an emergency. This, however, seemed unlikely: 'everything is as peaceful now, thank God, as we could wish'.[10]

Catherine, however, should have heeded the alarm bells, for the Huguenot leaders were indeed stirring. They had

---

6 Parker, *Dutch Revolt*, pp. 105–10; N.M. Sutherland, *The Massacre of St. Bartholomew and the European Conflict, 1559–1572* (London, 1973), pp. 59–74.
7 D'Aubigné, *Histoire universelle*, vol. 1, bk. 4, ch. 7.
8 Mariéjol, pp. 160–1.
9 *Lettres*, iii. 53, 56–7.
10 *Lettres*, iii. 58–9.

heard from someone highly placed at court that a secret council meeting had decided to arrest their leaders, the prince de Condé and Admiral Coligny: the one was to be executed, and the other imprisoned. The 6,000 Swiss mercenaries were to be distributed between Paris, Orléans and Poitiers; and the Edict of Amboise was to be rescinded. After a lively discussion, the Huguenot leaders decided to launch a pre-emptive strike. According to La Noue, they set themselves four objectives: to seize a few important towns; to raise a strong army; to 'cut to pieces' the Swiss troops; and to drive away the Cardinal of Lorraine, who was said to be continually pressing the king to destroy all the Protestants.[11] A Huguenot force was ordered to meet at Rosay-en-Brie in late September.

Even now, Catherine suspected nothing. On 24 September she urged M. de Gordes to ensure that the peace accord was enforced in Dauphiné.[12] That same evening, however, news reached her of the armed force at Rosay. The council met that night and summoned the Swiss, who were stationed at Château-Thierry, to come in haste. Catherine and her son took shelter within the walls of Meaux. She could not understand what had prompted the Huguenot action. Her councillors debated the pros and cons of staying put or moving to Paris. The Constable and L'Hôpital favoured the first option, but the Guises carried the day after the Swiss had confidently predicted that they would easily force a passage through the rebels.[13] Next day, as the court left at dawn for the capital, Charles IX vented his anger. He declared that he would never allow anyone to frighten him again and swore to pursue the culprits into their houses and beds. He intended, henceforth, to lay down the law to everyone great and small.[14] On reaching Paris, Catherine expressed her surprise and rage in several letters. Writing to Matignon, the king's lieutenant-general in Normandy, on 27

---

11 F. de La Noue, *Discours politiques et militaires*, ed. F.E. Sutcliffe (Geneva, 1967), p. 682.
12 *Lettres*, iii. 59.
13 F. Decrue, *Anne duc de Montmorency connétable et pair de France sous les rois Henri II, François II et Charles IX* (Paris, 1889), p. 462.
14 BN, ms. fr. 3347. Bochefort to Renée of Ferrara. Cited by Hector de La Ferrière in *Lettres*, iii, pp. ix–x.

September 1567, she said that she could not understand what had prompted the Huguenot action.[15] In a letter to Fourquevaux, she denounced it as an 'infamous enterprise' and spoke of her sadness at seeing the kingdom revert to the troubles and misfortunes from which she had taken such pains with God's grace to deliver it.[16] 'I could not have imagined', she wrote to the duke of Savoy, 'that such ambitious and unfortunate designs could have entered the hearts of the subjects regarding their king.' The unprovoked rebellion was, in her opinion, the 'greatest wickedness in the world', an act of 'unmitigated treason' which threatened to subvert the entire state and endangered the royal family.[17]

After daring to pursue the king and his mother as far as Paris, the Huguenots compounded their offence by blockading the capital. On the night of 1 October they burned several windmills outside the Porte Saint-Denis. Parisians rushed to take up arms and broke into Protestant homes looking for suspected arsonists.[18] From his pulpit, Simon Vigor denounced the Huguenots as traitors. Their religion had been established by the sword, he ranted, and would be destroyed by the sword.[19] Catherine had every reason to feel let down and angry. At a meeting of the *conseil privé*, she allegedly rounded on Chancellor L'Hôpital as he proposed making concessions to end the crisis. 'Your advice is to blame', she said, 'for landing us in the present mess.' Yet she still wanted peace. She offered a full amnesty to Condé if he would lay down his arms, but he arrogantly posed as a champion of the people's rights: he called for the re-enactment of the Edict of Amboise, a meeting of the Estates-General and a lowering of taxes. The people, he claimed, were being fleeced for no other reason than to satisfy the greed of Italians and other foreigners. He was evidently thinking of those bankers who were helping to

---

15 *Lettres*, iii. 60.
16 *Lettres*, iii. 61.
17 *Lettres*, iii. 62.
18 B.B. Diefendorf, *Beneath the Cross: Catholics and Huguenots in sixteenth-century Paris* (Oxford, 1991), pp. 80–1. The author suggests that this event was a rehearsal for the Massacre of St. Bartholomew five years later.
19 M. Simonin, *Charles IX* (Paris, 1995), pp. 174–5.

subsidize Catherine's lavish court entertainments. The remark was hardly tactful. While continuing to negotiate, she appealed to Philip II, the duke of Savoy, the duke of Florence and the pope for financial or military aid. Charles IX, meanwhile, assembled an army.[20]

Paris began to feel pangs of hunger as food supplies were cut off by the Huguenots. On 7 October the king sent a herald to the rebel camp at Saint-Denis. In time-honoured fashion he ordered Condé, Coligny and d'Andelot to disarm and surrender or stand condemned as rebels. In their response, they disclaimed any intention of harming the king or his kingdom. They explained that they were acting under constraint from their enemies and were still ready to serve the king if only their freedom of worship and personal safety could be guaranteed. Encouraged by these words, Montmorency made one last attempt at negotiation, but upset the Huguenots by saying that the Edict of Amboise had only been granted by the king provisionally and that he would never accept two religions in his kingdom. The talks were consequently broken off.

On 10 October the old Constable (he was seventy-four years old) rode out of Paris at the head of a large army to engage the rebels. The ensuing battle on the plain of Saint-Denis proved indecisive, but Montmorency was fatally wounded. He died a few days later and was accorded an almost royal funeral lasting several days. His loss, by removing a political heavyweight from the king's council, undoubtedly facilitated the mounting influence of the Guises, led by the Cardinal of Lorraine.[21] On 11 November the Huguenots lifted their blockade and retreated eastward. They planned to meet a large force of German *reiters* led by duke Casimir, the son of the Count-Palatine. Catherine hoped to see them crushed in another battle or at least routed; but this was not to be. Condé, perhaps as a delaying tactic, offered new peace terms. Catherine set off early in January to Châlons-sur-Marne, headquarters of the king's army. 'I am going to our camp', she wrote to Fourquevaux, 'in order, if possible, to close the door on those who are

---

20 Mariéjol, p. 162.
21 Decrue, *Anne, duc de Montmorency*, pp. 469–76.

being driven out of the kingdom.' She found the king's captains squabbling over tactics. After settling their divisions, she made contact with the renegade Cardinal Châtillon, who acted as negotiator for the rebels.

When the queen returned to Paris on 15 January, the public mood was vehemently hostile to a peaceful settlement. The Parisians offered Charles IX 600,000 *livres* to continue the war and Philip II offered a larger sum for the same purpose. So the talks with Châtillon had to take place at night and in secret. The papal nuncio added to Catherine's difficulties by asking for Châtillon to be handed over for punishment by the Holy See. When she pointed out that he had come to Paris under a royal safe-conduct, the nuncio retorted that human laws did not apply to heretics. To her credit, however, she kept faith with the cardinal, but he pitched his demands so high that the talks were broken off.

. . .

THE PEACE OF LONGJUMEAU (22–23 MARCH 1568)

The Protestant army succeeded in meeting Casimir's *reiters*. Condé and Coligny then marched on Auxerre, crossed the Loire at La Charité and entered the Beauce. Catholics everywhere were thrown on the defensive. On 5 February 1568 the royal army, now officially commanded by the king's brother Anjou as lieutenant-general, fell back on Nogent-sur-Seine. Paris, once again, felt threatened. Charles IX, who was jealous of his brother, announced that he was ready to lead his forces himself. On 21 February Condé laid siege to Chartres, but, being virtually penniless, begged the king to resume talking. This time, though, the negotiations were successful. The Peace of Longjumeau, signed on 22 and 23 March, restored the Edict of Amboise in full. The king also agreed to advance money due to Casimir's *reiters*. But the treaty was not as favourable to the Huguenots as it seemed. While they agreed to disarm and hand over towns which they had seized, Charles was allowed to keep his army for the time being. Coligny saw the flaw, but had to fall in with Condé's wishes and those of most Protestant leaders.

The peace, however, was not easily enforced. In Rouen, it was followed by three days of rioting. A Catholic mob burst into the parlement and expelled the councillors. Protestant houses were sacked and looted. When the edict was eventually registered and Huguenots who had left the city returned, there was more violence. The lieutenant-general appealed for more troops urgently.[22] The disorder was repeated elsewhere in France. According to the Protestant historian, La Popelinière, more of his co-religionists were killed during the so-called peace than during the two first civil wars combined. Catholics, too, were given cause to complain. On 4 April the Venetian envoy, Correro, reported that none of the towns which should have been surrendered to the king had yet been handed over. On the 27th he stated that Protestants had destroyed a large number of churches and killed many priests.

Charles IX and his mother did their best to enforce the pacification. She advised Monluc not to provoke Jeanne d'Albret, the queen of Navarre, and ordered Tavannes to restore peace to Burgundy. But no troops were at hand to enforce the peace once urban garrisons had been disbanded. Catherine called a meeting of the *conseil privé* for 1 May to discuss the current crisis, but was unable to attend on account of a high fever which kept her in bed for some weeks. In her absence, the councillors argued for and against repression. Some, like L'Hôpital, advocated conciliation; others, like Lorraine, pressed for severity. In the end, the king decided to send councillors and the *prévôts des maréchaux* to the various *gouvernements* to impose order.

During the queen's illness, the crisis deepened. Anjou warned against a new Huguenot uprising. All eyes were fixed on Condé, who had gone with a strong escort to Picardy. 'As long as the Cardinal of Lorraine remains at court', he allegedly said, 'the peace will not hold. I will fetch him and stain his gown red with his own blood.'[23] Catherine's recovery was urgently needed. On 24 May she was well enough to dictate a letter to Coligny. He had complained bitterly after one of his men, who was carrying 50,000 *livres* to Casimir's *reiters*, was attacked by royal troops garrisoned at Auxerre. Catherine promised that the culprits would be

---

22 P. Benedict, *Rouen during the Wars of Religion* (Cambridge, 1981), p. 120.
23 *Lettres*, iii. p. xxvi.

punished, the king's intention being to administer justice fairly to all his subjects.[24] The Admiral had also complained of plots against his own life. Catherine asked him for the names of his informants, but he declined, pointing out that she had often said that he owed his life to her. She ought to punish those who had offered to kill him and disclose their names so that he might know how best to defend himself.[25]

. . .

CATHERINE AND THE HUGUENOTS

What precisely was Catherine's policy at this stage? Did she have a 'secret plan' to crush the Huguenots, as Cloulas would have us believe, or was she still committed to peace through compromise?[26] Two schools of thought exist on this question. The traditional view, represented by Mariéjol and more recently by Cloulas, is that Catherine turned against the Huguenots after the *Surprise de Meaux* and abandoned her policy of pacification through compromise in favour of repression. The change of policy was reflected in a change of ministers. Instead of relying on L'Hôpital, the queen turned to Lorraine, who looked to Catherine's favourite son, Anjou, to carry out the new hard-line policy aimed at wiping out the Huguenot leadership once and for all. As Mariéjol writes: 'the queen did not follow suggestions; she used the cardinal as she had used l'Hôpital. Having changed her policy, she changed her servants.'[27]

However, according to Nicola Sutherland, Catherine was not responsible for the hard line taken by the French government after the peace of Longjumeau. She argues that it was Lorraine, not Catherine, who instigated the new policy. Ever since his return from the Council of Trent, he had been reasserting his authority in the king's council. Shortly after the *Surprise de Meaux* he had sent an agent to Alba with a request for help and a proposal to advance Philip II's

---

24 *Lettres,* iii. 142 and 142 n. 2. Coligny's letter to the king is in BN, ms. fr. 3193, f. 35 and that to d'Andelot is on f. 121.
25 Mariéjol, p. 168.
26 Mariéjol, p. 164; I. Cloulas, *Catherine de Médicis* (Paris, 1979), p. 234.
27 Mariéjol, p. 167.

claim to the French throne. This Sutherland takes as evidence that Catherine was no longer a free agent. Lorraine, she writes, 'regarded himself as an agent of the papacy and universal catholicism rather than as a nobleman of France and a servant of the crown'. It follows that Catherine 'must inevitably have opposed Lorraine'. 'While she strove for peace,' Sutherland writes, 'the cardinal strove for war.' It was thanks to Catherine's efforts that moderates on the council were able to conclude the treaty of Longjumeau. Lorraine, however, 'never entertained the notion of a proper peace' and used the temporary cessation of hostilities 'to recover the initiative and control the circumstances of the war'. Taking advantage of Catherine's illness in May 1568, he held a council meeting which decided to wipe out the Huguenot leaders. He also planned to seize the young king, but was foiled by the queen's recovery in mid-May. He then decided 'to rise upon the established authority and dawning ambition of Anjou'.[28]

Sutherland's thesis, which rests on a close acquaintance with the contemporary sources, has been accepted by many historians; yet some of her sources are biased and her conclusions rely heavily on supposition. Lorraine certainly became a powerful figure at the French court following his return from Trent and was regarded by Protestants everywhere as one of their principal foes. He was also the senior member of the house of Guise following the assassination of the second duke. This gave him a personal reason for hating Admiral Coligny, whom the Guises continued to regard as the instigator of the duke's assassination. Lorraine was also the uncle of Mary, Queen of Scots, who had a claim to the English throne. For all these reasons, he was a particular *bête noire* of the Protestants and of the English. He was thus singled out for particular attention by English diplomats in France. It does not necessarily follow, however, that he was as dominant in the French king's council as they liked their own government to think. Sutherland also attaches considerable importance to the strained relations betwen Catherine and the cardinal, which are reflected in the queen's correspondence. He seems to have conducted his

---

28 Sutherland, *Massacre*, pp. 61–2, 65–6, 70, 75–6.

own foreign policy behind her back. However, it is by no means proven that he ousted her from policy-making or that she necessarily disagreed with him over the measures needed to solve France's domestic problems. Lorraine was undoubtedly a hard-liner, but can we be sure that Catherine did not also become one after the *Surprise de Meaux*? Sutherland herself admits that the Huguenots had blotted their copybook by trying to ambush the king and then blockading the capital. 'It seems probable', she writes, 'that neither the king nor the capital – not to mention Lorraine – ever forgave them for this dual outrage.'[29] Why, then, should Catherine have forgiven them? She had most cause to feel aggrieved and betrayed. Why should she have clung to a policy which had so conspicuously failed? Nothing could be expected from the Huguenots, she said to the Venetian envoy, except deceit and treachery. Nor can we assume that Lorraine was virtually running the government. According to Correro, political activity was almost suspended during the queen's illness.

On 11 June 1568 the queen gave audience to the Venetian ambassador. 'There are circumstances', she said, 'which oblige one to turn upon oneself and to submit to what one did not want in order to avoid greater ills.' 'See what a miserable situation we have fallen into again. Whereas we had got used to going about the kingdom in safety, now we cannot take a step out of doors unless we are surrounded by guards.' Lowering her voice, she added: 'In this very room there may be people who would like to see us dead and would kill us with their own hands, but God will not allow this to happen; our cause is His and that of all Christendom; He will not abandon us.'[30] At this juncture, however, Catherine was informed that a large force of Huguenots under the sieur de Cocqueville was marching towards the border of Flanders, where they hoped to assist their hard-pressed co-religionists. But they were intercepted and routed by marshal Cossé, Cocqueville himself being taken prisoner

---

29 Ibid., p. 60.
30 *Lettres*, iii, pp. xxvii–xxviii.

and summarily executed. Catherine instructed Cossé to hand over his Flemish captives to Alba so that they might be punished as they deserved. As for his French prisoners, she wrote: 'I think some of them should be punished by execution and the rest sent to the galleys.'[31] As Mariéjol writes: 'One can see how worked up she has become; she is no longer the same woman.'[32] In a conversation with the Spanish ambassador, Alava, Catherine described the execution of Egmont and Hornes in Brussels on 5 June 1568 as 'a holy decision', adding that she hoped soon to take a similar one in France.[33]

. . .

THE HUGUENOT FLIGHT TO LA ROCHELLE

Towards the end of July 1568 the French government seemed ready to spring a trap for the Huguenot leaders, Condé and Coligny, who were staying together at the château of Noyers in Burgundy.[34] Norris reported that Charles IX had decided to send his army to Burgundy to deter William of Orange from coming to Condé's aid. Tavannes, he wrote, had promised to send the heads of Condé and the Admiral 'by the last of this month'.[35] Tavannes tells us in his Memoirs that he warned Condé of the plot by arranging for certain messages to fall into his hands, but this may be a fabrication of Tavannes' son, who edited the Memoirs, aimed at saving his father's reputation. Condé was certainly forewarned but we do not know by whom. On 23 August he and Coligny fled from Noyers with their families. 'We are thinking of nothing else', wrote Catherine on 8 September, 'than to gather as soon as possible a sizeable force with which to run them to earth, defeat them and destroy them before they can regroup and do

31 *Lettres*, iii. 166–7.
32 Mariéjol, p. 168.
33 Cloulas, *Catherine*, p. 235.
34 The château ('le plus bel chastel du royaume') was dismantled by Henry IV. I. Dunlop, *Burgundy* (London, 1990), pp. 81–3.
35 *CSPF, 1566–68*, pp. 526, 534.

something worse.'[36] Condé informed the king of his departure, adding that he could not see how a journey undertaken by 150 unarmed people could be construed as a rebellion, but the Huguenot exodus soon became a flood. At every stage of their journey westward, Condé and Coligny were joined by large numbers of Huguenots. As they passed through Berry, La Châtre wrote to the king: 'all the Huguenots of the towns and villages are following them. There are carts and waggons galore . . .'. Their objective, he thought, was to bring their families to safety in La Rochelle, then to mobilize for an attack on towns in the Loire valley.

On 15 August Jeanne d'Albret returned precipitately to Nérac from Tarbes. Realizing that the government was effectively at war with the Huguenot movement, she now placed herself at its head. At the same time she stood up for the rights of the princes of the blood: her son and all the Bourbons, whose right to sit in the king's council was far greater than that of the foreigners – Lorrainers (the Guises) and Italians (Retz, Birague, Gonzague-Nevers) – surrounding the queen. Jeanne's war was more than a religious one; it was a 'war of the public weal' similar to those France had experienced several times in the fifteenth century. She left Nérac with her two children and some fifty nobles. As she did so, she sent La Mothe-Fénelon, Catherine's envoy, back to his mistress with an explanation of her action: she was taking up arms for three reasons: 'the service of My God and of the true faith'; 'the service of my King and the observance of the edict of pacification'; and 'the right of blood', that is the defence of the rights of the illustrious race of Bourbon, true sprig of the fleur-de-lis. On 24 September, near Cognac, Jeanne met Condé and Coligny; four days later they entered La Rochelle together. Now aged fifteen, Henri de Navarre assumed the official headship of the Huguenot cause. The effective leader, however, was Condé.

Condé's letter to the king elicited no reply. Instead, orders were given to raise an army against him. Catherine appealed to the 'little man', as he was called, to stay at some place where she might talk to him. Some have seen this as a trap to allow Tavannes to overtake him, but Sutherland

36 *Lettres*, iii. 178 (BN, ms fr. 10752, p. 1463).

dismisses the idea. Tavannes, she says, was 'a supporter of Catherine'.[37] Be that as it may, a royal proclamation on 1 September ordered the mobilization of the *gendarmerie* at Orléans under Anjou. On 19 September, at a meeting of the king's council, L'Hôpital refused to seal orders for the alienation of church property to help pay for the new campaign. He also resisted a papal demand for the revocation of the edict of Longjumeau. Only Marshal Montmorency saved him from being physically molested by Lorraine.[38] But the hard-liners on the council carried the day. The edict was revoked and replaced by another which banned the exercise of any religion other than Catholicism and ordered Protestant ministers to leave the kingdom within a fortnight. L'Hôpital withdrew to his house at Vignay before surrendering the seals on 7 October.[39]

Catherine returned to Paris on 28 September in time to witness a solemn procession, customary on the eve of a new military campaign, in which the body of Saint Denis was carried. On 4 October Anjou, the commander-in-chief, set off for Etampes accompanied by the Cardinals of Bourbon, Lorraine and Guise. He was soon joined by Catherine, who gave him his final instructions before returning to Paris in order to complete preparations for the forthcoming campaign. The Huguenots, meanwhile, consolidated their hold on La Rochelle and captured a number of towns in Poitou. Catherine rejoiced on 2 November when she heard that a Huguenot army marching north from Provence had been defeated by Montpensier and Martigues.[40] But the Huguenots could expect help from outside France. On 17 November the prince of Orange crossed the frontier from the Netherlands. A few days later, Charles IX urged Nemours to form a second royal army to cover Paris.

---

37 Sutherland, *Massacre,* pp. 89–90.
38 *CSPF, 1566–68,* p. 554.
39 Ibid., p. 91. I cannot see why Sutherland should take the quarrel in the council as evidence that 'Catherine, and possibly the king, opposed Lorraine's determination to make war'. The fact that the Chancellor was forced to resign suggests rather a lack of royal support.
40 *Lettres,* iii. 200.

On 7 January 1569 Alava called on Catherine at Saint-Maur-les-Fossés. She seemed terribly tired as she left a council meeting and the ambassador asked her why. Replying with tears in her eyes, she said: 'I may well seem tired, as I have to carry the whole burden of government alone.' 'You would be very surprised', she continued, 'if you knew what has just happened. I no longer know whom to trust. Those whom I believed to be wholly devoted to the service of the king, my son, have turned around and are opposing his wishes.' 'I am scandalized', she explained, 'by the conduct of members of the council; they all want me to make peace.'[41] To avoid such pressure, she soon retired to Montceaux, where she remained till 14 January. Thence Catherine travelled to Châlons, where she announced that Orange had retreated beyond the Moselle. On 1 February Sir Henry Norris, the English ambassador, had an audience with her at Joinville, home of the Guises. She complained of the help Queen Elizabeth was sending to the rebels in La Rochelle. Norris tried to shift the blame on to disobedient subjects, who, he suggested, were common to both nations. Catherine briskly rejected the comparison. 'In England', she said, 'all the subjects share the queen's religion; in France it's quite another matter.'[42]

On 13 March Marshal Tavannes defeated the Huguenots at Jarnac. The battle is mainly significant on account of Condé's death. He was not killed in action, however, but murdered by one of Anjou's men after surrendering. The duke informed the king thus: '*Monseigneur,* you have won the battle. The prince de Condé is dead. I have seen his body.' The duke could not resist a pun recalling the *Surprise de Meaux:* 'Alas,' this poor man has caused so much trouble' (*tant de maux*).[43] After the battle, Jeanne d'Albret presented the young prince de Condé and her own son, Henri de Navarre, to the Huguenot army.[44] Though only fifteen and sixteen years old respectively, they were acclaimed as its new

---

41 AGS, K. 1514. Cited in *Lettres,* iii, pp. xxxvii–xxxviii.
42 *Lettres,* iii, p. xl.
43 P. Chevallier, *Henri III* (Paris, 1985), p. 119.
44 N. Roelker, *Queen of Navarre: Jeanne d'Albret, 1528–1572* (Cambridge, Mass., 1968), p. 308.

leaders. Being princes of the blood, they conferred a certain legitimacy on the Huguenot rebellion. The new effective leader of the Huguenots, however, was Admiral Coligny.

. . .

THE 'POLICY OF ELIMINATION'

On 7 May d'Andelot, Coligny's brother, died, some said 'of a fever', others of poison. Coligny and La Rochefoucauld also fell seriously ill at the time, but recovered. On 10 June Cardinal Châtillon, who had fled to England, wrote to Frederick III, Elector-Palatine. His brother, he said, had been poisoned. As evidence, he mentioned the findings of a post-mortem and the boasts made by an Italian to several people in Paris and at the French court. Claiming that he had administered the poison, he demanded his reward.[45] A report reached Alava from England that d'Andelot had been poisoned by a Florentine who had sought a reward from Charles IX. On 27 May Norris reported that an Italian was boasting that he had poisoned d'Andelot and 'had made him and the Admiral drink from the same cup'.[46] How far, if at all, was Catherine implicated in the plot? A conversation with Alava dating back to 7 April suggests that she was far from innocent. The ambassador advised her to ring the death knell for Coligny, d'Andelot and La Roche-foucauld. She replied that she had done so three days before, having offered 50,000 *écus* for the Admiral's murder as well as 20,000 and 30,000 for the other two.[47] Sutherland does not think that the queen's 'judicious replies' to the 'detested ambassador' should be taken as evidence that she supported 'his policy of elimination'. In her view, Catherine was 'bound to avoid the humiliation of openly admitting to Alava that the crown was constrained to perform, or submit to, the will of Lorraine'. What is more, 'having been gravely ill for a good two months, she herself is unlikely to have played any effective part in recent affairs at all'. Sutherland

---

45 Kluckhohn, *Briefe Friedrich des Frommen, Kürfürsten von der Pfalz* (Brunswick, 1870), vol. 2, 1st part pp. 334–8. Cited by Mariéjol, p. 172.
46 Sutherland, *Massacre*, pp. 100–1.
47 Ibid., p. 99.

suggests that Catherine could not afford to upset Philip II, who could assist or impede Charles IX's marriage to the Emperor's daughter. The deaths of the Protestant leaders would also 'have left her even more disastrously in the power of Lorraine'. Therefore, Sutherland concludes that there is no reason to suppose that Catherine's replies to Alava 'represented any change of policy on her part'.[48] This reads like special pleading. The evidence against Catherine is almost overwhelming. Lorraine's control of government policy and Catherine's exclusion from power are not proven. Her letters suggest that she was in close touch with events, even during her illness, and rejoiced at the discomfiture of the men who had humiliated her at Meaux and destroyed the peace which she had so painstakingly re-stored. Writing to Fourquevaux on 19 May, she said: 'We greatly rejoiced over the news of d'Andelot's death ... I hope that God will mete out to the others the treatment they deserve.'[49]

Tactically, the battle of Jarnac was of minor significance. The royalists tried unsuccessfully to capture Cognac, then Angoulême. Coligny, meanwhile, reorganized his forces, which had only been marginally reduced at Jarnac, as the infantry had not been used. He rested his hopes on German troops – 6,000 *reiters* and almost as many landsknechts – levied by the Elector Palatine and led by Wolfgang, duke of Zweibrücken. Nearly 250 miles separated the two armies and the risk of interception by the royalists was high, but Wolfgang eluded Nemours and Aumale, who were waiting for him on the Meuse, by marching through Montbéliard and Franche-Comté.

On 26 May Anjou wrote to his mother complaining bitt-erly about Lorraine and Aumale. His *reiters* had not been paid although Aumale had received the money due to them. As a result, they had allowed Zweibrücken to slip past him. By now Catherine was well enough to join Anjou in his camp. Writing to the king from Limoges on 11 June, she reported that Zweibrücken had given the royalists the slip and had linked up with Coligny. In the days that followed,

---

48 Ibid., p. 101.
49 *Lettres,* iii. 241.

she watched skirmishing between the two armies. After sacking Beaune, Zweibrücken crossed the Loire on 20 May, but died on 11 June, just before his army joined Coligny at Saint-Yriex. Catherine wrote to the king: 'You see, my son, how God helps you more than men do. He makes them die without a blow being struck.'[50] She threw herself heart and soul into the war. On 18 June she inspected 1,000 troops sent by the pope, and on the 21st wrote to the Cardinal de Guise, who was in Spain, asking him to hasten the dispatch of troops promised by Philip II.[51]

Although the royalist army was larger than its rival, its morale was at a low ebb. The troops felt that their victory at Jarnac had been wasted and that the Germans should not have been allowed to slip past them. Five weeks after Coligny's junction with them, he defeated a small royalist force at La Roche l'Abeille, capturing Filippo Strozzi, colonel-general of the infantry. The Admiral took few prisoners and caused hundreds of peasants to be slaughtered. Following his success, he wanted to take Saumur, but was persuaded to besiege Poitiers instead. This was a grave blunder: for the siege lasted from 24 July until 7 September. The king's army, in the meantime, received reinforcements from the pope, Florence and Spain.

It seems that a concerted effort was now made to undermine the Huguenot rebellion by destroying its leader. On 18 July Norris wrote to Cecil: 'I am told that a captain Haijz, a German, is sent from there to kill the Admiral by means of poison and that he has been paid the same salary as others who have undertaken a similar mission.'[52] On 8 August Alava reported to Philip II that a German was staying at his *hôtel*. He had come from the Admiral's camp and seemed well informed about the situation there. He had spoken of a plot to kill Coligny. Alava had offered to send him to Charles IX and his mother, but they had declined. Instead, they had enjoined Alava not to tell anyone what he had heard. They were expecting good news at any moment. 'Do not ask anything now,' they said; 'you will soon know everything.' They begged Alava to commit the German to remain silent,

---

50 *Lettres*, iii. 251.
51 *Lettres*, iii. 254.
52 *CSPF, 1569–71*, p. 96.

by bribery if necessary. Their furtive behaviour coupled with their joyful anticipation convinced the ambassador that they had plotted the Admiral's murder.[53] A month after this extraordinary scene, a servant of Coligny, called Dominique d'Albe, was stopped by Huguenots as he was on his way to the duke of Bavaria. On him were found a *laissez-passer* issued by Anjou and some white powder which was identified as poison. D'Albe admitted that he had been suborned by one of Anjou's guards to poison the Admiral. He was duly tried by a military court, found guilty and executed on 20 September.[54]

That Catherine should have instigated Coligny's murder is hardly surprising. Since Condé's death, he was the supreme commander of the Huguenot forces. The two young princes, Henri de Navarre and Henri de Bourbon, theoretically led the Huguenot movement but everyone knew that they were only 'the Admiral's pages'. Coligny's removal would effectively decapitate the Huguenot movement. Catherine had no reason to spare him. In her eyes, he was a rebel and no amount of excuses on his part could expunge his guilt: an outlaw could be legitimately killed by any subject. Poison had long been a favourite political weapon in Italy. It is unlikely that Catherine would have felt any scruples about its use, if this could speed up the return of peace. The attitude taken by the Parlement of Paris was equally drastic. On 13 September Coligny was sentenced to death in his absence, a price of 50,000 *écus* being placed on his head. He was to be strangled and hanged on the Place de Grève.[55] An additional decree, on 28 September, offered a reward to anyone who handed him over 'dead or alive'.[56]

---

53 ASG Simancas, K. 1512, no. 43. A translation is given in P. de Vaissière, *De quelques assassins* (2nd edn. Paris, 1912), pp. 100–1.

54 Mariéjol, p. 175; Sutherland, *Massacre*, pp. 102–3.

55 J. Shimizu, *Conflict of Loyalties. Politics and religion in the career of Gaspard de Coligny, Admiral of France, 1519–1572* (Geneva, 1970), pp. 134–5; Sutherland, *Massacre*, p. 104.

56 J. Delaborde, *Gaspard de Coligny, amiral de France* (Paris, 1879–82), iii. 145–7.

Pope Pius V congratulated Charles IX for condemning this 'detestable and execrable man'.[57]

On 9 October 1569 a new twist was given to the murder plot, when a young nobleman, called Louviers de Maurevert, shot the seigneur de Mouy, one of the Admiral's captains, in the back, killing him instantly. Maurevert was a former page of the Guises, who had gone into exile after murdering his tutor. He had planned to murder the Admiral but, as yet, no opportunity had presented itself. He now fled to the royal camp, where he was quite well received by Anjou and other councillors. However, Brantôme tells us that Maurevert was 'abhorred' by the rest of the army because he had betrayed his master and benefactor. The royal family had fewer scruples. On 10 October Charles IX wrote from Pléssis-lez-Tours to his brother, Alençon, in Paris, asking him to reward Maurevert with the collar of the Ordre de Saint-Michel.[58]

. . .

MONCONTOUR (3 OCTOBER 1569)

On 3 October 1569 Coligny took up a position near Moncontour in Poitou, where he thought he might engage the enemy with advantage, but a flanking movement by Tavannes forced him to fight on different ground. The two sides were fairly evenly balanced numerically, both having a large force of mercenaries. During the cavalry mêlée that ensued, Coligny was so badly wounded that Louis of Nassau had to take command. On the royalist side, Anjou was unhorsed and only saved by his bodyguard. Nassau charged the Swiss but failed to disperse them. In the end, the Huguenots gave up the fight. Their cavalry left the field, abandoning the landsknechts. The Swiss fell upon them with glee, killing them to a man. About half the Huguenot infantry were massacred; the rest escaped. The royalists lost few infantry, but more cavalry than the Huguenots.[59]

---

57 Sutherland, *Massacre,* p. 103.
58 Ibid., pp. 104–5; Mariéjol, p. 176; de Vaissière, *De quelques assassins,* pp. 112–13; Delaborde, *Gaspard de Coligny,* iii. 159.
59 J.W. Thompson, *The Wars of Religion in France, 1559–1576* (New York, 1909), pp. 388–9; Sir C. Oman, *A History of the Art of War in the XVIth Century* (London, 1937), pp. 448–55.

Tavannes wanted to pursue the Huguenots as they fled from the field, but Charles IX, who had come to Anjou's camp in the hope of sharing his victory, decided against a course of action which he thought demeaning. He decided instead to lay siege to the Huguenot strongholds covering the approaches to La Rochelle, which might offer scope for staging of triumphal entries. While the royal army exhausted itself besieging Saint-Jean-d'Angély (16 October–2 December), Coligny fled to the Midi. After spending the winter in the lush surroundings of Agen and Montauban, he rebuilt his forces, adding to them the army of Montgomery, which had just reconquered Béarn from the Catholics. In the spring of 1570, the Admiral moved across Languedoc as far as the Rhône, leaving a trail of destruction in his wake.

Meanwhile, during the siege of Saint-Jean-d'Angély, Catherine opened talks. Despite their recent defeat, the Huguenots needed peace less than the crown, their financial predicament being far less serious. As the Florentine ambassador put it, the king was driven to negotiate by 'a total lack of money'. The Huguenot leaders were united and their morale was high, while Catherine had to cope with new rivalries among the royalists: jealousy between Monluc and Damville, the commanders in the south, and growing hostility between her two sons, Charles IX and Anjou. Pope Pius V and Philip II did all in their power to hinder the peace negotiations. Catherine wrote to her ambassador in Spain: 'Please make the Catholic King, my good son, believe that extreme necessity has obliged us to take the path of pacification rather than that of force.' Charles IX painted an even darker picture of the state of his kingdom. Of the proposed peace, he wrote: 'it is a beginning . . . after which I shall lead [the Huguenots] bit by bit . . . to the Catholic religion'.

Catherine offered the Huguenots peace with freedom of conscience (February 1570), but they insisted on freedom of worship as well (March 1570). Jeanne d'Albret, who exerted an important influence on the talks, distrusted Catherine's advances. She pointed to the French crown's relations with Spain and, as evidence, produced a letter, intercepted by one of her agents, from Lorraine to Alba. The queen of Navarre did not want 'a peace made of snow this winter that would melt in next summer's heat'. No

131

lasting peace was possible, she explained, unless Charles IX conceded to the Huguenots freedom of conscience, the public exercise of their faith and the restitution of their estates, honours and dignities. 'I can scarcely persuade myself,' she wrote to Catherine, 'having once had the honour of knowing Your Majesty's sentiments intimately, that you could wish to see us reduced to such an extremity or to profess ourselves of no religion whatever . . . We have come to the determination to die, all of us, rather than abandon our God, and our religion, the which we cannot maintain unless permitted to worship publicly, any more than a human body can live without meat or drink.'[60]

On 10 February 1570 Jeanne begged Catherine not to let herself be fooled 'by those who do not wish the kingdom to be at peace . . . but wish instead civil war to continue until all is ruined'. The real aim of the king's advisers, she claimed, was to exterminate the Huguenots. She dwelt on 'the lying inventions originating in the hard, black heart of the cardinal de Lorraine'. Citing letters and dispatches intercepted by her agents, she warned Catherine and Charles that their wishes were being disregarded and changed by the cardinal. 'I know for a fact', she added, 'that he sent three assassins to kill my son, my nephew and the Admiral, and I do not doubt he has me marked out also, but we are all in the hand of God.'[61] These allegations bear out the Sutherland thesis, but they should be treated with caution. It had become customary for the Huguenots to affirm their loyalty to the crown and to claim that they were only trying to liberate it from its 'evil counsellors'. Lorraine filled that role admirably. Little purpose would have been served by accusing Catherine of complicity in the so-called 'policy of elimination'. As Nancy Roelker has pointed out, the cardinal 'had no such power, for instance in the royal Council, as Jeanne attributed to him'. 'By the nature of their respective positions Jeanne had few dealings with the Cardinal; what she says about him is largely myth.'[62]

---

60 Roelker, *Queen of Navarre*, pp. 332–5.
61 Ibid., pp. 335–7; *Lettres*, iii. 346–52.
62 Roelker, *Queen of Navarre*, p. 305.

Charles IX, though sickly, was beginning to assert himself. He reacted violently on 25 April when the Protestant negotiators presented their terms, but became more conciliatory as Coligny advanced northwards along the Rhône valley. Peace terms were almost agreed when Téligny, the chief Huguenot representative, demanded Calais and Bordeaux as surety towns. The king flew into a temper and, reaching for his dagger, exclaimed: 'I will show you that I am not the man of straw that the Huguenots take me for.' He would have stabbed Téligny if he had not been restrained by his entourage. The Admiral, meanwhile, was drawing closer to Paris. After a lengthy stopover at Saint-Etienne, he resumed his march, avoiding marshal Cossé, who tried to bar his way at Arnay-le-Duc (26 June) and set up a strong camp at La Charité-sur-Loire, whence he threatened the suburbs of the capital. In the west, La Noue, the 'Huguenot Bayard', captured Niort, Brouage and Saintes.

Catherine by now was tired of war. The struggle seemed to go on endlessly and government funds were running low. On 4 July Cossé warned that the king's army was on the verge of disintegration. Spain was sending no more help. The queen's task of peace-making was facilitated by Coligny's readiness to lay down his arms. On 29 July he wrote to Catherine: 'When your Majesty will study all my actions since first she knew me until now, she will admit that I am quite different from the portrait that has been painted of me. I beg you, Madam, to believe that you have no more devoted servant than I have been and have wanted to be.'[63] Catherine invited him to come to court, but he excused himself. On 5 August the king's council met three times. Lorraine was not present. For some reason, he had fallen into disgrace, and had gone back to his diocese. Sutherland offers no satisfactory explanation of this extraordinary development. She writes that the Cardinal 'evidently regarded peace as inevitable' and was 'fast losing, or had already lost, his vital control of the council'. She does, however, hint at the reason: 'the duc de Guise also fell into disgrace for aspiring to marry Marguerite . . . '.[64]

63 BN, ms fr. 3193, p. 41. Cited in *Lettres,* iii, p. lxv.
64 Sutherland, *Massacre,* pp. 115–16.

. . .

THE FALL OF LORRAINE

Catherine was an inveterate matchmaker. In 1568 two events had a major bearing on her matrimonial strategy: the first was the incarceration on 18 January of Don Carlos, the demented son of Philip II, who had been earmarked for the hand of Anna, the Emperor's eldest daughter; the second was the death on 3 October of Elisabeth de Valois, Catherine's daughter and Philip II's queen. The two events occurring so close together gave rise to the story that Carlos and Elisabeth had been lovers and that Philip had had them murdered. The story was nothing more than malicious gossip, but from it has sprung Schiller's play, *Don Carlos,* and Verdi's magnificent opera of the same name.[65] The removal of Don Carlos from the marriage market opened up the possibility of Charles IX marrying Anna instead, and Elisabeth's death created a vacancy on the Spanish throne which Catherine hoped to fill by marrying her younger daughter, Marguerite, to Philip II. Much of her political thinking in 1568 and 1569 was geared to these objectives, which carried important implications for France. As far as Catherine was concerned, the kingdom's religious troubles were an unwelcome distraction which needed to be resolved as quickly and effectively as possible.

The Cardinal of Lorraine, as senior member of the house of Guise, zealously promoted its interests, which were not necessarily the same as those of the royal house of Valois. Indeed, in 1568, they cut right across them. For in that year, on 19 May, Lorraine's niece, Mary Stuart, was forced by her rebellious Scottish subjects to flee to England. Although she was still Bothwell's wife (he did not die till 1578), she was, it seems, regarded by Lorraine as an eligible match for Charles IX or his brother, Anjou. Such a marriage would have restored the tie between the French crown and the house of Guise which had been severed when Francis II, Mary's first husband, had died in 1560. Mary was also highly desirable on account of her claims to the Scottish and

---

65 P. Pierson, *Philip II of Spain* (London, 1975), pp. 55–7.

English thrones. Lorraine tried to dazzle Anjou with the prospect of rescuing Mary and bringing her back to France. He suggested that if he married her she would cede him her estate in France as well as her rights in England and Scotland. In July 1568 Norris reported that great diligence was being made in France to rescue Mary. Catholics on the Continent considered Elizabeth I to be not only a heretic but a bastard and a usurper. As a prince of the Roman church, Lorraine undoubtedly hoped that Elizabeth would be overthrown, and he did his best to bring this about. Coligny and d'Andelot warned her against certain Italians sent by Lorraine 'to practise against her'.[66] Sutherland regards these moves as part and parcel of a great Tridentine crusade against Protestantism, but they also served the interests of the house of Guise, and, as such, they did not suit Catherine. She had always disliked Mary Stuart and did not wish to see her back at court as her daughter-in-law.

Catherine, as we have seen, was hoping to marry Marguerite to a sovereign prince. Once Philip II had turned her down, she looked for someone of comparable status. But Marguerite was seventeen years old and flirtatious. She may not have slept with Henri de Guise, who was roughly the same age, but she seems to have encouraged his advances, as did Lorraine. It was Anjou who allegedly got wind of the affair and informed his mother. Charles IX was deeply affronted by his sister's deceitfulness and Guise's presumption. Alava relates in a dispatch to Philip II an extraordinary scene which then took place at the French court. Early one morning, the king, still in his nightshirt, and Catherine summoned Marguerite and beat her up so fiercely that her clothes were torn and her hair was dishevelled. Catherine took one hour to repair the damage.[67] Highly coloured as this story may seem, it is not incredible. Charles IX also allegedly ordered his half-brother, the bâtard d'Angoulême, to murder Guise. The latter, to deflect the blow, hastily married Catherine de Clèves, princesse de Porcien, a young widow whom he had also been courting. The Cardinal of

---

66 *CSPF, 1566–68*, pp. 476, 500, 502.
67 ASG Simancas, K. 1514; *Lettres,* iii, p. lxiv; E. Viennot, *Marguerite de Valois* (Paris, 1995), p. 41.

Lorraine retired in disgrace to his diocese. Thus, it seems that it was not so much the impending peace as a conflict of matrimonial interest between Catherine and the Guises which precipitated Lorraine's fall in 1570.

. . .

THE PEACE OF SAINT-GERMAIN (8 AUGUST 1570)

The king's council, as we have seen, met three times on 5 October 1570. At the third meeting, which lasted till 11p.m., Villeroy read out the peace terms agreed by both sides. Charles IX, admitting that he had failed to end the troubles by force, expressed the hope that in future his subjects would be more obedient and his laws better observed than in the past. He asked the councillors to swear faithful observance of the terms and to ensure strict observance of the edict of pacification soon be published. Catherine added: 'I am glad that my son is now old enough to see that he is better obeyed than in the past. I will help him with my counsels and with all my power; I will assist him in enforcing the terms which he has conceded, as I have always wanted to see the kingdom restored to the state it was in under his royal predecessors.'[68]

The Edict of Saint-Germain was not quite a 'sell-out' to the Huguenots, although regarded as such by many Catholics. Protestantism was still banned at court and in Paris, but the settlement did mark a significant advance on earlier treaties, for the Huguenots were granted four security towns (*places de sûreté*) – La Rochelle, Montauban, La Charité, and Cognac – for two years. They were allowed freedom of conscience throughout the kingdom and freedom of worship where it had existed before the war, in two towns per *gouvernement* and in the homes of nobles with rights of high justice. Huguenots were also to be admitted to all universities, schools and hospitals; they were to have their own cemeteries and were given certain judicial privileges to protect them from biased judgments. All confiscated property and offices were to be handed back.[69]

---

68 *Lettres*, iii, p. lxvi.
69 N.M. Sutherland, *The Huguenot Struggle for Recognition* (New Haven, 1980), pp. 358–60.

Many Catholics did not think the Huguenots were in a sufficiently commanding position to exact such generous terms. 'We have beaten them time and again,' Monluc wrote, 'but notwithstanding they had so much influence in the king's council that the edicts were always to their advantage. We won by force of arms; they did so by these devilish writings.'[70] Pasquier was more philosophical: 'We have ended where we should have begun if we had been sensible; but in such matters we behave as we do in trials: we never come to an agreement until our purses have been emptied.'[71]

---

[70] *Commentaires de Blaise de Monluc,* ed. P. Courteault (Paris, 1925), iii. 374.

[71] E. Pasquier, *Lettres historiques pour les annés 1556–1594,* ed. D. Thickett (Geneva, 1966), p. 201.

Chapter 7

THE PHONEY PEACE
(1570–72)

There are two ways of looking at the peace of Saint-Germain: either as a genuine attempt to heal the religious division of France or as a trap designed to lure the Huguenots into a false sense of security in order to exterminate them more easily. Arguments can be advanced in support of either reading, though historians generally believe that the French crown was sincere in its efforts to reconcile the Huguenots and Catholics. Denis Crouzet believes that the peace inaugurated a humanistic 'dream' intended by the king to bring about a golden age of happiness and love for all his subjects.[1]

. . .

MARRIAGE PLANS

The pacification enabled Catherine to attend to what she liked doing best: arranging prestigious marriages for her children. Having taken the Emperor's eldest daughter as his new wife, Philip II of Spain no longer opposed a marriage between Charles IX and her younger sister, Elizabeth. This took place at Mézières in November 1570, Catherine seized the opportunity to hand over power, at least symbolically, to her son. On 6 March he made his formal entry into Paris. The programme, devised by Ronsard, Dorat and Pibrac, and the monuments designed by famous artists, like Niccolò dell'Abbate and Germain Pilon, celebrated the themes of Empire and Peace. The union of two great royal lines, both claiming descent from Charlemagne, was seen as an event of enormous significance which might lead to a universal religious peace. Ronsard had a programme for the entry ready to hand in the form of his epic poem, the *Franciade*, in which the origins of the Most Christian King are traced back to

---

1   D. Crouzet, *La nuit de la Saint-Barthélemy. Un rêve perdu de la Renaissance* (Paris, 1994), p. 183.

138

Francus, a mythical Trojan prince. One of his descendants, Pharamond, was supposed to have been the first king of France. Thus the first triumphal arch erected for Charles IX's entry was adorned with giant statues in stucco of Francus and Pharamond. The other theme celebrated in the entry was the religious peace recently achieved by Catherine de' Medici. One of the street decorations showed a woman, resembling her, who was holding up a map of Gaul. Around her were hieroglyphs referring to Catherine's vigilance and promptitude. One of four classical heroines seated below was Artemisia, the widow of King Mausolus. The theme of the pious widow was carried on at the next arch, which was topped by a heart and an urn carried by four children. A colossal statue of Juno referred to Catherine's skill in arranging splendid matches for her children. The imperial splendours of the union of Charles IX and Elizabeth of Austria were emphasized by eagles below the statue and by Catherine's own device, the rainbow.[2] On 11 March the king addressed the Parlement. 'After God,' he declared, 'I am most obliged to my mother. Thanks to her tenderness towards me and my people, her application, her zeal and her prudence, the affairs of the state have been so well managed when I was too young to attend to them myself that the storms of civil war have not damaged my kingdom.' The queen's coronation took place at Saint-Denis on 25 March and was followed four days later by her entry into the capital, which again celebrated the Franco-Imperial union.

Two other marriages envisaged by Catherine for her children proved more difficult. She had hoped to marry her flighty daughter, Marguerite, to Sebastian, the young Portuguese monarch, but he seemed uninterested, so Catherine turned to Henri de Navarre as an alternative match for her daughter. He was, of course, a Protestant, but Catherine never allowed religion to obstruct her matrimonial designs. In any case, a marriage between Henri and Marguerite might serve either to bring him into the Catholic fold or to bridge the gap between the two religious camps in France. Henri

---

2   F. Yates, *Astraea. The Imperial Theme in the Sixteenth Century* (London, 1975), pp. 127–48.

was at this moment in La Rochelle with his mother, Jeanne d'Albret. If he were to marry Marguerite, however, a papal dispensation would be required on two counts: his religion and the degree of consanguinity between the two parties. Jeanne was a zealous Protestant who disliked the French court and its lax morals. She was afraid that her son would be forced to abjure his faith in addition to picking up bad habits. Her suspicions were encouraged by her principal lieutenant, Admiral Coligny, who thought Catherine's proposal was a ruse to separate the princes of the blood – Navarre and Condé – from the Huguenot party. His own preference was for Navarre to marry the English queen. This would strengthen the ties between the Huguenots and England at a time when their co-operation was needed to assist the Dutch rebels in their struggle with Spain.[3]

Catherine was also keen to marry her favourite son, Henri, duc d'Anjou (the future King Henry III), to the English queen, Elizabeth I. This too was a controversial idea. As the daughter of Henry VIII and Anne Boleyn, Elizabeth was viewed by the Catholic world as a heretic and a bastard. What is more, the match was strongly resisted by Anjou himself. Elizabeth was twenty years his senior (he was seventeen and she thirty-seven) and had been excommunicated and deposed by the pope (25 February 1570). Her flirtation with the earl of Leicester had caused scurrilous mirth at the French court. Anjou could not see that his honour would be enhanced by marriage to 'a whore' (*putain publique*), as he called her, and he told his mother that he would never take her as his wife.[4] Catherine was nevertheless dazzled by the prospects held out for the marriage by the vidame de Chartres, who had fled to England with Cardinal de Châtillon, during the last civil war. As Elizabeth's consort, he said, Anjou would be able to conquer the Netherlands and

---

3   J. Shimizu, *Conflict of Loyalties: Politics and religion in the career of Gaspard de Coligny, Admiral of France, 1519–1572* (Geneva, 1970), pp. 150–2.

4   P. Champion, *La jeunesse de Henri III, 1551–1571* (Paris, 1941–2), i. 316; P. Chevallier, *Henri III* (Paris, 1985), pp. 143–5; D. Crouzet, *La nuit de la Saint-Barthélemy. Un rêve perdu de la Renaissance* (Paris, 1994), p. 282.

would command more influence in the Empire than the Habsburgs themselves.[5] When it became clear that the duke could not be moved, Catherine offered Elizabeth the hand of her youngest son, François, duc d'Alençon. Misshapen, heavily pock-marked and only sixteen years old, he was not much of a catch for Elizabeth, and Catherine did not press the proposal too far at this time. Her ambassador in England urged her to secure a defensive pact with England first. This was achieved in March 1572 when the treaty of Blois was signed. It proved to be 'a diluted and nearly worthless alliance', yet Catherine did not completely abandon hope of a marriage between her youngest son and Elizabeth.[6] Two French agents, who were sent to England in June 1572, carried a formal offer of marriage to the English queen, but, much to Catherine's irritation, Elizabeth refused to give a definite reply.[7] On 23 July she instructed her ambassador in France to decline the offer on account of the age difference between herself and Alençon. Yet four days later she wrote that the marriage might still take place if she could see the duke in person.[8]

· · ·

THE DUTCH QUESTION

In 1571, while Catherine was busy with her matrimonial schemes, the idea of an armed intervention by France in the Netherlands on the side of the Dutch rebels was being keenly promoted in France. William of Orange, their leader, had left France to prepare an invasion of his country from Germany, but his brother, Louis of Nassau, and many Dutch exiles had stayed behind. They organized raids on Spanish shipping from their base at La Rochelle, and, with Huguenot help, they prepared an attack on the Netherlands from the south, timed to coincide with another, led by Orange, from the east. Such an expedition, however, required the backing of King Charles IX, who had so far shown more interest in

5   Cloulas, *Catherine*, p. 262.
6   M.P. Holt, *The Duke of Anjou and the Politique Struggle during the Wars of Religion* (Cambridge, 1986), p. 22.
7   *Lettres*, iv. 105.
8   Holt, *Duke of Anjou*, p. 24.

hunting than in affairs of state. However, he had become jealous of Anjou's military reputation and saw the attractions of meddling in the Netherlands while Philip II of Spain was tied down by a serious revolt in Andalusia. The negotiations for an Anglo–French marriage opened up the possibility of English co-operation in a Dutch enterprise. The absence of the Guises from the French court facilitated Charles IX's readiness to participate in a Dutch conflict. After a brief visit to the court to attend the coronation of Charles IX's queen, on 25 March, the Guises again withdrew. While Henri, duc de Guise went to the family seat at Joinville, his younger brother, Charles, duc de Mayenne thought of fighting the Turks, and the Cardinal of Lorraine retired to his diocese at Reims.

Catherine did not want France to be dragged into a war with Spain, if only because she knew that it could not afford it. Yet she allowed herself to be drawn into secret talks with Nassau, possibly because he had influence with Jeanne d'Albret, whose consent was needed for the Navarre marriage. On 12 July he was received by Charles and his mother at the château of Lumigny (Brie). Another meeting took place at Fontainebleau at the end of the month, when a plan was drawn up for the partition of the Netherlands: France was to get Flanders and Artois; the Empire: Brabant, Guelderland and Luxemburg (under Orange's authority); and England: Holland and Zeeland. Nassau prophesied that many Dutch towns would open their gates on the approach of an army of liberation.

Sutherland thinks a bargain may have been struck at Lumigny whereby Catherine and Charles IX agreed to support a Dutch campaign in return for Nassau's consent to the Navarre marriage. She admits, however, that Catherine's 'position . . . in the summer of 1571 is rather obscure'. She suggests that the queen-mother may have been kept in 'partial ignorance' until her intercession was needed to obtain financial support from her cousin, Cosimo de' Medici, Grand Duke of Tuscany. 'If Catherine was ignorant of anything,' writes Sutherland, 'it must have been the details of the partition plan. It is difficult to believe that she could have supported it . . .'[9] In fact, no one knows.

---

[9]   N.M. Sutherland, *The Massacre of St. Bartholomew and the European Conflict, 1559–1572*, (London, 1973), p. 175.

. . .

COLIGNY'S RETURN TO COURT (12 SEPTEMBER 1571)

Admiral Coligny believed that the best way to end civil war in France was to revive the old Habsburg–Valois rivalry which had given so many French nobles the opportunity to acquire glory and booty in foreign fields. The Dutch rebellion seemed to him a worthwhile cause, particularly as so many of the rebels were Protestants like himself, but the Admiral's biographer, Shimizu, believes that religion mattered to him less than personal ambition.[10]

Coligny could not hope to win over Charles IX without returning to the French court, but this posed many risks to his personal safety, for France, despite the peace, was still being disturbed by violent clashes between Catholics and Protestants. Catherine needed the Admiral's support for the Navarre marriage. He would have preferred another, as we have seen, but had come round to the view that Henri's marriage to Marguerite was an essential prerequisite to French intervention in Flanders. He also believed that it would serve to protect his person at court.

No one knows for certain how sincere the king and his mother were in respect of Coligny, who had, after all, led the Huguenot rebellion against them. Had they really forgiven him or were they seeking to lure him to court in order to have him killed and the Huguenot party weakened? In November 1571 the nuncio Frangipani told Cardinal Rusticucci that the Admiral would be drawn to court in order to neutralize him. The protonotary, Francesco Bramante, went further: he alleged that Charles IX had promised Cardinal Pellevé to have Coligny assassinated. Jeanne d'Albret believed that the Admiral would be walking into a trap if he went to court.[11]

Both Charles IX and Catherine urged the Admiral to come to court. The queen-mother told Petrucci, the Tuscan ambassador, that she was ready to receive the Huguenot leaders with open arms provided they gave 'some reliable

---

10   Shimizu, *Coligny*, p. 154.
11   C. Hirschauer, *La politique de Saint Pie V en France, 1566–1572* (Paris, 1922), p. 131; N.L. Roelker, *Queen of Navarre: Jeanne d'Albret, 1528–1572*, (Cambridge, Mass., 1968) p. 349.

demonstration of their loyalty and obedience'.[12] Charles IX and his brothers gave the Admiral a written undertaking that he would be safe in their company. He, for his part, promised to obey the king and his mother and forget past injuries, yet he could not but notice that everywhere in France the edict of pacification was being flouted and no effective action being taken by the crown despite its promises.[13]

The Admiral returned to the court at Blois on 12 September and remained there for five weeks. He was given 100,000 *livres* by the king as compensation for losses suffered in the civil war as well as one year's income from the benefices held by his late brother, Cardinal de Châtillon. Coligny was also granted the princely privilege of being escorted everywhere by fifty noblemen and was readmitted to the king's council, but his standing at court was less secure than these royal favours would suggest.[14] Although the young king was anxious to break away from his mother's tutelage, her influence remained paramount. She distrusted Coligny and his plans for a war with Spain. He was still regarded by most Frenchmen as a rebel and a heretic, and the Guises had never forgiven him for the murder of their second duke in 1563 in spite of royal declarations of his innocence. Several attempts had been made to murder him; he could not be sure that there would not be another.

In the meantime, Catherine pressed on with her plans for the Navarre marriage. She still had to win Jeanne d'Albret's consent and was anxious that she too should come to court. When the Admiral remarked that he understood Jeanne's hesitations and suspicions, having experienced them himself, Catherine replied: 'We are too old, you and I, to deceive each other . . . she has less reason to be suspicious than you because she cannot believe that the King would be trying to

---

12 A. Desjardins, *Charles IX: Deux années de règne, 1570–1572. Cinq mémoires historiques d'après des documents inédits* (Douai, 1873), pp. 50–1.
13 Michel de La Huguerye, *Mémoires inédits*, ed. A. de Ruble (Paris, 1877–80), i. 48.
14 Crouzet, *La nuit de la Saint-Barthélemy*, pp. 288–9; Shimizu, *Coligny*, p. 147.

marry his sister to her son in order to harm her.'[15] Charles IX, meanwhile, tried to reassure the Huguenots by instructing his officers throughout the kingdom to apply the edict of Saint-Germain strictly and fairly. Perhaps under pressure from Coligny, he ordered the demolition and removal of the cross of Gastines.

In January 1569 Philippe and Richard Gastines had been arrested in Paris on a charge of holding a Protestant service in their house in the rue Saint-Denis. Their arrest prompted a riot in which fifty people were killed. In July the Gastines were hanged, their property confiscated and their house razed to the ground. On the site, a monument – a stone pyramid topped by a cross – was erected to symbolize the triumph of Catholic orthodoxy. Under the Edict of Saint-Germain such reminders of denominational conflict were to be destroyed, but the Parisians would not allow the cross to be torn down. In 1571, however, it was removed under an armed guard to the Cimetière des Innocents. Serious disturbances continued, which the Parlement blamed on poor labourers, women and children. Historians have looked for *agents provocateurs*, such as Spain or the Guises, but, as Barbara Diefendorf has shown, if such agents were involved, they merely 'took advantage of already present, long-festering hatreds and encouraged their expression'.[16]

On 7 October Spain won a resounding victory over the Turks at Lepanto, thereby justifying Catherine's opposition to a Franco-Spanish conflict. She instructed the French ambassador in Spain to assure Philip II of France's desire to live at peace with him and to explain that the recent talks with Nassau had been aimed at dissuading him from invading the Netherlands. Admiral Coligny, however, was not deterred from pressing on with his bellicose plans, and Charles IX seems to have continued to support them in spite of his mother's opposition. Lepanto has often been taken to mark the start of a serious rift between her and the king, but, as Denis Crouzet, has suggested, they may have been playing a game of contradictions so that neither the

---

15 Desjardins, *Négociations de la France avec la Toscane*, iii. 711.
16 B.B. Diefendorf, *Beneath the Cross: Catholics and Huguenots in sixteenth-century Paris* (Oxford, 1991), p. 88.

Catholics nor the Huguenots should feel marginalized.[17] The hypothesis is intriguing.

If the crown really wanted reconciliation in France, both religious camps needed to be won over. It was not sufficient to bring Coligny to court; the Guises had to be there too. Charles IX accordingly sent his steward to Henri de Guise to persuade him to come back. Catherine declared that she wanted the court to be a 'theatre of reconciliation' between the houses of Châtillon and Guise. She considered this to be essential to the peace of the kingdom and assured the Guises that they ought not to feel any sense of shame about coming to court since they would be obeying the king.[18] They were not so easily won over, however. At the end of December they were reported to be mobilizing for an attack on the Admiral's house at Châtillon. This was allegedly part of a grand design worked out with Spain. According to Walsingham, the English ambassador, it involved the dukes of Anjou and Nevers. Coligny warned Charles IX that the Guises were trying to foil his sister's marriage to Henri de Navarre. He added: 'I do not know, Sire, what else they will dare to do if they attack Your Majesty.' Charles tried to defuse the crisis by ordering the Guises and Coligny to stay in their respective houses. Téligny now became the link between the king and the Admiral.[19]

. . .

CATHERINE AND JEANNE D'ALBRET

Catherine had achieved only one of her objectives by bringing Coligny to court. She still needed to persuade Jeanne d'Albret to do the same and to gain her consent to her son's marriage to Marguerite de Valois. In 1570 Jeanne fought hard for the full implementation of the Edict of Saint-

---

17 Crouzet, *La nuit de la Saint-Barthélemy,* p. 292.
18 R. de Bouillé, *Histoire des ducs de Guise,* ii. 486.
19 Sutherland, *Massacre,* pp. 203–13; Crouzet (*La nuit de la Saint-Barthélemy,* p. 294) thinks that Sutherland exaggerates the crisis. In his view it was probably no more than a wave of suspicion ('une poussée du système du soupçon') triggered by the victory at Lepanto.

Germain. She wrote several times to the king and his mother complaining of breaches of the edict, and was particularly incensed by the refusal of the royal governor of Lectoure, capital of Armagnac, to hand the town over to her. The first meeting early in 1571 of royal and Huguenot commissioners, charged with supervising the edict's enforcement, offered Catherine a chance to press on Jeanne the proposed marriage of her son with Marguerite de Valois. She urged her to come to court. Writing on 8 January, Catherine assured her of Charles IX's intention 'to embrace the affairs of the Prince of Navarre, whom the King and I infinitely desire to see here with you'.[20] But the queen of Navarre stood firm. While expressing her devotion to the crown, she accused it of deception. 'I am not enjoying the fruits of your Edict', she wrote, 'in the majority of my strongholds, Lectoure, Villemur, Pamiers . . . you can judge from this how well you are obeyed.'[21]

Catherine kept up pressure on Jeanne. 'It seems to me', she wrote to the king, 'that it would do no harm to send Marshal de Cossé to her with a letter in your own hand . . . requesting that she meet you in Blois, bringing her son, in early September.'[22] Cossé was sent accordingly, but, on reaching Béarn, found that Jeanne had gone to take the waters at Eaux-Chaudes. He was followed by Biron, who joined the queen of Navarre at Nérac on 10 December. He reported that many of her nobles were casting doubt on the crown's good faith and had persuaded her to delay her departure to the French court. Some contemporaries believed the Jeanne was totally opposed to her son's marriage to Marguerite, but this may not be strictly true. She may have been willing to accept it as a confirmation of Henri's rights as first prince of the blood. The merest hint that he might lose them may have swayed her final decision. The evidence for this is obscure, but Catherine may have suggested that the pope, who was known to be hostile to the marriage, might decide to consider Henri's legitimacy. This was not beyond dispute as he was the son of Jeanne's second marriage,

---

20 Roelker, *Queen of Navarre*, p. 346.
21 Ibid., p. 347.
22 Ibid., p. 355.

which was itself of questionable validity. If the pope were to declare Henri a bastard, he would automatically lose his right to the French throne. Such a threat may have prompted Jeanne to fall in with Catherine's wishes. Even so, she laid down terms: Charles IX was to give Guyenne to his sister as part of her dowry; Jeanne was to negotiate alone in Paris, and towns which were hers by right yet continued to be occupied by royal troops, were to be returned to her.[23]

Early in January 1572 Jeanne recovered the fortress of Lectoure and, soon afterwards, set off for the French court, but Cardinal Alexandrini, who had been sent by the pope to frustrate the Navarre marriage, arrived ahead of her. While she waited at Tours for his departure, she was invited by Catherine to Chenonceaux. The negotiations between them, focusing on the religious implications of the marriage, proved difficult. Jeanne imparted her first impressions to her son on 21 February: 'I urge you not to leave Béarn', she wrote, 'until you receive word from me. If you are already en route, find some pretext ... to return ... It is evident that [Catherine] thinks everything I say is only my own opinion and that you hold another ... When you next write, please tell me to remember all that you have told me and especially to sound out Madame [Marguerite] on her religious views, emphasizing that this is the only thing holding you back, so that when I show it to her she will tend more to believe that such is your will. This will be very useful. I assure you I am very uncomfortable because they oppose me strongly and I need all the patience in the world.'[24]

On 2 March Charles IX welcomed Jeanne to Blois; but the ensuing weeks turned into an ordeal for her. Her health was fast declining and only her indomitable spirit carried her through. On 8 May she wrote: 'I am not free to talk with either the King or Madame, only with the Queen Mother, who goads me [*me traite à la fourche*] ... Monsieur [Anjou] tries to get around me in private with a mixture of mockery and deceit ... As for Madame [Marguerite], I only see her in the Queen's quarters, whence she never stirs except at hours impossible for me to visit her ... Perceiving that

---

23 Ibid., pp. 359–62.
24 Ibid., p. 368

nothing is being accomplished and that they do everything possible to bring about a hasty decision instead of proceeding logically, I have remonstrated on three separate occasions with the Queen. But all she does is mock me, and afterwards tells others exactly the opposite of what I have said, with the result that they blame me. I do not know how to give her the lie, because when I say "Madame, it is reported that I have said such and such to you" – and she knows perfectly well that she herself said it – she denies everything, laughing in my face . . . She treats me so shamefully that you might say that the patience I manage to maintain surpasses that of Griselda herself. She [Catherine] decides everything herself, which is the main reason, my son, that I am sending the present bearer – to beg you to send my Chancellor. I have no man here who can equal him in knowledge or ability. If he does not come, I shall give up. I have come this far on the sole understanding that the Queen and I would negotiate and be able to agree. But all she does is mock me. She will not yield at all on the subject of the Mass, which she speaks of in an entirely different tone from formerly . . . Take note that they are making every effort to get you here, my son, and watch it carefully. For if the King is determined to bring you here – as is rumoured – it makes me more troubled than ever . . . I am sure that if you knew the pain I feel you would pity me, for they treat me with all the harshness in the world and with empty and facetious remarks instead of behaving with the gravity the issue merits . . . She [Marguerite] is beautiful, discreet and graceful, but she has grown up in the most vicious and corrupt atmosphere imaginable. I cannot see that anyone escapes its poison . . . Not for anything on earth would I have you come to live here. Therefore I wish you to be married and to retire – with your wife – from this corruption. Although I knew it was bad, I find it even worse than I feared. Here women make advances to men rather than the other way round. If you were here you would never escape without a special intervention from God . . . You have doubtless realized that their main object, my son, is to separate you from God, and from me.'[25]

---

25 Ibid., pp. 372–4.

In a letter written to the Sieur de Beauvoir three days later, Jeanne was equally bitter: 'In truth you are right to pity me . . . I have never been treated with such disdain. They still do me honour on the surface . . . hoping to get round me with subtleties . . . but I shall win out by being even more subtle. If anything good is to be obtained here, it must be done by surprise, before they realize it . . . Anything they promise, they renege on . . . M. de Beauvoir, the heart of my letter is to pray you to pity me as the most put-upon and harassed person in the world . . . I say again that if I have to endure another month like the past one I shall fall ill. I do not even know whether I am already sick, because I am not at my ease.' In a postcript Jeanne repeats: 'I do not know how I can stand it: they scratch me, they stick pins into me, they flatter me, they tear out my fingernails, without let-up . . . I am badly lodged, holes have been drilled in the walls of my apartment, and Madame d'Uzès spies on me.'[26]

On 14 March 1572 Alava's secretary wrote to the duke of Alba: 'The Queen of Navarre would rather see her son burn than married according to the rites of the Roman Catholic Church.'[27] The form of the ceremonies was the major stumbling block in the negotiations: it tested the king's sincerity regarding Huguenot rights. On 24 March the English ambassador wrote: 'The Queen of Navarre remains so hard and unmoving in the negotiations that even Count Louis [of Nassau] is in despair and many Huguenots have turned away from her . . . ' Then, in the midst of the talks, Charles IX decided to press on with the Navarre marriage without the pope's dispensation. He let it be known that he would yield to Jeanne on all other issues, provided Henri would come to Paris for the wedding, This cut the ground from under her feet. On 4 April she at last consented to the marriage. The contract was drawn up on 11 April. Four days later J.-B. Alamani, bishop of Mâcon, wrote to Antonio Salviati, the papal nuncio: 'the Queen Mother . . . has abased the haughtiness of the Queen of Navarre, overcome her shiftiness and made her accept the conditions. This is a beginning from which Your Reverence can be assured that

---

26 Ibid., p. 376.
27 AGS, K. 1526, no. 11. Cited by Roelker, *Queen of Navarre*, pp. 376–7.

we will soon see the Prince returning to the bosom of Holy Church.'[28]

At the end of April Jeanne returned to Vendôme for a brief rest. Henri was supposed to join her, but was prevented by illness. So Jeanne had to go to Paris without him. She stayed at the vidame's house and filled her days with preparations for the wedding: buying jewels for Marguerite and clothes for Henri. The comte de Retz was deputed by Catherine in her absence to make Jeanne feel at home. On 4 June, however, she was taken ill and, five days later, she died.[29] She had been in poor health for some time and an autopsy revealed tuberculosis and an abscess in the right breast. No one mentioned poison until after the Massacre of St. Bartholomew, when Catherine was accused of causing Jeanne's death. Her Florentine perfumer, René Bianco, had allegedly sold Jeanne some lethal gloves.[30]

Jeanne's death was a serious blow to the Huguenot cause. As the Venetian envoy, Cavalli, put it: 'She was a very bold woman and her death is causing the greatest possible setback to Huguenot affairs.' Catholics were, of course, jubilant. The nuncio Frangipani believed that her death had cleared the way for her son's conversion. 'Her death, a great work of God's own hand,' he wrote, 'has put an end to this wicked woman, who daily perpetrated the greatest possible evil. Her son and daughter are in the hands of the crown.'[31]

· · ·

THE GENLIS FIASCO (17 JULY 1572)

In mid-July 1572 a Huguenot nobleman, Genlis, invaded the Netherlands from France with about 4,000 infantry and fewer than 1,000 cavalry. According to the Venetian envoy,

---

28 Roelker, *Queen of Navarre*, pp. 377–83.
29 Ibid., pp. 387–90.
30 Ibid., pp. 391–2. The accusation was first made in the *Discours merveilleux* (1574). See the edition by N. Cazauran (Geneva, 1995), pp. 200–1.
31 Kervyn de Lettenhove, *Les Huguenots et les Gueux* (Bruges, 1883–88), ii. 449; B. Fontana, *Renata di Francia, Duchessa di Ferrara* (Rome, 1889–99), iii. 254–6; C. Hirschauer, *La politique de St. Pie V en France* (Paris, 1922), pp. 185–6.

Giovanni Michieli, he had been sent secretly by Coligny with the connivance of Charles IX. D'Aubigné says that he went without the king's permission and does not mention Coligny. Shimizu believes that the Admiral may have connived at the expedition for two reasons: first, the prince of Orange had crossed the Rhine on 8 July and planned to enter Brabant. Secondly, Charles IX may have given Genlis his secret backing despite his refusal to declare war on Spain[32]. It is difficult to believe that he did not know about it, for it was an open secret at the French court. Even the Spaniards knew about it, hence the ease with which they intercepted Genlis near Mons. The Huguenots were heavily defeated. Those who survived the battle were butchered by the local peasants. Some 200, including Genlis, were taken prisoner. To compound the embarrassment for the king of France, a letter was found on Genlis proving the king's complicity in the activities of his countrymen in Flanders. On 21 July Charles denied that he had sanctioned the Genlis expedition; he even congratulated Philip II on his victory.

By threatening to provoke a Franco-Spanish war, the Genlis fiasco sent ripples of fear across the political map of Europe. The Venetians were particularly upset as they dreaded the possibility of losing Spanish support against the Turks. They sent Michieli, one of their most skilful diplomats, to Paris in an effort to avert a conflict and, in his presence, Catherine caused Charles IX to declare that his subjects had disobeyed his orders by going to Flanders and that he wished to live at peace with his neighbours. But his insincerity resurfaced after his mother had gone to Châlons to see her daughter, the duchess of Lorraine, who had fallen ill on her way to Paris for her sister's marriage. Taking advantage of Catherine's absence, Coligny pressed Charles to declare war. Retz and Birague warned Catherine, who returned in haste to Paris. A violent scene followed, as she accused her son of leaning on those who had tried to kill him and of handing over his kingdom to the Protestants by blindly engaging in a war with Spain. Not wishing to be a witness to the kingdom's collapse after all that she had done to bring up her son and to preserve his crown, Catherine asked for permission to retire to her birthplace if he

---

32 Shimizu, *Coligny*, pp. 165–8.

persisted with his bellicose policy. Two council meeetings then took place on 9 and 10 August in which the military commanders – Montpensier, Nevers, Cossé, Anjou and perhaps Tavannes – spoke in favour of peace. Finding himself in a minority of one, Coligny allegedly muttered to Catherine: 'Madam, if the king decides against a war, may God spare him another from which he will not be able to extricate himself.'[33] No one knows how the remark was taken by Catherine. She was sufficiently reassured by the council's decision to rejoin the duchess of Lorraine at Montceaux. However, on returning to Paris on 15 August, she discovered that nothing had changed. Alba was demanding to know why 3,000 Huguenots had gathered on the frontier near Mons, and why Coligny was raising 12,000 arquebusiers and 2,000 cavalry. According to the Venetian ambassador, it was common knowledge that the Huguenot nobles, who had come to Paris for Navarre's wedding, were under orders to go on to Flanders afterwards.

The wedding of Henri de Navarre and Marguerite de Valois took place at Notre-Dame on 18 August without the benefit of the long-sought-after papal dispensation. The ceremony, which had taken a long time to prepare, was unusual on account of the difference of religion between the bride and groom. Henri did not attend the Mass, his place being taken by Anjou. The nuptial blessing was given by the Cardinal of Bourbon in full view of the public on a wooden platform which had been specially erected across the cathedral's west front. During the wedding, Coligny apparently noticed Huguenot flags, taken at Moncontour, hanging in the cathedral. 'We must take them down soon,' he said, 'and replace them with more suitable ones.'[34] He doubtless had Spanish flags in mind. A nuptial lunch served in the bishop's palace was followed by several days of festivity in the form of balls, masques and tournaments. These had been organized by Anjou and legend has it that he devised mock battles in which the Huguenots were deliberately humiliated.

---

33 E. Albèri, *Relazioni degli ambasciatori veneti al Senato* (Florence, 1839–63), Series 1a, Francia, vol. iv, p. 285; Brantôme, ed. Lalanne, iv. 299; J.-H. Mariéjol, *Cathérine de Médicis* (Paris, 1920), p. 189; Crouzet, *La nuit de la Saint-Barthélemy*, p. 395.
34 D'Aubigné, iii. 303; De Thou, iv. 570.

With hindsight we can say that Coligny would have been wise to go home after the wedding. His cousin, Marshal Montmorency, who left the capital on 20 August apparently advised the Admiral to do likewise, but he preferred to stay put. Writing to his wife on 18 August, he explained that 'the King has promised me to give several days for settling matters relating to many pleas from various places in this kingdom about the breaches of the Edict, for which I should employ myself as much as possible although I very much wish to see you ...'[35] More violent clashes between Huguenots and Catholics had taken place since early August. The Admiral wanted to see justice done, but his main concern remained the Netherlands.

. . .

THE ATTEMPTED ASSASSINATION OF COLIGNY (22 AUGUST 1572)

On 22 August, between 10 and 11 a.m., Coligny was returning on foot from a council meeting at the Louvre to his residence in the rue de Béthisy, when he was hit by an arquebus bullet fired from the first floor of a house.[36] He was bending over to adjust his shoe at the time; otherwise he would surely have been killed. Instead, he lost the index finger of his right hand and his left arm was fractured. His companions rushed into the house and found the arquebus still smoking at an open window. However, the assailant had taken flight. He has never been identified for certain, but is generally believed to have been the seigneur de Maurevert, who had tried to kill the Admiral in 1569. Catherine received news of the assassination attempt without any display of emotion: she rose from table and retired in silence to her chamber. The Spanish ambassador, however, thought that she looked as though she expected the news. Meanwhile, the famous surgeon, Ambroise Paré, was rushed to the Admiral's bedside in the Hôtel de Béthisy where many shocked and angry Huguenot nobles had gathered. Coligny's index finger was amputated and the bullet extracted from

---

35 Shimizu, *Coligny*, pp. 171–2. The letter is in BN, nouv. acq. fr. 5214, f. 140.

36 For different accounts of the atempted assassination, see Crouzet, pp. 378–9.

his elbow. That afternoon the king, Catherine and all the leading courtiers, but not the Guises, called on the Admiral. Charles promised to punish his assailant. The President of the Parlement, de Thou, and a councillor, Cavaignes, were ordered to hold a judicial enquiry. On 22 August the king informed all foreign ambassadors of what had happened. Writing to La Mothe-Fénelon, his ambassador in England, he blamed the Guises for the crime. 'This wicked deed', he said, 'has come from the enmity between the houses of Châtillon and Guise.' This was confirmed by the enquiry: the house from which the shot had been fired belonged to the duchesse de Nemours. The assailant had been posted there by the seigneur de Chailly, *surintendant des affaires* of the duc de Guise. The horse on which the assailant made his escape came from the Guise stables. Without waiting to be incriminated, Guise asked the king for permission to leave Paris. This was granted, but, instead of leaving the capital, the duke shut himself up in the Hôtel de Guise. Knowing that Paris was a hotbed of Catholic extremism, Coligny asked the king for armed protection. Anjou sent 50 arquebusiers under captain Cosseins (a personal enemy of the Admiral) to the rue de Béthisy. The picket's real purpose may have been to prevent Coligny's friends from removing him to the country, as some wanted to do.

Catherine has been accused by many historians of insti-gating Coligny's murder. Her most recent biographer, Yvan Cloulas, is in no doubt. His account, which repeats a long tradition, can be summed up as follows. Catherine had reached the end of her tether. All her past efforts to pre-serve the kingdom for her children seemed about to be destroyed for the sake of a mad adventure in the Nether-lands which the Admiral was promoting to assist his Dutch co-religionists. He had obstructed her policy of pacification at every turn, had organized rebellions and was now threatening to take her place as the king's mentor. Was she going to allow him to supplant her, even perhaps to drive her into a Florentine exile? 'The removal of Coligny', writes Cloulas, 'was for Catherine not only a measure of personal salvation but also one of public salvation.'[37] Having taken

---

37 Cloulas, *Catherine*, pp. 283.

the decision, she applied herself to the task with all the appetite for revenge which in the past had led her to employ murderers and sorcerers to eliminate the Admiral. She did not have to look far for a cover: the Guises and their clients had flocked to Paris for her daughter's wedding. Catherine reached an understanding with the duke's mother, Anne d'Este, duchesse de Nemours, who longed to avenge the death of her first husband. Maurevert was sent for and ordered once again to kill the Admiral. The deed was to take place after the wedding. With Coligny out of the way, Henri de Navarre would be held as a hostage to prevent any Protestant reprisals.

So much for the traditional story, which is still widely followed. Recently, however, an attempt has been made to exculpate Catherine. In 1973 Nicola Sutherland undermined the traditional story by focusing attention on the international context. Using many contemporary sources, including ambassadorial dispatches, she has revealed a vast and bewildering network of relationships and interests involving the Guise family, Spain, the papacy, England, Venice, Turkey and others. It seems that a grand ultra-Catholic conspiracy was afoot aimed at preventing French intervention in the Netherlands, frustrating the Navarre marriage, and 'eliminating' the Huguenots generally. The plan was forcefully presented by the papal nuncio in Spain to the Cardinal of Como in a letter written on 5 August 1572. The time was ripe, he argued, for Charles IX to rid his kingdom of the Huguenots. The Admiral was in Paris, whose Catholic inhabitants would be easily roused. Philip II would then employ all his strength (viz. Alba's forces) to restore France to her former glory, thereby enhancing the security of his own kingdom.[38]

Sutherland also rejects what she describes as 'the fatuous maternal jealousy theory', which derives from the *Discours du roy Henri III*, a work unknown before 1623. Sutherland argues that Coligny's influence on the king has been exaggerated by historians, who have relied on the *Mémoires de l'Estat de France*, a contemporary work marred by careless

---

38 Sutherland, *Massacre*, pp. 295–6.

chronology. The Admiral, she affirms, did not return to court after his initial five weeks' stay until 6 June 1572. He cannot, therefore, have been high in the king's favour in May. Nor can his influence have been great in June, when his advice was rejected by the king, or in August, when affairs of state were virtually suspended on account of the wedding celebrations.[39] But, as Marc Venard has shown, the 'maternal jealousy' theory may not be so 'fatuous' after all. On 2 September the nuncio Salviati reported from Paris that the Admiral had aroused the queen-mother's jealousy (*grandissima gelosia*) by gaining so much credit with the king that he effectively ruled him. Venard also challenges Sutherland's assertion that the Admiral had no opportunity of influencing the king after he had returned to court in June. Salviati mentions two lengthy meetings between Coligny and Charles. 'The other evening (21 July),' he writes, 'as the king said that he was undressing for bed and as soon as everyone had gone, the admiral entered his chamber and remained alone with the king for a very long time.' On the second occasion (5 August) Coligny remained locked up with Charles and four secretaries of state from 11.30 p.m. until 2 a.m. This prompted a rumour that war was about to be declared.[40]

Building on Sutherland's research, Jean-Louis Bourgeon has argued that the Spanish government was behind the attack on the Admiral. 'The plot set up against Coligny', he writes, 'seems to me to be on a quite different scale from that of a vulgar settlement of accounts between rival feudal clans.'[41] He points out that, as early as September 1571, Philip II regretted that Charles IX was not taking advantage of Coligny's return to court to arrest him and cut off his head. Early in August 1572 the Spanish ambassador wrote

---

39 Ibid., pp. 315–16. Cf. Crouzet, *La nuit de la Saint-Barthélemy*, p. 293, who states that the Admiral returned to court at the beginning of November 1571.

40 M. Venard, 'Arrêtez le massacre!', *Bull. d'hist. mod. et contemp.*, 39 (1992), 645–61; *Correspondance du nonce en France Antonio Maria Salviati*, éd. P. Hurtubise (Rome, 1975), i. 162, 182–3, 217.

41 J.-L. Bourgeon, *L'assassinat de Coligny* (Geneva, 1992), p. 45.

about 'several things' which were brewing and would happen after the wedding festivities. Whereas most people were riddled with anxiety, Philip II and Alba maintained a calm exterior as if they already knew that a coup was in the offing. Bourgeon takes Philip's attitude as evidence of his diplomatic mastery, which, in his judgment, left Catherine, for all her duplicity, no taller than his ankle. He also takes as an admission of guilt the blame so swiftly levelled at Charles IX and his mother by the Spanish ambassador after the attack on Coligny.[42]

The truth is unlikely ever to be known. What is evident is that many people, including Catherine, had strong reasons for wishing to be rid of Coligny. She has perhaps received more than her fair share of blame. Catherine has been the target of Huguenot propagandists angered by the Massacre of St. Bartholomew and powerfully influenced by misogyny and xenophobia. It is also true that several sources (e.g. the memoirs of Tavannes, those of Marguerite de Valois and the *Discours du roy Henri III à un personnage d'honneur et de qualité*) on which generations of historians have relied were not published until the 1620s and are for that reason suspect; yet if the stories they tell sometimes seem excessively coloured, they cannot always be refuted. Whitewashing Catherine can be taken too far. She was no saint and had certainly dabbled in political assassination. Her responsibility for the attempted murder of Coligny remains an open question and is likely to remain so.[43]

. . .

THE MASSACRE OF ST. BARTHOLOMEW'S DAY
(24 AUGUST 1572)

The attempt on Coligny's life was followed two days later by the Massacre of St. Bartholomew's Day. Once again the truth is not easily sifted from the mass of partisan accounts. It seems unlikely that the attack on the Admiral was intended to be

---

42 Ibid., pp. 51–4.
43 Venard believes that 'Catherine and doubtless some members of the council were in the plot. They had only to leave its execution to the Guises' ('Arrêtez le massacre', p. 661).

the opening shot in a campaign against the Huguenots in general. Even if it had been successful, it would have been a major tactical blunder, for it would have warned the Huguenot leaders of the threat hanging over them. They would probably have left Paris and started a new civil war.

The failure of the attack caused panic at court. According to Tavannes, the king and his council, meeting at the Louvre on 23 August, decided that civil war had become inevitable. They thought 'it preferable to win a battle in Paris, where all the leaders were, than to risk one in the field and to fall into a dangerous and uncertain war'. Tavannes' memoirs, which were written up by his son long after the events described, may not be wholly reliable, yet Catholics did fear a Huguenot uprising after the attack on their leader. Rumours of a plot to murder the king and his family and to sack the capital were rife, and Charles IX doubtless recalled the *Surprise de Meaux*. The idea of a pre-emptive strike may have commended itself to him. Be that as it may, we can be reasonably sure that on 23 August he ordered the Huguenot leaders to be wiped out and Catherine was almost certainly a party to that decision. The prime responsibility for the massacre was given to the king's guards and to those of the duc d'Anjou serving under Guise, Aumale and other Catholic captains. The role played by the municipal authorities is less clear. The *prévôt des marchands*, Jean Le Charron, was summoned to the Louvre late on 23 August and ordered to take all necessary steps to secure the city.

The massacre started before dawn on 24 August when members of the king's guard, led by the duc de Guise, burst into the Hôtel de Béthisy and murdered Coligny, tossing his body out of a window. Wiping blood from the face, Guise said: 'It's him; I recognize him.' He then kicked the body. Someone cut off Coligny's head and took it to the Louvre to show to the king and his mother. It was later embalmed and sent to Rome for the pope and cardinals to see.[44] Meanwhile, the rest of the Admiral's body was mutilated by a Catholic mob and dragged for days through the streets of Paris before it was hanged from the gibbet at Montfaucon. It

---

44 The head was apparently intended for the duke of Alba. See Bourgeon, *L'assassinat de Coligny*, p. 117.

was eventually cut down and secretly buried. The Admiral's cruel fate secured him a place in the pantheon of Protestant martyrs.

As Coligny was being murdered, the tocsin of Saint-Germain-l'Auxerrois gave the signal for a mass slaughter of Parisian Huguenots. The killers may have been encouraged by Guise, who was overheard saying that the slaughter had been ordered by the king. Parisians were only too willing to believe that Charles had at last thrown his authority on the side of God's purpose and national purification. At 11 a.m. Le Charron called on him to complain of the bloodshed and destruction. That afternoon, Charles ordered the killing to stop, but it continued for almost a week. Greed and jealousy often fuelled the violence, as did alcohol. But only a minority of Parisians shared in the violence; the rest stayed behind closed doors. Even so, many approved of the slaughter. The sudden flowering of a hawthorn bush in the Cimetière des Innocents was seen as a miracle indicating God's pleasure at the destruction of Coligny and his friends. The Huguenots appear to have offered little resistance. Most of them were dragged from their beds and killed before they could assemble in self-defence. Some accepted their ordeal as a trial imposed by God; others saved themselves by abjuring or paying a ransom. At court, the princes of the blood – Navarre and Condé – were spared, but they were given three choices: abjuration, death or life imprisonment. Navarre abjured; Condé did so after a show of resistance.

The massacre was not confined to Paris. Huguenots were slaughtered in many towns, usually on receipt of news of the Parisian event. In some towns the killing was carried out by the local authorities in a cold-blooded, methodical way; in others, it was the work of rampaging mobs; but everywhere the murderers thought they were obeying the king's wishes. Some nobles apparently rushed off to the provinces from the capital with the message that Charles IX wanted all Huguenots wiped out. His orders, when they were eventually issued, were by no means clear or consistent.[45]

Was the massacre premeditated? Many contemporaries,

---

45 P. Benedict, 'The St. Bartholomew's massacres in the provinces', *HJ* xxi (1978), 201–25.

both Catholic and Protestant, believed that it was. Lorraine, for one, wanted his family to be given the credit; he hinted that it had been planned by the Guises. Protestants, like the Genevan pastor, Simon Goulart, were equally certain that the massacre had been planned, perhaps for years. He claimed that the planning had begun in 1570 with the Edict of Saint-Germain, whose generous terms had been cleverly designed to lull the Huguenots into a false sense of security. The government had lured Coligny and his friends to Paris ostensibly to prepare war against Spain but, in reality, to kill them.[46] The idea that the massacre was premeditated also has its modern advocates. 'Despite its unfolding in two stages (22 and 24 August),' writes Bourgeon, 'nothing, it seems to me, was less improvised than the massacre of St. Bartholomew.' He sees it as part of a well-orchestrated campaign to force a complete change of royal policies in France: the annulment of the Navarre marriage, the abrogation of the Edict of Saint-Germain, the return to power of the Guises, the exclusion of Huguenots from the king's council, the parlements and other bodies, a curb on taxation, the abandonment of French interference in the Netherlands and a realignment of French diplomacy in line with that of Philip III of Spain and Pope Gregory XIII. However, Crouzet rejects premeditation, arguing that the massacre was a hasty reponse by the king's advisers to the threat of a Huuenot rising after the attempted assassination of Coligny, He even sees it as 'a crime of love' aimed at salvaging the 'dream' of a golden age initiated in 1570.[47]

Where does all this leave Catherine? Outside France, Catholics greeted news of the massacre with jubilation. Gregory XIII held a *Te Deum,* which was followed by a celebration in the French church of St. Louis under the direction of the Cardinal of Lorraine. A special commemorative plaque was struck showing an angel, carrying a cross and superintending the killing of Coligny and his friends. Catherine was suddenly acclaimed as the Mother of the kingdom and the Conservator of the Christian name. Cardinal Orsini was sent by the pope to congratulate her on her

---

46 R.M. Kingdon, *Myths about the St. Bartholomew's Day Massacres, 1572-1576* (Cambridge, Mass, 1988), pp. 42-3.
47 Crouzet, p. 183.

Catholic zeal. Philip II 'praised the son for having such a mother . . . then the mother for having such a son'.[48] Revelling in this adulation, Catherine asked Alba's envoy: 'Am I as bad a Christian as Don Frances de Alava used to claim?'[49] She was happy to let the Catholic powers believe that she had long planned the massacre. Her claim, however, was contradicted by the nuncio Salviati. Writing from Paris on 24 August, he said: 'If the Admiral had been killed by the arquebus which was fired at him, I cannot believe that there would have been such a great carnage.'[50] The Spanish ambassador, Zuñiga, gave a similar opinion: 'The Admiral's death', he wrote, 'was a planned action; that of the Huguenots was the result of a sudden decision.'[51]

Catherine hoped to gain something from the massacre. She tried to arrange the marriage of the duc d'Anjou in Spain, but Philip II failed to oblige; so she turned to the Protestant powers. On 13 September she instructed Schomberg, who was going to Germany as ambassador, not to allow the princes to believe that the Admiral and his accomplices had been killed out of hatred for their religion, but only as a punishment for their wicked conspiracy.[52] She also continued to negotiate with England over the Alençon marriage, and resumed relations with Nassau and the prince of Orange. The papal legate, who had come to congratulate her, was kept waiting for some time in Avignon before she would see him; when eventually she did so, she refused his invitation to join a league of Mediterranean powers against the Turks or even to publish the Tridentine decrees.[53]

Catherine never showed regret or remorse over the massacre. In fact, she seems to have thoroughly enjoyed its results. The Huguenot party had lost its leaders. Henri de Navarre was her son-in-law and a king in his own right. What

---

48 G. Van Prinsterer, *Archives ou correspondance inédites de la maison d'Orange Nassau,* First Series, Supplement (1847), pp. 125* and 127*.
49 *Lettres,* Introduction, iv, p. xciv.
50 A. Theiner, *Annales ecclesiastici,* i (1856), p. 329.
51 F. Decrue, *Le parti des politiques* (Paris, 1892), p. 175; Mariéjol, p. 193.
52 Van Prinsterer, *Archives de la maison de Nassau,* First Series, Vol. iv, Supplement, p. 12*.
53 Holt, *Duke of Anjou,* p. 25; Mariéjol, pp. 194–5.

is more, he and Henri de Condé had become Catholics. The queen-mother's joy became manifest during a ceremony held by the chapter of the Ordre de Saint-Michel on 29 September. As she watched Navarre kneel before the altar like any good Catholic, she turned to the foreign ambassadors present and burst out laughing.[54] On 3 October he wrote to the pope asking for forgiveness and on the 16th issued an edict restoring Catholicism to Béarn. Thereafter he behaved as if the massacre had never taken place, fraternizing with Guise and others who had murdered his friends.

. . .

THE BLACK LEGEND

When the prince de Condé issued his manifesto in 1562, he justified his rebellion by accusing the Guises of usurping the government. He soon had to shift his ground, however, as the government, headed by Catherine, gave up its conciliatory efforts. Condé could no longer maintain that he and his friends were simply defending the government against the Guises. In a second manifesto, he professed to be defending the nation's constitution against the government. The same argument was taken up by several Huguenot pamphlets in the late 1560s, but it was the massacre of St. Bartholomew's Day and the role played by the king and his mother in that tragic event which made it impossible for the Huguenots to justify their armed opposition in terms of defending the monarchy. Charles IX had, on his own admission, ordered the slaughter of their leaders, even if he had not sanctioned the mass slaughter that ensued. Huguenots could no longer profess loyalty to a monarchy tainted by such a monstrous crime; a line could no longer be drawn between the king and his 'evil counsellors'. The hands of both were soaked in the blood of God's children.[55]

As Huguenot survivors of the massacres threw off their allegiance to the ruling dynasty, they had to find a new justification for their action. They all believed that the massacres had been planned in advance by Catherine and her

---

54 Forneron, *Histoire de Philippe II*, ii. 332 n. 1; Mariéjol, p. 195.
55 Q. Skinner, *The Foundations of Modern Political Thought* (Cambridge, 1978), ii. 302–4.

sons, particularly Anjou. Xenophobia, or at least a deep suspicion of Italy, permeates much of the polemical literature produced by the Huguenots after 1572. 'Among all the nations', wrote Henri Estienne, 'Italy carries off the prize for cunning and subtlety, so it is in Italy with Tuscany, and in Tuscany with Florence.' Catherine was seen as a disciple of Machiavelli, the quintessential Florentine, whose spectre had begun to haunt Protestant Europe. It was said that she had brought up her children on Machiavelli's *Prince*, and that Anjou always carried a copy in his pocket. The massacre was interpreted as the application of Machiavelli's precept to commit all necessary cruelties in a single blow. Innocent Gentillet's *Anti-Machiavel* (1576) helped to create the legend of Machiavelli as the author of text-books for tyrants. He was blamed directly for the French government's 'infamous vices'. By so doing, Gentillet helped the Huguenots to present their struggle as a legitimate act of self-defence.[56]

Many Huguenot pamphlets published after the massacres extended to the royal family, and to Catherine in particular, attacks which had previously been directed only at the Guises. A notable example is the *Discours merveilleux de la vie, actions et déportements de Catherine de Médicis, Royne-mère*, which purports to be a factual account of her life.[57] We find in it most of the stories, notably the poisonings, which eventually became part of the so-called Black Legend. Unfortunately, the untruths, if such they are, cannot always be refuted for lack of evidence; they can only be doubted. The task of sifting the work is all the more difficult because the author, whoever he was, evidently had personal knowledge of the French court in the 1560s. He seems not to have been a Huguenot, but someone who wished to promote an alliance between the Huguenots and malcontent Catholics against the house of Valois.[58] The *Discours* was first published anonymously in 1575 and two years later in a revised edition, which shows signs of Huguenot tampering. This may have been done by Simon Goulart, who included it in his

---

56 Ibid., ii 308.
57 *Discours merveilleux de la vie, actions et deportements de Catherine de Médicis, Royne-mère*, ed. N. Cazauran (Geneva, 1995). See also Kingdon, *Myths*, pp. 200–11.
58 *Discours merveilleux*, ed. Cazauran, pp. 31–54.

Mémoires de l'estat de France. The *Discours* was an immediate success in France and abroad, running through several editions in French and other languages. As propaganda against female rulers, its impact was long-lasting: it was used against Marie de' Medici in the seventeenth century and against Marie-Antoinette in the eighteenth.

The *Discours* was used as a rich quarry by historical novelists in the nineteenth century. Perhaps as a reaction to the cult of Henry IV after 1815, a veritable vogue for the Wars of Religion and Catherine de' Medici in particular swept France in the 1820s. Charles d'Outrepont, a justly forgotten writer, wrote a play in 1826 on the Massacre of St. Bartholomew in which Catherine is described as 'an execrable woman whose memory will remain wrapped in a bloody crape till the end of time'. Balzac, who at an early stage of his career hoped to become a French Walter Scott, wrote three essays, one of them a conversation between Catherine and Robespierre. They were subsequently published together under the title *Sur Catherine de Médicis.* In the author's judgment her guiding stars were 'love of power and astrology'. Unlike most historians, he dismissed her predilection for her son, Henri d'Anjou. 'Her conduct', he writes, 'proved the total hardness of her heart.' Historical fiction found its genial champion in Alexandre Dumas, who, as early as 1829, wrote a play, called *Henri III et sa cour,* in which Catherine is portrayed as the real ruler of France.[59] Better known is his novel *La reine Margot,* in which Catherine is portrayed as a malevolent spirit presiding over a debauched court. It has recently (1993) been turned into an extremely gory film by Patrice Chéreau and Danièle Thompson, which will doubtless serve to extend the life of the Black Legend.

---

59 *Henri III et son temps,* ed. R. Sauzet (Paris, 1992), pp. 16–19; see also Sutherland, *Princes, Politics and Religion,* 1547–89 (London, 1984), pp. 237–48.

Chapter 8

THE FAVOURITE SON
(1573–77)

Catherine was in for a rude shock if she imagined that peace had returned to France. Although the massacres had wiped out many high-ranking Huguenot nobles, enough lesser ones survived in the provinces to work out a new defensive strategy. They were strongest in the south, where they held several towns, including Nîmes and Montauban. Further north, they controlled La Rochelle, whence they could communicate easily with friends and allies in England and the Netherlands. A few weeks after the massacre in Paris, the people of La Rochelle refused to admit marshal Biron as their governor. Acting on orders from the king, he laid siege to the town in February 1573 and was soon joined by an army led by the duc d'Anjou. Charles IX's younger brother, Alençon, was there too, as were Henri de Navarre and the prince de Condé, the dukes of Guise and Aumale and many other nobles. From the start of the siege they squabbled among themselves, a major source of discord being the rivalry between the houses of Guise and Montmorency. As cousins of the late Admiral Coligny, the Montmorencies felt threatened by the triumph of the Catholic party and the return to power of the Guises. Marshal Montmorency and his brother, Damville, the governor of Languedoc, were prepared to remain loyal to the crown as long as their lives and honour were not at risk, but some of their younger kinsmen – Méru, the son-in-law of marshal Cossé, Guillaume de Thoré and the vicomte de Turenne – were more impetuous in defending their rights. They and other 'malcontents' rallied round Alençon, who was allegedly 'most dissatisfied at finding himself in the army without any

166

responsibility whatsoever'. As a prince of the blood, second in line to the throne, he could confer a certain legitimacy on a rebellion, but his followers as yet lacked cohesion; they were 'not a movement at all, but a heterogeneous group of malcontent nobles who harboured various ambitions . . . '.[1]

. . .

ANJOU BECOMES KING OF POLAND (10 MAY 1573)

The siege of La Rochelle dragged on through the spring, its resistance being stiffened by the arrival of refugees from the recent massacres, including fifty-four Calvinist pastors. At times the entire population was mobilized, including women who pelted the royal troops with stones from the ramparts. La Rochelle had to endure a fierce bombardment by Anjou's guns and repulsed several assaults by his troops. Curiously, the town was saved by an event in eastern Europe. On 7 July Sigismund-Augustus, king of Poland, died, bringing the Jagiellon dynasty to an end. Catherine, who had tried unsuccessfully to marry the duc d'Anjou to two queens, now put him forward as a candidate for election to the Polish throne. But a difficulty needed to be overcome. Anjou was reputed to be a fanatical Catholic and the main instigator of the St. Bartholomew's Day massacre. Poland, by contrast, was the only country in Europe where religious toleration existed under the constitution. If Anjou were to be seriously considered, he needed to alter his image. Catherine advised him to temper his religious zeal. 'Beware of Master Aymont, the Jesuit [Edmond Auger],' she wrote, 'for he writes everywhere that you have promised to extirpate all the people who have been Huguenots and that he knows this on account of his being your confessor.'[2] She also had to convince her entourage of Poland's desirability. When Tavannes dismissed it as a desert inhabited by savages, Catherine retorted that the Poles were civilized and cultured. Their kingdom, she said, was fine and contained 100,000 horses. She derided Tavannes for preferring to remain on

---

1   M.P. Holt, *The Duke of Anjou and the Politique Struggle during the Wars of Religion* (Cambridge, 1986), p. 30.
2   *Lettres*, iv. 228.

his own 'dunghill' (*son fumier*).[3] Catherine was also cross with the Cardinal of Lorraine, who was dragging his feet about levying 300,000 *livres* from the French clergy to help pay for Anjou's Polish adventure. When he moaned that it was a very large sum to send out of France, Catherine pointed out it that it was far less than all the money he had dispatched to Scotland. The returns would also be considerable: France would gain a new kingdom and enlarge her foreign trade. Her son, she believed, would become a great eastern European monarch, fully capable of standing up to the Habsburgs.[4]

Catherine's emissary to the Polish diet, Jean de Monluc, bishop of Valence, arrived almost at the same time as news of the Massacre of St. Bartholomew. He tried to play down Anjou's involvement by blaming the Parisian mob for the bloodshed. Fortunately for the duke, his main rivals – the Russian tsar, Ivan the Terrible, and the Austrian archduke, Ernest – were even less attractive to the Polish electors. On 10 May, after nearly a month of intensive electioneering, Anjou was duly chosen as king. Monluc, however, had to subscribe to two documents: the *Pacta conventa* and the *Articuli Henriciani*, which regulated relations between the king and the Senate, and proclaimed freedom of conscience and worship.

News of Anjou's election, which reached him on 29 May in his camp outside La Rochelle, offered him an honourable excuse for lifting the siege. Though he cared little about Poland as such, he liked the idea of being a king in his own right instead of living in the shadow of his elder brother. On 17 June Polish ambassadors arrived at La Rochelle and Anjou soon came to terms with the Rochelais: Protestant worship was allowed in La Rochelle, but only in private houses; Protestant nobles were allowed to hold Calvinist services in their homes. Baptisms and weddings, however, could not be attended by more than ten people. The same concessions were extended to Montauban and Nîmes.

On 19 August a distinguished Polish delegation consisting of twelve Catholics and Protestants with a suite of 250 nobles

---

3   *Lettres*, iv. 181.
4   *Lettres*, iv. 225.

and a host of servants arrived in Paris. As they made their way to their lodgings, they passed under triumphal arches erected in their honour. Parisians were much amused by their bonnets and bulky fur coats, but the French court was dazzled by their learning and their command of languages, particularly Latin. After they had rested for two days, the envoys were received by Charles IX and his mother. On 22 August they called on Anjou at the Louvre and congratulated him on his election, but they also reminded him of the need to subscribe to the engagements which Monluc had taken in his name. They demanded his adherence to the promise to maintain religious peace in Poland and even spoke on behalf of the relatives of Huguenots killed in the St. Bartholomew's Day massacre. Anjou tried to avoid endorsing the *Pacta* and *Articuli*, but was warned by one of the envoys: 'either you will swear the oath or you will not reign'. After further meetings, he signed the documents on 9 September. That same evening he entertained his Polish guests at a banquet and, next day at Notre-Dame, solemnly swore to keep his promises. Three days later he received the decree of his election, a superb document bearing the arms of Anjou and Poland. Meanwhile, Catherine took steps to prevent a *coup d'état* by Alençon in the event of Charles IX dying during Anjou's absence in Poland. At her instance Charles appointed Anjou as his heir. On 14 September the new king of Poland made his entry into Paris, which was followed by a magnificent banquet given by Catherine at the Tuileries palace. The meal was followed by an elaborate ballet and by a ball which lasted all night.[5] Next day the city of Paris gave Henri a chariot of silver gilt and enamel drawn by two white horses and carrying 'the God Mars behind a laurel bush'.

Henri was not keen to go to Poland. He tried to delay his departure for as long as possible, but was eventually obliged to leave by Charles IX, who wanted him out of the way. The court escorted him to the frontier, but illness detained Charles at Vitry-en-Perthois. Henri surrendered his seals as lieutenant-general of the kingdom on 12 November. The

5   F. Yates, *The Valois Tapestries* (London, 1975), p. 68. See also below, pp. 283–9

three brothers – Charles, Henri and François – put up a great show of sadness as they parted. At Nancy, Charles III, duke of Lorraine welcomed Henri and Catherine. She was delighted to see the duchess, her daughter Claude, again. She had just given birth to a boy, whom the bishop of Poznan now christened, Catherine being the godmother. It was at this time that Henri first saw Charles III's beautiful niece, Louise de Vaudémont, who was to become his wife. After leaving Nancy, he and Catherine travelled to Blamont, a small town close to the imperial border, where they met Louis of Nassau and Christopher, the son of Frederick III, Elector-Palatine. Catherine was anxious to ease Henri's passage through the territories of German Protestant princes, which is why she now resumed negotiations for a possible French involvement in the Netherlands on the side of the rebels. Having already sent a subsidy of 300,000 *écus* to enable Nassau to assist his brother William of Orange, she now promised 'to embrace the affairs of the said Netherlands as much and as far as the Protestant princes may wish'.[6] In return for a league between France, the house of Orange, the German princes and eventually Poland, Catherine, it seems, demanded the complete submission of the Huguenots to the French crown. As for Alençon, he told Nassau that he would join a force of Huguenots who were at Sedan preparing to go to the aid of William of Orange.[7]

. . .

TWO CONSPIRACIES AT COURT

On returning to court, Alençon hoped to acquire the office of lieutenant-general recently vacated by Anjou. He was promised this post by Charles IX on 25 January 1574, much to the annoyance of the Guises, who disliked Alençon's friendship with marshal François de Montmorency. They devised a scheme to discredit them both. On 16 February the duc de Guise attacked the sieur de Ventabren, one of

---

6   Groen Van Prinsterer, *Archives ou correspondance inédites de la maison d'Orange-Nassau*, First Series (Leiden, 1835–96), iv. 279.

7   F. Yates in *The Valois Tapestries,* pp. 73–81 suggests that one of the tapestries ('The Journey') refers to the meeting at Blamont with the Dutch leaders. See also below, p. 243.

Alençon's nobles, in the Louvre. He claimed that Ventabren had been hired by Montmorency to assassinate him. Although the charge was repudiated by the parties involved, Montmorency had to leave the court, and Charles IX broke his promise to Alençon. Charles III, duke of Lorraine, a cousin of the Guises, was appointed lieutenant-general instead. He was apparently the choice of Catherine, who was afraid that Alençon might use the authority of lieutenant-general to mount a coup if Charles IX died during the absence of his brother Henri in Poland. Lorraine's appointment, however, failed to pacify the court.

On the night of 27–28 February 1574 the court fled in confusion from Saint-Germain-en-Laye after a sizeable Protestant force had been spotted nearby. Its purpose, it seems, was to free Alençon and Navarre and allow them to assist Nassau and Orange in the Netherlands. The plot, however, misfired, as one of the conspirators arrived on the scene prematurely. Fearing a repeat of the *Surprise de Meaux,* Charles IX ordered the court to go to Paris. On 8 March it moved to the greater security of the fortress at Vincennes. When Alençon was questioned about the plot in the presence of the king, Catherine and Chancellor Birague, he claimed that it had been aimed at the Guises, who had blocked his appointment to a responsible position in the government. Birague wanted him and Navarre to be executed as traitors, but Charles IX and his mother were not prepared to take such a drastic step. The two princes were simply put under heavy guard and made to sign an oath of loyalty to the crown. Their supporters, however, remained at large.

Early in April 1574, as Charles IX succeeded in persuading marshal Montmorency to return to court, Catherine was told of another escape attempt by Alençon and Navarre. This time, they planned to flee to Sedan, where they hoped to meet a force of cavalry under Turenne. On learning of the plot, Charles placed the two princes and Montmorency under closer security than before and ordered the arrest of some fifty people, including the seigneur de La Mole and the comte de Coconas, the alleged ringleaders. When they were interrogated by the council on 11 May, La Mole denied all knowledge of the plot, but Coconas revealed that Alençon had planned to meet Condé and Thoré at La Ferté

171

before joining Louis of Nassau and Christopher of the Palatinate at Sedan. He accused the Montmorencies of being behind the plot and of trying to destroy the kingdom. Two days later, the two princes were questioned. Alençon admitted that he had intended to go to the Netherlands, while Navarre explained that he and Alençon had acted out of fear of another massacre. Once again Birague asked for their heads, but Charles IX decided to spare them. However, La Mole and Coconas were tried by the Parlement, found guilty of *lèse-majesté*, and executed. As an additional safety measure, marshals Montmorency and Cossé were imprisoned in the Bastille, but Damville, younger son of the late Constable Montmorency, remained free. Soon afterwards, the king revoked his commission as governor of Languedoc and appointed the Prince-Dauphin, Montpensier's son, in his place. Damville, however, was not easily removed as he disposed of an army and a numerous clientèle. On 29 May he signed a truce with the Huguenots in the Midi, and later he formed a Union of moderate Catholics and Huguenots – in other words an alliance of 'malcontents' of both religions against the government. Meanwhile, Condé fled to Germany and abjured his Catholic faith. As for the Huguenot captain, Montgomery, who had invaded Normandy from England, he was forced to surrender after being besieged in Domfront for seventeen days. Catherine, who had never forgiven him for killing her husband, conveyed her joy to Charles IX, but he was too ill to care. On 30 May 1574 the young king (he was only twenty-three years old) died at Vincennes in his mother's arms after he had signed an act appointing her as regent. Catherine sent Monsieur de Chémerault to Anjou in Poland to inform him of his brother's death and of his own accession as King Henry III. Next day, she wrote to him, describing his brother's sad end. 'I am grief-stricken', she wrote, 'to have witnessed such a scene and the love which he showed me at the end. He could not leave me and begged me to send for you in great haste and pending your return to take charge of the government and to punish the prisoners who, he knew, were the cause of all the kingdom's ills.' His last words were '*Eh, ma mère*'. 'My only consolation', she wrote, 'is to see you here soon, as your kingdom requires, and in good health, for if I were to lose you, I would have myself buried alive with you.'[8] She urged Henry to return by the safest route: namely through the Empire and Italy, and not to let the Poles detain him. She suggested that he might promise to send them his brother or his own second son by a future marriage. In the meantime, the Poles might be left to rule themselves with the assistance of an elected Frenchman. 'I think this would please them well,' she added, 'as they would be their own kings.' Catherine then advised Henry to treat his servants well but impartially. 'I beg you', she said, 'not to give anything until you are here, for only then will you know who has served you well or not; I will tell you their names and point them out to you. I will keep all benefices and offices that will fall vacant. We shall tax them as there is not an *écu* left to do all the things you need to do to maintain your kingdom. Your late brother has entrusted me with that task, and I will not let you down: I will do my best to hand it over to you entire and at peace so that you should not have to work for your greatness and to allow you a little pleasure after so much worry and care . . . The experience you have gained from your voyage is such that I am sure that there has never been a king as wise as you . . . since you left I have had only worry on top of worry: thus I believe that your return will bring me joy and contentment on top of contentment and that I will no longer have trouble or annoyance. I pray God that it may be so and that I may see you in good health and soon.'[9]

One of Catherine's first moves as regent was to move to the Louvre, where she tightened security by ordering all the gates save one to be walled up.[10] On 3 June the Parlement ratified her new powers as regent, which Alençon and Navarre endorsed in writing. Catherine then took steps to pacify the kingdom, pending Henry's return. The two marshals imprisoned in the Bastille were not set free, but Montgomery was swiftly tried and executed. At the end of June a truce was arranged with the Rochelais in return for a payment of 70,000 *livres*. Catherine assumed that the truce would last until the king's return. He would then have to

---

8   *Lettres,* iv. 310–12; Simonin, p. 434
9   *Lettres,* iv. 311–12.
10   P. de L'Estoile, *Registre-Journal du règne de Henri III,* ed. M. Lazard and G. Schrenk (Geneva, 1992), i. 57.

decide whether to resume the war to make peace. Finally, Catherine raised a loan of 100,000 *écus* to help pay for Henry III's return from Poland.[11]

. . .

HENRY III'S ACCESSION

Henry was in Cracow on 15 June, when news reached him of his brother's death. He promptly consulted his companions, Villequier, Pibrac, Bellièvre and Miron, and decided to leave Poland secretly during the night of 18–19 June. His flight did not pass unnoticed, but he managed to reach Imperial territory before Polish dignitaries could intercept him. After being warmly received in Vienna by Emperor Maximilian II, Henry entered Venetian territory on 11 July, where he was joined by the dukes of Nevers, Ferrara and Savoy. On 18 July he was greeted by doge Mocenigo and taken across a lagoon crowded with galleys and gondolas. He took up residence at the Palazzo Foscari on the Grand Canal and for the next eight days was magnificently entertained. At night, he would sometimes venture out in disguise to explore the city: he would call on famous courtesans or buy jewels and perfume on the Rialto. He called on the painter Veronese, still active at ninety-seven, and sat for his portrait in Tintoretto's studio. On 27 July, after attending a magnificent ball, the king left. He gave the doge a diamond ring worth 1050 *écus,* and received in return the statutes of the Order of the Holy Ghost, founded in 1352 by Louis of Anjou, king of Naples.[12] Knowing her son's extravagant tastes, Catherine had taken steps to provide him with a suite worthy of the first ever visit paid by a French monarch to the Serenissima. She had sent him 35,714 Venetian *écus* and he himself had borrowed 12,000 more. Over ten days he spent almost the entire amount: 29,188 *écus* on personal needs; 1,400 as a gift to the Venetian ambassador in Poland; and 13,216 (more than one year's expenditure by Catherine on her building projects) on gifts to various people ranging from rowers and gon-

---

11 I. Cloulas, *Catherine de Médicis* (Paris, 1979), pp. 373–4.
12 P. Chevallier, *Henri III* (Paris, 1985), pp. 236–44.

doliers to the doge. Such spending did not augur well for Henry's future management of France's finances.

From Venice, Henry travelled to Padua, Ferrara, and Mantua. Wherever he passed, he received messages from Catherine pressing him to come home. He nevertheless chose to spend twelve days in Turin, capital of the duchy of Savoy, as the guest of his aunt, Marguerite (the sister of Henry II) and of her husband, duke Emmanuel-Philibert. As a mark of friendship, Henry ceded to them the last three towns (Pinerolo, Savigliano and Perugia) still held by France in Piedmont, thereby leaving the marquisate of Saluzzo as the only French possession beyond the Alps. The king's generosity has generally been denounced by historians as irresponsible, but it did fulfil an undertaking given by France at the peace of Cateau-Cambrésis.[13] However, it did not go down well in France: Chancellor Birague refused to endorse it, and the duc de Nevers, who was governor of the French possessions beyond the Alps, protested loudly, but Catherine did not criticize Henry's action. On 1 October, she assured Emmanuel-Philibert that Henry would honour his word.[14]

Henry and Catherine were reunited at Bourgoin, near Lyon, on 5 September. The queen-mother had come down from Paris, bringing with her in her own coach Alençon and Navarre, presumably to keep an eye on them. Next day, Henry III made his entry into Lyon and began organizing his government. He seems to have followed advice contained in a letter from Catherine, which he had received in Turin. She advised him 'to show that he was now the master and not the companion'. People should not be allowed to think that they could take advantage of his youthfulness. He should stop making gifts to people who pressured him; if he started by refusing two or three lords, who were full of themselves, others would soon learn how to behave. Royal favours should be given only to good servants. Henry should also be careful not to give offices to unworthy individuals. Catherine warned him against allowing a favourite too much patronage, for this could leave him at the mercy of a few

---

13 Ibid., pp. 247–51.
14 *Lettres*, v. 99.

powerful nobles; he would do better to harness the assistance of the greatest and ablest men in the provinces by means of offices, dignities and benefices. He should also follow the example of Louis XI and Francis I by winning over the bishops, 'who control their dioceses'. Regarding his own court, he should set an example by rising at a regular time and asking for dispatches to be brought to him forthwith so that he might read them and dictate replies to the secretaries of state. Petitioners should address him alone, not the secretaries; they should be made to understand that he alone is the source of favours. This would make them grateful to him and inclined only to follow his lead. The council had become too large and ought to be reformed. The *conseil des finances*, which Catherine had herself set up, should be suppressed and there should be a return to the *conseil privé*, as it existed under Francis I. This had examined public affairs in the morning, leaving private matters to be dealt with in the afternoon. Finally, Catherine urged Henry to carry out these reforms immediately; otherwise he would never do so. She explained that she would have carried them out herself, if only she had disposed of his authority. 'He can do everything', she concluded, 'but he must have the will.'[15]

Henry III reduced the size of his council, which now had only eight members in addition to the princes. Bellièvre was appointed *surintendant des finances*, which was tantamount to suppressing the *Conseil des finances*. Important posts were given to friends who had been with Henry in Poland. Villequier and Retz shared the post of first gentleman of the chamber, each serving for six months in rotation. Bellegarde was promoted marshal of France and Ruzé became secretary of state. Furthermore, Henry began to read dispatches and to answer them himself, thereby down-grading the role of the secretaries of state, who had been in the habit of opening dispatches themselves and of taking decisions on their own authority. They were now expected merely to draft orders handed down by the king and his council. No royal favour was regarded as valid unless it carried the king's signature. Henry also tried to restrict access to his chamber

---

15 *Lettres*, v. 73–5.

and set up a barrier around his dining table, but these moves, which were evidently intended to enhance his dignity, proved so unpopular with courtiers that they had to be shelved. Henry again encountered opposition when he tried to revive them in 1585.[16]

Henry III, it seems, wanted to restore peace to his kingdom following his arrival in Lyon. 'I have no greater desire and wish', he wrote to the governor of Saintes on 1 October, '. . . than to recall my subjects to me and to the natural obedience which they owe me by gentleness and clemency rather than other means . . .'.[17] However, this was not to be. Members of the council, who pressed for a showdown with Damville and the Huguenots, managed to get their way. Damville was ordered on 14 October to disband his army and either go to the king in Lyon or retire to Savoy without prejudice to his property. He replied in a manifesto, issued on 13 November, which blamed foreigners in the council for all the kingdom's misfortunes. They were accused of taxing the people unfairly and of using religion to stir up unrest. Damville vowed to take up arms against them and to seek aid from abroad. He pleaded for at least limited freedom of conscience, for a General Council to settle religious differences and for a meeting of the Estates-General.[18]

Damville's manifesto coincided with a great flurry of polemical writings. In 1576 Innocent Gentillet, a Huguenot who had fled to Geneva, published a furious tirade, called *Anti-Machiavel,* in which Machiavelli was blamed for the French government's 'infamous vices'. Some pamphlets directed their fire at Catherine. *Le Discours merveilleux de la vie, actions et déportements de Catherine de Médicis, Royne-mère* (see above, p. 164–5), was so popular that it had to be reprinted several times. After reciting the queen's many crimes, it called on God to punish her like the Frankish queen, Brunhilda, who had been dragged to death by a wild stallion. Among other charges, she was accused of helping Italian financiers to line their own pockets at the expense of

---

16 Chevallier, *Henri III,* p. 262.

17 *Lettres de Henri III,* ed. M. François (Paris, 1965), ii. 24.

18 C. Tievant, *Le gouverneur de Languedoc pendant les premières guerres de religion (1559–1574): Henri de Montmorency-Damville* (Paris, 1993), pp. 312–13.

the French people. Other pamphlets called for the over-throw of the Valois dynasty. The *Reveille-matin des français* offered a daring solution to France's problems: in addition to an armed alliance of Protestant powers, it proposed a new constitution for France amounting to its dismemberment and ended with an appeal to all Frenchmen, whatever their religion, to overthrow tyranny and reassert their ancestral rights. Another pamphlet, the *Politique,* argued that the prince or ruler may be deposed for making unjust laws and adduced many historical precedents, ranging from the kings of the Old Testament to Mary Stuart. Another pamphlet, the *Francogallia,* offered a historically-based theory of popular sovereignty designed to discredit the Valois and to gain wide support for their overthrow.[19]

From Lyon, the court travelled to Avignon, where Catherine tried to negotiate with Damville, while the king took part in penitential processions. Damville meanwhile consolidated his position in Languedoc. On 22 December the king obtained from the local estates at Villeneuve-lès-Avignon a large subsidy to pursue the war, but each day showed the superiority of the enemy. Damville's military successes – notably the capture of Saint-Gilles and Aigues-Mortes – served to tighten the bonds between the Huguenots and the 'peaceful' Catholics in the Midi. On 10 January 1575 they signed a treaty of union at Nîmes and organised a republic – 'a state within the state' – grouping the provinces of the south and centre under Damville's command and the supreme authority of Condé.[20] The latter had spent the winter of 1574–75 in Heidelberg, negotiating with John-Casimir, son of the Elector-Palatine. In return for their help, the Elector and his son hoped eventually to gain control of the sees of Metz, Toul and Verdun, which the French had taken over in 1552. Condé also looked for assistance to England.

On 10 January the court left Avignon for Champagne. Having signally failed to impose his authority on the Midi,

---

19 R.M. Kingdon, *Myths about the St. Bartholomew's Day Massacre, 1572–76* (Cambridge, Mass., 1988), pp. 70–87, 140–9, 161–8, 202, 210–11.

20 J. Garrisson-Estèbe, *Les protestants du Midi, 1559–1598* (Toulouse, 1980), pp. 191–3.

the king was anxious to be crowned and married. His coronation took place at Reims on 13 February and was followed, two days later, by his marriage to Louise de Vaudémont. Catherine may have been disappointed for she had been seeking the hand of the daughter of the king of Sweden for her son. If she had succeeded, he might have been better able to retain his Polish throne. Louise's prospects were negligible by comparison, but Catherine put on a brave face, allowing people to believe that she had arranged Henry's marriage.

Meanwhile, Frenchmen continued fighting among themselves. In the west the duc de Montpensier, acting for the crown, managed to recapture a number of small towns commanding the approaches to La Rochelle, but he failed to seize the Ile de Ré, which would have threatened the town's maritime communications. As the war seemed to be getting nowhere, Henry tried to negotiate. On 11 April 1575 he received a deputation from Damville to whom he explained that he had come back from Poland intending to embrace all his subjects without religious discrimination. But the deputies were not impressed: they demanded freedom of Protestant worship throughout the kingdom, bi-partisan lawcourts in all the parlements, secure towns, the release of marshals Montmorency and Cossé, a meeting of the Estates-General, punishment of the perpetrators of the St. Bartholomew massacre and the rehabilitation of their victims. Angered by these demands, Henry would only offer strictly limited freedom of worship to Protestants in certain areas. Catherine told the delegates that the king would never go back to the Edict of January (1562). An assembly of the Union was then called by Damville to consider Henry's reply to its demands. This resulted in another deputation being sent to him, which laid down two prerequisites for further talks: freedom of worship for Protestants throughout France and the liberation of the two marshals in the Bastille.

.   .   .

A DIVIDED FAMILY

Despite his mother's advice, Henry III continued to fraternize with the young men who had accompanied him to Poland, while his brother Alençon had his own distinct circle of friends, as did their brother-in-law, Navarre. The ladies of the court were equally divided, often manipulating their husbands or lovers and being themselves used to advance a relationship or stratagem. Causes did not loom large in this mélée, low intrigue mingled with violence being the order of the day. Henry III and his brother, Alençon, hated each other. The king believed, rightly, that Alençon had had designs on his throne during his absence in Poland. He forgave him at their mother's instance on returning to France, but continued to distrust him. He suspected Alençon of having secret dealings with Damville, La Noue, Condé and other rebels. Such was the ill-feeling between the brothers that, in June 1575, as Henry fell seriously ill, he instructed Navarre to seize power in the event of his death.

The king had also become alienated from his sister, Marguerite, as she explains in her memoirs.[21] About 1570 he told Catherine that Marguerite was engaged in a politically dangerous flirtation with the duc de Guise. Marguerite vowed never to forgive her brother for his betrayal, and from this time onward she sided with her other brother, Alençon. After his return from Poland, Henry accused Marguerite of deceiving her husband, Navarre. Catherine was furious with her until it became clear that the king had been misled by malicious gossip. The next scandal involved Louis Béranger, sieur du Guast, a favourite of Henry and an enemy of Marguerite. He set a trap for Bussy d'Amboise, a dashing young courtier, who had joined Alençon's circle and was almost certainly Marguerite's lover. One night, as he left the Louvre, twelve men fell upon him, but he escaped unhurt. He vowed to be avenged, but on the king's advice left the court for a time, accompanied by many young nobles.[22]

Henry next accused his sister of being too friendly with Thorigny, one of her ladies, and persuaded Navarre to expel

---

21 Marguerite's *Mémoires* were written at Usson between 1585 and 1605. They were dedicated to Brantôme and first published in Paris in 1628. See H. Hauser, *Les sources de l'histoire de France, XVIe siècle* (Paris, 1912), iii. 34–5.
22 E. Viennot, *Marguerite de Valois* (Paris, 1995), pp. 80–1.

the lady from his household. At the same time the king drove a wedge between Navarre and Alençon by exposing them to the charms of Charlotte de Sauve, the wife of a secretary of state. As both fell madly in love with her, they longed to be rid of each other.[23] 'The court is the strangest I have ever known,' wrote Navarre to a friend. 'We are nearly always ready to cut each other's throat. We carry daggers, wear coats of mail and often a cuirass beneath a cape . . . The king is as vulnerable as I am . . . All the band you know wants my death on account of my love for Monsieur and they have forbidden for the third time my mistress (Charlotte de Sauve) to speak to me. They have such a hold on her that she does not dare to look at me. I am waiting for a minor battle, for they say they will kill me, and I want to be one jump ahead of them.'[24]

· · ·

ALENÇON'S ESCAPE (15 SEPTEMBER 1575)

On 15 September 1575 Alençon slipped quietly out of Paris in spite of assurances he had given to his mother.[25] She was taken aback by his conduct and, writing to the duke of Savoy, said that she wished she had not lived long enough to see such a day. She suggested to the duc de Nevers that Alençon might be kidnapped, but, when she found that so many people had gone to join him, she decided to follow him herself in order to bring him to reason. He, in the meantime, reached Dreux, a town in his apanage some 40 miles west of Paris, where he issued a manifesto.[26] Without attacking the king directly, he echoed three of Damville's earlier demands: the removal of foreigners from the government, a religious pacification pending a church council, and a meeting of the Estates-General. The government was alarmed at the prospect of a link-up between an invading force from Germany and the rebels in the south and west of

---

23 Ibid., pp. 81–2.
24 *Recueil des lettres missives de Henri IV*, ed. Berger de Xivrey, i. 92.
25 Holt, *Duke of Anjou*, p. 51.
26 BN, ms. fr. 3342, ff. 5–6; Holt, *Duke of Anjou*, pp. 52–4.

France, particularly if Alençon, as prince of the blood, decided to put himself at the head of the rebellion. It was in the hope of averting such a catastrophe that Catherine met him at Chambord at the end of September.[27] Alençon asked for the release of marshals Montmorency and Cossé, which Henry reluctantly conceded on 2 October, but peace depended on Catherine agreeing to further demands. Meanwhile, Thoré, who had invaded northern France with a force of German *reiters*, was defeated by Guise at Dormans. This took some of the pressure off Catherine. Alençon, it seems, had been ready to cast his lot with the Huguenots, but was too penurious to bargain with Catherine. On 21 November they signed a six months' truce at Champigny. Alençon was granted five towns (Angoulême, Niort, Saumur, Bourges and La Charité), while Condé was promised Mézières. Freedom of worship was granted to Protestants in all the towns under their control and in two more per *gouvernement*. A payment of 50,000 *livres* was promised to the *reiters* provided they did not cross the Rhine.[28] Catherine hoped that a lasting peace would follow, but Ruffec and La Châtre, the governors of Angoulême and Bourges, refused to hand their towns over to Alençon. Condé and John-Casimir also continued to threaten France's frontier. On 9 January 1576 their army, numbering 20,000 men, passed from Lorraine into France, taking Henry III completely by surprise. He watched helplessly as the invaders pushed south, destroying everything in their path. At court, critics of the truce accused Catherine of having capitulated to Alençon in return for empty promises. Indignantly rebutting the charge, she argued that she could not be blamed for La Châtre's disobedience. The king, she insisted, must punish him. If he did not do so, she begged to be allowed to go to her patrimonial lands in Auvergne in order to raise a force herself with which to punish those who had betrayed him.[29] Catherine reminded Henry that she had repeatedly pressed him to arm himself while she negotiated. 'I can boast', she wrote to Henry 'of having begun, if I had not been inter-

---

27 Holt, *Duke of Anjou*, p. 56.
28 Ibid., p. 59.
29 *Lettres,* v. 175.

rupted, the greatest service a mother has ever given to her children.'[30] She stressed the necessity to treat at all costs. 'I beg you', she wrote,'to offer Casimir a pension and even lands in this kingdom.'[31] She warned Henry not to repeat the mistake of Louis XI, who had fought his brother instead of seeking a reconciliation, only to be forced to accept worse terms than if he had settled sooner.[32]

Catherine hoped that Alençon would remain neutral, but he still had not been given the towns which he had been promised in the truce. In January 1576 he accused Birague of trying to poison him and made this an excuse for repudiating the agreement.[33] He moved to Villefranche, where he was joined by Turenne with 3,000 arquebusiers and 400 horse. On 5 February Henry III's predicament deepened as Navarre escaped from court. He blamed Marguerite for this new setback and placed her under close guard. 'If he had not been restrained by the queen my mother,' she wrote, 'I believe that his anger would have led him to commit some cruelty against my life.' Catherine tried to placate her offspring. While explaining to Marguerite that considerations of security had obliged her brother to curb her natural desire to join her husband, she warned Henry that he might need to employ his sister's services one day. She persuaded him that Alençon would not negotiate as long as Marguerite remained a prisoner. Henry accordingly called on her and assured her of his love.[34] Meanwhile, Navarre, who had gone to his apanage of Alençon, formally abjured the Catholic faith in favour of Calvinism.[35] Within a fortnight, a delegation representing him, Alençon, Condé and Damville submitted a lengthy remonstrance to Henry III. They demanded freedom of Protestant worship through-out France, the establishment of bi-partisan courts in every parlement, a number of surety towns and payment of the German *reiters*. Alençon asked for the duchy of Anjou,

30 *Lettres,* v. 176-7.
31 *Lettres,* v. 177.
32 Ibid.
33 Holt, *Duke of Anjou,* p. 61.
34 J.-H. Mariéjol, *Catherine de Médicis* (Paris, 1920), pp. 268-9.
35 J.-P. Babelon, *Henri IV,* (Paris, 1982), pp. 213-19.

Navarre for certain rights and privileges in Guyenne, and Condé for Boulogne. Henry III lacked the resources needed to resist the forces ranged against him. After hesitating for a time, Alençon issued another manifesto on 9 April 1576. 'We have decided . . .', he said, 'to win by force the peace and tranquillity that we could not achieve by reason.'[36] This left Henry with no choice but to seek peace, and again he called on his mother to treat for him.

Catherine left Paris on 26 April 1576, bearing the king's reply to the princes' remonstrance. She met them at Chastenoy, near Sens, and conceded virtually all their demands. The resulting Edict of Beaulieu was proclaimed on 6 May and registered a week later by the Parlement. It became known as the 'Peace of Monsieur' (the title traditionally given to the king's younger brother) because it was generally assumed that Alençon had forced it on the king. For the first time Huguenots were given freedom of worship throughout France except within two leagues of Paris or the court. They were allowed to build churches almost anywhere and admitted to all professions, schools and hospitals. For the first time too, bi-partisan courts were to be set up in all the parlements. The massacre of St. Bartholomew was condemned as a crime and its victims, including Coligny, rehabilitated. Eight surety towns were ceded to the Huguenots. Finally, Henry promised to call the Estates-General within six months. Alençon was granted an annuity of 100,000 écus and became duc d'Anjou.[37]

Henry III allegedly wept as he signed the peace. Catherine, on the other hand, wrote to Damville, expressing her joy at the removal of the obstacle which had stood in the way of the unity and friendship which ought to bind together all the king's subjects.[38] She urged her son not to delay in paying 300,000 livres which the reiters had been promised; otherwise, she said, they would not leave. She was right: the peace did not immediately rid France of foreign troops. Henry III needed to pay them off. On 6 May he wrote to his ambassador in Venice: 'All that is required is money to rid

---

36 Holt, *Duke of Anjou*, pp. 63–5.
37 Sutherland, *Huguenot Struggle*, pp. 228–31, 361–2.
38 *Lettres*, v. 193.

my kingdom of the oppression and ruin of war.'[39] Bellièvre made frantic efforts to raise the cash needed to satisfy Casimir. The dukes of Savoy and Lorraine were asked for large loans. Caught between the rapacity of the mercenaries and the greed of the moneylenders, the king was close to despair. 'I can assure you', he wrote to Bellièvre, 'that if I could only extricate myself at the cost of my own blood, I would not spare myself, given my strong desire to rid my kingdom of ruin and desolation.'[40] On 5 July an agreement was reached with Casimir, but he demanded hostages. Six went to Nancy, but two refused to be handed over, whereupon Casimir detained Henry III's envoys, Bellièvre and Harlay. Catherine was appalled: 'We would never have thought', she wrote, 'that duke Casimir would have shown so little respect to the king, my son, who has treated him so well.'[41]

·   ·   ·

THE HOLY LEAGUE

The Peace of Monsieur was regarded as a 'sell-out' by the majority of French Catholics and many began to see that only by forming a party would they ever succeed in defending their interests effectively. The Holy League, which was set up in 1576, was prompted by a clause in the peace treaty which granted Condé the governorship of Picardy as well as the town of Péronne. Jacques d'Humières, the town governor, refused to hand it over and formed an association of Picard nobles and soldiers to defend it. At the same time, he called on all the princes, nobles and prelates of France to form a holy and Christian union against the heretics. Henry denounced d'Humières' initiative, claiming that no one was a better Catholic than himself. Meanwhile, as the League spread from Picardy to other parts of France, the duc de Guise issued a declaration setting out its aim of implementing the law of God and maintaining the king 'in the state, splendour, authority, duty, service and obedience owed

---

39   *Lettres de Henri III*, ed. François, ii. 414.
40   Ibid. 466–7.
41   *Lettres*, v. 215.

to him by his subjects'.[42] All Catholics were invited to join the League and provide it with arms and men according to their ability. Members would help each other judicially and militarily. They would also pledge themselves to obey any leader chosen to accomplish the League's sacred mission. People rallied to Guise from all parts of France. Among the League's chief recruiting agents were the mendicant friars and the Jesuits. Much of its propaganda was disseminated from the Hôtel de Guise in Paris: this argued that the Guises, as descendants of Charlemagne, were better suited than the Valois, physically and spiritually, to fight and destroy heresy.

One of Henry III's main objectives in 1576 was to detach his brother, Anjou, from his alliance with the Huguenots and the Catholic malcontents in the Midi. Indeed, the Peace of Monsieur may have been primarily intended to achieve this end. Several months later, Catherine told Nevers that she and the king had signed the peace only 'to get back Monsieur, not to re-establish the Huguenots'.[43] Henry made similar statements. He tried to win over his brother by pointing to the danger posed to the Valois dynasty by Guise ambitions. Anjou proved responsive. Advances he was receiving from Catholics in the Netherlands and the prospect of a foreign crown caused him to sever his alliance with the Huguenots and to seek Henry III's backing. The brothers were reconciled at Ollainville in November 1576.

. . .

THE ESTATES OF BLOIS
(DECEMBER 1576–MARCH 1577)

Catholic opposition to the implementation of the peace forced Henry III to act: instead of opposing the League, he decided to put himself at its head. The success of this policy was tested at the Estates-General of Blois in December 1576.

---

42 Chevallier, *Henri III*, pp. 335–7.
43 Holt, *Duke of Anjou*, p. 69 citing the private journal of the duc de Nevers in 1576–7. Labourcé and Duval (eds), *Recueil des pièces originales et authentiques concernant la tenue des Etats Généraux*, 9 vols. (Paris, 1789), iii. 18.

Although the Huguenots had been agitating for such a meeting since the massacre of St. Bartholomew, they virtually excluded themselves from it by boycotting the elections on the ground that they were rigged. A majority of the deputies consequently supported the League. As they gathered in Blois, Henry ordered the establishment of armed leagues in every part of the kingdom. Huguenots were assured of freedom of conscience and respect for their lives and property as long as they complied with the estates' decisions. Opening the estates on 6 December, Henry expressed his desire for peace among his subjects. He paid fulsome tribute to his mother for all that she had done to promote the kingdom's prosperity, and promised to devote himself unsparingly to eradicating abuses and restoring order.[44] Next day, the three estates chose their respective spokesmen. On 11 December the only Huguenot deputy, Mirambeau, asked if it were true that another massacre of Protestants was being planned. Henry indignantly denied the rumour. His greatest wish, he reaffirmed, was that all his subjects should live in peace and harmony. That same day the estates asked the king to accept as definitive any unanimous decision which they might take. He naturally refused to give such an undertaking, which would have undermined his authority. Instead, he put on a show of Catholic zeal and incited the estates to propose the restoration of religious unity in the kingdom. This was bound to provoke a new civil war, which may have been what the king wanted, for if the estates could be made to break the peace, they would be morally obliged to assist him with subsidies.

On 19 December the nobility decided in favour of religious unity and of measures against Protestant pastors and any nobles who offered them protection. Three days later the clergy voted for the suppression of Protestantism. The third estate was divided on the issue, but in the end called for a ban on Protestant worship and the banishment of all pastors. A few deputies, including Jean Bodin, author of the *Six Books of the Republic*, spoke against war and the raising of more taxes, but they were overruled. Historians have claimed that these so-called 'politiques' formed a party

---

44 Chevallier, *Henri III*, p. 344.

dedicated to religious toleration; but, as Mack Holt has shown, such a party did not yet exist.[45] Bodin and his colleagues were not opposed to religious uniformity as such; they merely believed that civil war would destroy the kingdom. Henry III, however, did not share this view. At a council meeting, on 29 December, he explained that he had signed the Peace of Monsieur simply to win back his brother and to rid France of foreign troops. He expressed the hope that he would restore the Catholic religion to the place it had occupied under his predecessors and promised never again to break his coronation oath.[46]

Henry's new stance was, in effect, a repudiation of his mother's peace-making efforts, yet she made no attempt to oppose him openly. She wrote to him, on 2 January, praising his decision to restore the Catholic faith to his kingdom and to suppress the sect whose toleration was 'so displeasing to God', but she also expressed the hope that this could be accomplished without resorting to arms. She advised Henry to inform Condé, Navarre and Damville of his purpose. If Navarre proved obdurate, the duc de Montpensier should be asked to win him over. Navarre was most likely to trust him as he belonged to the same family and generation. Montpensier might flatter Navarre by proposing a marriage between his sister and the duc d'Anjou. Catherine estimated that Condé would soon treat if he found himself alone, but she was less sure of Damville: 'It is he', she wrote, 'whom I fear the most in as much as he has more sense, experience and consistency.' If all these approaches failed and war became inevitable, Catherine advised Henry to set up three armies, one to be led by himself into Guyenne. He should also send reinforcements to the various provincial governors, strengthen town defences, levy *reiters* in Germany and send an embassy to dissuade the German princes from intervening in France.[47]

Henry III could do nothing without money. The estates, however, seemed unwilling to assist him. While the clergy and nobility invoked their traditional right of tax exemption, the third estate pleaded poverty. In the end, the clergy

---

45 Holt, *Duke of Anjou*, p. 81.
46 Chevallier, *Henri III*, p. 347.
47 *Lettres*, v. 232.

offered 450,000 *livres*. An attempt by the king to alienate crown lands was foiled by the third estate. His predicament was compounded by the League's distrust. The Picard nobles would only take his oath of association if they were guaranteed their franchises and privileges. Meanwhile, the war, which Catherine hoped might be avoided, had already begun. In Provence and Dauphiné the Huguenots were gaining ground. Before entering the fray, however, Henry III wished to appear justified. At his suggestion, the estates invited Condé, Navarre and Damville to come to Blois for talks, but Condé refused, and Navarre asked the estates to reconsider their demand for religious uniformity. On 2 March the king's council took another look at the question of religious unity. While Nevers remained intransigent, Catherine pressed for peace. Her attitude had changed since 1574. If Marguerite de Valois is to be believed, the queen-mother condemned the bishops for advising the king to 'break his promises and undo all that she had promised and agreed in his name'. She also complained about Henry's policy in private. On 14 January she confided to Villequier and Nevers: 'I am almost sorry that I gave way to my son, for his advisers will carry the blame. He should never have committed himself so absolutely.' A few days later, she spoke to Cardinal de Bourbon in favour of peace, and complained to Queen Louise that her son was no longer listening to her: 'He disapproves of everything I do', she said; 'clearly I am not free to do as I wish.'[48]

Yet Catherine was largely responsible for detaching Damville from his alliance with the Huguenots. She asked the duke of Savoy to reassure the marshal as to the king's good intentions and urged Damville's Catholic wife, Antoinette de La Marck, to detach him from the Huguenots. But, distrusting Henry, Damville required solid guarantees. Eventually, he accepted the promise of the marquisate of Saluzzo in return for restoring Languedoc to the king's obedience. Catherine stood surety for the accord, assuring Damville that Henry would rather die than break his word.

---

48 *Lettres*, v. 348.

. . .

THE SIXTH WAR (1577)

Despite the estates' refusal to provide the funds needed by Henry III to fight the Huguenots, he did manage to raise a sizeable army, but could only pay for it for one month. Now that the Huguenots had lost the support of Anjou and Damville, they were weaker than formerly, except in the south of France, where they controlled many fortified towns. On 2 May Anjou captured and sacked La Charité-sur-Loire, thereby earning a hero's reception at court. Catherine offered him a splendid banquet at her château of Chenonceaux. On 28 May Anjou rejoined the king's army, as it laid siege to Issoire in Auvergne. As the garrison resisted, he was instructed by the king to punish it severely for its disobedience, and duly obliged by sacking the town mercilessly after it had capitulated on 12 June. Anjou, who had not been implicated in the St. Bartholomew's Day massacre, now joined his mother and brother in having hands stained with blood; the Huguenots never trusted him again.

Being jealous of his brother's military success, Henry recalled him to court, and gave his command to the duc de Nevers, but he was soon informed that the king could not pay his troops. Yet the war was still far from won. Many Huguenot strongholds were intact, and Navarre and Condé remained at large with their forces. After the Huguenots had seized the Atlantic port of Brouage and had begun to receive aid from England, Henry III decided to treat. In spite of his financial plight, he managed to repair some of the humiliation which his mother had incurred for him in the Peace of Monsieur. Under the peace of Bergerac (17 September 1577), the Huguenots were allowed to worship only in one town per *bailliage* as against two and in those towns which they held on 17 September. The exclusion zone around Paris was enlarged and half the bi-partisan courts were abolished and the proportion of Huguenot judges in the rest reduced to a third. But the Huguenots were allowed to keep eight 'surety towns' for six years. Catholic worship was to be reinstated throughout the kingdom and all leagues and confraternities were banned. Henry III felt that he had jettisoned his mother's tutelage and could, therefore, hold his head higher.

Chapter 9

PEACEMAKER
(1578–84)

Although France now had a mature king, his mother re-mained extremely active politically, travelling widely across the kingdom, often enduring severe physical hardship, in order to help her son impose his authority. If she had ever expected France's denominational divisions to be solved by the destruction of the Huguenot party, she lived long enough to learn that the kingdom's problems required other, less violent, solutions. Having tried conciliation, persecution and marriage in turn, Catherine now sought peace by compromise. Unfortunately, she was not helped by her wayward sons, Henry III and François, duc d'Anjou, each of whom liked to go his own way regardless of consequences.

. . .

ANJOU AND THE DUTCH REVOLT

Events in the Low Countries soon threatened the peace in France. After the fall of Namur to the Spaniards on 24 July, the Dutch rebels renewed their efforts to gain Anjou's support. The last thing Henry III wanted at this stage was to be dragged into a war with Spain by his foolish brother. He forbade his subjects to join the Dutch rebels, but Anjou kept in touch with them. Meanwhile, his position at court became intolerable, as his turbulent followers, led by Bussy d'Amboise, picked quarrels with the king's equally violent favourites or *mignons*. The quarrels reached a farcical climax when the king burst into his brother's bedchamber one night and turned over the bedclothes, looking for evidence of treason-able plotting. He gleefully snatched a letter from Anjou's hands, only to find that it was a *billet doux* from Madame de Sauve. Catherine, who had witnessed the scene, succeeded in reconciling her sons, but Anjou continued to feel insecure. On 14 February 1578 he fled from the court with the connivance of his sister, Marguerite. After reaching his apanage of Angers, he began to raise troops.[1] Catherine set off in pursuit and, catching up with the duke, tried to make him see sense. He promised not to prejudice the king or to upset the peace of the kingdom, but would not return to court. Early in May Catherine met him again at Bourgueil and secured a written promise from him to abandon his Dutch enterprise unless the States-General agreed to make him their prince and to hand over to him the principal towns which they held. In that event, Catherine and Henry promised not to stand in his way; they even allowed him to keep 2,400 troops on the Norman border.[2]

Perhaps in the hope of diverting Anjou's attention from his warlike schemes, Catherine tried to interest him in marriage. She offered him several possible brides, each with a potentially substantial dowry. One was the daughter of the duke of Mantua, who might receive Montferrat. If joined to Saluzzo, which was in Henry III's gift, Anjou would gain a sizeable principality in Italy. An even more alluring prospect was a Spanish infanta, who might be given Franche-Comté by her father, Philip II. If the marriage produced children, he might even give them the Low Countries or the duchy of Milan. If neither match could be realized, Catherine and Henry were ready to accept one between Anjou and Catherine de Bourbon, the sister of Henri de Navarre.[3] The queen-mother wanted her younger son to see that he could achieve his princely ambitions without dragging Henry III into a conflict with Spain and a quarrel with England. For Elizabeth I was strongly opposed to a French presence in the Low Countries and threatened to do her utmost to frustrate Anjou's enterprise.[4] As he pressed on with his plans, Catherine

---

1 J.-H. Mariéjol, *Catherine de Médicis* (Paris, 1920) p. 278; E. Viennot, *Marguerite de Valois* (Paris, 1995), pp. 103–6; *Mémoires de Marguerite de Valois*, ed. I. Cazaux (Paris, 1971), pp. 133–49.
2 *Lettres*, vi. 9–10, 20, 25.
3 Mariéjol, pp. 284–5.
4 *Lettres*, vi. 12–13, 28.

apologized to Philip II for his 'youthfulness' and assured Elizabeth that Henry III wanted only peace with his neighbours. At the same time, she was anxious not to drive Anjou into rebellion. It seems that while she openly disapproved of his conduct, she secretly instructed provincial governors to allow free passage to his troops.[5]

On 12 July Anjou arrived at Mons at the head of an army that was little better than a rabble. He informed William of Orange that he had come to assist the States-General in their just quarrel. A month later he signed a treaty with them: in return for his military assistance over three months, they appointed him 'Defender of the liberty of the Netherlands against the tyranny of the Spaniards and their allies'. The title, however, carried no authority. Moreover, such hopes as the Dutch had placed in the duke evaporated as his unpaid troops began to desert, ravaging the countryside on their homeward path.[6] In the autumn of 1578 he reopened his marriage negotiations with Elizabeth I. When she indicated that she would never marry a man without seeing him first, Henry and Catherine urged Anjou to go to England, if only to remove him from the Low Countries.

. . .

PACIFYING THE SOUTH

Although France was now officially at peace, the real situation, especially in the Midi, was tantamount to anarchy. Henry III was pressing Damville to hand over the *gouvernement* of Languedoc to marshal de Bellegarde in return for the marquisate of Saluzzo, but Damville refused. Bellegarde, who had resigned his command in haste, now tried to get it back by force with the help of Lesdiguières, leader of the Huguenots in Dauphiné. Meanwhile, Damville's lieutenants – Châtillon (Coligny's son), the governor of Montpellier, and captain Parabère, who held Beaucaire – rebelled against their superior. In Provence, nobles, called *Razats,* were fighting the comte de Carcès, leader of the local Catholic

---

5 Mariéjol, pp. 285–6; *Lettres,* vi. 30.
6 M.P. Holt, *The Duke of Anjou and the Politique Struggle during the Wars of Religion* (Cambridge, 1986), pp. 101–5.

nobility. The king's lieutenant-general, the comte de Suze, failed to command obedience. In Dauphiné, the conflict between Huguenots and Catholics was exacerbated by another between the third estate and the nobility over taxation. From Guyenne to Dauphiné, Huguenot leaders were refusing to hand over strongholds which they had occupied during the last war. Henri de Navarre complained that he was governor of Guyenne in name only and accused the lieutenant-general, marshal de Biron, of acting independently. He asked for the return of his wife Marguerite, whom the king seemed to be holding hostage at court. Meanwhile Huguenot soldiers throughout the Midi were randomly attacking castles and churches as well as merchants and travellers.[7]

For some reason – either insouciance or dislike of travel – Henry III left the task of pacifying the south to his long-suffering mother. She set off with a miniature court on a mission which she believed might last two months. Travelling with her were Marguerite de Valois, the Cardinal de Bourbon, the duc de Montpensier, the secretary of state, Pinart and some of the king's ablest councillors: Saint-Sulpice, Paul de Foix and Jean de Monluc. For a time Catherine also enjoyed the company of her close friend, the duchesse d'Uzès, the duchesse douairière de Condé and the duchesse de Montpensier. Her suite also included a number of beautiful young ladies. On reaching Bordeaux, Catherine wrote to Bellièvre, urging him to stop at all cost an invasion of France by John Casimir. She, for her part, would try to avert a storm by convincing Navarre and the Huguenots that the king was not planning their ruin. 'I hope', she explained, 'to do far more for the service of the king and the kingdom here, than I would do by staying with him and giving . . . bad (i.e. unpalatable) advice.'[8] Catherine, seemingly anxious to regain Henry III's trust and affection which recent events had damaged, vowed not to leave the Midi until she had restored peace to the region.

One of Catherine's first acts was to dissolve a Catholic confraternity in Bordeaux.[9] On 2 October she and Marguerite

---

7   *Lettres*, vi. 29, 57, 98, 401; Mariéjol, pp. 286–7.
8   *Lettres*, vi. 38–9.
9   *Lettres*, vi. p. 40.

met Henri de Navarre near La Réole. They soon agreed on peace terms, notably the restoration of occupied strongholds; but there were some 200 of these, and many of their captains refused to be dislodged.[10] Nine days later, the queen-mother explained the reasons for her coming to a large gathering of Catholic nobles at Agen: acting on the king's orders, she intended to restore Henri de Navarre's prerogatives as governor, and offered to work with the nobles to promote the reconciliation of all the king's subjects. Should they encounter difficulties, Catherine urged them to look to Marguerite, who would intercede for them with the king, her brother.[11] However, Navarre, for all his show of affability, remained deeply distrustful of the queen-mother and the king. He continued to look abroad for support, notably to John Casimir and Philip II. He was exasperated by Biron's presence in Bordeaux and quarrelled violently with him in Catherine's presence. For all these reasons, negotiations with Navarre and Turenne in Toulouse did not promise well. On 20 November the queen-mother moved to Auch, hoping that Navarre might feel safer there. He agreed to come, but became so infatuated with one of Catherine's beautiful ladies that he seemed unwilling to end the talks. One night, however, as a ball was in full swing, Navarre was told that Catholics had seized La Réole. Slipping away unnoticed, he retaliated by capturing the small Catholic town of Fleurance. On 4 December Catherine had formally to restore La Réole to the Huguenots.[12]

On 15 December Catherine arrived at Nérac, but talks with representatives of the Protestant churches did not start in earnest until 3 February 1579. Moreover, they submitted so many demands that some of the queen's councillors collapsed under the strain of dealing with them. The Huguenots asked for freedom of worship throughout the kingdom and also for sixty 'surety towns'. As the talks seemed to have stalled, the Huguenot representatives decided to go home. When they called on Catherine to take their

---

10 *Lettres*, vi. 451.
11 *Lettres*, vi. 75, 398–400.
12 Mariéjol, pp. 288–90; I. Cloulas, *Catherine de Médicis* (Paris, 1979), p. 420; Viennot, *Marguerite de Valois*, pp. 112–13.

leave, she exploded with fury, accusing them of having wasted her time and of never seriously wanting an agreement. She threatened to have them all hanged as rebels, but relented after a tearful intervention by Marguerite. As the talks continued, the Huguenots were persuaded to reduce their demands. Under the convention of Nérac (28 February), they obtained only fourteen surety towns for a period of six months and a bi-partisan court in Agen.[13]

Catherine would have liked to return to Paris now, but she still had work to do in the south. Leaving her daughter with her husband in Gascony, she continued to travel through the harsh winter months. In spite of frequent bouts of 'colic', a continual catarrh and rheumatism, Catherine could still enjoy her surroundings. As spring returned, she enthused over 'the flowering beans, the hard almonds, the fat cherries'.[14] Sometimes she abandoned her litter to ride a mule. 'I think', she wrote to a friend, 'that the king will laugh when he sees me riding with him on a mule like marshal de Cossé.'[15] Catherine also had to put up with some primitive accommodation on her travels, even sleeping under canvas on occasion. Such was her energy that she thought of travelling to England. In January 1579 she advised Anjou to resume his negotiations with Elizabeth I. Only by doing so, she said, would he acquire a crown. If need be, she would meet Elizabeth to arrange the marriage. As she confided to the duchesse d'Uzès in April: 'Although our age is more suited to rest than to travel, I must go to England.'[16] But the pacification of the Midi had to be completed first. On 18 May Catherine spoke of the hazards that lay ahead of her: plague, the sea, above all the Cévennes, where 'there are birds of prey, like those who stole your horses [the duchess's]. But I put my trust in God, who will always, it seems, protect me from danger. I trust Him completely.' She thanked her friend for telling her of the good understanding that now existed between the king and Anjou. Her

---

13 Mariéjol, p. 290; *Lettres*, vi. 260, 282; vii. 446; Viennot, *Marguerite de Valois*, p. 114.
14 *Lettres*, vi. 325.
15 *Lettres*, vi. 360.
16 *Lettres*, vi. 337.

children seemed at last willing to give her satisfaction. 'My daughter is with her husband,' she went on. 'I had news from them yesterday: they are the best couple anyone could wish for. I pray God to maintain it in this happy state, and to keep you until the age of 147 so that we may dine together at the Tuileries without hats or bonnets.'[17] Catherine could still smile in the midst of her woes.

On 29 May the queen-mother entered Montpellier, a Huguenot stronghold, which had recently rebelled against the king. Showing remarkable courage, she slipped between two rows of arquebusiers, brushing past the muzzles of their weapons. The local magistrates received her courteously and even agreed to restore the Mass on Sundays in the church of Notre-Dame. Writing to the duchesse d'Uzès, Catherine rejoiced over her success: 'I have seen all the Huguenots of Languedoc,' she said. 'God, who always backs me, has given me so much favour that I have got the better of them [here] as well as in Guyenne. There are plenty of nighthawks (*oiseaux nuisants*) here, who would readily steal your horses if you still have some fine ones; the rest are good company who danse the volta well.' Yet Catherine remained apprehensive: 'I am so worried about the quarrels in Provence that my mind can only conjure up anger . . . I do not know the people of Dauphiné will be any better. If the proverb that the sting is in the tail is true, I am much afraid that I may find it so; but my hope is always in God.'[18]

Unrest in Provence was as much social as religious. The nobles were divided into two factions: the *Razats* and the *Carcistes*, followers of the comte de Carcès. In May the *Razats* had captured the château of Trans and slaughtered the garrison; whereupon the *Carcistes* had retaliated by killing 400 people. Ordering both sides to lay down their arms, Catherine summoned their representatives to Marseille and offered them an amnesty, covering all their past offences, except the worst crimes, which would be left to the judgment of royal commissioners. The comte de Carcès would henceforth have to obey a new resident governor, Henri d'Angoulême. Eventually, Catherine's plan was acc-

---

17   *Lettres*, vi. 367.
18   *Lettres*, vi. 381.

epted. On 1 July fifteen deputies from either side swore to observe it. 'After playing my part and allowing them to play theirs', Catherine wrote, 'I made them all kiss each other.' During the next week she chose councillors from the Parlement of Aix and a president to judge crimes committed during the recent troubles, and asked Henry III to add eight or nine councillors from the Parlement of Paris as well as the president, Bernard Prévost, a man noted for his severity.[19]

While the queen-mother was hard at work in the south of France, Henry III was trying in his own way to bring order to the kingdom. He did not, as some historians have suggested, simply fritter the time away in lascivious pleasures. In November 1579 he created the Order of the Holy Ghost, a sort of militia aimed at establishing new ties of allegiance and fidelity between himself and a princely élite. In May 1579 two years of intensive legislative activity by the king and his council culminated in the great Ordinance of Blois, an ambitious up-dating of the law in response to the wishes of the Estates-General of 1576; and in February 1580 a new financial agreement, prolonging the Contract of Poissy, was signed with the clergy.[20] Although Catherine was often left to act alone, she always kept Henry informed of her actions and consulted him whenever possible. He, it seems, was duly grateful. Writing to his ambassador in Venice, he said: 'The queen, my lady and mother, is at present in Provence, where I hope that she will restore peace and unity among my subjects as she has done in Guyenne and Languedoc, and that, as she passes through Dauphiné, she will be able to do likewise. By this means will she implant in the hearts of all my subjects a memory and eternal recognition of her benefactions which will oblige them for ever to join me in praying God for her prosperity and health.'[21] This was only one of many letters in which the king expressed his filial gratitude.[22] It was a case of absence making the heart grow fonder. On 3 September 1578 he wrote to the duchesse

19 Cloulas, *Catherine*, p. 426.
20 *Lettres de Henri III*, ed. M. François (Paris, 1984) iv, p. xii.
21 Ibid. iv. 197.
22 Ibid., Nos. 3224, 3370, 3401, 3450, 3486, 3569.

d'Uzès: 'Above all bring back our good mother in good health, for our happiness depends upon this.'

Unrest in Dauphiné was much concerned with taxation. The third estate wanted the *taille personnelle* – a direct tax assessed on a person's social status – to be replaced by the *taille réelle*, one that was assessed on the status of land. This would have effectively suppressed the tax exemption traditionally claimed by the nobility. The change was not favoured by the crown, for whom the nobility was the chief bulwark against the common people. On reaching Montélimar, Catherine revealed her sympathies by praising the nobility in a speech to a distinguished assembly. This did not go down well with commoners in Valence and Romans, yet they agreed to abandon all 'leagues and associations'. They also promised to obey the lieutenant-general, Maugiron. Moving on to Grenoble, Catherine heard the grievances of all the estates. She roundly castigated Jean de Bourg, the spokesman of the third estate, who had dared to ask that differences between the estates should be judged by the king, not by the councillors who were accompanying her. Describing de Bourg as 'very factious', she said that he deserved to be severely punished for stirring up trouble.[23] She ordered a few trouble-makers to be arrested.

Peace in Dauphiné hung by a thread. In March 1579 Bellegarde had forcibly occupied Saluzzo after a quarrel with the governor, Charles de Birague. Henry III thought of sending an army against him, but this would have ignited a civil war. Catherine preferred to seek the duke of Savoy's mediation. A meeting was arranged with Bellegarde at Montluel-en-Bresse within the duke's domain, and on 17 October an agreement, wholly favourable to Bellegarde, was reached. After he had begged for the king's forgiveness, he was given the marquisate, but he died two months later, causing gossip-mongers to say that Catherine had poisoned him. On 20 October she made peace with several Huguenot communities in Dauphiné. In return for a promise to lay down their arms, she assured them that the king would attend to their particular grievances. She also allowed them

---

23 Mariéjol, pp. 302–4; *Lettres*, vii. 49–50; E. Le Roy Ladurie, *Carnival. A people's uprising at Romans, 1579–1580* (London, 1980), p. 75.

to occupy nine 'surety towns' for six months and promised to pay one month's wages to the captains of the garrisons, provided they allowed Catholics to return to their homes. In November a truce effectively brought hostilities to an end.

The king, meanwhile, had fallen seriously ill. He had an ear abscess similar to that which had killed his elder brother, Francis II. Catherine nearly went out of her mind.[24] Happily, the king recovered. '*Ma commère*,' she wrote to the duchesse d'Uzès, 'I have been deeply affected and not without cause, for he [Henry] is my life, and without him I wish neither to live nor exist. I believe that God has taken pity on me. Seeing that I have suffered so much from the loss of my husband and children, he has not wanted to crush me by taking this one. When I think of his complaint, I don't know who I am. I praise God for returning him to me and I beg that it should outstrip my life, and that I shall not see him unwell for as long as I live. It is a terrible pain, dreadful, believe me, to be far from someone whom one loves as much as I love him, knowing him to be ill; it is like dying on a slow fire.'[25]

On 9 October mother and son were reunited at last at Orléans, and on 14 November Catherine returned to Paris after an absence of nearly eighteen months. The king expressed his joy in a letter to Du Ferrier and also his gratitude for 'all the good she had sown wherever she has passed'.[26] Outside Paris, Catherine was met by the Parlement and the people, as if in tribute for her pacification of the kingdom. 'She is', wrote the Venetian ambassador, 'an indefatigable princess, born to tame and govern a people as unruly as the French: they now recognize her merits, her concern for unity and are sorry not to have appreciated her sooner.'[27] The ambassador, however, reckoned that Catherine had only appeased, not solved, the troubles of the south. Nor was the situation better elsewhere. Henry and Anjou had again fallen out. The duke, after an unsuccessful trip to the English court, was now sulking at Alençon. As a new civil war seemed imminent, Catherine once more took to the road.

---

24 *Lettres*, vii. 163–4.
25 *Lettres*, vii. 134.
26 *Lettres*, vii. 194 n. 2; 195 n. 1.
27 *Relations des ambassadeurs vénitiens*, ed. Tommaseo, ii. 449–51.

Calling on Anjou, she obtained a promise that he would not rally malcontents as he had done in the past, but he refused to return to court. Writing from Évreux on 25 November, the queen-mother warned Henry of impending catastrophe. 'I see things in a greater muddle than one thinks,' she said. 'I beg you to remedy them and to urge your financiers to set up a fund so that you may find support without further burdening your subjects, for you are on the eve of a general revolt. Anyone who tells you differently is a liar.'[28] In mid-December Catherine set off again, this time to Fère-en-Tardenois, where Condé was living. She wanted him to go to Saint-Jean-d'Angély, but he would not budge. Meanwhile, in the Midi, her good work was being undone. A Huguenot captain seized the town of Mende. Navarre apologized to the king, saying that the deed had been done without his consent; but he did nothing to repair the situation.

. . .

THE 'LOVERS' WAR'

In April 1580 Catherine called on the duc d'Anjou at Bourgueil to discuss his marriage prospects. She no longer favoured his marrying Navarre's sister, Catherine de Bourbon, on the ground that such a match would antagonize Catholics everywhere. This prompted Anjou to ask why she and Henry III did not raise the same objection to his marrying the English queen, who was also a Protestant. Catherine retorted that a marriage that would bring him a great kingdom was not to be compared with one that would only bring him an income of 50,000 *livres*.[29] Anjou was still interested in the English marriage and showed his mother several affectionate letters which he had received from Queen Elizabeth. He also allowed Henry III to send an official request on his behalf to the English government and to appoint commissioners to examine the terms of a possible marriage alliance. Catherine also wished to ascertain the state of Anjou's relations with the Huguenots. Denying that he had any secret dealings with them, he offered his

---

28 *Lettres*, vii. 202.
29 *Lettres*, vii. 241.

mediation if the king would appoint him lieutenant-general. In his opinion, all would be well if Henry would only persuade the nobility to take an oath before the Parlement to keep the peace and grant them a general pardon. Catherine urged Henry III to act on this advice.[30]

Anjou's assessment of the situation in the south was naïve, to say the least. In July 1579 a Huguenot assembly at Montauban decided to keep fifteen fortified towns, which should have been surrendered under the Nérac accord. They felt sure that Catherine would continue to treat with them, even if they seized a few châteaux. In April 1580 they suddenly launched an offensive for no apparent reason. According to Agrippa d'Aubigné, their action had been prompted by an affair between Navarre's wife, Marguerite, and his chief lieutenant, the vicomte de Turenne, and by offensive remarks which the king had made about it. For this reason the conflict has been called 'The Lovers' War', but, in fact, it was more probably a response to Catholic attacks in the south. If Marguerite had been partly to blame for the war, Catherine would surely not have asked her to help restore the peace; nor would Navarre have apologized for his predicament.[31] Catherine urged him to abide by his agreement with the king. 'I will never believe', she wrote, 'that having come from such a noble race [the Bourbons] you should wish to be the chief and general of the kingdom's brigands, thieves and criminals.' It was necessary, in her view, to restore the peace, as reason demanded, so that he should not be accused of breaking it. If he continued to prepare for war, Catherine did not doubt that God would abandon him. 'You will find yourself alone,' she wrote, 'accompanied by brigands and by men who deserve to hang for their crimes . . . Please believe me and see the difference between the advice of a mother, who loves you, and that of people, who loving neither themselves nor their master, want only to sack, destroy and ruin everything.'[32] Catherine also appealed to Marguerite to bring Navarre to his senses, but in vain.

---

30 *Lettres*, vii. 246.
31 Mariéjol, pp. 318–19.
32 *Lettres*, vii. 252–3.

As civil war broke out anew, Marguerite urged Anjou to mediate. Catherine, too, pressed for new talks, but in June she succumbed to *la coqueluche*, a serious epidemic which swept across much of France, killing thousands.[33] On 12 June she complained that she had not felt so unwell for a long time. In July, as the *coqueluche* was followed by plague, Catherine fled to Saint-Maur, while the king took the court to Fontainebleau. Anjou's interest in the Low Countries revived in the meantime, and, in September, representatives of the States-General called on him at Pléssis-lez-Tours. They offered him sovereignty over their provinces if he brought them Henry III's alliance. But Catherine and Henry insisted on peace being restored to France first. The duke accordingly set off, accompanied by Catherine's advisers, Bellièvre and Villeroy, to meet the king and queen of Navarre. On 26 November 1580 a peace treaty was signed at Fleix, which effectively confirmed the Nérac accord. The Huguenots retained their surety towns for another six months; everywhere they were to recover their property, honours and dignities.[34] Catherine thanked Bellièvre effusively for his successful diplomacy. Writing to the duchesse d'Uzès, she expressed her happiness at being reunited with her children in a kingdom once more at peace.[35]

. . .

DUKE OF BRABANT

While waiting at Coutras for Henry III to endorse the peace, Anjou learnt that the duke of Parma had laid siege to Cambrai, and immediately began raising troops to go to the town's relief. When Villeroy returned on 6 January with Henry's acceptance of the peace, he brought Anjou a letter from Catherine, urging him to remain in the Midi until the peace could take effect and to give up his Flemish

---

33 *Journal de l'Estoile pour le règne de Henri III*, ed. L.-R. Lefèvre (Paris, 1943), p. 248.
34 N.M. Sutherland, *The Huguenot Struggle for Recognition* (New Haven, 1980), pp. 363–4; Holt, *Duke of Anjou*, pp. 140–1.
35 *Lettres*, vii. 302.

enterprise. News that he was preparing to advance on Cambrai had turned her 'joy into a marvellous perplexity'. She felt sure that Anjou's expedition would bring nothing but ruin and desolation to the kingdom and would change her into 'the most afflicted and desolate mother'. He could not have picked on a worse time for his enterprise, Catherine went on, for if he ceased to oversee the peace of Fleix, the Huguenots of Languedoc and Dauphiné would rise up again and the king would have too much trouble in France to assist him. Nor would Anjou receive any help from abroad, for Elizabeth I did not wish to antagonize Philip II. The Swiss would not help him either, for they were still owed money by France. Spain had friends within France and also a powerful army whereas Anjou had only ruffians in his service. The obligation, which he claimed he had towards the people of Cambrai, had been assumed without the king's consent. Would he really dare to destroy the kingdom simply to honour that obligation? 'Although you have the honour of being the king's brother,' Catherine continued, 'you are nevertheless his subject; you owe him complete obedience and must give preference over any other consideration to the good of the kingdom, which is the proper legacy of your predecessors whose heir presumptive you are.'[36]

Catherine's anxieties were compounded by the king's health. Henry had been unwell since June. In January 1581 he went to Saint-Germain-en-Laye to undergo forty days of purgation. Before retiring, he asked his mother 'to send, command and sign everything for six weeks'.[37] Catherine tried to smother speculation about the king's possible demise by denying that she had been appointed regent, yet uncertainty remained.[38] Anjou promptly resumed preparations for his march on the Low Countries. He planned to raise twenty companies of light cavalry and hoped to receive the necessary funding from his brother, England and the

---

36 *Lettres*, viii. 304–9; Mariéjol, pp. 322–23; Holt, *Duke of Anjou*, p. 143.
37 A. Desjardins, *Négociations diplomatiques de la France avec la Toscane*, iv. 345; Mariéjol, pp. 336–7.
38 *Lettres*, vii. 328.

States-General. His mother was urging him to revive the marriage negotiations with Elizabeth I, which had almost stalled over the question of his rights of worship. On 28 February 1581 French commissioners were appointed to discuss terms with the English government. Catherine hoped that the talks would divert Anjou's attention from the Low Countries, but the reverse happened. Taking advantage of Henry III's absence, Anjou sent his favourite, Fervaques, to relieve Cambrai. He informed Catherine on 1 April that, having given up hope of ever seeing the handover of towns in the Midi completed, he had decided to cease his mediation. Three weeks later, he arrived at Alençon. Panic-stricken, Catherine sent her confidant, the *abbé* Guadagni, to plead with him, and she herself followed close behind. For three days (12–15 May) she begged Anjou to stay in France, but he was obdurate.[39] Soon afterwards, he joined his troops at Château-Thierry.

Catherine, however, had not yet given up hope of winning Anjou over. Early in July she called on him at Mantes, then, on 7 August, at La Fère. Marshal de Matignon, who accompanied her, warned the duke that he was heading for disaster, only to be told by Anjou that he would have had him beaten and thrown out of a window but for Catherine's presence. Since the battle seemed lost, Catherine changed her tack. Feeling that she could not abandon Anjou to his fate, she advised Henry III to support him covertly, but the king was furious with his brother for arming without his permission and for poisoning his relations with Spain. He ordered troops to assemble at Compiègne and ordered the sieur de La Meilleraye to scatter Anjou's army. In order to protect France from a possible counter-attack by Spain, he sent Biron to guard the frontier of Picardy. Catherine, meanwhile, tried to buy off Anjou by pandering to his ambitions. She tried to raise 300,000 *écus* for him, and ordered Puygaillard, who commanded the king's army in Picardy, to cover Anjou's force against a possible Spanish attack. Thus protected, he was able to relieve Cambrai on 18 August, and captured Cateau-Cambrésis on 7 September.[40] Even so,

---

39 Mariéjol, p. 327.
40 P. Chevallier, *Henri III* (Paris, 1985), p. 480; Mariéjol, pp. 328–9.

Catherine was deeply worried. 'I am extremely anxious', she wrote to Du Ferrier on 23 August, 'about the outcome of the voyage on which my son has embarked.'[41]

The queen-mother, meanwhile, continued to press for Anjou's English marriage, but Elizabeth made an Anglo-French alliance against Spain the essential prerequisite to any match. On 30 August Catherine and Walsingham had a conversation in the gardens of the Tuileries. The ambassador expressed surprise that Henry III was not doing more to help his brother. Catherine replied that the king had been assisting Anjou. While she and Henry did not desire a war with Spain, she felt that it would be in the interest of France and England 'to find some means of restoring the Dutch to their liberties'.[42] On 10 September Henry met Walsingham, who made one last attempt to secure a league with France without a marriage. Since his key to success seemed to lie in England, Anjou decided to return there. He landed at Rye on 31 October, accompanied by several gentlemen of his household.

Within a fortnight of Anjou's arrival in England, he and Elizabeth exchanged reciprocal promises and signed a pact without mentioning marriage. On 22 November, however, an extraordinary scene took place at Whitehall palace. As Anjou and Elizabeth were strolling along a gallery, accompanied by the earl of Leicester and Walsingham, the French ambassador asked the queen what he should say to Henry III about her marriage. 'You can write to the king', she replied, 'that the duke of Anjou will be my husband.' At the same moment, she kissed the duke on the mouth and gave him a ring from her finger, whereupon he gave her one of his own. Soon afterwards Elizabeth, addressing her lords and ladies, repeated what she had said, but on the very next day she told Leicester, Hatton and Walsingham that she had no intention of marrying.[43] Anjou, who was probably more interested in her money than in her hand, seemed unperturbed, but Catherine protested to Walsingham about Elizabeth's twists and turns. Most observers, however, believed

---

41 *Lettres,* vii. 391.
42 *Lettres,* vii. 492–7; Holt, *Duke of Anjou,* p. 159.
43 Holt, *Duke of Anjou* pp. 161–2.

that the English marriage had fallen through. On 1 February Anjou left London for the Netherlands, escorted by an imposing array of English lords. He was greeted in Flushing by William of Orange on 10 February, and next day arrived in Antwerp, where he was acclaimed as duke of Brabant.[44]

. . .

THE PORTUGUESE SUCCESSION

On 4 August 1578 King Sebastian of Portugal was killed fighting the Moors in North Africa. He was succeeded by his elderly uncle, Cardinal Henry, whose brief reign was spent trying to sort out the royal succession. Among numerous claimants was Catherine. Dismissing the entire Portuguese royal family as illegitimate, she proclaimed herself the lawful heir of Alfonso III (died 1279) and his wife, Matilda of Boulogne.[45] Henry III formally laid out her claim in a memorandum which was sent to Lisbon. 'It would be no small thing', Catherine wrote on 8 February 1579, 'if these things were to succeed and I was to have the joy of bringing this kingdom to the French by myself and on the basis of my claim (which is not a small one).'[46] Following Cardinal Henry's death on 15 January 1580, she ordered a solemn requiem mass at Notre-Dame from which Henry III absented himself so that everyone should realize that his mother was the chief mourner.

As the cardinal-king had no chosen successor, a regency commission was set up to examine the various claimants to the Portuguese throne. Catherine appointed the bishop of Comminges to present her case. However, Philip II, who had a much stronger claim, was, in any case, determined to unite the Iberian peninsula under his rule. As he threatened force, the Portuguese looked to France for help. Henry III agreed to supply this and his mother set about preparing an

---

44 Ibid., pp. 166–7.
45 For a clear statement of the queen-mother's claim see the 1582 relation of the Venetian ambassador, Lorenzo Priuli in E. Albèri, *Relazioni degli ambasciatori veneti al senato*, 1st series, France, iv. 427–8.
46 *Lettres*, vi. 256.

expeditionary force at Nantes under the command of her cousin, Filippo Strozzi. In June 1580 the Portuguese chose Don Antonio, prior of Crato, as their king, whereupon Philip II promptly invaded their country. On 25 August the duke of Alba entered Lisbon, and Don Antonio fled. He sent money to France so that more troops might be raised for Strozzi's expedition. Later, after Don Antonio had been defeated at Oporto (22 October), he sent an envoy to Catherine, who received him well, proudly declaring to a Spanish witness that she reserved the right to defend her claim to the Portuguese crown, which Philip II had usurped.[47]

Strozzi set sail in December only to be driven back by storms. Catherine, meanwhile, sent a spy to assess the situation in Portugal, while seeking a loan in Venice to pay for Strozzi's army. At the same time she offered asylum in France to any Portuguese subject threatened by persecution from Spain. In March 1581 Don Antonio's agent, the count of Vimioso, met Anjou for talks at Coutras. He carried valuable jewels, hoping to sell them and to hire mercenaries with the proceeds. On 21 April Henry III and Catherine received him at Blois. Rejecting a protest by the Spanish ambassador, Henry III declared that Vimioso was his mother's subject and that she had not given up her claim to the Portuguese throne. He allowed the count to organize an expedition aimed at capturing the Azores, which had not yet fallen into Spanish hands.

Two commanders of the expedition were appointed: Filippo Strozzi, colonel-general of the infantry, and Charles de Cossé, comte de Brissac. Both were the sons of marshals of France; neither had any experience of naval warfare. While Strozzi raised 5,000 troops in Guyenne, Brissac levied 1,200 in Normandy. When the Spanish ambassador complained of their activities, Catherine replied that Portugal belonged to her and that the army was being sent to enforce her rights, but she also hinted that she would give up her claim to the Portuguese crown if Philip II would agree to give one of his daughters in marriage to Anjou.[48] She hoped

47 *Lettres*, vii. 401.
48 Ibid.

that the Low Countries would be part of the dowry. In March 1582, when Catherine felt sure that Anjou's marriage to Elizabeth I was definitely off, she repeated her proposal, but Philip II rejected it as extravagant.[49] Force seemed to be the only option left to the queen-mother.

On 18 March Catherine submitted a long memorandum to Henry III which was a strange mixture of realism and wishful thinking. She explained that she had tried in vain to deter Anjou from going to the Netherlands. He had been warned not to expect help from his brother or to risk losing his favour by levying troops at the expense of his subjects, who had been so hard hit by the civil wars. Yet Anjou needed to withdraw honourably from the Netherlands. His best course of action, Catherine believed, was to return to England and marry Elizabeth. She could no longer refuse him on the ground of not wishing to provoke Philip II, since she had already compromised herself by assisting Anjou's passage to the Netherlands. If the duke was afraid of being turned down by Elizabeth, he ought still to seek her help in finding a wife and establishing a general peace in Christendom. Henry III, too, should urge Elizabeth to help decide Anjou's future. The time was ripe, Catherine argued, for such an initiative. Philip II had neither the will nor the strength to attack France: he was too busy conquering Portugal and holding on to Flanders. One could always guard against the possibility of a surprise attack by fortifying Provence, Saluzzo and Picardy. 'If your brother can maintain himself where he is', Catherine continued, 'and we can keep the Portuguese islands, I firmly believe . . . that he [Philip II] will be willing to treat.' She did not think he would want to bequeath a war with France to his heirs, but she urged Henry not to rely on her advice alone; he should also consult worthy men (*gens de bien*) in his entourage. 'It would grieve me if on my advice alone things were not to materialize as I wish them to do, and if the kingdom were to suffer and you were to be denied the satisfaction which I wish for you.'[50]

Henry III had no intention of ruining himself or jeopardizing his relations with Spain by supporting his brother.

49 Kervyn de Lettenhove, *Les Huguenots et les Gueux* (Bruges, 1883–88),vi. 173 n. 1.
50 *Lettres*, vii. 341–4; Mariéjol, pp. 342–5.

He did not, however, prevent Catherine from alienating some of her revenues and patrimonial lands in order to raise more troops for Anjou. She also sent Bellièvre to advise him on how to manage his affairs. Meanwhile, she tried to hasten the departure of Strozzi's expedition. In October 1581 Catherine met Don Antonio and persuaded him to promise her Brazil, if he should gain the Portuguese throne.[51] On 3 May 1532 she instructed Strozzi to make for Madeira first, then the Azores and, after planting garrisons there, to go on to Brazil. Brissac was to occupy the Cape Verde islands in the meantime.[52] But what exactly was in the queen-mother's mind? Was she seriously interested in founding a colonial empire, or did she have some other motive? Italian observers, who had come to regard her as peace-loving and prudent, were baffled by her policy. A Florentine viewed it as a feminine whim, while Priuli spoke of her 'great desire for glory' (*desiderosissima di gloria*). Spaniards believed that she was trying to give herself a noble ancestry after all those jibes about the 'merchant's daughter'. But, as Catherine herself explained to Priuli, her sole aim was to put pressure on Philip II so that he might reach some 'good composition by means of a marriage'. Now that Anjou's marriage to Elizabeth seemed unlikely, she wanted Philip II to give one of his daughters to her son.[53]

Strozzi's expedition, comprising 55 ships and more than 5,000 men, set sail from Belle-Île on 16 June 1582 and was soon joined at the Sables d'Olonne by another eight ships carrying 800 troops. Among 1,200 noblemen on the expedition were Don Antonio and the count of Vimioso. Strozzi, however, turned out to be a disastrous choice as commander. Instead of obeying Catherine's instructions, he

---

51 Mariéjol, p. 347, who cites H.T.S. de Torsay, *Le vie, mort et tombeau de . . . Philippe Strozzi* (Paris, 1608). See Cimber and Danjou, *Archives curieuses,* 1st series, ix. 444.
52 *Lettres,* viii. 28 n.
53 Mariéjol, p. 349; Albèri, *Relazioni,* 1st series, France, iv. 426. According to C. de la Roncière, 'Le secret de la Reine et la succession du Portugal, 1580–1585', in *Revue d'histoire diplomatique,* xxii (1908), pp. 481ff., Catherine planned to found an overseas empire, but this finds no contemporary echo and seems, on balance, unlikely.

landed on San Miguel, the only island which the Spaniards had so far occupied, and was soon challenged by a large Spanish fleet commanded by the marquis of Santa-Cruz, one of the victors of Lepanto. On 26 July Strozzi attacked, only to be heavily defeated. He himself was killed, as were more than a thousand of his men. Eighty noblemen and 300 soldiers and sailors were captured, but Santa-Cruz had them all executed as pirates. Don Antonio survived, as he was on another island at the time. News of the massacre caused outrage at the French court. Even Henry III, who had so far kept a low profile in respect of Strozzi's expedition, declared that the slaughter must be avenged.[54] Catherine accused Santa-Cruz of poisoning his prisoners before putting them to death. 'If men do not seek revenge,' she declared, 'I hope that God will do so Himself and not allow to go unpunished an act more inhumane and barbaric than any that have been spoken of for a long time between men professing to be soldiers.'[55]

Refusing to be defeated, Catherine decided on a new expedition to the Azores. To lead it, she chose Brissac, but Henry III insisted on the choice being left to his favourite, Joyeuse, who was Admiral of France. The expedition was finally entrusted to Aymar de Chastes. As Henry refused to supply any ships, Catherine asked the French ambassador in Denmark to look for about twenty armed vessels in the Baltic ports. She also asked the king of Sweden to lend her some. When the Spanish envoy, Tassis, protested, she repeated her willingness to sacrifice her own 'private interest' to the peace of Christendom.

The new expedition to the Azores was no more successful than the first. The French landed on Terceira but were hopelessly outnumbered, and on 26 July Chastes made an agreement with Santa-Cruz which allowed his men to be repatriated. They were packed into old hulks with inadequate supplies and half of them died on the way back to France, taking with them Catherine's Portuguese hopes. As

---

54 Mariéjol, pp. 349–50; *Lettres*, viii. 61 n. 2; 405; C.-A. Julien, *Les voyages de découverte et les premiers établissements* (Paris, 1948), pp. 270–5.
55 Cloulas, *Catherine*, p. 462.

the imperial envoy remarked, she had to accept Cambrai as the settlement of her Portuguese claim.

. . .

ANJOU'S DISCOMFITURE

Anjou's installation as duke of Brabant in Antwerp on 19 February 1582 was his finest hour. He revelled in public adulation such as he had never received at home, but once the jubilation had abated, he had to face the daunting task of fighting the duke of Parma. His main concern was the lukewarm support which was reaching him from France. Henry III, who wanted to avoid provoking Spain at all cost, publicly denied any complicity in his brother's activities. 'I will continue to do everything I can', he wrote, 'to persuade him to leave the Netherlands before he suffers the fickleness of its people.' Few, however, believed in the king's honesty. As Cardinal Granvelle wrote to Philip II, 'Anjou does nothing and could do nothing other than what his mother and brother desire, since they are the ones who are paying.' This was true enough. In May, Bellièvre came to Antwerp with 50,000 *écus* for Anjou from Henry III and the promise of more when the king could afford it. The Venetian ambassador believed that the money was 'in order not to alienate his brother completely'.[56] It was not sufficient, however, to maintain Anjou's army; nor was the asssistance provided to the duke by the Dutch States and Elizabeth I. His troops soon began to desert and, by June, Anjou had only about 6,000 foot and 1,000 horse. He tried to hire mercenaries, but they were expensive, yet, at the same time, he squandered his meagre funds on high living. On 9 June he warned Bellièvre that his army was on the verge of mutiny. 'If money is not delivered promptly,' he wrote, 'I will be ruined.' In August he advised Bellièvre that the war would end unless he were given the means to carry on. His anxieties grew as a plot to poison him was discovered. In September his plight was eased somewhat when Elizabeth sent him money, yet by late autumn his army, which was camped outside Antwerp, had shrunk to 3,000 men. Many

---

56 Holt, *Duke of Anjou*, pp. 197–8.

were dying of hunger and cold; others went about begging. 'Everything is falling apart in ruin,' Anjou wrote, 'and the worst part of it is that I was given hopes which have led me too far to back down now ... Thus, I say, that it would be better to promise me only a little money and keep your word than to promise so much and not send anything at all.'[57] On 27 November intensive lobbying by the prince of Orange was rewarded when the States-General agreed to provide 4 million *livres* per year to fund the war, but the money proved difficult to levy. In December Anjou received troop reinforcements from France led by Biron and Montpensier, but they did not solve the shortage of food and supplies in the midst of a harsh winter.

On 17 January 1583 Anjou, now at the end of his tether, tried to seize Antwerp only to see his troops massacred by the inhabitants.[58] News of the event – called 'the French fury' – sent shock waves through the French court. Catherine refused to hold Anjou responsible. Villeroy urged Henry III to strengthen his army. Meanwhile, Orange persuaded the Dutch Estates to negotiate with Anjou, but he refused their terms. He insisted on being given control of a North Sea port whence he might escape more easily if necessary; but he was in no position to bargain. Henry and Catherine, meanwhile, grew extremely nervous. In an attempt to ward off a reprisal attack by Spain, Henry reminded Parma of the numerous attempts he had made to dissuade his brother from going to the Netherlands and promised to persuade him to come home, if he could be assured of a free and safe passage across the frontier. Henry also apologized to the States for the 'French fury' and sent Bellièvre to mend Anjou's relations with them. He carried to Anjou 15,000 *livres* from Catherine and 150,000 *livres* from the king. Greatly cheered by this windfall, the duke signed a provisional treaty with the States in March under which he was allowed to move to Dunkirk. As evidence of their good faith, the States gave him and Biron some money and invited the latter to march to the relief of Eindhoven. Henry III congratulated Bellièvre on his achievement. On 23 April,

---

57 Ibid., p. 179.
58 Ibid., pp. 181–3.

however, Eindhoven capitulated, an event which Anjou once again blamed on the States. Biron moved to Roosendaal, but ran out of cash. After begging and pleading almost daily, he threw up his hands in despair as his men began to desert.[59]

In June, Anjou fled from Dunkirk towards Calais, where he hoped to meet his mother. It was not, however, until 12 July that he met her at Chaulnes. He explained that, without more help from Henry III, Dunkirk and Cambrai would fall to the enemy. In fact, Dunkirk surrendered four days later. Anjou begged his mother for 60,000 *écus* immediately in order to raise more troops in France. She replied that the king was willing to help, but would find it difficult to send any money right away. Moreover, it would not be to raise new troops, but to bring the French army home from the Netherlands. Biron, meanwhile, blamed the States of Flanders for everything. 'The fact is,' he wrote to Catherine, 'Monseigneur your son has been very badly and most unworthily served.'[60] Orange, too, was upset, but his influence was limited. Even Holland, where he was stadholder, was hostile to Anjou on religious grounds. The duke, meanwhile, spent the summer in Picardy, trying to raise new levies. He managed to obtain money from the citizens of Cambrai, but not enough to save Biron's army. His activities, moreover, angered his brother, who was ever fearful of Spanish reprisals. Although unwell, Catherine returned to Picardy early in August accompanied by two secretaries. On 9 August, at La Fère, she scolded Anjou for disobeying the king's orders, but promised him money if he would come home at once. Henry, she said, intended to hold an important council meeting in September and wanted Anjou to be present, but he refused to come. Catherine urged him to negotiate with both the Dutch and the Spaniards and to insist on keeping Cambrai. She sent him money but made sure that he used it to pay his Swiss mercenaries and to bring back Biron's army. Anjou complained that he was not left with enough to pay Cambrai's garrison. In November he moved to Château-Thierry, but was taken ill. Catherine went to see him, but apparently underestimated the gravity of his

---

59 Ibid., p. 191.
60 Ibid., pp. 192–3.

condition. Her main concern was to prevent him coming to terms with the Spaniards; for it was rumoured that he planned to sell them Cambrai. 'The report alone brings so much shame and infamy to France', she wrote, 'that I am dying of discontent and worry at the thought.'[61]

. . .

FAMILY PROBLEMS

In the midst of so many political problems, Catherine also had to sort out troubles within her own family. Her daughter, Marguerite, queen of Navarre, who had returned to the French court without her husband in 1582, was living scandalously. She offended the king by spurning his favourites, Joyeuse and Epernon, and by showing affection to her brother, Anjou. She also became infatuated with the duke's *grand écuyer*, Harlay de Champvallon. In August Henry III was angered by a report that she had been delivered of a bastard. The king, who was on a religious retreat at the time, ordered Marguerite to leave Paris instantly and to rejoin her husband. She promptly decamped with two of her ladies, but Henry sent his archers after them. Marguerite's litter was searched and her ladies sent to a nunnery, where the king interrogated them in person about their mistress. When they failed to incriminate her, they were released and Marguerite was allowed to continue her journey south. Catherine, who learnt of the rumpus rather late in the day, was content to leave its resolution to Henry's 'judgment and discretion'. But his overreaction provided Henri de Navarre with an opportunity to make mischief. He demanded proof of his wife's misconduct and threatened to cast her off unless Henry publicly declared her innocence. Henry had no explanation to offer when Navarre's agent, Duplessis-Mornay, met him in Lyon. Instead, he left his mother to sort out the mess. She sent Bellièvre to Gascony, where Navarre was threatening war and sending appeals for help to his allies in England and Germany. He seized the town of Mont-de-Marsan and demanded that royal troops be removed from the vicinity.

---

61   *Lettres*, viii. 157.

Eventually, he was given satisfaction and forgave Marguerite, who joined him at Porte-Sainte-Marie on 13 April 1584.[62]

Catherine did not blame Henry III for what he had done. 'You know his character,' she wrote to Bellièvre, 'which is so open and honest that he cannot conceal his displeasure.' By contrast, she tried to teach Marguerite good behaviour. Thanking Bellièvre for his efforts, she asked him to admonish Marguerite on her behalf. She was to ensure that her reputation was not endangered by the company she kept, to follow her mother's example and not to provide her husband with an excuse for being unfaithful. Nor should she allow him to take liberties with her ladies-in-waiting. Anticipating a possible rejoinder, Catherine explained that she had only put up with her husband's mistress, Diane de Poitiers, out of obedience and love for him. She urged Marguerite also to obey her husband, while showing him what her love and dignity would not tolerate. Catherine believed that he would respect and love her all the more for doing so.[63]

. . .

THE DEATH OF MONSIEUR (10 JUNE 1584)

Although Anjou was too ill to attend the Assembly of Notables at Saint-Germain on 18 November, he nevertheless kept in touch with events in the Netherlands. While negotiating with Parma, he kept Orange and the States informed of his every move. He may have used the talks as a lever to extract money from Henry III, who sent him 50,000 *écus*. After the garrison of Cambrai had been paid, Anjou's talks with Parma were broken off. The States then informed him that they were prepared to keep him as their prince in exchange for a firm commitment of support from Henry III.[64] This prompted Catherine to return to Château-Thierry on 31 December, but failing to accomplish anything, she soon returned to Paris and fell ill. Anjou went to see her and was warmly received by Henry III. For three days the brothers

---

62 Mariéjol, pp. 356–8; Cloulas, *Catherine*, pp. 469–71; *Lettres*, viii. 171.

63 *Lettres*, viii. 181

64 Holt, *Duke of Anjou*, pp. 200–2.

celebrated carnival together. 'I praise God from the bottom of my heart', wrote Catherine, 'to see them so happy together, which can only be for the good and prosperity of the kingdom's affairs.'[65] Following Anjou's departure on 21 February, she wrote to Bellièvre that her sons were 'so satisfied with each other that I have cause to praise God and to hope for peace and contentment for the rest of my days. I can assure you that this has greatly assisted my recovery and the end of my fever, which was brought on by the worry and sadness that I experienced throughout their separation.'[66]

On his return to Château-Thierry, Anjou informed Orange that Henry III was ready to support his enterprise in the Netherlands, but that his offer was contingent on French troops replacing Dutch ones in several border towns. On 14 March the States warned the duke that Parma had laid siege to Ypres; they urged him to add his forces to theirs without delay. By now, however, his health had seriously deteriorated: he was running a fever and vomiting blood. Catherine rushed to his bedside, as doctors tried to save his life. As late as 18 April she believed that he would have a long life provided that he avoided excess (*quelque grand désordre*). We know that he was dying of consumption but Catherine continued to hope: on 10 May she announced that he had recovered, and, on a subsequent visit to Château-Thierry, she thought his condition had improved. She returned to Saint-Maur only to learn that he had died on 10 June. It has sometimes been suggested that Catherine did not grieve much over Anjou's death. This is disproved by a letter she wrote on 11 June. 'I am so wretched', she wrote, 'to live long enough to see so many people die before me, although I realize that God's will must be obeyed, that He owns everything, and that he lends us only for as long as He likes the children whom He gives us.' Her only solace was the good understanding between her two surviving children – Marguerite and Henry – and the hope that Henry would have children. On 19 June Anjou's embalmed body was taken to Paris by marshal Biron and given a magnificent funeral by Henry III. After a requiem mass at

---

65 *Lettres*, viii. 174.
66 *Lettres*, viii. 175.

Notre-Dame, a procession involving hundreds of people from all walks of life (it took five hours to file through the streets of the capital) carried the body to the basilica of Saint-Denis. Anjou had asked to be buried as 'the duke of Brabant and lord of the Netherlands', but Henry III, ever anxious to avoid upsetting Philip II, decided otherwise, so the duke was buried in a white pall bearing only the arms of Anjou and Alençon.[67]

Anjou, in his will, had left Cambrai to the king of France, but Henry renounced the bequest in favour of his mother. She accepted it and, leaving aside the question of sovereignty, promptly informed the inhabitants of Cambrai that she was taking them under her protection. When Parma demanded the city's return, Catherine's only response was to send marshal de Retz to engage in peace talks with him. Meanwhile, she refused to meet representatives from the States-General and on 29 July, following the assassination of the prince of Orange, merely asked them to keep up their friendship with the French crown. Cambrai was but a crumb crumb compared with the thrones which Catherine had hoped to gain for Anjou in England, the Netherlands and Portugal, yet it was not without importance. For more than ten years it provided France with a forward position against the might of Spain. Far from provoking immediate retaliation by Spain, its occupation actually facilitated the conclusion of a truce with Parma on 15 December 1584.[68]

Anjou's death was an event of tragic significance for France; for Henry III had no children and seemed unlikely to have any after ten years of a sterile marriage. His heir presumptive was his brother-in-law, Henri de Navarre, the leader of the Huguenots. Catholics had reason to fear persecution similar to that which their English co-religionists were suffering at the hands of Elizabeth if he came to power. Even the possibility of his conversion did not placate their doubts, for he had already changed his religion four times. The Guises had already announced their determination to keep a heretic off the throne. Their candidate was the Cardinal de Bourbon. Anjou's death played into the hands

---

67 *Journal de l'Estoile*, pp. 355–6; Holt, *Duke of Anjou*, pp. 206–11.
68 Cloulas, *Catherine*, pp. 484–6.

of the Guises. As the diarist, Pierre de L'Estoile, writes: 'It came at a very opportune time for them, facilitating and advancing the designs of their League, which from that moment grew stronger as France grew weaker.'[69]

---

69 *Journal de l'Estoile,* p. 357.

Chapter 10

THE NEW ARTEMISIA

Historians have all too often assumed that Catherine de' Medici was a superlative patron of literature and the arts because of her Italian birth and her membership of the Medici family, which had produced so many outstanding patrons. We should remember, however, that she left Italy at the age of thirteen never to return, although she remained in touch by correspondence and personal contacts. Her recollections of the villas and palaces in Tuscany and Rome can only have been blurred. Her taste, such as it was, is more likely to have been formed at the court of Francis I, which outshone all the courts of northern Europe during the Renaissance. Here she would have met Italian artists in plenty as well as their French colleagues. Catherine employed Primaticcio, but she is also closely associated with a number of distinguished French artists, including the architects, Philibert de l'Orme and Jean Bullant, and the sculptor, Germain Pilon.

Catherine's intellectual interests were mainly scientific. Ronsard, as we have seen, praised her expertise in geography, physics and astronomy. She was also a fervent believer in astrology, which in the sixteenth century was held to be a respectable science. The poets of the Pléiade celebrated the 'virtues' of the planets, and one of their number, Pontus de Tyard, affirmed the truth of this kind of divination in his *Mantrice*. Believing that the fate of human beings was determined by the stars, Catherine owned a book with pages of bronze on which rotating disks represented the constellations. By manipulating them, she could easily work out the conjunctions essential to the reading of horoscopes and

220

noted down carefully those under which each of her children was born. She frequently consulted leading astrologers of her day and had some of her own, called Régnier and Cosimo Ruggieri. When the queen-mother visited Provence in November 1564, she made a point of calling on Nostradamus at Salon de Crau. He was regarded as the leading prophet of his age after publishing a poem of impenetrable obscurity, called *Centuries*. He pleased Catherine by telling her that her son, Charles IX, would live as long as the Constable Montmorency, who would himself not die before the age of ninety. Alas, on this occasion the prophet was too precise for his own good: Montmorency died, in his seventies, three years later and Charles passed away when he was only twenty-three. Catherine, however, did not hold astrology responsible for the errors of its practitioners, realizing that they were as fallible as other scientists.

Catherine was believed to have had prophetic powers of her own. Numerous witnesses speak of her foreseeing the deaths of her husband and of the prince de Condé. Her daughter, Marguerite, writes in her Memoirs that a bright flame appeared to Catherine each time one of her children was about to die. She would wake up with a start, crying: 'God, defend my children!' (*Dieu, garde mes enfants!*).[1] D'Aubigné states in his *Histoire universelle* that, on 24 December 1574 at Avignon, the queen-mother suddenly woke up, saying: '*Monsieur le cardinal*, I have no need of you!' The Cardinal of Lorraine died at that very moment.[2] For several weeks thereafter, according to L'Estoile, Catherine complained to her chambermaids of seeing the Cardinal's ghost.[3]

The queen-mother also believed in black magic. She became very suspicious of the astrologer Cosimo Ruggieri, after he had become involved with the conspirators around the duc d'Alençon in 1574. A wax doll was found among the personal effects of his friend, La Mole, and Catherine was afraid that Ruggieri might have been sticking pins into it to

---

1   *Mémoires de Marguerite de Valois*, ed. Y. Casaux (Paris, 1971), p. 64.
2   A. d'Aubigné, *Histoire universelle*, ed. A. de Ruble (Paris, 1890), iv. 300–1.
3   *Journal de l'Estoile pour le règne de Henri III*, ed L.-R. Lefèvre (Paris, 1943), p. 55.

bring about the king's death. She informed the chief prosecutor that Ruggieri had asked some very strange questions about Charles IX's health as he was being arrested. 'Make him confess everything . . .', she wrote, 'so that the truth may be known about the king's health and that he may be made to undo any spell that he has cast to endanger his health or to make my son fall for La Mole.'[4] Ruggieri inspired so much fear that he was sentenced to only nine years in the galleys. He was soon released and restored to royal favour.

In addition to believing that the stars could influence the health and lives of human beings, Catherine and her contemporaries were particularly attentive to unusual celestial phenomena, such as comets and eclipses, viewing them as signals of divine wrath or as portents. Her life was particularly susceptible to such happenings. A comet was seen in 1533 at the time of her marriage and another in 1560, when her son, Francis II, died. The birth of Charles IX in 1550 was soon followed by an eclipse of the sun. In addition to an exploding star between 1572 and 1574, comets appeared in 1577, 1580, 1582 and 1585, a frequency which disturbed even the most hardened sceptic. The year 1582 was particularly prolific in heavenly manifestations, leading to what Denis Crouzet has described as 'a spectacular pulsation of eschatological anguish which seized France on the eve of the League's creation'.[5] It may have been at this time that Antoine Caron painted his *Astronomers observing an eclipse of the sun*, containing symbols which may point to the destiny of Catherine's two surviving sons.[6]

One of the strangest features of the Hôtel de la Reine, which Catherine built in Paris, was a tall Doric column, commonly known as *la colonne de l'horoscope*. It survives today next to the domed Bourse du Commerce. Inside the hollow

---

4   *Lettres*, iv. 296–7.
5   D. Crouzet, *Les guerriers de Dieu* (Paris, 1990), ii. 287.
6   *L'Ecole de Fontainebleau* (exhibition catalogue, Grand Palais, Paris, 1972), pp. 32–3; L. Golson, 'The approach to science of a Renaissance painter. Research into the theme and background of the Astronomers Studying an Eclipse by Antoine Caron', G.B.A. (1963), pp. 202–14.

column is a staircase leading to a platform, capable of carrying three persons, topped by an iron cage, from which one could observe the sky. The purpose of the column has never been explained, but, as it was the only one of its size in Paris, it would have been a useful observation post. According to tradition, it was also used by Catherine's astrologers to scan the heavens.[7]

. . .

THE NEW ARTEMISIA

Catherine was acutely superstitious. She fussed over dates and would never do business on a Friday, which she described to Henry III as 'my unlucky day, for it was the day your father was wounded, which brought us – to me principally and to the whole kingdom – so much harm that I cannot see myself ever doing anything worthwhile on that day'. Although Henry II had not been the best of husbands, Catherine mourned him for the rest of her life. She never put aside her widow's weeds, except for the marriages of her sons, and she directed much of her artistic patronage towards the immortalization of her grief.

Thus the column at the Hôtel de la Reine, in addition to its possible use as an observatory, was also a memorial. Embedded in the fluting are various ornaments carved in the stone – fleurs-de-lis, cornucopias, shattered mirrors, torn love-knots and the letters 'C' and 'H' intertwined, all of them symbols of Catherine's conjugal piety.

In February 1562 Nicolas Houël, a Parisian apothecary, scholar, philanthropist and art patron, published a long poem, called *L'Histoire d'Arthemise*.[8] He intended it to be a fitting monument to Henry II and to Catherine's achievement as queen and regent. Artemisia II was the widow of Mausolus,

---

7   D. Thomson, *Renaissance Paris. Architecture and growth, 1475–1600* (London, 1984), pp. 175–6; J.-P Babelon, *Paris au xvie siècle*, pp. 141–2; J.-H. Mariéjol, *Catherine de Médicis* (Paris, 1920), p. 215.

8   Houël created a school of pharmacy in Paris in 1576 and four years later a botanical garden, the ancestor of the present-day Jardin des Plantes. See Babelon, *Paris au xvie siècle*, pp. 83, 254.

prince of Caria (352–350 BC), who built the Mausoleum of Halicarnassus, one of the seven wonders of the ancient world, to commemorate her grief over his death. She also vanquished his enemies and educated his children, five of whom became kings. The parallel with Catherine is obvious. Each of the four books into which Houël's poem is divided plays on three themes: contemporary events and artistic achievements, descriptions of Artemisia's life and times, and the elaborate funeral ceremonies and monuments which she erected. Houël is particularly interested in architecture, giving over whole chapters to the construction of pyramids, obelisks, ancient epitaphs, the temple of Diana and so forth. In his dedication to Catherine, he writes: 'You will find here the edifices, columns and pyramids that she had constructed and built both at Rhodes and Halicarnassus, which will serve as remembrances for those who reflect on our times and who will be astounded at your own buildings – the palaces at the Tuileries, Montceaux, and Saint-Maur, and the infinity of others that you have constructed, built, and embellished with sculptures and beautiful paintings.'[9]

Seventy-four drawings, representing important events in the life of Artemisia, were commissioned from the painters Niccolò dell'Abbate and Antoine Caron to illustrate Houël's poem, of which fifty-nine survive. Each of Caron's forty-four drawings has a fine border, showing the arms of France and of the Medici with the motto *Ardorem Testantur / Extincta Vivere Flamma*. Catherine's tears, though abundant, were not enough to extinguish the flame of her love for Henry II. Also visible in the borders are scythes, broken mirrors, scattered pearls and floods of tears.[10] The drawings were subsequently turned into tapestries, but, if any were woven for Catherine, they have not survived. The same theme, however, was used for tapestries made in the seventeenth century for two other royal widows who served as regents, Marie de' Medici and Anne of Austria. Among the scenes represented in the drawings are the funeral procession of Mausolus, the burning of his body, the building of the

9 M. McGowan, *Ideal Forms in the Age of Ronsard* (Berkeley, Calif., 1985), p. 126.
10 *L'Ecole de Fontainebleau*, p. 37.

temple where his ashes were deposited, and the education of his son, Lygdamis. Other scenes depict Artemisia's works of peace: the building of palaces, the designing of parks and of gardens containing aviaries and menageries.

According to Vasari, Catherine wanted Michelangelo to carve Henry II's equestrian statue, but he excused himself on account of his age. The commission was accordingly passed on to Daniele Ricciarelli, alias Daniele da Volterra, who, overcoming many difficulties, managed to cast the horse in bronze before his own death in 1566.[11] Giambologna (Jean Boulogne), a Flemish sculptor employed by the Medici in Florence, was asked to provide the king's statue, but he failed to deliver. Only the horse ever reached France, where it eventually served for Louis XIII's equestrian statue in the Place Royale in Paris. It was melted down in 1793 during the French Revolution.[12]

Another of Catherine's commissions proved more successful. This was the marble monument designed to contain Henry II's heart, which was carved by Germain Pilon and Domenico del Barbiere. It was originally set up in the convent of the Celestins in Paris and is now at the Louvre. The statue consists of an urn (which is a nineteenth-century restoration) resting on the heads of the three Graces, representing the theological Virtues and standing back to back. With their long necks and small heads they remind one of Primaticcio's nymphs at Fontainebleau, while the folds of their drapery fall with exquisite grace. The monument has been described as 'one of the summits of our sculpture'.[13]

By far the most important memorial raised by Catherine to her late husband was the chapel of the Valois, a circular building which was to be added to the end of the north

---

11 G. Vasari, *Lives of the Painters, Sculptors and Architects*, ed W. Gaunt (London, 1963), iv. 79–80; C. Avery, *Giambologna* (London, 1993), pp. 159–61.

12 C. Avery, 'An equestrian statuette of Louis XIII attributed to Simon Guillain (1581–1658)', *The Burlington Magazine*, cxxvi (Sept. 1984), pp. 553–6.

13 H. Zerner, *L'art de la Renaissance en France* (Paris, 1996), p. 354. See also *Germain Pilon et les sculpteures français de la Renaissance*, ed. G. Bresc-Bautier (Paris, 1993), pp. 16–21, 284–7.

transept of the abbey of Saint-Denis. In the middle was to stand the tomb of the king and queen, which was begun in 1563 on Primaticcio's design, the sculpture being carried out by Pilon. Very little, it seems, was erected by the time Primaticcio died in 1570. Two years later, Jean Bullant took charge of the work, and, when he died in 1578, he was succeeded by Baptiste du Cerceau. The building was carried up to the top of the second Order by 1585, but was then abandoned, presumably because of the political situation. It was left to decay, then demolished. The chapel in its general design harked back to Italian models by Bramante or Michelangelo, but it was different in having six chapels – one for each of Henry II's sons and two for the altar and entrance – instead of four or eight. The external division into two storeys, each with its Order, from which emerges the drum that carries the dome recalls Sangallo's design for St. Peter's in Rome, which Primaticcio must have seen in 1540–41.[14]

Although the chapel of the Valois was never completed, several of the monuments which it was to house survive. The tomb of Henry II and Catherine, designed by Primaticcio and executed by Pilon, stands among the other royal tombs in the basilica of Saint-Denis. It has been called 'the last and most brilliant of the royal tombs of the Renaissance'.[15] Like those of Louis XII and Francis I, it carries two sets of effigies: on the top, the *priants* – the king and queen, as living effigies in bronze, kneeling in prayer – and, below, their *gisants* or cadavers in white marble. However, the monument is generally simpler than its predecessors. Narrative bas-reliefs have been eliminated and the mortuary chamber opened up so as to offer a better view of the *gisants*. By limiting ornamentation, the sculpture has been enhanced. The *gisants* have also been treated in a novel way: the king recalls the body of Christ as shown in Renaissance *pietàs*, while his queen seems to be asleep rather than dead.

---

14 A. Blunt, *Art and Architecure in France, 1500–1700* (Harmondsworth, 1957), pp. 54–5; H. Zerner, *L'art de la Renaissance en France. L'invention du classicisme* (Paris, 1996), pp. 351–4.

15 Zerner, *L'art de la Renaissance*, p. 349.

The cardinal Virtues – tall statues in bronze – stand at each corner of the monument. The base is adorned with marble reliefs of the theological Virtues, the fourth side being given over to the first of the works of charity: giving drink to the thirsty.

The *priants* are unconventional in one major respect. Henry II instead of clasping his hands in prayer, as Catherine is doing, holds his right hand up to his chest and stretches out the left. His gesture is incomprehensible in the absence of a missal resting on a prie-dieu, which were removed and melted down during the French Revolution. Zerner questions the common assumption that the *priants* represent the king and queen in their earthly existence. He suggests that they are already beyond death and are presenting themselves to God in anticipation of His judgment. The king's gesture may thus be taken to refer to his defence of Catholic orthodoxy. Such a radical departure from traditional iconography is unlikely to have been made by the artists without consulting Catherine or her councillors.

The anomaly may be related to another pair of *gisants*, also of Henry II and Catherine, which Pilon executed as from 1583. Whereas the imagery of Henry's tomb is almost sensual, these additional *gisants*, ostentatiously draped in their coronation robes and wearing crowns, are as rigid as any thirteenth-century ones. They are also cruelly realistic: Catherine is portrayed with her face bloated over a double chin. These *gisants* were meant to flank the high altar of the chapel. Fixed in motionless prayer, they would have attended the eternal round of masses which the priests of the abbey were expected to say for them. The absence of any religious ornamentation from Henry's tomb, apart from the theological Virtues, should not be taken as evidence of a secular trend. The tomb was intended to face a chapel containing Pilon's grandiose *Resurrection*. If the chapel had been completed, the tomb would have been part of 'a grand ritualistic drama which would have filled the rotunda's celestial space and in which the visitor/spectator would have participated fully'.[16]

---

16   Ibid., pp. 349–54.

. . .

CATHERINE'S BUILDINGS

Ronsard criticized Catherine de' Medici for preferring masons to poets, and it is a well-attested fact that she favoured architecture above all the arts. Both Jacques Androuet du Cerceau the Elder, the first of an important dynasty of architects, and Philibert de l'Orme dedicated treatises to her in the certain knowledge that she would read them. In the dedication of his *Architecture* (1567), Philibert expresses his admiration 'as your good judgment (*bon esprit*) shows itself more and more and shines as you yourself take the trouble to project and sketch out (*protraire et esquicher*) the buildings which it pleases you to commission'. Elsewhere, Philibert writes of the queen-mother, who with 'an admirable understanding combined with great prudence and wisdom' has taken the trouble 'to order the organization of her said palace (the Tuileries) as to the apartments and location of the halls, antechambers, chambers, closets and galleries, and to give the measurements of width and length'. Catherine was not content with a cold classicism; as Philibert explains, she ordered him 'to make several encrustations of different kinds of marble, gilded bronze and of minerals, like marcassites' both externally and internally. He liked to decorate his Orders, but at the Tuileries she compelled him to take down some Ionic columns which were not rich enough for her taste.[17]

Catherine's earliest foray into architecture was at the château of Montceaux-en-Brie, which Henry II had given her in August 1556. It consisted of two long wings with a pavilion at each end. They were linked by a third wing with a central pavilion containing a straight staircase. An important feature of the garden was an alley for playing *pall-mall*, a form of croquet. As Henry was particularly fond of this game, Catherine thought of covering the alley with a wooden roof, and turned to Philibert de l'Orme, who had recently invented a new method of building such a roof at minimum expense. However, she commissioned something more ambitious: namely, a 'grotto' comparable to that which the

---

17   A. Blunt, *Philibert de l'Orme* (London, 1958), p. 99.

Cardinal of Lorraine had just built at Meudon. The Montceaux 'grotto' took the form of a tall two-storey building standing on a base made to look like a natural rock. A reception room or *salle,* on the same level as the garden alley served as a vantage point from which people might follow a game in progress while taking refreshments. Nothing survives of this 'grotto', which was completed in the spring of 1558.[18]

Following her husband's tragic death, Catherine abandoned the old palace of the Tournelles, which had become hateful to her.[19] She had it destroyed and sold the site. In 1563 she decided to build a new residence close to the Louvre but outside the walls of Paris. This was the Tuileries, named after the tile factory formerly on the site. As architect, Catherine surprisingly employed Philibert de l'Orme, who had been dismissed as *surintendant* after Henry II's death. She may have been touched by his *Instruction,* a work written during his disgrace in which he rebutted the charges levelled by his enemies and pleaded for fairer treatment.[20] If an engraving by the contemporary artist Jacques Androuet du Cerceau is to be believed, the Tuileries was to be a vast palace with three courtyards, the two smaller ones being divided by large oval halls. But, as Blunt has demonstrated, du Cerceau's plans and elevations 'are not consistent among themselves, and . . . do not agree in detail with what was already built'. Some of the features shown (e.g. the two oval halls) 'have no parallels in the work of De l'Orme and their peculiar curved forms are contrary to his general principles'.[21] It is likely, in fact, that de l'Orme never intended the scheme shown by du Cerceau. Instead, he may have planned a smaller palace based on a single courtyard with double pavilions on one side and single ones on the other. Little of this scheme, moreover, was actually built, for de l'Orme died in January 1570 and, two years later, Catherine stopped the work. It has been suggested that she did so under the influence of a fortune teller who had told

---

18 J.-P. Babelon, *Châteaux en France au siècle de la Renaissance* (Paris, 1989), pp. 691–2.
19 Babelon, *Paris au xvie siècle,* p. 240.
20 Blunt, *Philibert de l'Orme,* pp. 88–9.
21 Ibid., pp. 92–3.

her that she needed to avoid Saint-Germain if she wanted to live for a long time. The Tuileries was in the parish of Saint-Germain l'Auxerrois. But the story is suspect, since Catherine continued to visit the palace, notably in 1573, when she received the Polish ambassadors who had come to offer the Polish crown to the duc d'Anjou. She probably abandoned the Tuileries for security reasons. Being outside the walls of Paris, it was vulnerable to attack in a period of civil unrest.[22] For whatever reason, the Tuileries was never finished; much of it was pulled down under Louis XVI and the rest destroyed by the Communards in 1871.

According to du Cerceau, Catherine decided before 1576 to connect the Louvre with the Tuileries. The first part of this link was the *Petite Galerie*, designed by de l'Orme or Lescot. Only the ground floor, however, was built in part or completely in Catherine's lifetime. At some time after de l'Orme's death work also began on a pavilion at the southern end of the incomplete de l'Orme wing of the Tuileries. The architect was Jean Bullant, who evidently planned to extend the Tuileries to the river Seine, whence a gallery might be run towards the southern extremity of the *Petite Galerie*. The style of Bullant's pavilion is far less adventurous and experimental than de l'Orme's wing.[23]

In 1572 Catherine began looking for the site of a new residence within the walls of Paris, but she wanted it big enough for a garden. She evidently wanted a residence of her own, distinct from the king's residence at the Louvre. But she retained her apartment at the Louvre and divided her household between the two establishments. It seems to have doubled in size as a result. Between 1575 and 1583 the number of her ladies-in-waiting rose from 68 to 111 and other categories of personnel followed suit. In 1585 Catherine's household comprised nearly 800 persons, including 86 ladies-in-waiting, 25 maids of honour and 40 chambermaids and nurses.[24] Those who could not be accommodated under her roof took up lodgings close by.

22　I. Cloulas, *Catherine de Médicis* (Paris, 1979), p. 323; Babelon, *Paris au xvie siècle*, p. 210.

23　Thomson, *Renaissance Paris*, pp. 172–4.

24　Cloulas, *Catherine*, pp. 330–1.

Catherine created a space for her new residence by sweeping away an entire built-up area in Paris. She began by purchasing the Hôtel Guillart, near the church of Saint-Eustache. With the pope's permission, she moved the convent of the *Filles Repenties,* an order dedicated to reclaiming young girls from prostitution, to the rue Saint-Denis.[25] The convent was demolished, save for the chapel. Catherine also acquired and pulled down the Hôtel d'Albret and other houses nearby. On the site of all these buildings, Jean Bullant built a new palace for Catherine, called the Hôtel de la Reine. It has almost entirely disappeared, but its appearance is known from engravings by Israël Silvestre of about 1650 and a plan of about 1700. These show a central wing, a courtyard and gardens. In the middle of the central wing, consisting of three pavilions, was a large arch flanked by two tall projections decorated with pilasters. All that remains of the Hôtel de la Reine is the tall fluted Doric column, described above.[26]

Outside the capital, Catherine's building activity was mainly focused on two châteaux: Saint-Maur-les-Fossés and Chenonceaux. She purchased Saint-Maur from the heirs of Cardinal Jean du Bellay and employed de l'Orme to complete it. He submitted a plan which she rejected as inadequate for the needs of her large entourage, whereupon he added two pavilions at each end of the main block. On the garden side the pavilions were joined by a terrace carried by a cryptoporticus. Saint-Maur was unfinished when de l'Orme died. At some date after 1575 another project was launched by an unidentified architect. He doubled the pavilions on the garden side, raised them by two storeys and crowned them with high pitched roofs. Two more arches were built over the cryptoporticus and this part of the building was given a colossal, even grotesque, pediment; but this too was

---

25 Babelon, *Paris au xvie siècle,* pp. 229, 232.
26 F.-C. James, 'Jean Bullant, Recherches sur l'architecture française du xvie siècle', *Positions des thèses de l'Ecole des Chartes,* (1968), pp. 101–9; F. Boudon, A. Chastel, H. Couzy and F. Hamon, *Système de l'architecture urbaine: Le Quartier des Halles à Paris* (Paris, 1977).

only partially carried out and the house seems not to have been habitable until the late seventeenth century.[27]

In 1560 Catherine forced Diane de Poitiers to exchange Chenonceaux for Chaumont, but it was not until 1576 that she assigned large revenues to building work at Chenonceaux. This consisted of two galleries on the bridge which Bullant almost certainly designed. A drawing and engraving by du Cerceau show a vast scheme, which Catherine allegedly had in mind, but, as Blunt has argued, this may have been just a fantasy. Du Cerceau 'sometimes inserted in his book designs embodying ideas which he himself would have liked to see carried out rather than those of the actual designer of the building in question'.[28]

Catherine was fond of gardens, where she liked to conduct much of her business. Although work on the Tuileries stopped in 1572, the gardens were already laid out and were admired by visitors. In addition to flowerbeds, canals and fountains, there was a grotto adorned with animals – snakes, tortoises, lizards, frogs and birds – in glazed pottery by Bernard Palissy. A large walled garden attached to the Hôtel de la Reine included avenues of trees in addition to flowerbeds, a lake with a jet of water, an aviary and an orangery, 48 metres long and made of timber, which could be dismantled each winter for reassembly later. At Chenonceaux, Catherine did much to embellish the gardens. She brought water from neighbouring springs, created waterfalls, laid out three parks, set up an aviary of exotic birds and an enclosure of rare animals. She also added new stocks to the existing vineyard and planted mulberry trees for the rearing of silkworms. Chenonceaux had its own spinning-mill and in 1582 Catherine set up a silk factory at Orléans.

Catherine's building programme was expensive. An account for the year 1581 shows that she spent a total of 8,898 *écus* on the Hôtel de la Reine and 760 *écus* on Saint-Maur. The total cost of all her building activities that year was 10,027 *écus*.[29] Such extravagance did not endear the queen-mother among the king's subjects, especially the Parisians,

---

27 Blunt, *Philibert de l'Orme*, pp. 89–91.
28 Ibid., p. 64.
29 Cloulas, *Catherine*, pp. 328–30, 339.

who were continually being asked for contributions. Ronsard echoed their feelings in a poem dedicated to the Trésorier de l'Epargne:

> *Il ne faut plus que la reine batisse,*
> *Ni que sa chaux nos trésors appetisse . . .*
> *Peintres, maçons, engraveurs, entailleurs*
> *Sucent l'épargne avec leurs piperies.*
> *Mais que nous sert son lieu des Tuileries?*
> *De rien, Moreau: ce n'est que vanité*
> *Devant cent ans sera deshabité.*[30]

> *The queen must cease building,*
> *Her lime must stop swallowing our wealth . . .*
> *Painters, masons, engravers, stone-carvers*
> *Drain the treasury with their deceits.*
> *Of what use is her Tuileries to us?*
> *Of none, Moreau; it is but vanity*
> *It will be deserted within a hundred years.*

. . .

LITERATURE AND THE THEATRE

Catherine liked books and collected them, believing that they were an essential adornment of a royal palace. Until her day, the royal library had moved about a good deal, from Blois under Louis XII to Fontainebleau under Francis I. Pierre Ramus, the well-known mathematician and philosopher, begged Catherine to bring the library to Paris and to install it in the university quarter, where it might more easily accessible to scholars. She responded by moving it to Paris, but kept it at the Louvre, where it remained until Henry IV moved it to the Collège de Clermont.

Following the death of Piero Strozzi in 1558, Catherine acquired the collection of precious manuscripts which he had inherited from Cardinal Ridolfi, the nephew of Pope Leo X. She persuaded Piero's widow to sell it to her for 15,000 *écus*, but she never paid up. When Catherine died, her creditors tried to seize the collection, but scholars protested

---

30 Ibid., p. 322.

and Henry IV ordered the books and manuscripts – 4,500 volumes in all – to be added to the royal library.[31]

Catherine enjoyed the company of learned men. She had accredited poets – Pierre de Ronsard, Rémy Belleau, Jean-Antoine de Baïf and Jean Dorat – whom she protected and employed on writing the programmes of her court festivals. Although not as well read in the classics as Marguerite de Navarre or Marguerite de France, Catherine belonged to their intellectual circle. She was particularly interested in Italian literature. Tasso, who came to France in 1571 as the secretary of Cardinal d'Este, presented his *Rinaldo* to her, and she sent him her portrait as a token of her admiration. She must also have been generous to Aretino to qualify for his fulsome praise: 'Woman and goddess serene and pure, the majesty of beings human and divine'.

Shortly before Henry II's accidental death, he and Catherine attended a performance at Blois of *Sophonisba*, a tragedy by Trissino translated from the Italian by Mellin de Saint-Gelais. It was performed for royal marriages and persons of high rank, including princesses, who acted in it wearing magnificent costumes. The acts were divided, as in comedies, by musical interludes, unrelated to the plot, which praised the king and his court. According to Brantôme, Catherine became convinced after her husband's death that the play had brought him bad luck and refused thereafter to see any more tragedies. Thus it has been said that her conjugal piety inspired a new type of drama: tragicomedy. But the fact that tragedy went out of favour at the court after 1570 may have been part of a general revulsion from the violence of the times. The first tragicomedy to be performed at the French court was *Ginevra,* an episode from Ariosto's *Orlando Furioso* in a French version by an unknown poet. It was staged at Fontainebleau on 13 February 1564.[32]

Catherine was not responsible for bringing the *Comédie italienne* to France during the reign of Charles IX, as is sometimes claimed. The first well-organized troop of Italian players, who came to France in March 1571, were invited by

31 E. Frémy, *Les poésies inédites de Catherine de Médicis* (Paris, 1885), pp. 239–42; *Lettres*, i. 563.
32 M. Lazard, *Le théâtre en France au xvie siècle* (Paris, 1980), pp. 152, 220–30.

Louis de Gonzague, duc de Nevers, whose brother, the duke of Mantua, was passionately keen on the theatre. By February 1572 two companies of Italian players, calling themselves *I Gelosi*, were working in Paris. Charles IX invited them to Blois, where they helped him to pass the time during three weeks that he spent dieting. They returned to Paris in time for the celebrations in honour of the Navarre marriage in August. Under Henry III a more sophisticated troop, also called *I Gelosi*, came to France at the king's bidding after he had seen them perform in Venice on his return from Poland.[33] Catherine, we are told, greatly enjoyed their performances. She did not even mind their risqué humour, but she disapproved of obscenity. After seeing *Le Brave*, an adaptation by Baïf of a play by Plautus, at the Hôtel de Guise on 28 January 1567, she urged the author to look to the work of Terence, but to avoid the 'lascivious talk' of the ancients.[34]

In a famous letter of advice to her son, Catherine recalled the court of his grandfather, Francis I. The old king used to say that two things were necessary to live at peace with the French and to retain their love: they needed to be kept happy and occupied with some honest exercise, otherwise they were likely to engage in dangerous pursuits.[35] Taking this advice to heart, Catherine seems to have made a conscious effort to divert the French nobility from fighting each other by keeping them entertained at court. Among its principal adornments were her ladies-in-waiting, numbering about eighty, whom she recruited from the noblest houses in France. Some who regularly accompanied her on her progresses became known as her 'flying squadron' and were allegedly used by her to seduce courtiers for political ends.[36] According to Jeanne d'Albret, the court of France was a sink of iniquity where the women, not the men, made the sexual advances, but Jeanne was an austere Huguenot, who may

---

33 A. Baschet, *Les comédiens italiens à la cour de France* (Paris, 1882), pp. 1–70.
34 Mariéjol, pp. 223–4.
35 *Lettres*, ii. 92. La Ferrière dates this letter 1563, but Mariéjol argues (pp. 142 n. 1 and 269 n. 5) that it was actually written in 1576.
36 See BN, ms. fr. 7854, ff. 13–35 for a list of Catherine's ladies.

have exaggerated the temptations which Catherine's circle held for her son.[37] According to Brantôme, Catherine's court was not only an earthly Paradise but 'a school of all honesty and virtue', yet it seems that she could be very broad-minded at times. On 9 June 1577 she threw a banquet in the grounds of Chenonceaux in honour of her son, Anjou, following his capture of La Charité. The meal was served by topless young ladies.[38]

. . .

COURT FESTIVALS

Catherine's court was notable for its lavish entertainments. Brantôme writes of her liberality 'similar to that of her great uncle Pope Leo and of the magnificent lord Lorenzo de' Medici'. He singles out three occasions on which she displayed it: Fontainebleau in 1564, Bayonne in 1565 and Paris (the Tuileries) in 1573. It was at Fontainebleau, on the eve of her 'grand tour' of France, that Catherine first made an impact on the traditional chivalrous pastimes of the French court. The so-called 'magnificences' lasted several days and included 'a tournament and breaking of lances, combats at the barriers and all kinds of war games (*jeux d'armes*)'. Several were jousts in fancy dress and in allegorical settings. Twelve knights – six on each side – dressed as Greeks and Trojans fought over ladies imprisoned in an enchanted tower on an island. Another entertainment was a water-show in which sirens swam in the canals and greeted the king with songs. Neptune floated by in a chariot drawn by sea-horses. This plot of water-creatures doing obeisance to the monarch became something of a stereotype. Such entertainments have been construed as an attempt by Catherine to bring Huguenots and Catholics together in chivalrous pastime. At the same time, she may have been seeking to buttress the king's authority: the sirens were 'gentle deities of nature whose cosmic powers support the power of the French monarchy'.

The Bayonne summit in 1565 enabled Catherine to show

---

37 Mariéjol, p. 143.
38 Brantôme, *Oeuvres*, ed. L. Lalanne, vii. 377.

that France, in spite of her domestic troubles, was still capable of putting on a magnificent spectacle. If Brantôme is to
be believed, the 'magnificence was such in everything that
the Spaniards who are very contemptuous of all others, save
their own, swore that they had never seen anything finer'.[39]
But Alba's letters suggest that they merely served to irritate
him as distractions from the serious business which he
believed needed attention.[40] Several printed accounts exist
of the entertainments at Bayonne. Most were based on the
normal pastimes of the court, held to the accompaniment of
verse recitations, set to music and in splendid costumes. A
banquet held on the île d'Aigueneau on 23 June was particularly lavish. Guests were taken there in splendidly
decorated boats, enabling them to watch on the way fisher-
men harpooning an artificial whale which spewed red wine
from its wounds. They also encountered six tritons sitting on
a large turtle, blowing conch shells, Neptune in a chariot
pulled by sea-horses, Arion riding on two dolphins, and
sirens singing praises of the royal guests. On the island, they
were treated to regional dances performed by girls dressed
as shepherdesses, and invited by sirens to celebrate the
accord between France and Spain. The banquet was
followed by a ballet of nymphs and satyrs. Next day, a
tournament was fought between British and Irish knights,
Charles IX leading the former and his brother Henri the
latter. Cartels (challenges issued at the start of a tournament)
were recited to music, and the subject of the contest –
'Virtue and Love' – was represented by two chariots: one,
drawn by four white horses, contained ladies symbolizing
the five virtues; the other carried Venus and Cupid,
accompanied by many little cupids. The ladies distributed
devices similar to those displayed by the knights on their
shields. The climax came when the knights cut across one
another without touching, while little balls of fire were
thrown among the horses. The event, which took place in a
special enclosure, was accompanied by music and musical
recitation. The royal grandstand was adorned with superb

39 Ibid. x. 73.
40 *Papiers d'état du Cardinal de Granvelle* (Paris, 1852), ix. 281–330.

tapestries depicting the *Triumph of Scipio,* which Francis I had commissioned from Giulio Romano.[41]

No *Livret* or *recueil* was published describing the festivals given for the fateful wedding of Henri de Navarre and Marguerite de Valois. Nearly all that is known about them comes from Protestant writers who, in the light of the subsequent massacre, viewed them with grave suspicion. They seem to have followed the pattern already used in 1564 and 1565. One of the entertainments planned was a fort which was to be attacked by Coligny and his co-religionists and defended by the king and the Catholics, but it was dropped because Coligny did not feel well enough to take part. An entertainment which did take place was a procession of chariots shaped like rocks on which were perched marine gods and sea creatures. Another was the 'Paradise of Love' in which twelve nymphs were defended by the king and his brothers against Navarre and his Huguenot companions, who were sent to Hell but rescued by Mercury and Cupid. The nymphs celebrated, dancing a long and elaborate ballet. This was followed by a combat between the knights during which explosions of gunpowder filled the hall with fire and smoke. On the last day, before the attempted assassination of Coligny brought the festivities to an abrupt end, a running at the ring took place at the Louvre. Several groups of contestants presented themselves, including the king and his brother attired as Amazons, Navarre and his men as Turks wearing turbans and long golden robes, Condé and others as Albanian stradiots, and Guise and his friends, also dressed like Amazons.

In August 1573, one year after the St. Bartholomew's Day massacre, Paris was again *en fête,* this time for the Polish ambassadors who had come to offer their country's crown to the duc d'Anjou. They were treated to tournaments, mock combats, barriers and running at the ring or at the quintain. Catherine also treated them to a splendid 'festin' at the Tuileries, described by Jean Dorat in his *Magnificentissimi spectaculi.* This work, in Latin verse and including French verses by Ronsard and Amadis Jamyn, describes a ballet with illustrations. Sixteen nymphs representing each French

---

41   F. Yates, *The Valois Tapestries* (London, 1975), pp. 55–60.

238

province appeared on a moving rock from which they descended to dance a long and intricate ballet designed by Beaujoyeulx. They distributed devices to the spectators. Brantôme calls this 'the finest ballet that was ever given in this world' and defends Catherine's expenditure on such shows which bring France so much prestige.[42] D'Aubigné tells of the astonishment of the Poles, who declared that 'the ballet of France was something which no king on earth could imitate'.[43] Brantôme explains that 'all these inventions' were due to Catherine alone. Her 'magnificences' exceeded all others. She often said that she wished to imitate the Roman emperors, who set out to keep their subjects from misbehaving by giving them games and amusements. 'The question of Italian influence on the French *ballet de cour* seems solved,' writes Yates. 'It was invented, in the context of the chivalrous pastimes of the court, by an Italian, and a Medici, the Queen Mother. Many poets, artists, musicians, choreographers, contributed to the result, but it was she who was the inventor, one might perhaps say, the producer; she who had the ladies of her court trained to perform these ballets in settings of her devising.'[44]

Under Henry III a spectacular fête was given in the Salle Bourbon in Paris in celebration of the marriage of the duc de Joyeuse and Marguerite de Lorraine, Henry's sister-in-law, on 24 September 1581. About seventeen entertainments were given each day after the wedding for about a fortnight. They included tournaments in allegorical settings, a water fête, an equestrian ballet and a wonderful fireworks display. Elaborate temporary buildings, designed by the best artists of the day, were put up in the streets and squares and the various shows were accompanied by music. The dominant artist employed for the 'magnificences' was Antoine Caron, who was assisted by Germain Pilon. Jean Dorat designed their works, Ronsard and Desportes wrote the verses and Claude Le Jeune the music. According to a manuscript programme, a combat on foot between the king and the dukes of Guise, Mercoeur and Damville was staged on 19

42 Brantôme, 'Discours sur la Royne Mère', *Oeuvres complètes*, ed. P. Mérimée (Paris, 1890), x. 76.
43 A. d'Aubigné, *Histoire universelle*, ed. de Ruble, iv. 179.
44 Yates, *Valois Tapestries*, p. 68.

September. They fought over Love in what was, in effect, a musical dramatization of Petrarch's *Trionfi*. On 24 September another combat took place, this time between the king and the dukes of Guise and Mercoeur. The king's entry 'took the form of a marine triumph in which a great ship was preceded by Tritons and Sirens playing various instruments and sorts of music, with drums'. The programme announces another entertainment in which 'twelve torch bearers will be men and women disguised as trees ... the golden fruits of which will carry lamps and torches'. Dorat probably helped to design the visual decorations and to write the verses under the pictures and on the triumphal arches. One arcade, dedicated to the newly-weds, shone like the full moon, while the other, dedicated to the king, was like a flaming sun. Echoing the sun–moon theme were the white and yellow liveries of twenty-eight combatants. The arcades were linked to a great amphitheatre containing 'cabinets' representing the planets and constellations. Among these artificial heavens were allusions to Catherine's rainbow, Henry III's three crowns and to the twin stars of Castor and Pollux. The theatre, designed by Montjosieu, seems to have served as the background for a dramatic entry by the king, dressed as the Sun in a sun-chariot.[45]

The most famous of the Joyeuse 'magnificences' was the *Ballet comique de la reine,* which was offered by Queen Louise, who employed her own team of poets and musicians. The music, provided by ten groups of singers and players inside a 'golden vault', aimed at producing 'effects', while the plot and themes of the entertainment were an invocation of cosmic forces to come to the aid of the monarchy. The theme was the transference of power from the enchantress Circe to the royal family. At one end of the hall, where the entertainment was given before a large crowd of spectators, was Circe's garden before whom passed men who had been turned into beasts. The action opened with a man's escape from the garden. After crossing the hall, he begged the king to deliver the world from the sorceress. In the ensuing drama she was defeated by an alliance of the Virtues and

---

45 Ibid., pp. 82–8; F. Yates, *Astraea. The imperial theme in the sixteenth century* (London, 1975), pp. 149–72.

Minerva with the celestial world, expressed through ballets based on symbolic geometrical figures and danced by the queen, the bride and other ladies. When the Four Cardinal Virtues entered, wearing star-spangled robes, they appealed to the gods to descend from heaven. Circe's defeat was assured by the descent of Jupiter, sitting on an eagle signalled by a loud clap of thunder and accompanied by the 'most learned and excellent music that had ever been sung or heard'. Jupiter was a 'fortunate star' brought down by powerful music to protect France from the horrors of war and to strengthen and bless her monarchy.[46] At the end, all the performers knelt before Henry III, 'showing that they were ceding to this great king the power to command, the wisdom to govern and the eloquence to attract the hearts of the men furthest removed from duty; all of which virtues and powers he owed to the wise counsels, instructions and conduct of the queen his mother'. To round off the show, Catherine caused the queen to give her husband a gold medal on which was depicted a dolphin swimming in the sea, a clear expression of her fervent desire that he should soon have a male heir to carry on the dynasty.[47]

. . .

CATHERINE AS ART COLLECTOR

Catherine was an avid collector of works of art and curiosities of all kinds. This is borne out by an inventory of the movables at the Hôtel de la Reine, which was drawn up in August 1589, after her death.[48] Apart from tapestries, the contents of the her residence included, on the ground floor, twenty-five maps 'drawn by hand' of different parts of the world, more than 135 pictures and several works of sculpture. On the first floor were 341 portraits, many by Pierre and Cosme Dumoustier and Benjamin Foulon, Catherine's official painters. There were 259 pieces of Limoges ware. One room in the Hôtel de la Reine had walls covered with

---

46 F. Yates, *The French Academies of the Sixteenth Century* (rev. edn. London, 1988), pp. 236–50.
47 Cloulas, *Catherine*, p. 359.
48 E. Bonnaffé, *Inventaire des meubles de Catherine de Médicis en 1589* (Paris, 1874).

Venetian mirrors. Her study was lined with cupboards adorned with landscape paintings and filled with objects of all kinds: leather fans, dolls attired in different costumes, caskets, a stuffed chameleon, Chinese lacquer, numerous games and pious objects. Hanging from the ceiling were seven stuffed crocodiles and innumerable stags' heads. Around the room were a collection of minerals, some terracotta statuettes and four small cannon. In a cupboard between two windows were books – including a set of architectural plans – which Catherine liked to have readily accessible. Altogether she had about 4,500 books, including 776 manuscripts. The latter, however, were kept in a separate building in the rue Plâtrière with their own custodian. The printed books were at Saint-Maur. Finally the inventory lists many costly fabrics, ebony furniture inlaid with ivory and 141 pieces of china, probably from Palissy's workshop. The Hôtel de la Reine, in short, was 'as lavishly equipped and richly furnished as any of the palaces and châteaux belonging to the crown'.[49]

A major item missing from Catherine's inventory is the set of eight huge and magnificent tapestries, usually called the Valois tapestries, now in the possession of the Uffizi gallery in Florence (unfortunately they have not been on public display for several years). It is likely that they once belonged to Catherine and that she gave them to her grand-daughter, Christina of Lorraine in 1589 on the occasion of her marriage to Ferdinand de' Medici, Grand Duke of Tuscany.[50] No one knows for certain who ordered, designed and made the tapestries or for whom. However, certain facts are clear. They are based on six (originally eight?) drawings made during the reign of Charles IX by Antoine Caron and subsequently modified by another artist, who added groups of full-length figures in the foreground. Most of them are easily recognizable as Henry III and members of his family and court. His brother, François, duc d'Anjou, figures prominently in some of the tapestries. In all except one, Catherine de' Medici, dressed in her widow's weeds, occupies a more or less central position. Other recognizable

---

49 Thomson, *Renaissance Paris*, p. 20.
50 Yates, *Valois Tapestries*, pp. xxv–xxvi, 124–9.

figures include Henry's queen, Louise de Lorraine. The presence of the Polish ambassadors, who came to the court of France in 1573 and can be identified by their distinctive costumes, helps to date the tapestries. Other figures are not so easily identified. On the right of the tapestry showing the French court on the move outside the château of Anet is a group of three unknown noblemen. Nearly all the tapestries depict festivals that took place at the court of Charles IX, notably at Fontainebleau in 1564, Bayonne in 1565 and the Tuileries in 1573, yet Charles IX is absent, all the identifiable portraits belonging to the next reign.[51]

Among the scholars who have tried to explain the Valois tapestries, none has shown as much learned ingenuity as Frances Yates. She has identified the designer as Lucas de Heere, who had worked in France for Catherine during the reign of Francis II. He knew the geographer, Abraham Ortelius, and the topographical artist, Georg Hoefnagel, from whom he may have acquired the interest in topography and costume that is reflected in his modifications of Caron's drawings.[52] De Heere seems also to have consulted the published accounts of the festivals, so that he was able to represent them more accurately and bring them up-to-date. Yates reads into the tapestries allusions to the Joyeuse 'magnificences' of 1581.[53] She also identifies the three un-known noblemen as Louis of Nassau, Christopher of the Palatinate and Henry of Nassau, and argues that the court in that tapestry is shown travelling to Blamont, where they met and negotiated with Henry III and Catherine.[54] But who commissioned the tapestries? Yates suggests that they were made in Antwerp, paid for by the city, commissioned by William of Orange, and sent as a diplomatic gift to Catherine with a view to persuading her and Henry III to support Anjou in the Netherlands.[55] She also reads a 'politique' intention in the tapestries depicting the coming of the Polish ambassadors to the French court in 1573 and argues that Charles IX was deliberately excluded from the

---

51 Ibid., pp. 6–12.
52 Ibid., pp. 13–24.
53 Ibid., pp. 82–8.
54 Ibid., pp. 73–81.
55 Ibid., pp. 25–38.

tapestries because of his involvement in the St. Bartholomew's Day massacre. However, Yates' theory is difficult to accept. It is very unlikely that William of Orange would have relied on a gift of tapestry to bring about a major policy shift by the French crown. Catherine and Henry were afraid of intervening in the Netherlands for fear of provoking a war with Spain. They are unlikely to have changed their minds in response to a gift of tapestry, however magnificent. Yates' conviction that a 'politique' agenda, shared by Orange, Anjou, Catherine and Henry, needed only an artistic prompt to undergo a revival flies in the face of all the historical evidence. The notion that Catherine was an Erasmian is fanciful. The tapestries remain an enigma. Almost certainly they were meant to glorify the ruling house of Valois against the background of its spectacular festivals. Further we cannot go without indulging in wishful thinking.

Catherine's patronage was by no means outstanding. To call her 'the French Medici' is misleading. Unlike her father-in-law, Francis I, she never invited leading artists from Italy or elsewhere to work for her in France; she was content to employ native talent, which was often of a high order. Philibert de l'Orme was a great architect, who evolved a distinctively French style of building; Germain Pilon was a wonderful sculptor whose works are not only accomplished but also psychologically revealing. Painting seems to have interested the queen-mother far less, perhaps because it had sunk to a low ebb in her day. Portraits loom large in the inventory of her goods, and one suspects that she looked upon them rather as a mother today would cherish an album of family photographs. By accident or design her patronage has proved ephemeral. Even the chapel of the Valois, which she had intended as a lasting memorial to her adoptive dynasty, was never finished. Interested as she was in architecture, she seems to have quickly lost interest in a particular project, either because it was too expensive or unsuited to her needs of the moment. Thus the Tuileries palace was never finished. Her literary patronage was not particularly distinguished either. She employed some good poets and musicians, but her choice of bedside reading – *Les Abus du monde* by Gringore, the *Book of Sibyls,* the Gregorian calendar, and a genealogy of the counts of Boulogne (her maternal ancestors) – hardly points to a keen literary appreciation.[56] Only in the realm of extravagant court festivals, combining dancing, music and poetry, did Catherine leave her mark. She was a Renaissance impresario to whom ballet and opera in our own age are distantly indebted.

---

56 Bonnaffé, *Inventaire*, p. 85.

Chapter 11

APOCALYPSE

At sixty-six, Catherine de' Medici was very old by sixteenth-century standards. She was also in poor health, yet she continued to play an active role in politics. Her son, Henry III, behaved like a spoilt child, often crossing her and listening to his favourites, especially the duc d'Epernon, who made her out to be feeble or timid, or too well disposed towards the house of Guise. Yet Henry knew from experience that in a crisis he could depend on his mother's help. Never did he need her more than after the death of his brother, the duc d'Anjou, which precipitated a succession crisis. For Henry III had no children and seemed unlikely to have any after ten years of a sterile marriage. Under the Salic law, the heir presumptive was his brother-in-law, Henri de Navarre, the leader of the Huguenots. The prospect of being saddled with a Protestant monarch horrified Catholics, who had only to look across the Channel to see how their English co-religionists were being persecuted by their Protestant queen. Even if Navarre were to prove more tolerant than Elizabeth I, they could not believe that he could be lawfully king without being anointed with the sacred balm or crowned by a Catholic prelate.

Not every Catholic, however, was displeased by the new situation. Anjou's death was a godsend to the Guise family. As L'Estoile writes: 'It came at a very opportune time for them, facilitating the designs of their League, which from that moment grew stronger as France grew weaker.'[1] In

---

1   *Journal de l'Estoile pour le règne de Henri III (1574–1589)*, ed. L.-R. Lefèvre (Paris, 1943), p. 357.

September 1584 Henri, duc de Guise, his brothers, the duc de Mayenne and Cardinal de Guise, and two other noblemen, had founded an association at Nancy designed to exclude Henri de Navarre from the throne. They looked for support to Pope Gregory XIII, but he refused to back a movement hostile to Henry III, whose Catholic credentials were unimpeachable. Philip II of Spain, however, had no such scruples: he could not easily forgive the house of Valois for the support it had given, however imperfectly, to the Dutch rebels. Thus he allowed his representatives to sign a treaty with the Guises at Joinville on 31 December 1584. The parties undertook to defend the Catholic faith and to extirpate heresy in France and the Netherlands. They recognized Cardinal de Bourbon – Navarre's sixty-five-year-old uncle – as heir to the throne. On becoming king, he was to apply the decrees of the Council of Trent to France, renounce her alliance with the Turks and stop French privateering against Spanish shipping. Philip II, for his part, agreed to subsidize an armed rising by the League.[2]

Military operations began almost at once. Guise began to raise troops in many parts, hired 6,000 Swiss troops, recruited mercenaries in Germany and built up stocks of weapons everywhere. His kinsmen, the dukes of Elbeuf, Aumale and Mercoeur, led uprisings in Normandy, Picardy and Brittany. Mayenne occupied Dijon, Mâcon and Auxonne; La Châtre gave him Bourges, and Entragues, Orléans. The governor of Lyon, Mandelot, razed the citadel which had controlled the city. While southern and western France stayed loyal to the king or to the Protestant cause, nearly all the provinces in the centre and north declared for the League. By the end of May, Guise had assembled at Châlons 25,000 infantry and 2,000 cavalry. Henry III's response was to hire Swiss mercenaries and take steps to defend Paris against a surprise attack. At the same time, he looked to his mother to defuse the crisis diplomatically.

Catherine was alarmed in March 1585 when she learnt that troops disbanded by Parma were coming to France to serve under Guise. She had always been afraid of a war between France and Spain and viewed with serious mis-

---

2   J.-M. Constant, *La Ligue* (Paris, 1996), p. 115.

givings the alliance of the Guises with Philip II. She wrote to Guise, saying that she could not believe he was being disloyal to the crown after all the assurances he had given her.[3] On 31 March, however, the duke published a manifesto at Péronne urging Catholics to prepare to defend their faith. The king's ministers were accused of paving the way to the throne for a heretic and of depriving other nobles of titles and power so as to control the king's forces themselves. The manifesto also called for taxes to be reduced and for regular meetings of the Estates-General.[4]

.   .   .

THE PEACE OF NEMOURS (7 JULY 1585)

In March 1585 Catherine travelled to Epernay in Champagne hoping to meet Guise, but he was in no hurry to see her. When eventually he did turn up on 9 April, he complained that his actions had been misconstrued and of various dangers facing the Catholic faith, but Catherine thought he was using religion to cover his real purpose, though she could not elicit from him what precisely this was.[5] Following his departure, she turned for help to her son-in-law, the duke of Lorraine, who offered his mediation, which Catherine urged her son to accept.[6]

The queen-mother's stay at Epernay was bedevilled by ill-health. In addition to all her usual ailments (colics, catarrh, rheumatism), she now suffered from a persistent cough, an earache, a pain in her side and thigh, gout, toothache and bouts of sickness. On 22 April the king's physician, Miron, bled her to save her lungs from 'overheating', as he explained to the king. For much of the time Catherine had to negotiate from her bed. She also found writing difficult, but could count on the support of the secretary of state, Claude Pinart. Catherine's correspondence, which is remarkably complete for this period, is almost entirely in his hand. She dictated to him from her bed, often in a great

---

3   I. Cloulas, *Catherine de Médicis* (Paris, 1979), p. 498.
4   Ibid., pp. 499–500; J.-H. Mariéjol, *Catherine de Médicis* (Paris, 1920), pp. 368–9.
5   *Lettres,* viii. 245
6   *Lettres,* viii. 250–1.

hurry, while he sat at its foot. Pinart's despatches were received at court by his fellow secretary, Pierre Brulart, who acted as his intermediary with the king. He kept Catherine regularly posted on events in other parts of France.[7]

The leaders of the League, knowing Catherine's state of health, hoped that she would soon return to Paris, but this did not happen. However, as she grew tired of waiting for the Guises to return, she talked of negotiating with Henri de Navarre instead. The king had already sent Epernon to persuade him to change his religion, and Catherine may have been thinking along the same lines. The threat brought Guise and Cardinal de Bourbon back to the negotiating table, where, on 29 April, they offered a fortnight's truce. Catherine hoped to elicit from the garrulous cardinal some indication of the League's intentions, but he merely stressed the urgency of achieving religious unity. Henry III was, in fact, willing to revoke the edict of pacification, but was not prepared to hand over towns to the League as guarantees of his good faith. Catherine knew, however, that sooner or later he would have to give in.[8] This became obvious during a new round of talks with Guise and Cardinal de Bourbon at Jalons. News that Henry had banned the Protestant religion throughout France caused the cardinal to clasp his hands in thanksgiving, but he went on to explain that more was needed to satisfy the League; heresy, he insisted, had to be rooted out completely. In other words, the king needed to make war on the Huguenots. Guise then pointed out that the safety of the League had to be guaranteed. He demanded a written statement to this effect from the king. Catherine now understood that Henry's only hope of standing up to the League was to build up his forces, for, as she put it, 'peace is carried on a stick'.

When Catherine next met Guise and the cardinal, they asked for a large number of towns to be ceded to them as sureties and for governors and captains, who had joined the League, to have their offices confirmed or restored by the king. Catherine tried to curtail these demands before Henry

---

7   N.M. Sutherland, *The French Secretaries of State in the Age of Catherine de Medici* (London, 1962), pp. 258–9.
8   *Lettres*, viii. 275.

proceeded to do likewise. When his reply was read out, however, Cardinal de Bourbon flew into a towering rage. He claimed that the Leaguers had not demanded the sureties for themselves, only for their faith. When Catherine retorted that the duke and the cardinal ought to be pleased by the king's reply, they walked out in disgust. When they returned a few hours later, she offered a few concessions, but they refused to consider them. This time it was Catherine's turn to fly into a temper: she reproached them bitterly for wasting her time 'with so many disguises' and threatened to go next day, but the duke of Lorraine was able to save the talks. The queen-mother pointed out how unreasonable it was to expect her son to dismiss loyal servants in favour of Leaguers; but Guise repeated that his demands were meant to safeguard Catholicism. Catherine complained that her concessions were never enough to satisfy him and his friends.[9] The cardinal virtually admitted as much in a letter to Madame de Nevers: 'The queen talks of peace, but we ask for so much in the interest of our religion that I do not think our demands will be granted.'[10]

As she began to lose hope, Catherine instructed the secretary of state, Villeroy, to inform the king that he would never have peace unless he gave in to the Leaguers. She offered to give up her role of negotiator. 'I await in great devotion your instructions,' she wrote to Henry, 'for I dare not leave without knowing what they are.' She was anxious to speak to him alone even for only one hour. 'I only complain of my role,' she said, 'if it avails you nothing.'[11] The king had just received an ultimatum from the Leaguers, who claimed that they only wanted to promote and advance God's glory and to extirpate all heresy without damaging the state. They asked Henry for an unconditional edict against the heretics. They, on their part, offered to abandon all sureties except those that depended on his favour, on their innocence and on the goodwill of worthy men (*gens de bien*)[12]. As they delivered this ultimatum, the Leaguers

---

9 *Lettres,* viii. 310.
10 *Lettres,* viii. 292 n 1.
11 *Lettres,* viii. 316.
12 *Le Premier Recueil de pièces concernant les choses les plus mémorables advenues sous la Ligue . . .* 1590, p. 325; Mariéjol, p. 375.

moved their troops forward. Catherine feared an attack on Paris, where Guise enjoyed strong support. 'Take care,' she wrote to Henry, 'especially around your person; there is so much treachery about that I die of fear.'[13] The king promptly ordered the gates of Paris to be made more secure, purged the militia of potential traitors, and created a new royal bodyguard – the famous 'Forty-five' – young noblemen who were ready to die for him.

In June Henry III sent Villeroy to Epernay without having any clear idea of what he expected him to do. He hoped against hope that Villeroy might be able to avert a war. The upshot of his mission was the treaty of Nemours, signed on 7 July, which amounted to a humiliating capitulation by the king.[14] He agreed to pay for the League's army and conceded a number of surety towns. The lion's share went to Guise, whose clients also received favours, pensions and governorships. At a *lit de justice* on 18 July, the Parlement registered an edict banning all Protestant worship. All pastors were ordered to leave the kingdom immediately, their flocks being allowed six months in which to abjure or go into exile. Protestants were debarred from all public offices and were to hand over surety towns in their possession. Setting aside the Salic law, the edict deprived Navarre of his rights to the throne. Catherine's enemies accused her of complicity with the League, but her letters show that she accepted the peace only to avoid a damaging war. Henry III would not have been able to resist the League on his own; he would have had to ally with the Huguenots, which would have inflamed the situation. Catherine had chosen the lesser of two evils. Religion probably played no part in her decision. She gave way to the League on account of its superior strength, not because of its faith. Sacrifices, she believed, were necessary in order to gain time and allow Fortune's wheel to turn to one's advantage.[15] Other members of the king's entourage, however, were less sanguine. Villeroy believed that the peace would bring only

---

13 *Lettres,* viii. 290.
14 E. Haag, *La France Protestante* (Paris, 1846–59), x. 184–7; N.M. Sutherland, *The Huguenot Struggle for Recognition* (New Haven, 1980), p. 364.
15 Mariéjol, p. 376.

fire, blood and desolation to France. He likened the kingdom to a man, who, emerging from a fever, feels even more debilitated than during the crisis of his illness. He saw its total ruin as an inexorable process which had to be worked through.[16]

The peace of Nemours left the Huguenots with no option other than to fight for survival. Navarre was so shocked when told of the treaty that half his moustache turned white. In several letters to Catherine he refused to endorse the settlement. 'I am bound to oppose with all my strength', he declared, 'those who wish to cause the ruin of the crown and house of France.' On 10 August he and Condé met Damville near Lavaur and renewed the alliance between the Huguenots and the 'United Catholics'. In a joint manifesto, they accused the Guises of trying 'to extinguish the house of France and to take its place'. While affirming their belief that Protestantism was indestructible, the Huguenot leaders promised to respect Catholicism, its adherents, having always believed that consciences should be free. Reaffirming their loyalty to the crown, they explained that they had no choice but to fight the League.[17]

Henry III may have hoped to get round the peace of Nemours as he had evaded the Peace of Monsieur, but the situation had changed since 1576. Dissatisfaction was rife in the kingdom. The reforms contained in the Ordinance of Blois (1579) had been largely ineffective: justice was still poorly administered, civil war endemic, pillaging by soldiers common, taxes were heavier than ever, and offices continued to be sold. Furthermore, the price of bread had doubled since 1578, causing much hardship among the urban poor. All this, in addition to the personal unpopularity of Henry III and his *mignons*, played into the hands of the Leaguers. Among towns supporting them, Paris was the most radical. It had set up a League of its own in 1584 which was run by a committee, called the Sixteen (*Les Seize*). From the beginning it had close relations with Guise. Hundreds of printed pamphlets warned the people that the

---

16 Sutherland, *French Secretaries of State*, p. 264.
17 Mariéjol, p. 379.

Huguenots were planning a massacre of Catholics as well as Navarre's succession to the throne.[18]

Catherine advised Henry III to prepare for war, but he dragged his feet. He believed that he had been let down by his mother and resented the fact that the League had forced his hand. Pique may have prompted him to quarrel with the new pope, Sixtus V, who strongly favoured the League. He forbade a new nuncio to travel into France further than Lyon, whereupon the pope expelled the French ambassador from Rome. The dispute upset Catherine, who knew that Henry needed the pope's consent to tax the French clergy. 'If I had a voice,' she wrote, 'I would please kings and popes until I had forces to command and not to obey.'[19] She even offered to go to Rome to placate Sixtus, and complained when the bishop of Auxerre was sent instead.

On 9 September Sixtus V excommunicated Navarre and debarred him from the succession to the French throne.[20] Henry III refused to publish the bull, but copies circulated widely. On 11 October Navarre formally protested to the Parlement. Meanwhile, in alliance with Damville, his followers strengthened their hold on Guyenne and Languedoc. In Dauphiné, they seized several towns, and in Poitou, Condé repulsed an invasion led by Mercoeur, only to be soon defeated by Henri de Joyeuse (the favourite's brother). Catherine claimed this victory as a demonstration of Henry III's commitment to the Catholic faith. She suggested that Guise should join him in an act of thanksgiving, but the king was becoming more of a religious recluse each day and showing little enthusiasm for the war. In December he walked all the way to Chartres and refused to see anyone. Catherine followed him there to remonstrate with him. She warned Henry that he was damaging his health and giving his ministers an impossible task. He set to work for a week, but soon returned to Vincennes and asked not to be disturbed while he fasted and prayed.[21]

---

18 Constant, *La Ligue* pp. 25–32.
19 *Lettres,* viii,. 350–1.
20 J.-P. Babelon, *Henri IV* (Paris, 1982), pp. 345–7.
21 Sutherland, *French Secretaries of State,* pp. 264–5.

. . .

LA REINE MARGOT

The struggle between Henry III and the League was not Catherine's only concern. The reconciliation of her daughter, Marguerite, with her husband Henri de Navarre had been short-lived. He had fallen madly in love with Diane d'Andouins, better known as 'la belle Corisande', who evidently hoped to usurp Marguerite's place. In March 1585 Marguerite left Nérac to settle at Agen. Whether or not she joined the League is uncertain, but she certainly raised troops and fortified Agen. Catherine was, at first, sympathetic. She sent her daughter money after learning that she could not afford to feed herself properly. Their relations, however, soon turned sour. Henry III was furious to learn that Marguerite had applied to the duke of Lorraine for asylum and Catherine, too, was angered by her irresponsible behaviour. Writing to Bellièvre (15 June), she described Marguerite as 'this creature' whom God had sent to her as a punishment for her sins, and as her 'affliction', yet she did not abandon her completely.[22] After Marguerite had been expelled from Agen by the inhabitants, Catherine offered her asylum at Ibois, but she preferred to go to Carlat, a fortress deemed impregnable, where she remained until 13 October 1586. By now everyone knew that she had taken a lover in the person of a petty nobleman, the seigneur d'Aubiac. It was even rumoured that she had borne him a child. Appalled by her conduct, Catherine urged the king to arrest her without delay, 'otherwise', she said, 'she will bring shame upon us again'.[23] She urged Villeroy to ensure that Henry removed this 'insufferable torment'; but the king had already ordered Canillac, the governor of Upper Auvergne, to arrest his sister and to imprison her in the château of Usson. 'I want her to be referred to simply as "sister" in the letters-patent,' he instructed, 'not as "dear" or "well-beloved"; delete such words.' He added: 'The queen enjoins me to have Aubiac hanged and that this should be done in the presence of that wretch (*seste miserable*) in the courtyard of

---

22 *Lettres*, viii. 318.
23 *Lettres*, ix. 513.

the château of Usson.' Aubiac, however, was sent to Aigue-perse, where he was interrogated and executed.[24]

Believing that her days were numbered, Marguerite sent a valedictory letter to Catherine begging to be allowed a female companion who would vindicate her reputation one day. Any shame to which she was subjected, she warned, would tarnish her family's reputation. Finally, she asked for her servants to be paid their wage arrears. However, Marguerite's luck soon turned. After Canillac had met some prominent Leaguers in Lyon, he set Marguerite free. Had she seduced him? This is unlikely. Other, more prosaic, reasons may be suggested for her release. The Guises had an interest in Marguerite's survival for her elimination by murder or banishment to a nunnery would have left Navarre free to remarry, thereby dashing Guise hopes of eventually reaching the French throne. Marguerite may also have bribed her gaoler, for we know that she gave him all her rights in Auvergne, as well as money and a pension. Having regained her liberty, she turned for help to Philip II and to Charles IX's widow, Elizabeth of Austria. She may also have tried to mend her relations with Henry III, but she never returned to Paris. She spent the next fourteen years in Auvergne, outliving her mother and brother. Significantly, Catherine cut her out of her will.[25]

· · ·

HENRI DE NAVARRE

The queen-mother always underestimated Henri de Navarre, regarding him as a scatterbrain. Though certainly foolish in affairs of the heart, he was politically astute. For several months, Catherine hoped to persuade him to return to the Catholic faith, or at least to leave the Protestant camp. That was her purpose when she travelled south, accompanied by Pinart, in July 1586. Navarre agreed to meet her, while he secretly negotiated with marshal Biron, the royal commander in western France. Once he had signed a truce with

---

24 *Lettres*, ix. 108–9 n. 1 where the letter is wrongly dated Oct 1586 instead of 6 January 1587.
25 E. Viennot, *Marguerite de Valois* (Paris, 1995), pp. 175–8.

him in August, Navarre played for time. He knew that Henry III was under pressure from the German Protestant princes to renew religious freedom in France and that his armies were desperately short of cash. Catherine, however, was willing to endure any amount of fatigue for her son's sake; so, pressing on with her mission, she tracked down Navarre to the château of Saint-Brice, between Cognac and Jarnac. As her right arm continued to give her pain, nearly all her letters at this time were written by Pinart.[26] Meanwhile, Villeroy sent her news of the military situation in western France and gave her almost her only news of the king, who was hiding from the public. While he recalled his armies from the field and began to disarm, Guise remained under arms.[27]

Catherine's first encounter with Navarre was an ill-tempered exchange of recriminations. She was only able to secure a promise that he would consult his advisers. Next day, he and Condé asked for a two months' truce so that they might call representatives of the Protestant churches and write to their friends abroad. Two further meetings proved equally fruitless. Catherine vainly tried to persuade Navarre to become a Catholic again and to ban Protestant worship in towns under his control. She offered him a year's truce in return, but he explained that he lacked the authority to impose such a ban.[28] The subject of his marriage may also have cropped up at Saint-Brice. Catherine, as we know, had fallen out with her daughter and if Claude Grouard, president of the Parlement of Normandy, is to be believed, she suggested that Marguerite might be eliminated so that Navarre might be free to remarry. The allegation was later confirmed by Henry IV himself, though he sometimes liked to talk for effect. Marshal de Retz, to whom Grouard owed his story, had attended the talks at Saint-Brice, but was hostile to Catherine. More reliable is a letter written by Henry III to his mother in January 1587 in which he warns against Navarre being allowed to remarry in Marguerite's lifetime. Were he to do so, wrote the king, he would impugn

26 Sutherland, *French Secretaries of State*, p. 271.
27 Ibid., p. 273.
28 Babelon, *Henri IV*, pp. 369–72; Cloulas, *Catherine*, pp. 525–6.

the legitimacy of his line and would become Henry's 'chief enemy'.[29]

Navarre took care not to break off his talks with Catherine until a force of *reiters*, which he had been promised from Germany, was at hand. After dragging his feet for as long as possible, he sent the vicomte de Turenne to negotiate with the queen-mother. When Turenne offered her Protestant help to restore the king's authority which the League had destroyed, she understood that she had been taken for a ride and the talks ended on 7 March 1587. In the meantime, Catholic opinion in France was outraged by the execution in England of Mary, Queen of Scots. A torrent of abuse directed at Elizabeth I and her Huguenot allies poured out of the League's pulpits and presses. Henry III was accused of betraying Mary and it was rumoured in Paris that ten thousand Huguenots were preparing to avenge the St. Bartholomew's Day massacre. In February, Henry shut himself up in the Louvre after learning of a plot to kidnap him and to force him to hand over power. The League offered to defend the kingdom against the German *reiters*, who were about to invade France in order to join Navarre. While Guise besieged Sedan and Jametz, towns belonging to the duc de Bouillon, Aumale seized towns in Picardy, a province likely to become strategically significant, as Spain prepared to launch her Armada against England. Already it was becoming evident that a grand Catholic crusade, in which the League would co-operate with Spain, was under way.[30]

In May 1587 Catherine was sent on yet another abortive errand, this time to Reims, where Guise and Cardinal de Bourbon agreed to extend a truce recently signed with Bouillon, but refused to hand over the towns of Doullens and Le Crotoy to the duc de Nevers, whom the king had appointed as governor of Picardy. Catherine blamed her failure to achieve more on shortage of time.[31] In August

---

29 Ibid., pp. 526–7; Mariéjol, pp. 387–8.
30 De Lamar Jensen, *Diplomacy and the Catholic League: Bernardino de Mendoza and the French Catholic League* (Cambridge, Mass., 1964), pp. 152–9; G. Mattingly, *The Defeat of the Spanish Armada* (London, 1959), pp. 193–213.
31 *Lettres*, ix. 219.

1587 Henry III announced that he would take the field at the head of his army. He left Paris on 12 September and took up a position on the Loire with the aim of preventing a link-up between the German *reiters* and Navarre's forces. Meanwhile, he sent Joyeuse to fight Navarre in the west. Catherine was left in charge of the government in Paris and, working closely with Bellièvre and Villeroy, did all she could to assist the war effort.[32]

On 25 October Catherine was dismayed to learn that Joyeuse had been defeated near Coutras by Navarre, but better news followed: the relief army from Germany, after failing to cross the Loire, pushed westward towards the Beauce, only to fall apart. As the *reiters* set off on their own, they were defeated twice – at Vimory (26 October) and Auneau (24 November) by Guise. Meanwhile, the Swiss, who had fought the king, agreed to go home in return for four months' pay and, on 8 December, the *reiters* were bought off too. Henry III returned triumphantly to Paris on 23 December. He attended a *Te Deum* at Notre-Dame and organized a splendid funeral for Joyeuse. Catherine rejoiced over what she described as a miracle sent by God to show that He loved the king and his kingdom, but the real victors were the king's enemies: Guise and Navarre.[33] The League's preachers praised the duke's heroism without which 'the ark would have fallen to the Philistines'. The Sorbonne decreed that a ruler whose conduct was unacceptable could be deposed. The pope criticized Henry for using the clergy's money to buy off the kingdom's invaders. The king then provoked the League's fury by giving Epernon offices previously held by Joyeuse: he became governor of Normandy and Admiral of France. Guise had wanted the governorship as his reward for defeating the *reiters*.[34]

. . .

THE DAY OF THE BARRICADES (12 MAY 1588)

Early in 1588 Guise and other principal Leaguers met at Nancy and drew up a list of demands for the king. They

---

32 Mariéjol, pp. 391–2; *Lettres*, ix. 249, 251, 254–5, 260–1.
33 *Lettres*, ix. 312.
34 P. Chevallier, *Henri III* (Paris, 1985), pp. 610–12.

asked him to join the League unconditionally, to banish non-Leaguers from his council and all major offices of state, to publish the decrees of the Council of Trent and to establish the Inquisition in France. The Leaguers also asked for more fortified towns to be ceded to them and for the king to pay troops stationed in and about Lorraine. The goods of heretics were to be sold and a third or a quarter of the property of heresy suspects was to be confiscated for the duration of the war. Religious prisoners were to be executed unless they agreed to live as Catholics in future.[35] Henry III, however, avoided answering these demands. The League, meanwhile, made no secret of its alliance with Spain. In conjunction with Parma, Guise overran the territory of the duc de Bouillon, who had just died, and Aumale overran much of Picardy with a view to assisting the Spanish Armada with harbours and supplies, but he failed to capture Boulogne. He also tried to stir up trouble for Epernon in Normandy, ignoring a royal command to desist. 'We must henceforth be king,' Henry III wrote to Villeroy, 'for we have been the valet for too long.'[36]

Before mounting an attack on the king, the League concentrated its fire on the duc d'Epernon. A dispatch from the nuncio Morosini reveals how isolated the royal favourite had become. He called on Catherine one day and knelt before her, cap in hand, for an hour, but she never asked him to rise or cover himself. He told her that he intended in future to be her servant and to do anything to be reconciled with the duc de Guise.[37] But Epernon's enemies were implacable, believing that he was a supporter of Navarre and Damville. In March and April 1588 several attempts were made against his life. Henry accordingly reinforced security at the Louvre and brought 4,000 Swiss troops into the suburbs of Paris. On 20 April Catherine and Epernon clashed violently in the council over security. The duke suspected her of being pro-League and of trying to influence the king in its favour.[38] He may not have been wide of the mark, for she had close family ties with the

---

35 Mariéjol, pp. 393–4; Chevallier, *Henri III*, p. 616.
36 Chevallier, *Henri III*, p. 617.
37 Ibid., p. 618.
38 Ibid., p. 620.

house of Lorraine. Her daughter Claude was married to Charles III, duke of Lorraine, and Catherine, who cared little about the Salic law, liked the idea of their son, the marquis de Pont-à-Mousson, becoming heir to the French throne in the event of Henry III remaining childless. She had virtually adopted the marquis's sister, Christina. In addition to these family ties, Catherine was friendly with the duchesse de Nemours (Guise's mother) and other members of the Guise family. She shared Guise's hatred of Epernon, who had dared to displace her in her son's counsels and affection, as she thought. Moreover, as we have seen, Catherine did not care for her Protestant son-in-law Henri de Navarre. Yet, if she sympathized to any extent with the League, her prime loyalty was undoubtedly to her son; as her correspondence makes abundantly clear, all her actions were determined by what she took to be his interest.[39]

Tension between the king and Guise exploded in May when the duke defied a royal command banning him from Paris in response to a call for help from the Leaguers in the capital. He travelled there with a small escort, and promptly called on the queen-mother at her residence. She was ill in bed at the time, but got up and took the duke to the Louvre. There are conflicting accounts of what happened next. According to one source, Henry III rebuked Guise for his disobedience, whereupon the duke explained that he had come at Catherine's bidding. She confirmed this so that Henry was unable to punish Guise.[40] It is sometimes alleged that Catherine had indeed sent a verbal message to the duke at Soissons countermanding her son's ban on his coming to Paris, but this is uncertain.[41] The sequel, however, is amply documented. As reports reached Henry of an imminent coup by the League, he introduced several companies of

---

39 Cloulas, *Catherine*, pp. 542–3.
40 'Histoire de la Journée des Barricades de Paris, mai 1588' in Cimber and Danjou, *Archives curieuses de l'histoire de France*, 1st series, xi. 368–69; B. Zeller, 'Catherine de Médicis et la Journée des Barricades', *Revue historique*, xli (1889), p. 267; Mariéjol, p. 395.
41 Cloulas, *Catherine*, p. 575. The source of this story is P. Chaudon de Brialles, *Vie de Jean Chandon* (Paris, 1857). See Mariéjol, p. 396 n. 1.

French and Swiss troops into the capital early on 11 May, thereby contravening a jealously guarded privilege whereby Parisians were entitled to defend themselves in an emergency. Outraged by the presence of foreign troops in their midst, they took up arms, poured into the streets and erected barricades. The king's troops found themselves cut off and under attack from the mob. Some were killed and others injured as they came under fire from snipers or were pelted with stones from windows and roofs. Henry III sent out ministers to bring the troops to safety, but they did not find the task easy. Two later admitted that they had never been so frightened in their lives. In the end, Guise responded to an appeal from the king. Leaving his residence, he walked unarmed through the streets, appeasing his followers, As they shouted '*Vive Guise!*', he reprimanded them gently for not shouting '*Vive le roi!*'[42]

On 13 May Catherine found the streets barred as she tried to reach the Sainte-Chapelle for mass. An anonymous Leaguer tells us that she seemed quite happy as the barricades were opened up to let her through.[43] Yet, according to L'Estoile, she 'did nothing but cry' over her lunch that day. Later, at a meeting of the king's council, she alone pressed Henry to remain in Paris. Then, calling on Guise at his residence, she asked him to quell the mob, go to the Louvre and assure the king of his obedience. But the duke replied that he could not control the people, who were like 'excited bulls' (*taureaux échauffés*). As for seeing the king, he thought it would be folly to go to the Louvre, where he would be at the mercy of his enemies. Since he seemed immovable, Catherine sent Pinart to the Louvre to advise her son to leave, but the secretary found that Henry had already left for Chartres.[44]

The League tightened its control of the capital, while the queen and queen-mother were prevented from leaving the Hôtel de la Reine. Guise tried to secure a postponement of

---

42 Chevallier, *Henri III* pp. 630–8. See also Cimber and Danjou, *Archives curieuses*, xi. 327–63, 370–1; *Journal de L'Estoile*, ed. L.-R. Lefèvre (Paris, 1943), pp. 551–7.
43 Cimber and Danjou, *Archives curieuses*, xi. 387.
44 *Journal de L'Estoile*, p. 555.

the Parlement's session, which was due to meet on the 14th. When his request was refused, he turned to Catherine, who persuaded the few councillors present to disperse, while authorizing them to send a deputation to the king at Chartres. The Bastille surrendered on 14 May and a new governor was appointed. Royalist members of the municipal council were replaced by Leaguers. The leader of the Sixteen, La Chapelle-Marteau, became *prévôt des marchands*. After she had recognized the new administration, Catherine asked Guise, on 17 May, to draw up a list of demands for the king, but he said that he needed to confer with his colleagues first. Meanwhile, he occupied various towns around Paris so as to safeguard its food supplies in the event of a confrontation with the king. On 20 May the Leaguers presented Catherine with a draft of their demands, which they finalized and signed on 23 May. Henry III was to appoint Guise as commander-in-chief of the royal armies; dismiss and banish Epernon and La Valette as 'supporters of heresy', revoke the fiscal edicts, confirm the new government of Paris and replace the captains of major fortified towns by Guise clients. At the same time, the Parisians invited the other major towns to set up a federation against the enemies of the faith.[45]

On 16 May Henry III received the deputation from the Parlement. He promised to forgive the Parisians if they would submit and acknowledge their faults. He then received a procession of thirty-six penitents led by Henri de Joyeuse. They were followed by several more deputations, so that the king began to think that the Day of the Barricades had been no more than a brief outburst of popular hysteria. He tried to appease his subjects by revoking forty edicts under which offices had been created and sold. He also promised to summon the Estates-General and banished Epernon to Angoumois, but the Leaguers were not satisfied. They tightened security around the two queens in Paris. Catherine complained vehemently to Guise after she had been refused passage through one of the city's gates, and threatened a showdown by leaving the capital. This was only bluster, however, for she believed that Henry should give

---

45 Cloulas, *Catherine*, pp. 584–5.

way to the League rather than face catastrophe. 'I know it is a hard medicine for my son to take, given his stoutness of heart,' Catherine wrote to Bellièvre, 'but it would be harder still for him to lose all his authority and obedience. He would earn much praise by restoring himself in whatever manner he can at this stage, for time brings many things that cannot be anticipated . . . Never have I seen myself in such trouble or with so little light by which to escape. Unless God intervenes, I do not know what will happen.'[46]

On 15 June the League sent new demands to the king. He was to promise to recognize the Holy Union, concede six surety towns to the Leaguers, publish the Council of Trent, sell the goods of Protestants, and send two armies – one led by Guise, the other by Mayenne – against the Huguenots. On 5 June Henry capitulated and, soon afterwards, signed the Edict of Union, which in effect recognized the League as a state institutiom, while banning all other associations.[47] His subjects were to take an oath never to accept a heretical king and Henry forgave all who had taken part in the Day of the Barricades. Publication of the edict was celebrated by a *Te Deum* at Notre-Dame, attended by the two queens, the Cardinals of Bourbon and Vendôme, the duc de Guise, foreign ambassadors and councillors of the Parlement.

Henry's surrender released the two queens from their semi-captivity. They left Paris on 23 July and met Henry at Mantes. Catherine wanted him to return to the capital, but he chose to go back to Chartres with his queen. On 1 August Catherine called on him, accompanied by Guise and the Cardinals of Bourbon and Vendôme. As Guise knelt in obeisance, the king raised him up and kissed him 'tenderly' twice. That evening he offered to share his table with him and to toast 'the good barricaders of Paris'. On 4 August Henry began distributing favours to the Leaguers. Guise was appointed commander-in-chief of the king's armies; Cardinal de Bourbon was given the regal privilege of appointing a master in each town guild throughout the kingdom. Henry promised to seek the legateship of Avignon for the Cardinal

---

46 *Lettres,* ix. 368.
47 Sutherland, *Huguenot Struggle,* pp. 365–6; Haag, *La France Protestante,* x. 201–3.

de Guise, and to appoint the archbishop of Lyon as Keeper of the Seals.[48]

. . .

THE ESTATES-GENERAL OF BLOIS (1588)

Henry III's excuse for not going to Paris, as the League wanted him to do, was his need to attend the meeting of the Estates-General in Blois, which he had called. He arrived there on 1 September, accompanied by his mother and all the court. A week later he surprised everyone by sacking all his ministers. His letter to Villeroy read as follows: 'Villeroy, I remain satisfied with your services; yet fail not to return to your home where you shall remain until I send for you. Seek not the reason for my letter, simply obey me.' Villeroy's colleagues presumably received the same curt, albeit polite, missive. Most contemporaries interpreted the dismissals as a deliberate snub to Catherine, a view generally endorsed by historians.[49] According to the Spanish ambassador, Mendoza, Henry berated the ministers, when Catherine asked him to explain their dismissal. He described Chancellor Cheverny as corrupt, Bellièvre as a crypto-Huguenot, Villeroy as monstrously vain, Brulart as a nonentity and Pinart as a rascal who would sell his parents for money. He was altogether more circumspect in the reasons he gave to Morosini, the papal legate. He explained that he had sacked the ministers in anticipation of a demand from the Estates that he should do so.[50] But Catherine seems to have taken personal offence at Henry's action. Writing to Bellièvre, she deplored the harm that she had suffered as a result of the king having been taught 'that he must obey God's command to love and honour his mother but not to give her the authority and credit needed to prevent one from doing what one wants'.[51]

---

48 Cloulas, *Catherine*, p. 589.
49 Sutherland, *French Secretaries of State*, pp. 294–303. She writes (p. 303): 'The only credible explanation of the dismissal of the ministers. . . is that the king's original intention was first to appear to have disgraced them, and then to recall them after the States had been dissolved.' But this view is not generally endorsed.
50 Cloulas, *Catherine* p. 591.
51 *Lettres*, ix. 382.

Henry, it seems, blamed her and her ministers for his humiliation at the hands of the League. By sacking the ministers who had worked closely with Catherine and replacing them with men who owed her nothing, he demonstrated his resolve to be master in his own house.

After a series of preparatory meetings, the Estates-General met for the first time at the château of Blois on 16 September. In his opening address, Henry III paid fulsome tribute to his mother for her services to the kingdom. She deserved, he said, to be called not only 'mother of the king' but also 'mother of the state and of the kingdom'. He seemed to be thanking her for the last time. 'I am your God-given king,' he continued, 'only I can speak truly and lawfully.' After proclaiming his Catholic faith, he outlined an ambitious reform programme. He announced his intention to make war on the heretics, but explained that he needed money. For the rest, he implored his subjects to join him in the fight against lawlessness and corruption. 'Some great nobles of my kingdom', he said, 'have formed leagues and associations, but, as evidence of my habitual kindness, I am prepared in this regard to forget the past.' These words did not please the duc de Guise and his brother, who tried to have them deleted from the published version of the king's speech, but it had already been printed.[52] At the next session of the estates, the deputies swore to observe the Edict of Union, declaring it to be a 'fundamental law' of the kingdom. The crown's financial position then came under scrutiny. On 10 November Henry III submitted a sort of budget. He offered to reduce drastically his annual expenditure, but failed to impress the estates. In the end, the third estate offered him a meagre 120,000 *écus,* of which 100,000 were to be spent on the armies of Mayenne and Nevers.

Catherine took no part in these debates, being stricken with gout and rheumatism, and unable to shake off an exhausting cough. On 8 December, however, she found the strength to attend the signature of the marriage contract between her beloved granddaughter, Christina of Lorraine, and Ferdinand, Grand Duke of Tuscany. Afterwards, she

---

52 Cloulas, *Catherine*, pp. 588–9.

threw a ball in her apartment.[53] On 15 December, however, she had to return to her bed with a serious lung infection.

Finding himself increasingly under pressure from the estates, Henry began to think of ways of regaining his freedom of action. He believed that the deputies were being stirred up by Guise, who, it was said, was planning to take him to Paris, where the duke would be in an even better position to dictate to him. Guise did not help himself at this juncture by proposing that Epernon and his brother, La Valette, should be condemned as Huguenots and rebels. On 19 December Henry III and his advisers decided that the time had come to eliminate Guise. Early on 23 October the duke was summoned to the king's presence. As he entered the chamber, the Forty-five fell on him, piercing him fatally with their rapiers. Simultaneously, eight members of the Guise family were rounded up and imprisoned in the château. Next day, the duke's brother, Cardinal de Guise, was dragged out of prison and hacked to death. The bodies of the victims were then burnt to ensure that they would not be idolized.[54]

Immediately after the duke's murder, Henry went to his mother's chamber, situated immediately beneath his own. He found her in bed with her doctor, Filippo Cavriana, in attendance. The king asked how his mother was. Cavriana replied that she was well and had taken medicine. Approaching her bed, Henry said with a firm voice: 'Good day Madam. Please forgive me. Monsieur de Guise is dead. He will not be spoken of again. I have had him killed. I have done to him what he was going to do to me.' He then recalled the injuries he had received since 13 May, adding that he had endured them so as not to soil his hands with the rebel's blood, but had now decided to act since Guise was threatening his authority, life and state. After much hesitation on his part, God had inspired and helped him and he was about to give Him thanks. Henry went on to explain that he intended no harm to Madame de Nemours or other members of the Guise family, whom he knew to be

---

53 Mariéjol, pp. 401–3; *Lettres,* ix. 278.; A. Desjardins, *Négociations diplomatiques de la France avec la Toscane,* iv. 876ff.
54 Chevallier, *Henri III,* pp. 662–70.

loyal. 'But I do want to be king', he said, 'and no longer a prisoner and a slave . . .' He disclosed that the Cardinals of Bourbon and Guise as well as the archbishop of Lyon were under arrest. The king then left the chamber with a determined look on his face. A dispatch describing this scene, which Cavriana sent to the Florentine government, makes no mention of Catherine's reaction. He merely says that she had only just recovered from an almost fatal illness and that he is afraid that the departure of Christina of Lorraine for Tuscany and the 'funereal spectacle' of the duc de Guise may worsen her condition. The only indication of her feelings is a conversation which she had with a Capuchin friar on Christmas Day. Speaking of her son, she exclaimed: 'Oh! wretched man! What has he done? . . . Pray for him for he needs [your prayers] more than ever. I see him rushing towards his ruin. I am afraid he may lose his body, soul and kingdom.' On 31 December Cavriana reported that Catherine was much distressed (*turbarta*). Despite her prudence and her vast experience of affairs, she did not know how the kingdom's troubles might be cured either now or in the future.[55]

On 1 January 1589 Catherine called on her old friend, Cardinal de Bourbon, who was under house arrest. She wanted to tell him that Henry forgave him and that he would be set free, but the cardinal rounded on her, exclaiming: 'Your words, Madam, have led us all to this butchery.' Silently and in tears, Catherine returned to her apartment. Three days later, she ran a high fever, and on 5 January, said that she wanted to make her will and asked for her confessor. Later that morning her speech became so faint that the king had to dictate her last wishes. She died at 1.30 p.m. after taking communion.[56] Legend has it that she had once been told by a soothsayer to beware of Saint-Germain if she wished to live for a long time. She had accordingly avoided the château of Saint-Germain and the parish of Saint-Germain l'Auxerrois. But the prophecy caught

55 Ibid., pp. 671–2; Desjardins, *Négociations diplomatiques de la France avec la Toscane,* iv. 842–3.
56 Mariéjol, pp. 405–6; Cloulas, *Catherine,* pp. 599–600.

up with her, as the priest who gave her the last rites was called Julien de Saint-Germain.[57]

An autopsy revealed that Catherine had rotten lungs, a blood-soaked brain and an abscess in her left side. The modern verdict is that she died of pleurisy. While her body was embalmed and placed in a wooden coffin lined with lead, her life-like effigy, decked out in robes that had once served for the funeral of Anne of Brittany, was laid out for public view. On 4 February her funeral took place in the church of Saint-Sauveur in Blois. Reynault de Beaune, archbishop of Bourges, gave the eulogy. 'Acknowledge', he told his audience, 'that you have lost the most virtuous queen, the noblest of race and generation, the most excellent in honour, the most chaste among all women, the most prudent in government, the sweetest in conversation, the most affable and kindly to all who wished to see her, the most humble and charitable to her children, the most obedient to her husband, but above all the most devout before God, and the most affectionate to the poor of any queen who ever reigned in France!'[58]

News of Catherine's death aroused mixed feelings in Paris. The chronicler L'Estoile writes: 'She was seventy-one years old and well preserved for such a fat woman. She ate heartily and was not afraid of work (*affaires*) although she had to face as much as any queen in the world since the death of her husband thirty years before. She died leaving a debt of 800,000 *écus*, having been more prodigal than any prince or princess in Christendom . . . She was mourned by some of her servants and intimates and a little by her son the king . . . Those closest to her believed that her life had been shortened by displeasure over her son's deed. This was due not so much to her friendship for the victims (whom she liked in the Florentine way – that is to say, in order to make use of them) but because she could see that it would benefit the king of Navarre, her son-in-law, whose ruin she had sworn to bring about by any means. His succession was

---

57 E. Pasquier *Lettres historiques pour les années 1556–1594*, ed. D. Thickett (Geneva, 1966), p. 387.
58 *Oraison funèbre faicte aux obsèques de la Royne–Mère du Roy* (Blois, 1589); Cloulas, *Catherine*, pp. 601–2.

what she feared most in the world. Parisians, however, believed that she had given her consent to the murder of the Guises, and the Sixteen said that if her body were brought to Paris for burial in the magnificent sepulchre she had built for herself and her late husband, Henry, they would drag it through the streets or throw it in the river. So much for the Parisian view. In Blois, where she had been adored and revered as the court's Juno, she had no sooner passed away than she was treated with as much consideration as a dead goat.'[59]

Catherine's body had to stay in Blois until it could be safely transported to Saint-Denis, the traditional burial place of France's kings and queens. However, as Pasquier informs us, the embalming had been bungled owing to the absence in Blois of the requisite drugs and spices. As the corpse began to smell, it had to be buried at night in an unmarked grave within Saint-Sauveur.[60] There it remained for twenty-one years until Diane, the natural daughter of Henry II, and his mistress Filippa Duci, had it moved to the Valois rotunda at Saint-Denis. In 1719, after its demolition, the corpse was moved again within the abbey until 1793, when a revolutionary mob tossed it into a mass grave along with the bones of all the other kings and their consorts.[61]

59 *Journal de l'Estoile*, pp. 604–5.
60 E. Pasquier, *Lettres historiques*, pp. 386–7.
61 Cloulas, *Catherine*, pp. 604–5.

CONCLUSION

A single Doric column overlooking a former market area, a few architectural fragments tucked away in a corner of the Tuileries gardens and an empty tomb in the basilica of Saint-Denis are among the only material remains of Catherine de' Medici's forty-two years as queen of France, regent and queen-mother. Even those priceless tapestries which evoke the splendid festivals of her court are at present hidden from public view in a Florentine art gallery. Are we to read a message of failure into these relics of a woman who has achieved legendary status in France? She is portrayed in countless novels as a wicked and murderous schemer who would stop at nothing to feed her love of power. Traditionally, she has been held responsible for the Massacre of St. Bartholomew. Recently, however, a number of historians have tried to rehabilitate her. Nicola Sutherland has pointed to the difficult legacy which she inherited and to the intense international pressures under which she had to preserve her sons' interests. In her judgment, Catherine was 'the first to be confronted – in circumstances of peculiar difficulty – by some of the underlying problems of the *ancien régime*' and 'without her conservative achievements the later monarchy would have had no foundation upon which to build'.

Catherine certainly found herself in a particularly difficult situation when her husband was killed in July 1559. At the age of forty and without any significant experience of government, she was left to defend the inheritance of her children – four sons and a daughter. Two other daughters were already married, one to the duke of Lorraine, the other to Philip II of Spain. The eldest boy, Francis II, was only fifteen, but under French law he was considered old enough to be king. Consequently, Catherine could not be regent and had to work with the existing ministerial team consisting mainly of the powerful aristocratic house of Guise. Only when Francis died in 1560 was she able to act as regent for her son Charles IX, who was only ten years old. But, even as regent, Catherine lacked the authority of a king. While she depended on the support of the nobility, she had to maintain her independence in the face of the bitter aristocratic rivalries which flourished in the absence of a mature king. To further complicate her task, the French crown was virtually bankrupt. The tax system was both unfair and inefficient, and other means of raising money never sufficed to meet the government's needs in addition to encountering resistance. However, the most intractable part of Catherine's legacy was the religious disunity of the kingdom. For several years the old principle of 'one king, one law, one religion' had been breached by the steady growth of the Protestant movement. By 1559 it had won recruits, including many nobles, and the crown had decided to stamp it out. One of the first crises faced by Catherine was the Conspiracy of Amboise, an attempt by dissident nobles, many of them Calvinists, to seize power by overthrowing the Guises.

Catherine has for long been given credit for the relatively tolerant policy which she and her Chancellor, Michel de L'Hôpital, pursued in the wake of the conspiracy. Under a series of royal edicts, some more generous than others, the Huguenots were offered concessions which the government hoped would pacify them, but, as events were to demonstrate, they were never content to be second-class citizens. Believing that their faith was the true one, they wanted not only freedom of conscience, but also freedom of worship. While seeking to satisfy them, Catherine looked for a theological formula which would permanently unite Catholics and Protestants. She tried her best at the Colloquy of Poissy, but also revealed her profound ignorance of the theological issues at stake. The disagreement over the nature of the Eucharist could not be papered over as she seemed to imagine.

Following the Edict of Amboise in 1563, Charles IX became king and Catherine stepped down as regent. But she continued to be politically dominant and sought to buttress her son's authority by taking him on an extended tour of his kingdom so that his subjects might know him better. She actively sought the support of the provincial nobility and used her son's authority to see that the recent pacification was enforced. However, it was in the course of this progress that she committed the first of a long series of major political blunders. She wanted to marry her son, Anjou, to a Spanish infanta and tried to meet Philip II in Bayonne. He was not interested in her proposal and sent his minister, the duke of Alba, in his place. Nothing of substance was achieved by the negotiations at Bayonne, but they aroused the deepest suspicions among the Huguenots. Catherine, in short, threw away her chances of bringing peace to France by pursuing one of her many matrimonial will of the wisps.

A direct consequence of the Bayonne encounter was the *Surprise de Meaux* of 1567, whose significance has not always been sufficiently appreciated by historians. The event, as we have seen, was prompted by the Dutch revolt and Philip II's decision to send an army under Alba to crush it. Philip did not inform Catherine of his decision, so that no one in France knew exactly where Alba was going, as he marched north from Milan. Charles IX raised 6,000 Swiss troops to defend his kingdom, while the Huguenots feared that they were about to be attacked. Catherine, in the meantime, was congratulating herself on the success of her recent progress through France. She believed that she had given it peace. Her dismay, therefore, was all the greater, when the Huguenots, led by Admiral Coligny, launched a pre-emptive strike. Not only did they try to kidnap Catherine and her son, Charles IX, they also pursued them to Paris and blockaded the capital. As Catherine herself declared, this was 'the greatest wickedness of all time'. From this moment onwards, all talk of conciliation on her part was dropped. Henceforth, she determined to punish the Huguenots, who had not only betrayed her trust but challenged the king's authority. Historians who believe that Catherine consistently pursued an Erasmian or 'politique' line need to read her correspondence immediately following the *Surprise de Meaux*. It throws an entirely different light on the attempted assassination of Coligny and the massacre that followed.

Unless new evidence is forthcoming, Catherine's complicity in the plot to assassinate Coligny will never be firmly established. She did not really need to do much herself, for the Guises were committed to avenge the murder of their second duke, for which they blamed Coligny, and they would almost certainly have killed him regardless of Catherine's involvement. As far the massacre is concerned, her role seems clearer. All the available evidence suggests that she and Anjou were a party to the decision taken on 23 August to exterminate the Huguenot leadership. Bourgeon's suggestion that the decision was engineered by Spain with the backing of the papacy is no more than a hypothesis. Everyone at the time believed in Catherine's guilt and she herself, far from denying it, seems to have basked in the adulation of the Catholic world.

The last decades of Catherine's life witnessed the collapse of all that she had ever hoped for. In 1573 Huguenots who had survived the massacre held out in La Rochelle against a royal army commanded by the king's brother, the duc d'Anjou. Charles IX was dying of consumption, but his mother seems not to have realized it. She persuaded Anjou to offer himself as a candidate for the vacant throne of Poland. On being elected, he raised the siege of La Rochelle and reluctantly set off for Poland, whereupon Charles IX died. Catherine had to fill the power vacuum which her younger son, the duc d'Alençon, was longing to fill. She had herself declared regent and kept the throne warm for Henry pending his return from Poland. Her action has been acclaimed as her finest hour. By preserving the crown for Henry, she had upheld 'the principle of legitimacy' and saved the kingdom from destruction, but it is arguable that she herself had precipitated the constitutional crisis by sending Henry on a wild goose chase beyond the Elbe at a time when Charles IX's health was, at best, precarious.

Catherine's role in the kingdom underwent a profound change during the reign of Henry III. Her children, by now adolescents, were keen to break away from her tutelage. Henry continued to lean on her from time to time, particularly when the going was rough, but he often preferred to listen to his male favourites, Joyeuse and Epernon. Catherine willingly assumed invidious tasks in the hope of retaining his affection and esteem. Thus she tried to dissuade Alençon (now Anjou) from helping the Dutch rebels by interesting him in the search for a wife in England or Spain. But the English match was a non-starter, given Elizabeth's age and religion. When this avenue was closed, Catherine foolishly tried to put pressure on Philip II to offer his daughter's hand by challenging his claim to the Portuguese throne and sending an armed expedition to its doom in the Azores. In the end, Anjou remained single. Regardless of Catherine's wishes, he gave up the role she had given him of overseeing the pacification of the Midi, and marched to the assistance of the Dutch rebels. Although Henry III tried to stop him, Catherine sent him help, which had to be secret in order not to provoke retaliation by Spain. The effort was, in the event, wasted, as Anjou's bid to secure a kingdom ended in defeat and humiliation. In the meantime, Catherine tried to help Henry III by detaching his brother-in-law, Henri de Navarre, from the Protestant movement, but he was far too wily to succumb to her blandishments. He may have calculated that time would play into his hands. Events were to prove him right. In 1588, at Blois, Henry III committed the greatest blunder since the Massacre of St. Bartholomew and this time Catherine was not to blame. He presented her with a *fait accompli*: the duc de Guise had been eliminated. She was apparently deeply shocked by the news. After calling on her old friend, Cardinal de Bourbon, and being accused by him of responsibility for the recent carnage, she retired in tears to her chamber, saying, 'I can take no more; I must go to bed!' A few days later, she died.

No verdict on Catherine can ever be more than tentative and personal. Too much of her thoughts and deeds lie buried in the past and will never come to light. We are unlikely ever to know for certain whether or not she connived at the attempted assassination of Coligny or at the massacre that followed. However, there are grounds for thinking that her policy was less consistently pacific than her defenders have claimed. Yates' suggestion that her festivals were designed to promote peace in the kingdom is most unconvincing. Being confined to the court, they merely served to increase its unpopularity at a time when the king's subjects were experiencing severe economic hardship. Even the judicious Pasquier, who thought reasonably well of Catherine, criticized her extravagance. She certainly wanted peace, but may not have ruled out a draconian policy to achieve it once her early efforts at conciliation and co-existence had failed. In 1567 she seems to have favoured the suppression of the Huguenots or at least the extermination of their leaders after they had betrayed her trust at Meaux and defied the king's authority. The only consistent principle to which she adhered was a touching faith in the matrimonial solution to all political problems. She sought greatness for her children by arranging prestigious marriages for them and was largely successful. Two of her daughters became queens and one a duchess. But not all the marriages turned out well. That between Marguerite and the king of Navarre was nothing short of a disaster. Nor could Catherine do anything to ensure that her children were capable of filling the roles she intended for them. Her sons were with one exception riddled with disease so that she outlived them all except Henry III. He was intelligent enough to be a successful king, but had serious faults of character and threw away his chances by murdering the duc de Guise and his brother. This dreadful crime ensured that he himself would be assassinated and that his throne would pass into the hands of his Protestant brother-in-law. Such was the outcome of Catherine's painstaking efforts over forty years to bring eternal glory to the house of Valois.

BIBLIOGRAPHICAL ESSAY

The essential starting-point for research into sixteenth-century France is H. Hauser, *Les sources de l'histoire de France au XVIe siècle*, 4 vols (1906–16). This can be supplemented by P. Caron and H. Stein, *Répertoire bibliographique de l'histoire de France*, 6 vols (1923–38), then by the *Bibliographie annuelle de l'histoire de France*, published since 1953 by the Comité français des sciences historiques. The two principal collections of royal edicts and ordinances are A. Fontanon, *Les Edits et ordonnances des rois de France* 4 vols (Paris, 1611) and F.-A. Isambert, *Recueil général des anciennes lois françaises*, 29 vols (Paris, 1829–33). A useful compilation is *Edits des guerres de religion*, ed. A. Stegmann (Paris: Vrin, 1979). N.M. Sutherland lists the various religious edicts and analyses their significance in *The Huguenot Struggle for Recognition* (New Haven: Yale University Press, 1980). The *Archives curieuses de l'histoire de France*, ed. L. Cimber and F. Danjou, 6 vols (Paris, 1834–35) and G. Ribier, *Lettres et Mémoires d'Estat des Roys, Princes, Ambassadeurs et autres Ministres sous les règnes de François Ier, Henry II et François II*, 2 vols (Paris, 1666) contain some important documents. Events in Paris are covered by the *Registres des délibérations du Bureau de la Ville de Paris*, ed. P. Guérin *et al.*, 7 vols (Paris, 1835–96). Major printed sources for the history of Protestantism include *Ioannis Calvini Opera quae supersunt omnia*, ed. G. Baum, E. Cunitz and E. Reuss (Brunswick and Berlin, 1863–1900); *Histoire ecclésiastique des églises réformées au royaume de France*, ed. G. Baum and Ed. Cunitz, 3 vols (Paris, 1889), E. and E. Haag, *La France Protestante ou vies des protestants français*, 10 vols (Geneva, 1846–59; 2nd edn. Paris, 1877–88) and J. Crespin,

Histoire des martyrs, ed. D. Benoit and M. Lelièvre, 3 vols (Toulouse, 1885–89). The first edition has been reprinted in 10 vols (Geneva, 1966). For a contemporary view of events see Etienne Pasquier, *Lettres historiques pour les années 1556–1594*, ed. D. Thickett (Geneva: Droz, 1966). Much valuable information is to be gleaned from the reports sent by foreign ambassadors in France to their respective governments. They include *Relazioni degli ambasciatori veneti al Senato*, ed. E. Albèri, vols 1–4 and 15 (appendix) (Florence, 1839–63); *Négociations diplomatiques de la France avec la Toscane*, ed. A. Desjardins, vols 3 and 4 (Paris: Imprimerie impériale, 1865); *Relations des ambassadeurs vénitiens sur les affaires de France au XVIe siècle*, ed. N. Tommaseo, 2 vols (Paris: Imprimerie nationale, 1838) and the *Calendar of State Papers, Foreign: Edward VI, Mary, Elizabeth I*, 25 vols (London, 1861–1950). Letters sent by Walsingham from Paris in 1572 are contained in Sir Dudley Digges, *The Compleat Ambassador or two Treaties of the intended marriage of Qu. Elizabeth* (London, 1655). See also Bertrand de Salignac de La Mothe-Fénelon, *Correspondance diplomatique*, 7 vols (Paris, 1838–40). The reports of papal nuncios are published in *Actae nuntiaturae Gallicae*: vol. XII, ed. P. Hurtubise, 2 vols (Rome, 1975); vol. XIV, ed. J. Lestocquoy (Rome, 1977) and vol. XVI, ed. A. Lynn Martin and R. Toupin (1984). Franco-Dutch relations are illuminated by vol. 4 of *Archives ou correspondance inédite de la maison d'Orange-Nassau*, ed. Groen van Prinsterer, 14 vols (Leiden: Luchtmans, 1835–37); Antoine Perrenot de Granvelle, *Correspondance, 1565–86*, ed. E. Paullet and C. Piot, 12 vols (Brussels, 1877–96), and Franco-Spanish relations by *Papiers d'Etat du Cardinal de Granvelle*, ed. C. Weiss, 9 vols (Paris: Imprimerie royale, 1841–52). Memoirs proliferated in sixteenth-century France. For the Wars of Religion, see especially the *Mémoires de Claude Haton* (Paris, 1857), *Mémoires de Condé*, 6 vols (London and Paris, 1743), Michel de La Huguerye, *Mémoires*, ed. A. de Ruble, 3 vols (Paris, 1877–80), the *Commentaires* of Blaise de Monluc, ed. P. Courteault, 3 vols (Paris: Picard, 1911–25), François de La Noue, *Discours politiques et militaires*, ed. F.E. Sutcliffe (Geneva: Droz, 1967) and Gaspard de Saulx-Tavannes, *Mémoires*, in the *Collection complète des mémoires relatifs à l'histoire de France*, ed. M. Petitot, vols 23–25 (Paris, 1822). Among important early histories two stand out: Agrippa d'Aubigné, *Histoire universelle,* ed. A. de Ruble, 10 vols (Paris, 1886–1909); Jacques-Auguste de Thou, *Histoire universelle depuis 1543 jusqu'en 1607,* 16 vols (London, 1734).

The background of Catherine de' Medici's career is covered by several surveys of sixteenth-century France. The most up-to-date are Arlette Jouanna, *La France du XVIe siècle, 1483–1598* (Paris: PUF, 1996), F.J. Baumgartner, *France in the Sixteenth Century* (London: Macmillan, 1995) and my own *The Rise and Fall of Renaissance France* (London: Harper-Collins, 1996). Among older surveys J.H.M. Salmon, *Society in Crisis: France in the sixteenth century* (London: Benn, 1975) and R. Briggs, *Early Modern France, 1560–1715* (Oxford: OUP, 1977) are particularly useful. Though older still, J.-H. Mariéjol, *La Réforme et la Ligue: L'Edit de Nantes (1559–1598)* (Paris: Tallandier, 1983), which is a reprint of vol. 6 of the old *Histoire de France,* ed. E. Lavisse (Paris, 1903), remains useful. Four short introductions to the Wars of Religion are G. Livet, *Les guerres de religion (1559–1598)* (Paris: PUF, 1962); M. Pernot, *Les guerres de religion en France, 1559–1598* (Paris: SEDES, 1987), Mack P. Holt, *The French Wars of Religion, 1562–1629* (Cambridge: CUP, 1995) and my own *The French Wars of Religion, 1559–1598* (rev. edn, London: Longman, 1996). Two excellent local studies are P. Benedict, *Rouen during the Wars of Religion* (Cambridge: CUP, 1981) and Penny Roberts, *A City in Conflict: Troyes during the French wars of religion* (Manchester: Manchester University Press, 1996). J.-F. Solnon, *La cour de France* (Paris: Fayard, 1987), though mainly focused on a later period, contains some interesting material on the sixteenth-century court. Lucien Romier, *Le Royaume de Catherine de Médicis,* 2 vols (Paris: Perrin, 1922) is a general survey of France in the age of Catherine de' Medici. It is seriously out-of-date on social matters, notably on the economic status of the nobility. His errors are corrected in J.-M. Constant, *La vie quotidienne de la noblesse française aux XVIe–XVIIe siècles* (Paris: Hachette, 1985). Arlette Jouanna, *Ordre social: Mythe et réalités dans la France du XVIe siècle* (Paris, 1977) and her *Le devoir de révolte. La noblesse française et la gestation de l'État moderne, 1559–1661* (Paris: Fayard, 1989) are both scholarly and eminently readable. On the rise of Protestantism, two excellent introductions in English are M. Greengrass, *The French Reformation* (London: Historical Association, 1987) and

D. Nicholls in *The Early Reformation in Europe,* ed. A. Pettegree (Cambridge: CUP, 1992), pp. 120–41. For a more detailed treatment, see D. Crouzet, *La genèse de la réforme française, 1520–1562* (Paris: SEDES, 1996). On the visual arts in France during the Renaissance, the standard work remains A. Blunt, *Art and Architecture in France, 1500–1700* (Harmondsworth: Penguin, 1957). This can now be supplemented by A. Chastel, *L'art français. Temps modernes, 1430–1620* (Paris: Flammarion, 1994) and H. Zerner, *L'art de la Renaissance en France. L'invention du classicisme* (Paris: Flammarion, 1996). The kingdom's many palaces and country houses are comprehensively examined in J.-P. Babelon, *Châteaux de France au siècle de la Renaissance* (Paris: Flammarion/Picard, 1989) and *Le château en France,* ed. J.-P. Babelon (Paris: Berger-Levrault/CNMHS, 1986). For Paris generally in this period, see J.-P. Babelon, *Paris au XVIe siècle* (Paris: Hachette, 1986). On royal pageantry, see L.M. Bryant, *The King and the City in the Parisian Royal Entry Ceremony: Politics, ritual and art in the Renaissance* (Geneva: Droz, 1986) and J. Chartrou, *Les entrées solennelles et triomphales à la renaissance, 1484–1551* (Paris, 1928). Useful introductions to the literature of the period are J. Cruikshank, *French Literature and its Background,* vol. 1 (Oxford: OUP, 1968); I.D. McFarlane, *A Literary History of France: Renaissance France, 1470–1589* (London, 1974) and *The Oxford Companion to Literature in French,* ed. P. France (Oxford: Clarendon, 1995).

The essential source for the life of Catherine is *Lettres de Catherine de Médicis,* ed. Hector de la Ferrière and Baguenault de Puchesse, 10 vols (Paris: Imprimerie nationale, 1880–1909). N.M. Sutherland, *Catherine de Medici and the Ancien Régime* (London: Historical Association, 1966) – an excellent introduction aiming to undo the effects of the 'Black Legend' – is reprinted in *Princes, Politics and Religion, 1547–1589* (London: Hambledon Press, 1984), an important collection of essays, including one on 'The legend of the wicked queen'. Biographies of Catherine in French are too numerous to list here. Most of them are popular works of no scholarly merit. The first to make use of Catherine's bulky correspondence is Jean-H. Mariéjol, *Catherine de Médicis (1519–1589)* (Paris: Hachette, 1920), which has footnotes but no index. Yvan Cloulas, *Catherine de Médicis* (Paris:

Fayard, 1979), which draws heavily on Mariéjol's work, contains some new material as well as a substantial bibliography, but is long-winded, lacks footnotes and its conclusion is disappointingly tame. Jean Héritier, *Catherine de Médicis* (Paris: Fayard, 1940), which is available in an English translation (London, 1963), offers an effusively rhetorical defence of the queen. Paul Van Dyke's *Catherine de Médicis,* 2 vols (London, 1923) – the only substantial biography in English – is sound, but dull and inevitably dated. N.M. Sutherland, *The French Secretaries of State in the Age of Catherine de Medici* (London: Athlone, 1962) provides an original and carefully researched account of Catherine at work and of the ministers who served her. A contemporary admirer of Catherine was Brantôme, whose *Oeuvres* have been edited by Ludovic Lalanne in 11 vols (Paris: Renouard, 1864–82). Vol. 7 contains his account of Catherine in *Des dames.*

Relatively little is known about Catherine de' Medici's childhood in Italy. The only work that focuses upon it is A. de Reumont and A. Baschet, *La jeunesse de Catherine de Médicis* (Paris: Plon, 1866). Some light is shed on her education in K. Gebhardt, 'Catherine de Médicis (1519–1589) et la langue française' in *Henri III et son temps,* ed. R. Sauzet (Paris: Vrin, 1992), pp. 21–38. A useful introduction to her family background is J.R. Hale, *Florence and the Medici. The pattern of control* (London: Thames & Hudson, 1977). The best treatment of Leo X remains L. Pastor, *The History of the Popes,* vols 7 and 8, trans. R.F. Kerr (London, 1908). On Lorenzo de' Medici the Younger, see R. Devonshire Jones 'Lorenzo de' Medici, Duca d'Urbino "Signore" of Florence?' in *Studies in Machiavelli,* ed. M.P. Gilmore (Florence, 1972). Michelangelo's work for the Medici family is discussed in H. Hibbard, *Michelangelo* (Harmondsworth: Penguin, 1978). The fullest account of Clement VII's pontificate is that given by Pastor (as above), vols 9 and 10. For the political background to Catherine's marriage, see my *Renaissance Warrior and Patron: The reign of Francis I* (Cambridge: CUP, 1994) and Le P. Hamy, *Entrevue de François Ier avec Clément VII à Marseille, 1533* (Paris, 1900). Important primary sources for the reign of Francis I include *Catalogue des actes de François Ier,* 10 vols (Paris, 1887–1910), the *Journal de Jean Barrillon,* ed. P. de Vaissière, 2 vols (Paris: Renouard, 1897) and the *Mémoires du maréchal de Florange,* ed. R. Goubaux and P.-A.

Lemoisne (Paris: Renouard, 1913). M. François, *Le cardinal François de Tournon* (Paris: Boccard, 1951) and V.-L. Bourrilly, *Guillaume du Bellay, seigneur de Langey (1491–1543)* (Paris: Société nouvelle de librairie et d'édition, 1905) are important for Francis I's foreign relations. For the visual arts at his court, see Janet Cox-Rearick, *The Collection of Francis I: Royal treasures* (New York: Abrams, 1995) and Cécile Scalliérez, *François Ier et ses artistes* (Paris: Louvre, 1992). On architecture in the same reign, see M. Chatenet, *Le château de Madrid au Bois de Boulogne* (Paris: Picard, 1987); *La Galerie d'Ulysse à Fontainebleau,* ed. S. Béguin, J. Guillaume and A. Roy (Paris: PUF, 1985) and the special number 16–17 of the *Revue de l'art* (1972). Francis I's artistic dealings with Florence are considered by Caroline Elam in *I Tatti Studies – Essays in the Renaissance,* v (1993), 33–109. Cellini's activities at the French court are examined in J. Pope-Hennessy, *Cellini* (London: Macmillan, 1985).

I. Cloulas, *Henri II* (Paris: Fayard, 1985) and F.J. Baumgartner, *Henry II King of France 1547–1559* (Durham, NC, 1988) are good accounts of the reign. Four volumes have so far been published of the *Actes de Henri II:* vol. 1 (Paris: Imprimerie nationale, 1979); vols 2–4, ed. Marie-Noëlle Baudouin-Matuszek and Anne Merlin-Chazelas (Paris: CNRS, 1986–94). The first volume of L. Romier, *Les origines politiques des guerres de religion,* 2 vols (Paris, 1913–14), which draws heavily on the Este archives in Ferrara, is concerned with Henry II's Italian policies, the second with his struggle with the Protestants. On Henry II's policy of self-glorification, see Margaret McGowan, *Ideal Forms in the Age of Ronsard* (Berkeley: University of California Press, 1985). On the king's mistress, see F. Bardon, *Diane de Poitiers et le mythe de Diane* (Paris: PUF, 1963). See also *Lettres inédites de Diane de Poitiers,* ed. G. Guiffrey (Paris, 1866). On his principal minister see F. Decrue, *Anne, duc de Montmorency* (Paris: Plon, 1889) and B. Bedos Rezak, *Anne de Montmorency, seigneur de la Renaissance* (Paris: Publisud, 1990). On foreign affairs, see G. Zeller, *La réunion de Metz à la France (1552–1648):* pt. I (Paris, 1926) and M.J. Rodriguez-Salgado, *The Changing Face of Empire. Charles V, Philip II and Habsburg authority, 1551–1559* (Cambridge: CUP, 1988). On religious persecution in his reign, see N. Weiss, *La Chambre ardente, étude sur la liberté de conscience sous François Ier et Henri II,*

1540–1550 (1989) and D. Nicholls, 'The Theatre of Martyrdom in the French Reformation', *Past and Present*, 121 (1988), 49–73.

Important primary sources for the brief reign of Francis II include Pierre de La Place, *Commentaires de l'estat de la Religion et Republique soubs les Rois Henry et François second et Charles neuviesme, 1556–1561* (Paris, 1565); Regnier de La Planche, *Histoire de l'Estat de France sous le règne de François II*, ed. Buchon (Paris, 1836) and *Négociations, lettres et pièces diverses relatives au règne de François II*, ed. L. Paris (Paris: Imprimerie royale, 1841). Lucien Romier leads the field among historians of an older generation who have given detailed attention to some of the main events in which Catherine de' Medici was involved. His works include *La Conjuration d'Amboise* (Paris, 1923) and *Catholiques et Huguenots à la cour de Charles IX* (Paris, 1924). Other treatments of the Amboise conspiracy are H. Naef, *La Conjuration d'Amboise* (Geneva, 1922); L.R. Lefèvre, *Le Tumulte d'Amboise* (Paris, 1949). An essential treatment of the religious implications is R.M. Kingdon, *Geneva and the Coming of the Wars of Religion in France, 1555–1563* (Geneva: Droz, 1956). On the Estates-General, see J. Russell Major, *The Estates-General of 1560* (Princeton, NJ, 1951). For the dukes of Guise, see J.-M. Constant, *Les Guise* (Paris: Hachette, 1984), which is heavily indebted to R. de Bouillé, *Histoire des ducs de Guise*, 4 vols (Paris, 1849) and H. Forneron, *Les ducs de Guise et leur époque*, 2 vols (Paris: Plon, 1893). H.O. Evennett, *The Cardinal of Lorraine and the Council of Trent* (Cambridge: CUP, 1930) suggests that the cardinal was less fanatical in his Catholicism than is often believed. On Francis II's queen, see Antonia Fraser, *Mary Queen of Scots* (London: Weidenfeld, 1969) and Jenny Wormald, *Mary Queen of Scots. A study in failure* (London: G. Philip, 1988). On Antoine de Bourbon, see N.M. Sutherland, 'Antoine, king of Navarre and the French crisis of authority, 1559–1562' in *French Government and Society, 1500–1850. Essays in memory of Alfred Cobban*, ed. J.F. Bosher (London, 1973). M. Simonin, *Charles IX* (Paris: Fayard, 1995) is an interesting biography by a literary specialist. On Michel de L'Hôpital, see Seong Hak Kim, 'The chancellor's crusade: Michel de l'Hôpital and the *Parlement* of Paris', in *French History*, 7 (1993), 1–29; 'Michel de l'Hôpital revisited', in

Proceedings of the Annual Meeting of the Western Society for French History, 17 (1990), 106–12; 'Dieu nous garde de la messe du chancelier: The religious belief and political opinion of Michel de l'Hôpital', in *Sixteenth Century Journal,* 24 (1993), 595–620. The *Oeuvres complètes de Michel de L'Hospital,* ed. P.J.S. Dufey, 5 vols (1824–25) is an unsatisfactory edition. *Discours pour la majorité de Charles IX et trois autres discours,* ed. R. Descimon, gives four of the Chancellor's speeches. On the Colloquy of Poissy, see H.O. Evennett, *The Cardinal of Lorraine and the Council of Trent* (Cambridge, 1930); D. Nugent, *Ecumenism in the Age of the Reformation: The Colloquy of Poissy* (Cambridge, Mass., 1974) and N.M. Sutherland, 'The cardinal of Lorraine and the *Colloque* of Poissy, 1561: A reassessment', in *Journal of Ecclesiastical History,* 28 (1977), 265–89. On the Edict of January, see 'L'Hospital and the Edict of Toleration of 1562', in *Bulletin d'humanisme et Renaissance* (1952), 301–10.

On the Massacre of Vassy see H. Forneron, *Les ducs de Guise et leur époque* (Paris: Plon, 1893), vol. 1, pp. 306–26 and L. Romier, *Catholiques et Huguenots à la cour de Charles IX* (Paris, 1924), 318–27. On the assassination of François, second duc de Guise, see N.M. Sutherland, *Princes, Politics and Religion, 1547–1589* (London, 1984), P. de Veissière, *De quelques assassins* (Paris: Émile-Paul, 1912) and E. Marcks, 'Catherine de Médicis et l'assassinat du duc François de Guise', in *Bulletin de la société de l'histoire du protestantisme français,* xl (1891), 153–64. The entry of Charles IX into Paris is described by F.A. Yates, *Astraea: The imperial theme in the sixteenth century* (London: Routledge & Kegan Paul, 1975), pp. 127–48. Catherine's extensive progress through France is well described by P. Champion, *Catherine présente à Charles IX son royaume (1564–1566)* (Paris: Grasset, 1937) and is given the full *Annaliste* treatment in J. Boutier, A. Dewerpe and D. Nordman, *Un tour de France royal: Le voyage de Charles IX (1564–1566)* (Paris: Aubier, 1984). See also V.E. Graham and W. McAllister Johnson, *The Royal Tour of France by Charles IX and Catherine de Medici: Festivals and entries, 1564–66* (Toronto, 1979). F. Yates describes festivals of the reign of Charles IX, including that at Bayonne, in *The Valois Tapestries* (London: Routledge & Kegan Paul, 1975), pp. 53–72. On Admiral Coligny see J. Shimizu, *Conflict of Loyalties: Politics and religion in the career of Gaspard de Coligny, Admiral of France,*

283

1519–1572 (Geneva: Droz, 1970) and J. Delaborde, *Gaspard de Coligny*, 3 vols (Paris: Sandoz et Fischbacher, 1870–82). The *Actes du Colloque L'Admiral de Coligny et son temps (Paris, 24–28 octobre 1972)* (Paris: Société de l'histoire du protestantisme français, 1974) contains a large number of papers of variable quality on all aspects of his eventful political and military career.

The fraught relations between Catherine and Jeanne d'Albret, the mother of Henry of Navarre, are carefully examined by Nancy Lyman Roelker in *Queen of Navarre. Jeanne d'Albret 1528–1572* (Cambridge, Mass: Harvard University Press, 1968). Her son, the future Henry IV, has a large bibliography all to himself. For his early years, see J.-P. Babelon, *Henri IV* (Paris: Fayard, 1984), Janine Garrisson, *Henry IV* (Paris: Seuil, 1984) and, in English, D. Buisseret, *Henry IV* (London: Allen and Unwin, 1984). On the situation in Paris on the eve of the massacre of St. Bartholomew see Barbara B. Diefendorf, *Beneath the Cross: Catholics and Huguenots in sixteenth-century Paris* (Oxford: OUP, 1991) and P. Champion, *Paris au temps des Guerres de Religion* (Paris: Calmann-Lévy, 1938). The massacre itself remains highly controversial. The documentary evidence is examined in N.M. Sutherland, 'Le massacre de la Saint-Barthélemy: La valeur des témoignages et leur interprétation', in *Revue d'histoire moderne et contemporaine*, 38 (1991), 529–54. The government of Charles IX is blamed by Janine Estèbe (now Garrisson) in *Tocsin pour un massacre: La saison des Saint-Barthélemy* (Paris: Centurion, 1968) and her *La Saint-Barthélemy* (Brussels: Complexe, 1987). N.M. Sutherland, *The Massacre of St. Bartholomew and the European Conflict, 1559–1572* (London: Macmillan, 1973) places the event in its international context. She exculpates Catherine, as does J.-L. Bourgeon, *L'assassinat de Coligny* (Geneva: Droz, 1992) and his *Charles IX devant la Saint-Barthélemy* (Geneva: Droz, 1995), who blames the Guises, Spain and the papacy. An important article, which challenges the Sutherland–Bourgeon thesis, is M. Venard 'Arretez le massacre!' in *Revue d'histoire moderne et contemporaine* (1992), 645–61. *The Massacre of St. Bartholomew*, ed. A. Soman (The Hague: Nijhoff, 1974) includes various reappraisals and cites two contemporary Italian accounts. D. Crouzet, *La nuit de la Saint-Barthélemy. Un rêve perdu de la Renaissance* (Paris: Fayard, 1994) approaches the event in a highly original way, bringing into play the author's unique familiarity with the sensibilities of the age. R.M. Kingdon, *Myths about the St. Bartholomew's Day Massacres, 1572–76* (Cambridge, Mass: Harvard University Press, 1988) focuses on the collection of polemical pamphlets, some of them hostile to Catherine, assembled by the Calvinist pastor, Simon Goulart. The most vitriolic attack on her is the *Discours merveilleux de la vie, actions et deportements de Catherine de Médicis, Royne-mère*, ed. Nicole Cazauran (Geneva: Droz, 1995). On political ideas generally in this period, see Q. Skinner, *The Foundations of Modern Political Thought*, vol. 2 (Cambridge: CUP, 1978).

The best account of the career of Charles IX's younger brother, François, is Mack P. Holt, *The Duke of Anjou and the Politique Struggle during the Wars of Religion* (Cambridge: CUP, 1986). See also J. Boucher, 'Autour de François duc d'Alençon et d'Anjou, un parti d'opposition à Charles IX et Henri III' in *Henri III et son temps*, ed. R. Sauzet (Paris: Vrin, 1992), pp. 121–31. The duke's involvement in the Netherlands is chronicled in P. Geyl, *The Revolt of the Netherlands, 1555–1609* (5th edn London, 1980) and G. Parker, *The Dutch Revolt* (London: Allen Lane, 1977), and his courting of Elizabeth in W.T. MacCaffrey, 'The Anjou match and the making of Elizabethan foreign policy' in *The English Commonwealth, 1547–1640*, ed. P. Clark *et al.* (Leicester: Leicester University Press, 1979). On Montmorency-Damville, see Claude Tiévant, *Le gouverneur de Languedoc pendant les premières guerres de religion (1559–1574): Henri de Montmorency-Damville* (Paris: Publisud, 1993) but the publication date is misleading: it antedates work by J.M. Davies, M. Greengrass and R. Harding on the same subject. The popular success of the recent film, *La reine Margot*, has prompted the publication of two new biographies of Catherine's disreputable daughter. The best is Éliane Viennot, *Marguerite de Valois. Histoire d'une femme, histoire d'un mythe* (Paris: Payot, 1993/5). Janine Garrisson, *Marguerite de Valois* (Paris: Fayard, 1994) is marred by inaccuracy. See also *Mémoires de Marguerite de Valois*, ed. Y. Cazaux (Paris: Mercure de France, 1971), and *Mémoires et lettres de Marguerite de Valois*, ed. F. Guessard (Paris: Soc. de l'hist. de France, 1852).

On Catherine's interest in the occult, see E. Defrance, *Un croyant de l'occultisme, Catherine de Médicis: Ses astrologues et ses médecins envoûteurs* (Paris, 1911). In addition to the biographies of Catherine and the general works on the arts in sixteenth-century France listed above, the following have a bearing on her patronage. For a brief survey see my 'Royal patronage of the arts in France, 1574–1610' in *From Valois to Bourbon*, ed. K. Cameron (Exeter, 1989), pp. 145–60. Catherine's architectural activities are examined in A. Blunt, *Philibert de l'Orme* (London: Zwemmer, 1958). For her buildings in Paris, see D. Thomson, *Renaissance Paris* (London: Zwemmer, 1984). The contents of the Hôtel de la Reine are listed in E. Bonnaffé, *Inventaire des meubles de Catherine de Médicis en 1589* (Paris, 1874). F. A. Yates, *The Valois Tapestries* (2nd edn London: Routledge & Kegan Paul, 1975) needs to be read critically; the learning is impressive but the interpretation wildly imaginative. For sculpture, see *Germain Pilon et les sculpteurs français de la Renaissance*, ed. G. Bresc-Bautier (Paris: Documentation française, 1993) and C. Avery, *Giambologna* (London: Phaidon, 1993). The best general account of French painting in the late sixteenth century is S. Béguin, *L'école de Fontainebleau* (Paris: Gonthier-Seghers, 1960). See also J. Ehrmann, *Antoine Caron: Peintre des fêtes et des massacres* (Paris, 1986), though he too allows his imagination free rein.

The best recent biography of Henry III is P. Chevallier, *Henri III, roi shakesperien* (Paris: Fayard, 1985). The essential primary source is *Lettres de Henri III roi de France*, ed. M. François, 4 vols so far (Paris: Klincksieck, 1959–84). On the court see René de Lucinge, *Lettres sur la cour d'Henri III en 1586*, ed. A. Dufour (Geneva: Droz, 1966) and D. Potter and P.R. Roberts, 'An Englishman's view of the court of Henry III, 1584–5: Richard Cook's "Description of the Court of France"' in *French History*, 2 (1988), 312–26. One of the liveliest primary sources is the diary of Pierre de l'Estoile, a well-informed Parisian with a keen appetite for gossip and a zealous collector of pamphlets and other trifles. The *Journal de l'Estoile pour le règne de Henri III*, ed. L.-R. Lefèvre (Paris: Gallimard, 1943) is being superseded by *Registre–Journal du règne de Henri III*, ed. M. Lazard and G. Schrenk (Geneva: Droz, 1992–96), 2 vols so far. A selection, translated (not always correctly) into English, is *The Paris of Henry of Navarre as seen by Pierre de l'Estoile*, trans. and ed. Nancy L. Roelker (Cambridge, Mass: Harvard University Press, 1958). For the king's youth, see P. Champion, *La jeunesse de Henri III,* 2 vols (Paris, 1941–42). Jacqueline Boucher's thesis 'Société et mentalités autour de Henri III', 4 vols (Lille, 1981) seeks to redeem the king's reputation. She sums up her views in *La cour de Henri III* (Rennes: Ouest-France, 1986). Several useful articles, notably on Henry's reign in Poland, are contained in *Henri III et son temps,* ed. R. Sauzet (Paris: Vrin, 1992). Henry's controversial reputation is further considered in K. Cameron, *Henri III: Maligned or malignant king?* (Exeter: Exeter University Press, 1978) and his 'Henri III: The antichristian king' in *Journal of European Studies* 4 (1974), 152–63. See also S. Anglo, 'Henri III: Some determinants of vituperation' in *From Valois to Bourbon,* ed. K. Cameron (Exeter: Exeter University Press, 1989). This volume also includes N.M. Sutherland, 'Henri III, the Guises and the Huguenots' (pp. 21–34) and R. Cooper, 'The Blois assas- sinations: Sources in the Vatican' (pp. 51–72). On the king's favourites, see P. Champion, 'Henri III: La légende des mignons' in *Bulletin d'humanisme et renaissance,* vi (1939), 494–528. Henry's religiosity is sympathetically examined in F.A. Yates, *The French Academies of the Sixteenth Century* (revised edn. London: Routledge, 1988).

The terrible events leading up to the assassination of Henry III have received much attention from historians recently. The violence of the times and the eschatological mood that gripped the Catholic masses in the 1580s are captured in Denis Crouzet's monumental work, *Les Guerriers de Dieu,* 2 vols (Paris: Champ Vallon, 1990). Jean-Marie Constant, *La Ligue* (Paris: Fayard, 1996) is a convenient synthesis of recent research. An excellent introduction to the Parisian league is M. Greengrass, 'The Sixteen: Radical Politics in Paris during the League', in *History,* 69 (1984), 432–9. Spanish involvement in the activities of the League is stressed in De Lamar Jensen, *Diplomacy and Dogmatism: Bernardino de Mendoza and the French Catholic League* (Cambridge, Mass: Harvard University Press, 1964).

LIST OF MAIN ROYAL EDICTS CONCERNING RELIGION AND PEACE TREATIES

27 June 1551: Châteaubriant

A fiercely anti-Protestant edict. Heresy cases involving laity to be judged by parlements and presidial courts without appeal. Strict censorship. Appointment to offices restricted to Catholics. Informing made mandatory. Heretics to be tracked down in their homes. Property of religious exiles to be confiscated. Church attendance to be compulsory.

24 July 1557: Compiègne

Death penalty without appeal for all Protestant preachers, iconoclasts, trouble-makers, exiles and book-pedlars. Their property to be applied to charitable purposes.

2 March 1560: Amboise

Pardoned all past religious crimes on condition of abjuration, except by pastors and plotters against the crown.

May 1560: Romorantin

An edict more concerned with law and order than religion. The judgment of heresy cases left to church courts which could not impose death penalty. Bishops ordered to reside in their dioceses. Inquisitorial clauses of Edict of Châteaubriant removed. Illicit assemblies banned and informing on them made obligatory.

19 April 1561: Fontainebleau

Ban on mutual abuse and provocations. Religious prisoners freed. Religious exiles allowed to return and recover property if they abjured. No one to be persecuted at home.

11 July 1561: Saint-Germain

Cases of religious sedition to be judged by presidial courts. Ban on mutual provocations reaffirmed. All Protestant assemblies banned. Banishment the maximum penalty for heresy. Pardon for all religious offences since the death of Henry II. Strict ban on the carrying of weapons.

20 Oct 1561: Saint-Germain

All churches and church property seized by Protestants to be restored. Further seizures to be punished by death. Ban on mutual provocation renewed. Iconoclasts to be hanged. Ban on carrying of arms upheld. Provincial governors ordered to enforce justice.

17 Jan 1562: Saint-Germain

Usually called 'Edict of January'. It repeated ban on seizure of church property and upheld death penalty. Protestant preaching banned in all towns, but unarmed Protestants allowed to worship outside towns by day. All sedition to be prosecuted. Ban on all unauthorised synods or consistories. Catholic holidays to be observed. Mandatory death sentence for a second offence by printers and distributors of placards. Protestants forbidden to have their own churches.

19 March 1563: Amboise

The first 'edict of pacification'. Nobles with superior rights of justice allowed to worship in their own homes with their families and vassals; other fief-holders allowed to do so with their families only. Protestant worship allowed in one town per *bailliage*, also in towns where it existed before 7 March 1563. Confiscated church property to be restored as well as other property, status, honours and offices. Condé and his followers pardoned and rehabilitated. Amnesty for all injuries committed in the war. Ban on quarrels arising from them. Religious prisoners and POWs to be set free. Ban on all associations.

23 March 1568: Longjumeau

Edict which ended the second civil war. Peace of Amboise of 19 March confirmed.

8 Aug 1570: Saint-Germain

A seminal edict aimed at restoring peace. Mass to be restored where suspended. Protestant worship allowed in two named towns per *gouvernement* and in places where it was public on 1 August 1570. Banned within two leagues of royal court and nearer to Paris than Senlis, Meaux and Melun. Protestant burials allowed at night. Ban on associations. All property and offices restored. Religious discrimination banned in schools, universities and hospitals. Protestants made eligible to all offices and not to be taxed more than Catholics. All judgments against them since reign of Henry II suspended. Protestants given four surety towns (*places de sûreté*) – La Rochelle, Montauban, Cognac and La Charité-sur-Loire – for two years. All royal officials to swear to observe edict. Death penalty for anyone obstructing it by force.

[2] July 1573: Boulogne (Peace of La Rochelle)

Similar to Edict of Saint-Germain, but restricting religious privileges of nobility. Its aim was simply to extricate the duc d'Anjou from La Rochelle so that he might go to Poland.

6 May 1576: Beaulieu (Peace of Monsieur)

The most liberal edict. The free, general and public exercise of the Protestant faith allowed except within two leagues of Paris. Synods and consistories allowed in the presence of royal agents. Protestants to have their own churches (*temples*), but to observe church holidays. Clauses in edict of Saint-Germain *re* admission to offices and restoration of property confirmed. Bi-partisan tribunals set up in each parlement to judge cases involving Catholics and Protestants. Pardon for participants in the massacre of St Bartholomew and restoration of inheritance rights of the victims' relatives. No prosecution for non-payment of taxes since the massacre. No religious discrimination in taxation. Pardon for all acts of war since 1573. Ban on associations upheld and certain censorship rules revived. Eight surety towns permitted to Protestants, 2 each in Languedoc, Guyenne, Provence and Dauphiné. The marshals of France to enforce this edict; any obstruction by force to be punished by death.

17 Sept 1577: Poitiers (Peace of Bergerac)

A modification of Peace of Monsieur. King to pay garrisons of surety towns and the Protestants' German mercenaries. Certain religious privileges restored to nobility. Protestant worship allowed in one town per *bailliage*, in towns where it was public on 17 Sept. All judges of bi-partisan courts to be chosen by the king. Protestants allowed 8 surety towns in the same 4 southern provinces, this time for 6 years.

7 July 1585: Treaty of Nemours

All the earlier edicts of pacification rescinded. Exercise of Protestant faith banned. Pastors to be banished within a month and Protestants to abjure within 6 months or be exiled, but allowed to sell their property. Bi-partisan courts abolished. Protestants debarred from all offices. Death penalty for anyone opposing religious ban. Surety towns to be evacuated and their garrisons withdrawn. The Guises exonerated for their revolt and intrigues abroad.

July 1588: Edict of Union

The king's coronation oath to extirpate heresy reaffirmed. His subjects to take similar oath and to refuse obedience to a heretic should Henry III die childless. No Protestant to be appointed to any royal office. King's adherence to Catholic League proclaimed. Anyone refusing to sign Act of Union to be treated as a rebel.

LIST OF DATES

1518 Marriage of Lorenzo de' Medici, duke of Urbino, and
      Madeleine de La Tour d'Auvergne at Amboise
      (28 April)

1519 Birth of Henri, second son of Francis I (31 March)
      Birth of Catherine de' Medici (13 April)
      Death of Madeleine de La Tour d'Auvergne,
      Catherine's mother (28 April)
      Death of Lorenzo de' Medici, Catherine's father
      (4 May)

1520 Death of Raphael (April)

1521 Death of Pope Leo X (Giovanni de' Medici) (1 Dec)

1522 Election of Pope Hadrian VI (9 Jan)

1523 Death of Pope Hadrian VI (14 Sept)
      Election of Pope Clement VII (Giulio de' Medici)
      (19 Nov)

1524 Birth of Ronsard (11 Sept)

1527 Sack of Rome by imperial troops (6 May)
      Death of Machiavelli (22 June)

1530 Coronation of Charles V as Holy Roman Emperor
      (24 Feb)
      Medici rule restored in Florence (12 Aug)

1532 Alessandro de' Medici becomes duke of Florence
(27 April)

1533 Birth of Montaigne (28 Feb)
Francis I meets Pope Clement VII in Marseille
(13 Oct–12 Nov)
Marriage of Catherine de' Medici and Henri,
duc d'Orléans at Marseille (27 Oct)

1534 Death of Pope Clement VII (25 Sept)

1536 Death of the Dauphin François (10 Aug).
Henri d'Orléans becomes Dauphin

1537 Murder of Alessandro de' Medici by his cousin
Lorenzino (5 Feb)
Cosimo de' Medici becomes duke of Tuscany

1540 Edict of Fontainebleau (1 June)

1542 Death of King James V of Scotland and accession of
his infant daughter Mary Stuart (24 Nov)

1544 Birth of François, Catherine's first child by Henri,
duc d'Orléans (19 Jan)

1545 Birth of Catherine's daughter, Elisabeth, future
queen of Philip II of Spain (2 April)
Council of Trent opens (13 Dec)

1547 Death of Francis I and accession of Henry II
(31 March)
Birth of Catherine's third child, Claude, future
duchess of Lorraine (12 Nov)

1548 Henry II's entry into Lyon (23 Sept)

1549 Birth of Catherine's fourth child, Louis,
duc d'Orléans (3 Feb). He died on 24 Oct

1550 Birth of Charles-Maximilien, the future Charles IX
(27 June)

1551 Edict of Châteaubriant (27 June)
Birth of Edouard-Alexandre, the future Henry III
(20 Sept)

1552 Treaty of Chambord (15 Jan)
Henry II's 'German voyage' (April–July)
Rebellion of Siena (July)
Siege of Metz by Charles V

1553 Charles V raises siege of Metz (1 Jan)
Birth of Marguerite, future Queen of Navarre
(14 May)

1555 Birth of Hercule, later François, duc d'Alençon
(18 March)
Capitulation of Siena (17 April)
Pope Paul IV elected (23 May)
Peace of Augsburg (3 Oct)

1556 Abdication of Emperor Charles V (16 Jan);
Philip II becomes king of Spain

1557 Expedition of François, duc de Guise to Italy
Battle of Saint-Quentin (10 Aug)
Affair of the rue Saint-Jacques, Paris (Sept)

1558 Duc de Guise conquers Calais (6 Jan)
Marriage between Dauphin François and Mary,
Queen of Scots (24 April)
Accession of Elizabeth I, queen of England (Nov)

1559 Marriage of Catherine's daughter Claude to
Charles III, duke of Lorraine (22 Jan)
Peace of Cateau-Cambrésis (3 April)
Edict of Ecouen (2 June)
Marriage by proxy of Catherine's daughter, Elisabeth,
to Philip II, king of Spain (22 June)
Marriage of Henry II's sister, Marguerite, to
Emmanuel-Philibert, duke of Savoy (9 July)
Death of Henry II, king of France and accession of
Francis II (10 July)
Death of Pope Paul IV (18 Aug)
Execution of Anne du Bourg (21 Dec)
Pope Pius IV elected (25 Dec)

1560 Edict of Amboise (March)
Conspiracy of Amboise (March)
Edict of Romorantin (May)
Assembly of Fontainebleau opens (20 Aug)
Death of Francis II, king of France; accession of
    Charles IX and regency of Catherine de' Medici
    (5 Dec)
Opening of Estates-General at Orléans (13 Dec)

1561 Ordinance of Orléans (Jan)
Edict of Saint-Germain (11 July)
Colloquy of Poissy (9 Sept–18 Oct)
Edict of Saint-Germain (20 Oct)
Contract of Poissy (Oct)

1562 Edict of Saint-Germain (17 Jan)
Massacre of Vassy (1 March)
Protestants under Condé seize Orléans (2 April)
Treaty of Hampton Court between Elizabeth I
    and Condé (20 Sept)
Siege of Rouen (24 Sept)
Battle of Dreux (19 Dec)

1563 Assassination of François duc de Guise (18 Feb)
Peace of Amboise (19 March)
Charles IX's majority proclaimed at Rouen (17 Aug)
Council of Trent closes (4 Dec)

1564 Death of Michelangelo (18 Feb)
Charles IX's 'grand progress' begins (Jan)
Anglo-French treaty of Troyes (11 April)
Death of John Calvin (27 May)
Catherine meets duke of Alba at Bayonne
    (15 June–2 July)

1565 Charles IX's progress continues
Death of Pope Pius IV (9 Dec)

1566 Pope Pius V elected (7 Jan)
Ordinance of Moulins (Feb)
Henri d'Orléans becomes duc d'Anjou; his brother
    François becomes duc d'Alençon (8 Feb)
Death of Diane de Poitiers (22 April)
Charles IX's progress ends (1 May)

Dutch revolt against Spain begins (Aug)
Catherine's granddaughter, Isabel Clara Eugenia,
   born (15 Aug)

1567 *Surprise de Meaux* (26–28 Sept)
Battle of Saint-Denis; death of Constable Montmorency
   (10 Nov)

1568 Peace of Longjumeau (23 March)
Egmont and Hornes executed in Brussels (5 June)
Death of Catherine's daughter, Elisabeth de Valois
   (Oct)

1569 Death of Philibert de l'Orme (8 Jan)
Battle of Jarnac; death of Louis de Condé (13 March)
Battle of Moncontour (3 Oct)

1570 Battle of Arnay-le-Duc (27 June)
Edict of Saint-Germain (8 Aug)
Marriage of Charles IX and Elizabeth of Austria (Nov)
Affair of the cross of Gastines (Dec)

1571 Charles IX's entry into Paris (6 March)
Battle of Lepanto (7 Oct)

1572 Capture of Brill by the Dutch Sea-Beggars (1 April)
Death of Pope Pius V (1 May)
Election of Pope Gregory XIII (14 May)
Defeat of Genlis near Mons (17 July)
Attempted assassination of Admiral Coligny (22 Aug)
Massacre of St. Bartholomew's Day (24 Aug)

1573 Siege of La Rochelle by Henri d'Anjou (Feb–July)
Anjou elected king of Poland (11 May)
Peace of La Rochelle (Edict of Boulogne) (2 July)
Polish embassy to France (Aug-Sept)
Anjou leaves France for Poland (2 Dec)

1574 Anjou crowned king of Poland (21 Feb)
Death of Charles IX; accession of Henry III (30 May)
Henry III visits Venice (18–27 July)
Henry III returns to France (6 Sept)
Death of Charles, Cardinal of Lorraine (26 Dec)

1575 Montmorency-Damville allies with the Huguenots
(12 Jan)
Coronation of Henry III (13 Feb)
Marriage of Henry III and Louise de Vaudémont
(15 Feb)
François, duc d'Anjou escapes from court (15 Sept)
Anjou issues manifesto (18 Sept)
German *reiters* defeated by Henri de Guise at
Dormans (10 Oct)

1576 Henri de Navarre escapes from court (3 Feb)
Peace of Monsieur (Edict of Beaulieu) (7 May)
Formation of League at Péronne (June)
Opening of Estates-General at Blois (6 Dec)

1577 Estates-General of Blois close (Feb)
Anjou sacks La Charité-sur-Loire (2 May)
Anjou sacks Issoire (11 May)
Peace of Bergerac (Edict of Poitiers) (17 Sept)

1578 Anjou's second flight from court (14 Feb)
Anjou's first expedition to the Netherlands
Catherine's peace mission to the Midi (Oct)
Anjou fails to relieve Mons (23 Dec)

1579 Conference at Nérac between Catherine and Henri
de Navarre (3 Feb)
Treaty of Nérac (28 Feb)
Ordinance of Blois (May)
End of Catherine's peace mission in the Midi (June)

1580 Siege and capture of Cahors by Henri de Navarre
(26–31 May)
Treaty of Pléssis-les-Tours between Anjou and the
Dutch (19 Sept)
Peace of Fleix (26 Nov)

1581 Marriage of Anne, duc de Joyeuse and Marguerite
de Lorraine (24 Sept)

1582 Anjou given title of duke of Brabant
Defeat of Strozzi in the Azores (26 July)

1583 Anjou fails to capture Antwerp
Assembly of Notables opens at Saint-Germain-en-Laye
(18 Nov)

1584 Death of François, duc d'Anjou (10 June)
Formation of the second League (Sept)

1585 Treaty of Joinville between the League and Spain
(2 Jan)
League issues manifesto in Péronne (13 March)
Death of Pope Gregory XIII (10 April)
Election of Pope Sixtus V (24 April)
Treaty of Nemours between Henry III and League
(7 July)
New alliance between Navarre and Montmorency-
Damville (10 Aug)
Pope Sixtus V debars Navarre and Condé from the
French throne (9 Sept)
Death of Ronsard (27 Dec)

1586 Talks between Catherine and Navarre at Saint-Brice
(Dec)

1587 Execution of Mary, Queen of Scots at Fotheringay
(18 Feb)
End of talks between Catherine and Navarre (March)
Battle of Coutras; death of Joyeuse (20 Oct)
Guise defeats the German *reiters* at Vimory (26 Oct)
and Auneau (24 Nov)

1588 Death of Henri de Condé at Saint-Jean d'Angély
(5 March)
Day of the Barricades and Henry III's flight from
Paris (11–13 May)
Edict of Union (21 July)
The Spanish Armada defeated (Aug–Sept)
Henry III sacks his ministers (8 Sept)
Opening of Estates-General of Blois (16 Oct)
Murder of Henri, 3rd duc de Guise and his brother,
the Cardinal (23–24 Dec)

1589 Death of Catherine de' Medici (5 Jan)

MAPS AND
GENEALOGICAL TABLES

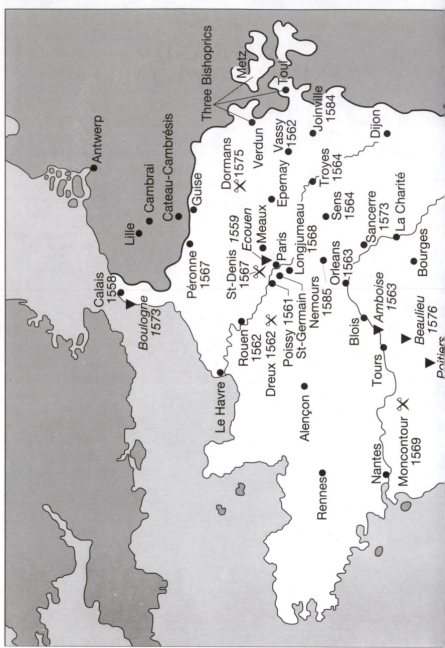

France, 1562–89

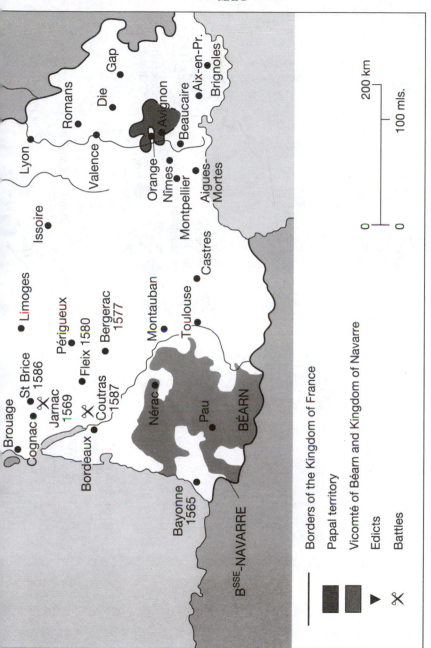

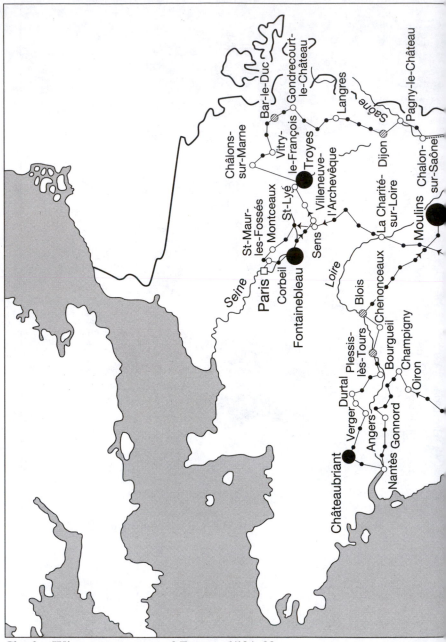

Charles IX's progress around France, 1564–66
Adapted from Jean Boutier, Alain Dewerpe and Daniel Nordman *Un tour d*
France royal. Le voyage de Charles IX (1564–1566) (Paris, 1984)

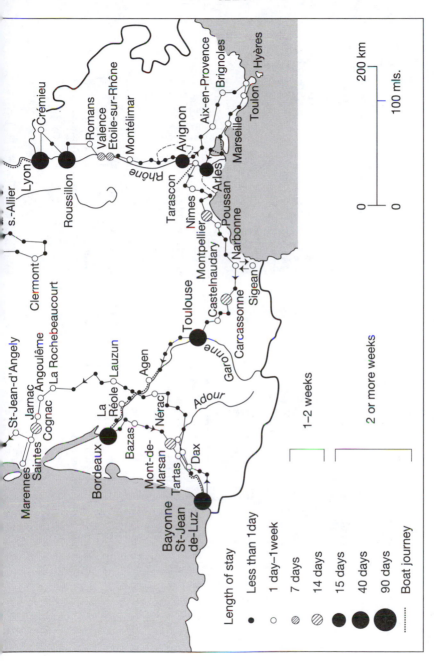

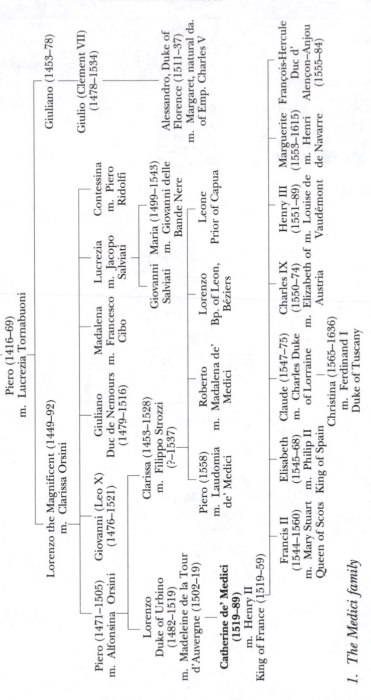

1. *The Medici family*

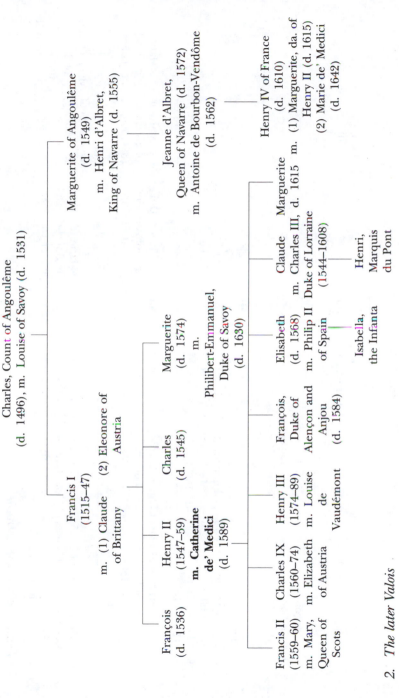

Charles, Count of Angoulême
(d. 1496), m. Louise of Savoy (d. 1531)

Marguerite of Angoulême
(d. 1549)
m. Henri d'Albret,
King of Navarre (d. 1555)

Jeanne d'Albret,
Queen of Navarre (d. 1572)
m. Antoine de Bourbon-Vendôme
(d. 1562)

Henry IV of France
(d. 1610)
m. (1) Marguerite, da. of
Henry II (d. 1615)
(2) Marie de' Medici
(d. 1642)

Francis I
(1515–47)
m. (1) Claude   (2) Eleonore of
of Brittany   Austria

François
(d. 1536)

Henry II
(1547–59)
m. Catherine
de' Medici
(d. 1589)

Charles
(d. 1545)

Marguerite
(d. 1574)
m.
Philibert-Emmanuel,
Duke of Savoy
(d. 1630)

Claude   Marguerite
m. Charles III, d. 1615 m.
Duke of Lorraine
(1544–1608)

Francis II
(1559–60)
m. Mary,
Queen of
Scots

Charles IX
(1560–74)
m. Elizabeth
of Austria

Henry III
(1574–89)
m. Louise
de
Vaudémont

François,
Duke of
Alençon and
Anjou
(d. 1584)

Elisabeth
(d. 1568)
m. Philip II
of Spain

Isabella,
the Infanta

Henri,
Marquis
du Pont

2. *The later Valois*

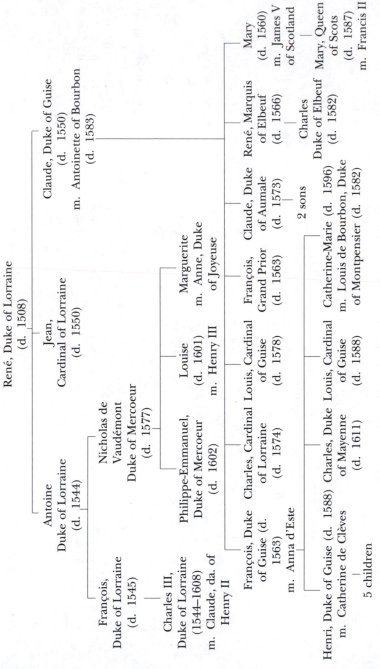

3. *The house of Guise-Lorraine*

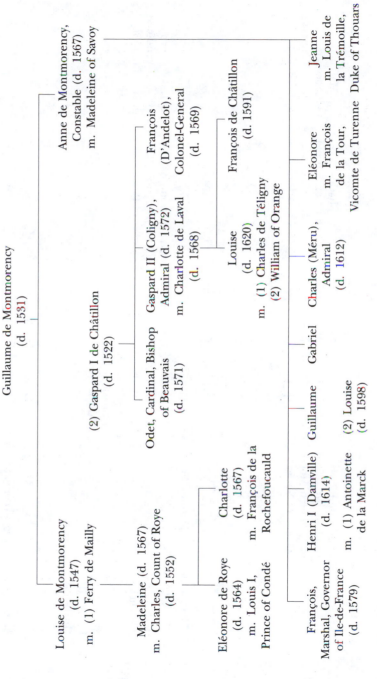

4. *The house of Montmorency*

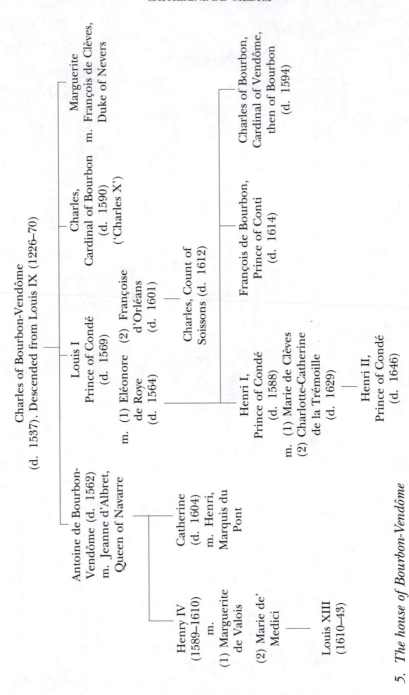

5. *The house of Bourbon-Vendôme*

INDEX

meets Navarre at
Saint-Brice, 256–7;
on day of the Barricades,
261;
offended by Henry III's
ministerial reshuffle, 265;
and assassination of duc de
Guise, 267;
her buildings, 41, 107, 174,
222, 228–33;
her correspondence, xiii,
88, 100, 106–7, 109, 120,
127, 248, 260;
her children, 34, 83, 85–6,
108, 134, 221, 275;
her device, 139, 240;
her health, xiii, 118, 120,
196, 203, 217, 248–9,
265–6, 268;
her household, 23, 230;
her inventory, 241–4;
her library, 233;
her court festivals, 234–41,
274;
her 'flying squadron', 235;
her matchmaking, 134,
138–9, 141, 143, 179, 210,
272, 275;
her patronage of literature
and the arts, 220–44;
and astrology, 220–1;
her superstitious nature,
223, 229–30, 234, 267–8;
her portraits, 14, 227;
her religious views, 53–4,
63, 80, 86, 251, 271;
her reputation, xi-xiii, 68,
163–5, 177, 268;
her statesmanship, 71;
her death, 267;
her post-mortem, 268;
her funeral, 268;
her tomb, 226–7;
her legacy, 270–1;

her mistakes, 272, 274–5;
her 'finest hour', 273
Catherine of Aragon
(1485–1536), queen of
England, 13
Cavaignes, Arnauld de, 155
Cavalli, Marino (1500–73),
Venetian ambassador in
France, 30
Cavalli, Sigismondo, Venetian
ambassador in France, 151
Cavriana, Filippo, Catherine
de' Medici's physician,
266–7
Cercamp, 54
Cecil, William (1520–98),
baron Burghley, 128
Cellini, Benvenuto
(1500–71), sculptor and
goldsmith, 24, 27–8
Chabot, Philippe
(1480–1543), Admiral of
France, 24, 32
Chailly, François de Villiers,
seigneur de, 155
Châlons-sur-Marne, 116,
125, 152, 247
Chambord, château of, 41,
182
Chambord, treaty of (1551),
43
Chambre ardente, 50
Champagne, 112, 178,
248
Champigny, truce of (1575),
182
Champvallon, Harlay de, 215
Chantonnay, Thomas de,
Spanish ambassador in
France, 75, 83, 85, 97, 99
Charles V, Holy Roman
Emperor (1519–56/58),
8–15, 18, 20, 28–9, 42–3, 45,
47

Juana, sister of Philip II of
Spain, 108
Julius II (Giuliano della
Rovere), pope (1503–13), 5
Julius III, pope (1550–55), 45

Knox, John, xii

La Bretonnière, Françoise, 54
La Chaise, barony of, 7
La Chapelle-Marteau, Michel,
prévôt des marchands, 262
La Charité-sur-Loire, 109,
117, 133, 136, 182, 190, 236,
290
La Châtre, Gaspard de, 123,
182, 247
Lainez, Diego, general of the
Jesuits, 78, 81–2
La Marck, Antoinette de,
189
La Meilleraye, sieur de,
marshal of France, 205
La Mole, Antoine de
Boniface, sieur de, 171–2,
221–2
La Mothe-Fénelon, Bertrand
de Salignac, marquis de,
123, 155
Landriano, battle of (1529),
10
Languedoc, 36, 51, 60, 95–6,
131, 166, 178, 189, 197–8,
204, 253; governor, 172,
193, 291
La Noue, François de
(1531–91), 114, 133, 180
La Planche, Régnier de, 67
La Popelinière, historian, 118
La Renaudie, Jean du Barry,
seigneur de, 64–5
La Réole, 195
La Rochefoucauld, François
III, comte de, 96, 126

La Roche l'Abeille, battle of,
128
La Rochelle, 122–5, 131,
136, 140–1, 166–8, 179, 273,
290
La Rochepot, seigneur de, *see*
Montmorençy, François de
La Tour, barony of, 7
La Tour, Jean III de, 7
La Tour d'Auvergne,
Madeleine de, comtesse de
Boulogne, mother of
Catherine de' Medici 7–8
Lautrec, Odet de Foix
(c. 1481–1528), marshal,
10
La Valette, Bernard de, 262,
266
League, Catholic or Holy,
185–6, 189, 222, 246–7, 249,
251–4, 257–60, 263, 292
Le Camus, 66–7
Le Charron, Jean, *prévôt des
marchands*, 159–60
Le Crotoy, 257
Lectoure, 147–8
Lefèvre d'Etaples, Jacques
(1450–1536), evangelical
humanist, 19, 54
Leghorn, 4, 13
Le Havre, 90, 93
Leicester, Robert Dudley
(1532?–88), earl of, 140,
206
Le Jeune, Claude
(1528–1600), musician, 239
Leo X (Giovanni de' Medici)
pope (1513–21), 1, 4–9, 22,
233, 236
Lepanto, battle of (1571),
145, 146n., 211
Lescot, Pierre (1500/15–78),
architect, 230
Lesdiguières, 193

332